JEWS AND HERETICS IN CATHOLIC POLAND

Jews and Heretics in Catholic Poland takes issue with historians' common contention that the Catholic Church triumphed in Counter-Reformation Poland. In fact, the Church's own sources show that the story is far more complex. From the rise of the Reformation and the rapid dissemination of these new ideas through printing, the Catholic Church was overcome with a strong sense of insecurity. The "infidel Jews, enemies of Christianity," became symbols of the Church's weakness and, simultaneously, instruments of its defense against all of its other adversaries. The beleaguered Church sought to separate Catholics from non-Catholics: Jews and heretics. This process helped form a Polish identity that led, in the case of Jews, to racial anti-Semitism and to the exclusion even of most assimilated Jews from the category of Poles. *Jews and Heretics in Catholic Poland* will be considered controversial in some circles not only because it challenges the historians' claim of the Church's triumph by emphasizing the latter's sense of insecurity, but also because it portrays Jews not only as victims of Church persecution but also as active participants in Polish society who, as allies of the nobles and placed in positions of power, had more influence than has been recognized.

Magda Teter is Assistant Professor of History at Wesleyan University. She is the recipient of the Koret Foundation Publication Prize and has been published in English, Polish, and Hebrew in such journals as *Jewish History*, *AJS Review*, and *Gal-Ed*.

Jews and Heretics in Catholic Poland

A Beleaguered Church in the Post-Reformation Era

MAGDA TETER
Wesleyan University

CAMBRIDGE
UNIVERSITY PRESS

CAMBRIDGE UNIVERSITY PRESS
Cambridge, New York, Melbourne, Madrid, Cape Town, Singapore, São Paulo, Delhi

Cambridge University Press
32 Avenue of the Americas, New York, NY 10013-2473, USA

www.cambridge.org
Information on this title: www.cambridge.org/9780521109918

First published 2006
This digitally printed version 2009

A catalog record for this publication is available from the British Library

Library of Congress Cataloging in Publication data
Teter, Magda.
Jews and heretics in Catholic Poland : a beleaguered church in the post-Reformation era /
Magda Teter.
p.   cm.
Includes bibliographical references and index.
ISBN-13: 978-0-521-85673-7 (hardback)
ISBN-10: 0-521-85673-6 (hardback)
1. Catholic Church – Poland – History.   2. Jews – Poland – History.
3. Heretics – Poland – History.   4. Counter-Reformation – Poland.
5. Poland – Church history.   I. Title.
BX1565.T48   2005
282′.438 – dc22   2005011720

ISBN 978-0-521-85673-7 hardback
ISBN 978-0-521-10991-8 paperback

Publication was made possible, in part,
by a gift from the Koret Foundation.

For my parents –
dla moich rodziców z wyrazami wdzięczności

In the Church of Christ, there is, and has to be, only one highest and visible Shepherd.... And just as there is only one shepherd, there is and has to be only one fold of Christ, outside of which no one will achieve redemption.

Adam Abramowicz, *Kazania Niedzielne* (Sunday Sermons), 1753

Q: And whom does the Catholic Church reject, condemn and curse?
A: The Catholic Church rejects, condemns and curses all pagan errors . . . heresies and all schisms. It condemns and excludes from the community of the faithful all pagans, Jews, heretics, schismatics, and bad and disobedient Catholics.

Bishop Krzysztof Szembek, *Krótkie zebranie nauki chrześciańskiej* (A short collection of Christian teachings), 1714

Contents

List of Illustrations

Preface and Acknowledgments

This book had begun long before I formally embarked on it. During my summer break of 1994, after my first year of graduate studies in Jewish history at Columbia University, I returned to Poland to visit my parents and my relatives in my father's hometown of Sandomierz. There, I had an encounter and a heated debate with a local priest about a painting in the local cathedral church depicting Jews in the act of murdering a Christian child. The discussion left me with many questions about Jewish-Christian relations, Jewish-Church relations, and the attitudes of the Catholic Church toward Jews in premodern Poland.

The following fall, it happened that Michael Stanislawski taught a graduate colloquium at Columbia University on the history of Jews in Poland before 1772. In researching Polish and Polish Church historiography on Jews and the Catholic Church in Poland, I found mostly silence about anything that dealt directly with Jewish-Church relations. This silence surprised me because, in my conversations with people in the United States, in Europe, and in Israel, I had found that most people had strong opinions about Polish Jews and the Catholic Church, opinions generally either accusatory or defensive. And thus began my journey that has led to this book.

Searching for answers to my questions on the Church's attitudes toward Jews in Poland in the seventeenth and eighteenth centuries, I found some answers. Yet, I also am acutely aware that there is more to be learned. More questions, in fact, emerged. The topic is rich and the materials abound. This book focuses on the Church's use of anti-Jewish rhetoric and imagery in post-Reformation Poland; it seeks to understand the mind-set of those who created them, and seeks to explore how the attitudes toward Jews harbored by the Catholic clergy and imparted to lay Catholics in Poland were shaped. The picture that emerged turned out to be more complex and fascinating than I had anticipated, a picture of a besieged Church, fearful of anyone opposing it.

My research took me to many archives and libraries, mostly in Poland and in Rome, but other libraries such as the Widener Library at Harvard, the Butler Library at Columbia University, and the Jewish National and University Library in Jerusalem were also crucial in this work. I am grateful to all those who enabled me to gain access to these collections. In many archives I received the warmest welcome. The Jesuit archives in Cracow and Rome were a pleasure to work in, as were the archives of the Dominicans and the Reformed Franciscan Friars in Cracow, the Metropolitan Archive of the Archdiocese in Cracow (Archiwum Kurii Metropolitalnej w Krakowie), and the Archive of the Collegium de Propaganda Fide in Rome. And, despite some bureaucratic stumbling blocks at the Vatican Archives (Archivio Segreto Vaticano), I was granted access to their collections.

Sometimes access was less easy, especially access to Church archives in Poland, where some Church officials are still distrustful of scholars, especially those coming from the outside, whether geographically or culturally. I tried to minimize the impact of that status. Sometimes it took several attempts, and at times I rephrased the topic to be less provocative to the archivists guarding the documents, while making sure that it was not deceptive or misleading to those responsible for granting me archival access and that it remained truthful to my intentions.

In my first try during the summer of 1996, for example, after I failed to gain access to one Church archive, which has since become open to all and very pleasant to work with, I realized that I should avoid the term "Counter-Reformation" in Poland because it had negative connotations grounded in Polish historiography. That particular archivist told me that there had been no Counter-Reformation in Poland. Sometimes, both in libraries and archives, I referred broadly to study of "religious minorities," or simply "religious history," rather than to "Jews" or "heresy." Some archives still remain locked, among them – most crucial for my own work – the archive of the cathedral chapter in Sandomierz. Some Polish clergy find scholarship threatening. One can only hope that now-closed archives will eventually be opened to allow scholars to peruse the important sources so that the history they write will be based on all available primary sources, thus leading toward greater understanding of the social dynamics of the past and helping to address the causes of today's continuing religious and ethnic prejudice to create a more open society.

The Jesuit archive in Cracow, which I used, possesses some copies of the materials collected in the Archivum Romanum Societatis Iesu (ARSI – the Roman Archive of the Society of Jesus) in Rome. The original sources were destroyed during a fire in Cracow. The ARSI, a true treasure trove of sources pertaining to the work of Jesuits in Poland, has collections of annual reports sent from Poland to the headquarters in Rome, chronicles, and correspondence. These materials are a wonderful, yet virtually untapped, source for investigating both the ideals and methods by which individual Jesuits worked toward their goals. There are chronicles of particular houses, reports on the numbers of converts, sermons delivered, confessions heard, marriages consecrated, and much more, many of which I used for this book.

The Metropolitan Archive of the Archdiocese in Cracow (Archiwum Kurii Metropolitalnej w Krakowie) and the Archives of the Cathedral Chapter at Cracow's Wawel Castle (Archiwum Kapituły) hold exceptionally rich sources, including records of trials in the episcopal courts, correspondence between the cathedral chapter and various Church and lay officials that elucidate the working of the Church bureaucracy of the time, and the social and political dynamic that the Church faced.

Archives of religious orders hold a vast number of unpublished sermons and collections of homiletic material used by preachers, allowing the researcher a glimpse into sermons preached in small churches – sermons that never made it into print. There is a difference worth noting in topics addressed in published and unpublished homiletic literature: published materials tended to be devotional or to address broader political issues, including the sins of the nobles, whereas the unpublished works, though also generally devotional, addressed more the "earthly sins" committed by lower-class people, in which drinking, sex, and violence predominate.

Facing the actual historical sources forces a historian to confront his or her own expectations, presuppositions, and biases. Most projects start with an idea, perhaps even with a thesis, and thus sometimes with expectations of what may be found. The heated debate I had with a priest in Sandomierz, the painting in the cathedral church, and the strong opinions about the subject held by most of my interlocutors along the way led me to expect to find in the archives abundant material filled with anti-Jewish sentiments and tales filled with hate. I expected to find countless sermons that disseminated these sentiments. But when I confronted the sources, or perhaps when the sources confronted me, I had to reassess my ideas. I did not find large quantities of anti-Jewish works; in fact, my first reaction was that I was reading large quantities of "boring" devotional works and sermons that "had nothing to do with Jews," most of which never found their way even to footnotes or the bibliography in this book. Jews were not even mentioned in the majority of the works I examined. I needed to switch gears. These works showed me the larger cultural context in which the post-Reformation Catholic attitudes toward Jews were shaped. The Jews were one of multiple concerns of the Church. Based on all my presuppositions and those of my opinionated interlocutors, I expected to find Jews as a central focus of the Church's thought and actions.

I faced a number of paradoxes that the reader will face as well. The Catholic clergy's attitudes toward Jews are central to the book, though not as central to the body of material as a whole produced by the Catholic clergy from that period of time. Jews had long been an important theological concern for the Church and Christianity; even though they did not dominate the literature of the period, they were a focus of the clergy's expressed fears and insecurities, one of the foes that had, for centuries, threatened the Church's ideal of being "one Church." In that long history of dealing with Jews as theological threats, the Church developed a wide range of measures, both legal and polemical, that were, in turn, used to combat other challengers to the Church's ideal. Thus, Jews became both central and peripheral to the Church's concerns. These paradoxes complicate a story that would have been much simpler if, as I had expected, I had found bins and boxes of materials filled with anti-Jewish texts, but they also make it more interesting than a simple tale of the Church's anti-Jewish sentiments.

ALONG THE WAY I HAVE ENCOUNTERED PEOPLE WITHOUT WHOM THIS WORK would have been impossible. I want first to thank those with whom my life began and to whom this work is dedicated – my parents, Alina and Zdzisław Teter. It was they who indulged my curiosity, encouraged reading and learning, and who have always supported my interests and the steps I have taken in life – even when they may have thought what I was doing was not practical. It was my father who, when I was six, gave me my first book about Jews in Poland, and it was he who showed me what was left of the *Kierkut*, a Jewish cemetery, in his hometown, Sandomierz. With my parents I explored whatever was left of Jewish life in Małopolska, the Little Poland, a region in southeastern Poland, when we drove from the town where we lived to Sandomierz. All of this undoubtedly sparked my interest in the life of Jews in Poland. My parents supported me when I wanted to study Hebrew at the University of Warsaw, and continued their support when, because of the political situation in the late 1980s in Poland, I could not formally study Hebrew there, and studied Mongolian instead. They supported me too when, after the end of the Cold War, I began to venture to the West to study Jewish languages and history, first to Amsterdam, then to Jerusalem, Oxford, and, finally, to New York. I thank them for their love and for letting me go far away from them to fulfill my dreams.

To continue on a personal note, I want to thank my partner and friend – my husband, Shawn Hill, who has given me endless encouragement and support in moments of despair, and shared the joy in moments of happiness. He has always encouraged me to be assertive and strong, to express my values, and to strive to achieve my goals. I thank him for spending long hours reading through my papers and early drafts. I thank him for his patience, and for enduring long stretches of loneliness, when I would go on research trips to Poland, Italy, or Israel. I thank him for his love.

Sometimes, it is difficult to separate the professional from the personal, and many of my colleagues became friends who provided constant words of wisdom and support, encouragement, and, as good friends do, also critiques. I thank my colleague and dear friend Jeremy Zwelling at Wesleyan University, who, along with his wife Vicky, made Wesleyan such a hospitable and welcoming place. Without them, being at Wesleyan would not have been the same. Jeremy's warmth, care, and personal and professional honesty have been a necessary nourishment. Deep-felt thanks belong to Edward Fram, of Ben-Gurion University of the Negev, who walked me through the complexities of rabbinic sources, and who sparked my interest in the history of printing. I thank him for spending long hours reading and commenting on my work at its various stages, for providing most pointed and necessary critiques, and for being an amazing mentor for more than ten years now.

I also thank him for forcing me to pay attention to the beauty of spring in New England when we spent a semester together at Harvard as Harry Starr Fellows. I thank him, too, for being a wonderful friend.

I thank Elisheva Carlebach of Queens College, CUNY, who has supported and mentored me ever since I asked her to be a member of my dissertation committee. Both Elisheva Carlebach and Edward Fram have been models of academic mentors; it is they who taught me to be open to constructive criticisms.

Very special thanks go to Michael Stanislawski and Yosef Hayim Yerushalmi of Columbia University for their confidence in my ability to succeed at Columbia. They taught me how to be a historian, and I am grateful for the privilege of having been their student; without them this work would not have been possible. They planted in me the idea of working on the Catholic Church and the Jews in early modern Poland. I thank them for their encouragement from the very early stages of my career as a historian of the Jews, and for their continuing support.

I want also to thank several people without whom I may have never come to the United States. Michał Friedman, who was my teacher of Hebrew and Yiddish in Warsaw, deserves special thanks. It was he who encouraged me to go to Amsterdam Summer University for a program in Eastern European Jewish History. There I met people who, in turn, persuaded me to apply to graduate schools in the United States and then supported me in my pursuits: Zvi Gitelman of the University of Michigan, Edward van Voolen of the Jewish Historical Museum in Amsterdam, and Molly and Nathan Deen of Utrecht. Without their encouragement I would not have had the confidence to try to reach across the Atlantic Ocean.

Many of my colleagues read this book or its parts. I thank Moshe Rosman of Bar Ilan University in Israel for taking the time and spending the energy, much needed in the midst of his illness, to read my manuscript. His persistent comments on certain points made this book better. I thank Gershon D. Hundert of McGill University for reading a few versions of this work, and Kenneth Stow of Haifa University for his invaluable comments, and for sharing his work with me.

I also want to thank my colleagues at Wesleyan University, both in my department and beyond. My colleagues from the history department were instrumental in my first steps in moving from a doctoral dissertation to a book. Special thanks go to Laurie Nussdorfer, David Morgan, Richard Elphick, Bruce Masters, Gary Shaw, and Michael Printy, all of whom read and commented on the book in its various stages. I am grateful to them for their criticisms, and to other colleagues for their support and confidence. I also want to thank the department of special collections at Wesleyan's Olin Memorial Library, especially Suzy Taraba and Jefferey Makala for their help and for giving me permission to publish a map of eighteenth-century Poland from a 1723 atlas in the University's collection. The staff at the Interlibrary Loan office have seen me much too often since my arrival at Wesleyan, and without them completing this book would have been much more difficult. Kathy Stefanowicz, Kate Wolf, and Lisa Pinette have all patiently filled my requests. Allynn Wilkinson and

Manolis Kaparakis of the Information Technology department helped me prepare images.

My students at Wesleyan University also deserve thanks. My thanks go especially to Ilana Cohn and Tal Beery for their thoughtful critique of my work. Two groups of students in my seminar "Eastern European Jewish Experience: History and Historiography" (HIST 156) read drafts of chapters from my book; their comments and responses have been invaluable.

Several institutions were crucial in the process of writing this book. I am grateful to Columbia University both for a generous fellowship enabling me to study the history of Jews and for the prestigious Salo and Jeanette Baron Prize for "the best dissertation in Jewish studies at Columbia University between 1996 and 2001." It has been an honor and a privilege to study at Columbia. I would like to express my appreciation also to the Memorial Foundation for Jewish Culture, the only foundation that provides generous support for non-U.S. citizens in predoctoral and postdoctoral stages, and to the Koret Foundation for support of the publication of this book.

My deep thanks go to Jay Harris and the Center for Jewish Studies at Harvard University for an unforgettable opportunity of working with other scholars of early modern Jewish history by the award of a Harry Starr fellowship in 2002. The fellowship allowed me to explore genres of sources I had not previously used, such as criminal court records, without which this book would have been weaker. I was privileged to learn from and to share my work with other Starr Fellows: Edward Fram, Elliott Horowitz, Boaz Huss, Anat Lapidot-Firilla, Elchanan Reiner, Michael Silber, and the faculty and students of the center. My long hours in the Phillips reading room at the Widener library will be long remembered. The last months of writing this book I spent in Israel as a Yad Ha-Nadiv Fellow. I want to thank the Yad Ha-Nadiv Foundation for affording me this opportunity.

Numerous libraries and archives allowed me to use their rich collections. My warmest thanks go to the rare book division of the Jagiellonian Library in Cracow whose rare book room was my home during waking hours for many months. The staff made my work there a true pleasure; they shared their knowledge with me and allowed extensive use of their collection, patiently filling out my numerous requests, and sometimes answering email questions after my return to the United States. Maria Dytko, Małgorzata Gołuszka, Jolanta Jakubiak, Marian Malicki, Romana Piech, Wanda Ptak-Korbel, Grażyna Stepien, and Zofia Wawrykiewicz were invaluable. I also thank the staff at the rare book division of the National Library in Warsaw, especially Maria Zychowiczowa and Bożena Ciepłowska, who on numerous occasions responded to email queries, and sometimes made sure that books would be waiting for me when I arrived. I thank the staff of the Czartoryski Library in Cracow, and the staff of the manuscript collection of the University of Warsaw, who gave me permission to see manuscripts when using the microfilmed versions was difficult.

Elżbieta Knapek of the Archiwum Kurii Metropolitalnej, and Idalia Rusnaczyk of the Archiwum Kapituły na Wawelu, both in Cracow, are a wonderful resource of archival knowledge from which I continue to draw. Archivists of Polish religious orders deserve my heartfelt thanks for granting access to their wonderful collections. I thank Cracow's Archiwum OO. Franciszkanów Reformatów, Archiwum Prowincji Polskiej OO. Dominikanów, Archiwum OO. Karmelitów, Biblioteka i Archiwum OO. Bernardynów, Biblioteka i Archiwum OO. Jezuitów – especially Stanisław Obirek, SJ, Ludwik Grzebień, SJ, and Sister Leonia, who graciously shared her office with me in the winter of 1996–7. In Rome I was granted access to the collections of the Archive of the Collegium de Propaganda Fide and the Roman Jesuit Archive (Archiwum Romanum Societatis Jesu), where Marek Inglot, SJ, was especially helpful. I also thank the staff at the state archives in Cracow, Przemyśl, Poznań, and the Archiwum Akt Dawnych in Warsaw for giving me access to their collections.

I am grateful to Roman Chyła of Sandomierz for helping me obtain archival materials and for helping me to photograph the series *Martyrologium Romanum* in the cathedral church there.

Very special thanks go to Jeannette Hopkins, whose sharp mind and wit forced me to hone my argument and to fill the gaping holes in my research. Her acutely pointed comments have been invaluable in writing this book. I appreciated her being my "academic therapist" in helping me to identify the problems and then forcing me to find a solution, a process sometimes painful but tremendously rewarding. Without her the book would also, no doubt, have been duller. She taught me a great deal about book writing and academic publishing; I feel tremendously privileged to have worked with her.

I thank Cambridge University Press, and especially Andrew Beck, for publishing this book.

All of these people, and many more, have made the book only better; any weaknesses and errors are solely my own.

Note on Terms, Spelling, and Translations

During the premodern period covered by this book, the Polish state was transformed from the independent states of the Polish Crown and the Grand Duchy of Lithuania into the Polish-Lithuanian Commonwealth. The actual unification took place in 1569. During the early modern period the Commonwealth was often referred to as the Polish Crown and the ruling elite identified as the Polish nation. "Poland," therefore, is sometimes used to denote the whole Commonwealth. In cases where the eastern territories alone are referred to, they are so described.

Towns and cities are identified throughout according to the terminology of the period, unless an English equivalent exists. So, for example, present-day Vilnius in Lithuania appears as Wilno and current-day Lviv in Ukraine as Lwów. But, for Kraków or Warszawa, for which English names exist, Cracow and Warsaw are used. In the bibliography the place names correspond to the place names on the publication itself, but current names are placed in brackets.

All translations within the text are mine unless otherwise noted.

Abbreviations

The following abbreviations have been used in notes:

AEp   Acta Episcopalia
AIVAK   *Akty Izdavaemye Vilenskoiu Arkheograficheskoiu Kommiseiu*
AKM   Archiwum Kurii Metropolitalnej in Cracow
AKW   Archiwum Kapituły na Wawelu in Cracow
ARSI   Archivium Romanus Societatis Iesu (The Roman Archive of the Society
        of Jesus)
ASV   Archivio Segreto Vaticano
BT   *The Babylonian Talmud*
Tur   *Arba'ah Turim ha-Shalem*

1. Carol de Prevot, *Martyrologium Romanum* series in the cathedral church in Sandomierz. The series of sixteen paintings depicts the martyrdom of Catholics in Sandomierz (four paintings) and in the history of the Church (twelve paintings). Detail from a side panel in the northern nave.

2. Carol de Prevot, *Martyrologium Romanum* series. Martyrdom of forty-nine Dominicans from the Church of St. Jacob in Sandomierz at the hands of Tatars in 1260 (detail). One of the four paintings in the series from the history of Sandomierz.

3. Carol de Prevot, *Martyrologium Romanum* series. Detail from a panel in the northern nave.

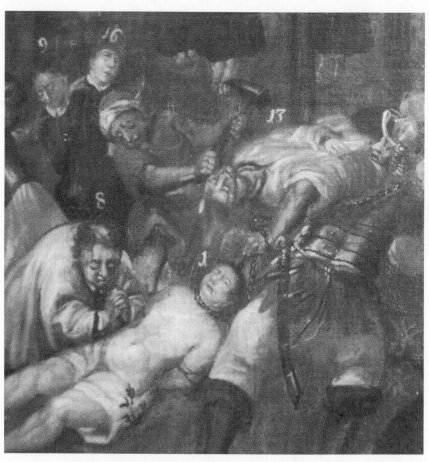

4. Carol de Prevot, *Martyrologium Romanum* series. Detail.

5. Carol de Prevot, *Martyrologium Romanum* series. The painting depicts the ritual murder of Christian children, which Jews of Sandomierz were accused of in 1710. Inspired by a trial of Jews that started in 1710. One of four paintings in the series from the history of Sandomierz.

6. Carol de Prevot, *Martyrologium Romanum* series. Detail from a panel depicting the destruction of the Sandomierz castle at the hands of Swedes in 1656. One of the four paintings from the history of Sandomierz.

PROCESS
KRYMINALNY
o Niewinne Dziecię
J E R Z E G O
KRASNOWSKIEGO.

Iuż to trzetie, Roku 1710. dnia 18. Sierpniá
W SENDOMIRZU
Okrutnie od Zydow zamordowane.
Dla odkrycia iawnych kryminałow Zydowskich,
Dla przykładu fprawiedliwości potomnym wiekom.
OD X. STEFANA
ZUCHOWSKIEGO,

Oboyga Prawa Doktorá, ARCHIDYAKONA,
OFFICYAŁA Y PLEBANA Sendomirskiego,
iako Roku 1698. o drugie, tak Roku tegoż 1710. o trzecie za
bite w Sendomirzu Sieroty
A K T O R A.
Zaczęty y dotąd fię toczący.
Z dozwoleniem Starfzych
Roku 1713. do Druku podany

7. Title page from Stefan Żuchowski's *Process Kryminalny*, a book written in response to the trial of Jews in Sandomierz accused of murdering a boy, Jerzy Krasnowski, in 1710. The book's date on the title page is 1713, but the final pages deal with the material from 1718.

8. Detail from the last page of Stefan Żuchowski's *Process Kryminalny*. A papal tiara with a skull and bones, a symbol usually placed under a crucifix to signify the first man, Adam.

9. Portrait of King Sigismund I from Piotr Hyacynth Pruszcz's *Forteca Duchowna* (1737). The text discusses the execution of Katarzyna Malcherowa for conversion to Judaism in Cracow in 1539.

10. The Polish-Lithuanian Commonwealth. A detail from "Map of Moscovy, Poland, Little Tartary, and ye Black Sea, &c." (plate 13) in Herman Moll, *The World Described, or, A New and Correct Sett of maps: Shewing the Several Empires, Kingdoms, Republics . . . in All the Known Parts of the Earth* (London: J. Bowles, 1709–1720). Courtesy of the Olin Library at Wesleyan University.

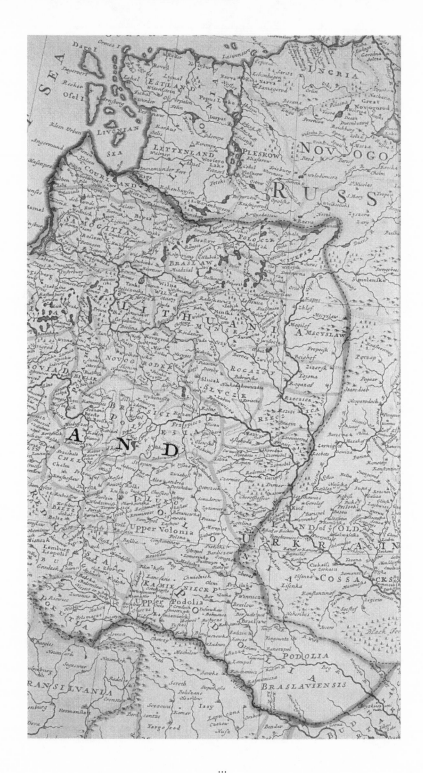

JEWS AND HERETICS IN CATHOLIC POLAND

Introduction

O N JANUARY 16, 2004, THE ASSOCIATED PRESS REPORTED THAT ISRAEL'S
chief rabbis, Yona Metzger and Shlomo Amar, had received an audience with
Pope John Paul II. The rabbis asked the pope to speak out against anti-Semitism
and to devote a day in the Catholic calendar "for study and reflection on the Jewish
faith."[1] The pope replied that he had "striven to promote Jewish-Catholic dialogue and to foster ever greater understanding, respect and cooperation." But, in
his native country of Poland, the Polish society and the Catholic Church continued to struggle with the difficult legacy of Polish-Jewish relations. Surrounded
by denial, condemnations, and apologetics, the question of relations between the
Polish Catholic Church and the Jews still stirs strong emotions and controversies
even though of the millions of Jews in Poland in 1939, when Nazi Germany invaded
Poland, fewer than twenty thousand remain.

One such controversy centered around a painting, formerly known as *Infanticidia*
or "Ritual Murder by Jews," in the cathedral church in Sandomierz, a small town
in southeastern Poland.[2] The painting depicts the murder of a Christian child by
Jews, a crime of which Sandomierz Jews were accused a number of times in the
seventeenth and eighteenth centuries. The painting itself is said to commemorate
a murder of 1710. These tales were popularized in two notorious books published
contemporaneously by the local priest, Stefan Żuchowski, instigator of one of the
trials of Jews for such alleged crimes[3] and commissioner of the painting.[4]

The painting portrays the episode as Żuchowski imagined it; it corresponds to
the sequence related in his book *Process kryminalny* [A Criminal Trial]: a Christian
woman's offering of the child to the Jews; torture of the child in a barrel lined
with protruding nails; extraction of the child's blood; and the culminating scene
of the child's body devoured and then vomited out by a dog. This image is a vivid
instance both of the Catholic perception of Jewish hostility toward Christians and
also of Catholic anti-Jewish sentiments in the premodern period.[5] Following the
reestablishment of diplomatic relations between Poland and Israel in the 1990s
and the appointment of a Jewish-Catholic committee on reconciliation, a demand
arose that this painting be removed from the church, as other paintings of this
sort had been in Poland, as in Kalwaria Zebrzydowska, near Pope John Paul II's
hometown of Wadowice. The painting was kept in place but a new description was
added, reading "The alleged ritual murder by Jews."

1

Most of those who called for the painting's removal had argued that it aroused anti-Semitism. They failed to note that the painting does not stand alone. It is one in a series of sixteen violent and evocative paintings, entitled "Martyrologium Romanum," covering the walls of the Sandomierz Cathedral.[6] In this series depicting Catholic martyrdom at the hands of non-Catholics, conceived and commissioned by Żuchowski, Sandomierz's castle explodes, blown up by Protestant Swedes. Bodies fly in the air. In a second painting, Muslim Tatars slaughter Sandomierz Dominicans. On the side panels, "infidels" butcher Catholics. Blood and body parts are scattered around. Elaborate methods of torture are conspicuously present in each painting. The series underlines the Polish Catholics' perception of non-Catholics, Jews, heretics, and other "infidels" as deadly enemies of the Church. Jews are but one of many, though central and most intimate in the series of paintings.[7]

These paintings, like the sermons and polemics of the time, tell a history that complicates the common view among modern historians that, by the early 1600s, the Counter-Reformation had triumphed in Poland.[8] The paintings, as well as other contemporary Church sources, reveal that the Church continued to feel not triumphant but threatened well into the eighteenth century. The Church in Poland had achieved nominal gains among the Polish nobility, most of whom after a short affair with Protestantism returned to Catholicism by the second half of the seventeenth century; but it had not triumphed, and it knew that it had not.

Indeed, the challenges of the Reformation had weakened the Church. Jakub Wujek, the popular sixteenth-century preacher and author of the Polish Catholic translation of the Bible, compared the Church to a boat in a storm imperiled by "heavy winds from Jews, Turks, pagans and heretics, and sometimes even bad Christians."[9] Well into the eighteenth century, the far-from-triumphant rhetoric of Polish Church leaders pleaded for recognition of the Catholic Church as the only legitimate religion. The pre-Reformation united Church had been "torn apart" by heretics, so a popular late seventeenth-century catechism explained. Heretics had introduced "different faith and different teachings."[10] They defied Catholic observances by vocal opposition to "confessions, [performing] last rites and accepting the Holiest Sacrifice [Mass]," rites that had existed since the beginning of "the Church of God."[11] Church writers claimed that Poland was being punished by God for tolerating this religious dissent, or as one argued because of the "varietas," religious diversity, and challenges to the legitimacy of Catholicism.[12] As late as 1733, during elections to choose the next monarch of Poland after the death of King August II, Bishop Jan Felix Szaniawski thundered:

The Catholic Religion has been abhorred by dissidents, schismatics and others, the churches and their immunity have been violated. Some [Catholics] have been killed, others taken prisoners. *Dualitas* [religious duality] did it.... Let us put our Crown on the Throne of God, which many will try to obtain but only one will achieve. Let us plead with God that he will place [the crown] on the head of one who is able to maintain the Catholic Faith, our Laws and Freedoms, and who is able to preserve the Unity of the Kingdom.[13]

The bishop was appealing to the protonationalistic feelings of the Polish nobility, according to which the nobles *were* the Polish nation.[14] Diverse in religious convictions in the sixteenth century, by the second half of the seventeenth century and into the eighteenth century the nobility, as a consequence of Poland's wars with its non-Catholic neighbors, had increasingly identified with Catholicism. Political threats from non-Catholics had come to symbolize threats to the country itself, which the nobles considered synonymous with themselves.

The religious diversity of Poland, or, as Bishop Szaniawski saw it, *dualitas* [duality], was expressed in a variety of ways but had a single central meaning: "we, Catholics," and they, the Others – heretics, Jews, schismatics, and sinners – all stigmatized as "foreign" and as a threat to the unity of the Church. In books and sermons that the clergy addressed to Polish nobles, these Others were described as a threat even to the well-being of Poland itself.[15] Such religious appeals with a political message are typical of published sermons and treatises, in contrast to unpublished sermons extant in manuscripts, which tend to focus instead on common sins of the flesh. The published works, some of which were sermons delivered at political occasions, sought to influence those in power, that is, the nobles, appealing to their sense of identity and to their fears for their country.[16] As one preacher asked: How can there be "a common good without the True Religion?" He declared that "heresies create discord in Kingdoms . . . they ruin kingdoms, unlike the True Religion, which consolidates them."[17]

The "True Religion" was identified as Catholicism. Opposed to that "True Religion" were all the non-Catholics – heretics, Jews, Turks, and schismatics, as the Eastern Orthodox were called – all outsiders and all seen as enemies of the Church. Thus, the series of paintings in the cathedral church in Sandomierz underlines these sentiments, as do Bishop Szembek's words in 1714: "The Catholic Church rejects, condemns and curses all pagan errors . . . heresies and all schisms. It condemns and excludes from the community of the faithful all pagans, Jews, heretics, schismatics, and bad and disobedient Catholics."[18] A late seventeenth-century Jesuit preacher, Wojciech Tylkowski, declared that it was not appropriate to pray in public for "the cursed heretics, schismatics, Jews and pagans," for "they do not belong to the Church" and, therefore, should derive no spiritual benefit from it.[19] Another Jesuit, Stefan Wielowieyski, did pray for sinners, schismatics, heretics, Jews, and pagans, but only in order to convert to Catholicism those who had fallen outside of Church control.[20] Jews, but not Jews alone, were attacked by the Church.

The Catholic Church of the post-Reformation period strove to reestablish its religious hegemony to become the "only one Church," but it failed in that mission. The vast Polish-Lithuanian Commonwealth continued to be religiously diverse. Even Poland itself was not to become homogeneously Catholic until the end of the Second World War, when it lost not only its Jewish population to the Nazi death camps but also, for different reasons, its Ukrainians, its Byelorussians, and its Lithuanians of the eastern territories of Poland, annexed by the Soviet Union after the war; it lost its Germans as well, expelled from the western areas that became part of modern Poland. Early modern Poland, in vivid contrast, had been a home to the largest Jewish community in the world. Jews had settled and flourished in the Polish-Lithuanian Commonwealth in response to its extensive economic opportunities. It was, in addition, a home to Eastern Orthodox Christians, Muslims, and Protestants. Catholics were not even a majority in early modern Poland.

The Church's post-Reformation influence in Poland was hindered, too, by the dynamics of power there. From the mid-seventeenth century, the Polish-Lithuanian Commonwealth had been ravaged by military and political conflicts with its non-Catholic neighbors: Orthodox Russia to the east, Protestant Sweden to the north, Protestant Prussia to the west, and the Muslim Ottoman state to the south. Only the Habsburg Monarchy was Catholic, and yet, because of complicated political alliances, Poland's relations with it were cold. The Polish-Lithuanian Commonwealth itself was weak; between the sixteenth and eighteenth centuries, its political structure had shifted from a strong monarchy to a state ruled by powerful nobles.[21] Although these ruling nobles supported many new Catholic churches and displayed religious devotion both by funding many new altars, paintings, and other religious art, and by leaving their private wealth to the Church in their wills, when it suited them they paid little attention to Church teachings, and often used their political power to limit the Church's political influence. They sought to end the Church's historically privileged fiscal status of freedom from taxation. Thus, even among the nobles, the "Counter-Reformation" victory was tenuous. The Polish Church longed for a strong Catholic monarch it could count on more easily than on the many – disobedient – lords. But the Church could not even count on a king. For a large part of the eighteenth century, the Polish-Lithuanian Commonwealth was headed by a king from Saxony, who was a convert from Lutheranism, and whose entourage included Lutherans.

One could argue that the Church never really held power and total control in Poland, even prior to the Reformation, for most of the society in that period was only nominally Christian; not all towns and villages had permanent parishes, and the level of education of both clergy and laity was far from satisfactory. The Polish Catholic clergy itself understood clearly that after the Reformation the Church had been permanently weakened. The Protestant Reformation had distanced the Church even farther from achieving its goal of religious hegemony, and had exposed its limitations and vulnerability. The Protestant Reformation boosted the number of perceived Church "enemies," which earlier, at least on a religious level, had been confined almost exclusively to Jews and, in a different way, to Muslims, or "the Saracens."

In its defensive, even reactionary, stance, the Catholic Church in Poland, as elsewhere, began in consequence to define and enforce more closely the social and religious boundaries that separated it from Others.[22] Its hostile rhetoric excluded those who did not accept that "there is only one Church" and sharpened religious commitments and identities. Historians have called this period the age of confessionalization.[23]

The nobles' relationship with Jews highlighted the failure of the Catholic Church to establish broader social control and discipline in Poland. For the Church, Jews had symbolic significance, for Jews had been seen by the Church as its earliest theological threat, and hence as its earliest "enemy." In the Church's ideal society, Jews may be tolerated but only in a circumscribed place that would remind them of their "exile" and of their divine punishment for their failure to accept Jesus and "the only one Church with its pastor," the pope. In Poland itself, the nobles often ignored this symbolism, and Jews became prominent leaseholders, merchants, and administrators of the nobles' estates, sometimes occupying positions of power over Christians themselves. In their insubordination to the Church's teachings, the nobles disrupted the order the Church had dreamed of establishing and controlling.

At the same time, Jews, as the most prominent theological and symbolic threat to the Christian Church from antiquity, provided a model for the Church's battles against its challengers. Anti-Jewish rhetoric became an instrument in the Church's wider struggle for domination. The Jewish presence in Poland made the Church's own rhetoric more relevant. References to Jews appeared, sometimes prominently, in Catholic sermons and polemical literature, usually not as the actual focus but rather as a symbol of the hostile forces Catholic clergy relentlessly attacked.

Jews were not the only ones against whom the Polish clergy fostered feelings of hostility, and they had a place, if a limited one, within Catholic Christianity. Christian heretics, such as Protestants and others, did not. Anti-Jewish rhetoric was employed against these heretics, and also against the nobles who, because of their political and economic power, could not be directly attacked. Symbolic Jews and their sins – even, indeed, their piety – were cited in moralistic Catholic sermons to illuminate the severity of the sins of "bad and disobedient Catholics," that is, Catholics such as those who preferred to go to a tavern on a Sunday rather than to attend a mass.

To place the Catholic Church's attitudes toward Jews in post-Reformation Poland into a niche of Church anti-Semitism is tempting. The Church did indeed have animosity toward Jews, and certain works by Polish Catholic clergy did contain vitriolic polemic against Jews. Yet, just as the painting, "Infanticide," in the cathedral church in Sandomierz, depicting Jews killing a Christian child, must be seen in the context of the other sixteen paintings of violent deaths of Catholics at the hands of non-Catholic enemies – Protestant Swedes, Muslims, Tatars, or ancient pagans – so too the Church's attitudes toward Jews have to be seen in an even broader context of anxieties that the Catholic clergy experienced and fostered.

Hostility toward Jews in post-Reformation Poland was part of the Church's desire for social and religious control, discipline, and influence. So too is it part of Catholic cultural history; with the invention of printing, the hostile anti-Jewish stereotypes entered literary culture in Poland with other books from the West and remained an important part of this culture into the eighteenth century. This occurred at least in part as a consequence of the cultural insularity of the post-Reformation Polish Church.

In the eighteenth century, when the Catholic Church in Rome and in France was facing the challenges of the Enlightenment, the Catholic Church in Poland was still waging the battles of the century-and-a-half before, when Martin Luther and other Reformers threatened the Church's hegemony. And even in the century of the Enlightenment, the Catholic clergy in Poland continued to turn back to centuries-old sources and methods, filling their literature with medieval tales and imagery that the Church in the West seems to have abandoned.

The Catholic Church's use of Jews, real or symbolic, as instruments for its wider struggles propagated anti-Jewish sentiments in Poland and ultimately disseminated a virulent animosity against those real Jews with whom Polish Christians had daily contacts. Vilified and dehumanized from premodern times, Jews eventually found themselves permanently excluded from a Polish nation that increasingly saw itself as Catholic. The creation of a Polish Catholic national identity had begun with the nobles in the early modern period and extended to other Polish Catholics in modern times, when the modern Polish nation refused to accept as Poles Orthodox Christians, Protestants, or Jews. But, in the modern era of nationalism, Eastern Orthodox Christians could identify as Ukrainians or Byelorussians, and Protestants, such as Lutherans, as Germans. Religious identity became increasingly linked to nationality and to the state. And, once religious identity, nationality, and the state became one, Polish Jews, after centuries in Poland, now found themselves regarded as strangers. The premodern anti-Jewish stereotypes that challenged the Jews' very humanity and extended beyond religion to permeate their very nature translated into racist anti-Semitism that denied even most assimilated Jews their identity as Poles.[24]

Such was the modern fallout of a process of the Church's search for religious hegemony that had begun in premodern times. Yet, it would be a mistake to say that this consequence was a conscious goal of the Church. The Church's intent was rather to prevent pollution and corruption of its own flock, to cripple its opponents, and to establish social and political control over the larger society. Its goal was to bring all groups under its embrace, to convert or to control. The permanent exclusion of Jews, especially of converted Jews, was a contradiction of the Church's theology and of its ideals.[25]

1

〇〜

"One Mystical Body . . . Only One Shepherd":
The Church Ideals of Social Order

*I*N 1302, POPE BONIFACE VIII WROTE IN HIS BULL *UNAM SANCTAM*, "WE
declare, we proclaim, we define that it is absolutely necessary for salvation
that every human creature be subject to the Roman Pontiff."[1] The bull was a cul-
mination of a theory of hierarchy of power developed over several centuries by
Church jurists and theologians. That theory established an ideal of a society, a
respublica Christiana, a broader Christian *ecclesia*. In its highest form that society
was to be entirely Christian, functioning according to Christian laws and dogmas. It
was to be, in the words of Pope Boniface VIII, "one sole mystical body whose Head
is Christ and the head of Christ is God, and his vicar Peter and Peter's successor."[2]
The pope claimed the supremacy of spiritual power and a hierarchy of power in
the world: "For with truth as our witness, it belongs to spiritual power to establish the terrestrial power and to pass judgment if it has not been good. Thus is
accomplished the prophecy of Jeremiah concerning the Church and the ecclesiastical power: 'Behold to-day I have placed you over nations, and over kingdoms and
the rest. . . . Therefore whoever resists this power thus ordained by God, resists the
ordinance of God' [Rom 13:2]."[3]

"TWO SWORDS . . . THE SPIRITUAL AND THE TEMPORAL"

Pope Boniface VIII justified the claim of papal supreme authority in his *Unam
Sanctam* by citing a medieval interpretation of an ambiguous verse in Luke 22:38,
"Behold, here are two swords." According to the theory of "two swords," the Apostle
Peter had received two swords from Jesus. In the eyes of medieval Church jurists,
one sword represented temporal power, the other, spiritual power. Church jurists
asserted that all temporal power and political authority derived from the Roman
pontiff, Peter's successor, in effect "Christ's vicar" on earth, the heir of the legacy of
two swords and the two powers they represented. Although the pontiff voluntarily
relinquished to the emperor the sword of temporal power, the emperor's power
(and, by implication, also that of other temporal rulers) derived from God through
the pope, who was the supreme authority over both temporal and spiritual matters.[4]

7

The bull *Unam Sanctam* left little ambiguity about the papal claims of power:

We are informed by the texts of the gospels that in this Church and in its power are two swords; namely, the spiritual and the temporal. For when the Apostles say: 'Behold, here are two swords' – that is to say, in the Church, since the Apostles were speaking, the Lord did not reply that there were too many, but sufficient. Certainly the one who denies that the temporal sword is in the power of Peter has not listened well to the word of the Lord commanding: 'Put up thy sword into thy scabbard' [Matthew 26:52]. Both, therefore, are in the power of the Church, that is to say, the spiritual and the material sword, but one ought to be administered for the benefit of the Church, the other by the Church; the one in the hands of the priest; the other by the hands of kings and soldiers, but *at the will and sufferance of the priest* [my emphasis]. However, one sword ought to be subordinated to the other and temporal authority [should be] subjected to spiritual power. For since the Apostle said: 'There is no power except from God and the things that are, are ordained of God' [Rom 13:1–2], but they would not be ordained if one sword were not subordinated to the other and if the inferior one, as it were, were not led upwards by the other.[5]

The legitimacy of temporal power was to remain perpetually subject to the Church's spiritual authority. Lay rulers were to serve the good of the *ecclesia*.

There were earthly implications of the Church's position on the superiority of the spiritual over the temporal power. Tithes, the monetary obligations to the Church, became a worldly symbol of recognition of the Church's ideal political order. "Hence we must recognize more clearly," *Unam Sanctam* asserted, "that spiritual power surpasses in dignity and in nobility any temporal power whatever, as spiritual things surpass the temporal. This we see very clearly also by the payment, benediction, and consecration of the tithes, by the acceptance of power itself and by the government even of things."[6]

But *Unam Sanctam* was an ideal. The reality was much more complex, as even the context surrounding this very bull revealed. *Unam Sanctam* was issued as a protest against the erosion of papal authority. Asserting the superiority of papal authority over that of the monarch, it reflected a conflict between Pope Boniface VIII and the king of France, Philip IV (the Fair). The king had taxed the clergy, and, in response, the pope issued first a bull, *Clericis Laicos*, forbidding such taxation, whereupon King Philip the Fair banned exportation of gold from France, thus depriving the papacy of revenue.[7] The French party, in turn, plotted to declare Boniface a heretic and depose him. It was in this context of crisis that Pope Boniface VIII issued his powerful bull. But, after Boniface's death, the cardinals, influenced by the French king, elected as pope Clement V, who in 1305, under pressure from the French, moved from Rome to Avignon to become the first of the Avignonese popes.[8] As Gordon Leff has argued, from the fourteenth century on the papacy and the Church as a whole "became less rather than more powerful."[9]

The Church and the Papacy would never return to the height of prestige and power it held during the rule of Pope Innocent III at the turn of the twelfth and thirteenth centuries.[10] But, even at that pinnacle, the Church was plagued with heresies and dissent.[11] Centuries of struggles between the Church – at times more specifically, the papacy – and the lay rulers ensued. The ideal of Church hierocracy proved unattainable, but the Church never ceased to strive to fulfill the ideal of its supreme power in the world of the spirit and in the world of flesh.

Reflecting the political reality of late antiquity and before the Church emerged as a visible power within the Roman Empire, ancient Christian jurists had agreed on the existence of parallel structures of temporal and spiritual powers, the former represented by the Empire, the latter by the Church.[12] As the Roman Empire was transformed in the West into separate independent principalities, and in the East into Byzantium, the Christian Church began to assume a stronger position of authority – especially in the fragmented West, where the office of the emperor disappeared. In the East, in the Byzantine Empire, where the imperial presence survived, the legacy of the emperor as source of both temporal and spiritual authority persisted. It lessened the intensity of the power struggle between the Byzantine emperor and Church patriarchs, such as that which developed in the West between emperors and kings and the papacy. In the East, the emperor continued to play an important role in affairs of the Church.[13]

It took the West several centuries to return to the very idea of the Roman Empire, with an emperor at its head. In the meantime, chaos caused by the breakup of the empire and the lack of imperial authority enabled the pope, the bishop of Rome, to emerge as the principal authority. Still, in Western Europe, the idea of the empire lingered, and by the ninth century it was back. It proved to be the source of conflicts between the Church and the state that were to last for centuries.[14] In 800, when Pope Leo III arranged to crown Charlemagne as the Holy Roman Emperor, Charlemagne was displeased; he understood that an act of papal coronation implied that his own imperial authority derived from the pontiff and hence was subordinate to it.[15]

The notion that temporal authority derived legitimacy from the spiritual authority of the Church had been tested a few decades earlier when the Frankish king, Pippin III, seeking legitimacy for his power, was anointed, first by Boniface, a missionary who later became a saint, and subsequently, in 754, by Pope Stephen III.[16] But if Pippin III needed such confirmation of his power, many other kings and subsequent emperors, like Charlemagne, were convinced that their authority needed no such papal endorsement. Centuries later the continuing conflict manifested itself in the form of controversies over appointments of bishops, taxation of the clergy, and even over who held authority over Jews.[17] These conflicts were never resolved in practice, and the Church found itself perpetually dependent on the lay powers. At times even the popes' own political and economic existence rested in the hands of monarchs, as did indeed that of Pope Boniface VIII.

By the end of the sixteenth century, the understanding of pontifical powers had changed and the Papal States, territories in central Italy where from 756 to 1870 the pope had political sovereignty, had been transformed into a real political state, with an army, a bureaucracy, and a well-organized diplomatic corps. In 1595 Paolo Paruta wrote in his report to the Senate in Venice: "The Roman Pontiff can be considered to embody two persons: the head and shepherd of all of Christianity, in the Catholic and Apostolic Church the Vicar of Christ and a true successor of Peter; and a temporal prince who controls a state in Italy. . . . The Pontiff rules the whole Ecclesiastic State with a supreme authority . . . relying regarding all things on solely on his will."[18] The symbolic spiritual power had become a real political power; in consequence, the mystical theology may have lost some of its allure. As Paolo Prodi has argued, the pope became the prince with the authority to apply Church laws in the papal territories that elsewhere had been left to the discretion of the secular authorities.[19] But beyond the Papal States, the Church leaders continued to demand obedience from temporal rulers.[20]

THE THREAT TO THE SWORD OF SPIRITUAL POWER: "THOSE WRETCHED AND MISERABLE JEWS"

Nor was the "sword" of spiritual authority of the Church securely held. From the earliest days of Christianity, centuries before the doctrine of two swords, Christian leaders felt threatened, first by Jews, and later also by Christian heretics. Christianity had emerged from among several Jewish sects during the last decades of the Second Temple period, and needed to validate itself in the light of Jewish persistence in rejecting Christianity's claims that the Messiah had already come.[21] Christian thinkers and theologians turned to the Hebrew Scriptures, which they began to call "the Old Testament," and pointed to passages that, in their opinion, "proved" their claim that Jesus was the Messiah foretold in the Jewish Scriptures. It resulted in a paradox. On the one hand, Christianity sought its validity in the Hebrew Scriptures; on the other hand, it sought to invalidate Jewish religious beliefs and practices based on the same texts.[22]

Jews dismissed Christians in the early period and attacked them for failing to observe Jewish law. For their part, the Romans persecuted the new sect, accusing them of immorality and cannibalism, a charge later Christians would raise against Jews. The second-century Christian writer Justin the Martyr[23] captured these challenges in his dialogue with Trypho, the Jew:

After they had finished their discourse on this subject [war in Judea], I thus began again, and said: Is there any objection, gentlemen, that you have to make against us, besides this, viz. that we do not live according to the law; that we are not circumcised as your ancestors were; nor observe the Sabbaths as you do? Do you find any fault with our lives and conversations? I mean, do you believe that we eat the flesh of men; and that after an entertainment, when the candles are put out, we are defiled with unlawful mixtures?[24]

Although the persecution of Christians and charges of cannibalism came primarily from non-Christian gentiles,[25] Justin lashed out against Jews:

For other nations are not so culpable for the injury that is done to us, and Christ himself, as you; who first caused them to entertain so great a prejudice against that Just One, and us his disciples and followers. For after you had crucified him, who alone was unblameable and just, by whose stripes they are healed who come unto the Father by him; after ye knew that he was risen from the dead, and ascended up into heaven, as the ancient prophecies foretold concerning him; ye were so far from repenting of those evil deeds which ye have committed that even then ye dispatched from Jerusalem into all countries select missionaries to inform them that the impious sect of Christians latterly sprung up worshipped no God; and to spread abroad those false and scandalous reproaches, which all that are unacquainted with us and our religion, do even to this day lay to our charge.[26]

Justin charged that Jews refused to accept Jesus not because they were unaware of the prophecies in Jewish Scriptures but because they were "afraid to acknowledge him to be the Christ, as the scriptures, and those things which are seen and done in his name, do plainly prove that he is, lest ye should suffer persecution from the princes of this world who at the instigation of that wicked and seducing spirit the serpent, will not cease from killing and persecuting those that call on the name of Christ, till he shall come again and destroy them all, and render to every man according to his desserts."[27] In early Christian history, when Christianity's status was lower than that of Jews in the Roman Empire, Justin suggested that Jews refused to accept the divine truth foretold by their own scriptures because of fear of Roman persecution.

The Hebrew Bible and history were to demonstrate, as the fourth-century Christian historian Eusebius argued, "The real antiquity, and divine character of Christianity...to those who suppose that it is recent and foreign, appearing no earlier than yesterday."[28] Christians interpreted passages of the Hebrew Scriptures Christologically. Already Paul the Apostle, himself a Christian Jew, had begun to interpret the Hebrew Scriptures in this manner, by comparing Hagar, the slave woman with whom Abraham had his first son, Ishmael, to Jewish law. In his Epistle to Galatians (4:21–5:1), Paul wrote:

Tell me you who desire to be subject to the law, will you not listen to the law? For it is written that Abraham had two sons, one by a slave woman and the other by a free woman. One, the child of the slave, was born according to the flesh, the other, the child of the free woman, was born through the promise. Now, this is an allegory: these women are two covenants. One woman, in fact, is Hagar, from Mount Sinai, bearing children for slavery. Now Hagar is Mount Sinai in Arabia and corresponds to the present Jerusalem, for she is in slavery with her children. But the other woman corresponds to the Jerusalem above, she is free and she is our mother.... Now you my friends are children of the promise like Isaac. But just as at that time the child who was born according to the flesh persecuted the child who was born according to the Spirit, so is it now also. But what does the scripture say? 'Drive the slave and her child for the child of the slave will not share the inheritance with the child of the free woman.' For freedom, Christ has set us free. Stand firm, therefore, and do not submit again to a yoke of slavery.

Paul's Christological reading of the Hebrew Scriptures and his comparison of Jewish law to slavery set a model that some later Christian theologians would follow.[29]

Jews' insistence on continuing observance of Jewish law challenged Christian theological claims. If those whose texts "prophesied" about Christianity refused to accept Christian dogmas, could it be that Christians were wrong and Jews right? After all, Jews could claim antiquity of their laws "from the time of Moses" and continuity of their adherence to those laws, whereas the Christian sect and its own claims were relatively new. It became even worse when theological dilemmas were translated into practice. Some gentile Christians did not understand why they should reject the laws Jews observed as taught in the scriptures, and they continued to value these laws, in some cases adhering to them for centuries.

In the fourth century, the Christian preacher John Chrysostom was infuriated by Christians who continued to celebrate Jewish festivals:[30] "Another malady, a most severe one, summons my tongue for its treatment, a disease which has infected the body of the Church. . . . The continuous and successive festivals of those wretched and miserable Jews – Trumpets, Tabernacles and the fasts – are about to begin and of those who belong to us and say they are loyal Christians, many are accustomed to attend these places where the festivals are held, and others, even to partake of the feasts and share in the fasts. This wicked practice I now desire to expel from the Church."[31] Chrysostom explained, "I know that many people hold a high regard for the Jews and consider their way of life worthy of respect at the present time. That is why I am hurrying to pull up this fatal notion by the roots."[32] Canon XLIX of the Council of Elvira in 300 demonstrated such a respect for the Jews, a respect that seems to have exceeded that of the Christian clergy itself: "Landholders are to be admonished not to suffer the fruits, which they receive from God with the giving of thanks, to be blessed by the Jews, lest our benediction be rendered invalid and unprofitable."[33]

Christian scholars responded in two ways to the Christian observance of some Jewish rituals, which they saw as transgressions of religious boundaries: by aggressive anti-Jewish rhetoric, like that by John Chrysostom, which aimed at invalidating Jewish practices and deterring Jewish-Christian interaction; and also by a complex theoretical scheme, like that developed by Chrysostom's contemporary, Augustine of Hippo,[34] who actually justified Jewish persistence in observance of their law, while affirming Christianity.[35]

Chrysostom demonized Jews and their places of worship, exclaiming that they did not worship God and that a synagogue was "not only a whorehouse and a theater; it is also a den of thieves and a haunt of wild animals."[36] Unlike the obvious pagan cults, Jewish worship attracted and confused Christians. Chrysostom wanted to remove the confusion. The synagogue was a place of blasphemy, he continued in his sermon:

[W]here the Christ-killers collect, where the Cross is rejected, where God is blasphemed, where the Father is unknown, where the Son is outraged, where the grace of the Spirit is disdained, and where, besides, real demons are present, is not the mischief much greater? For in the Temple of Apollo the godlessness is open and obvious and can scarcely seduce or deceive a thoughtful, sober person. But there, with their claims to worship God and spurn idols, to possess the prophets and honor them, the Jews prepare quantities of bait and entrap the naïve and senseless unawares. So the impiety of the Jews is equal to that of the Greeks, and the deception they achieve is far worse. For in their midst stands an altar of deception, invisible, on which they offer not sheep and calves, but the souls of men.[37]

Augustine of Hippo, on the other hand, tried to explain Jews' persistence in observance of their law as part of the divine plan. Jews had a historical and theological role to play, and that role, Augustine argued, in fact buttressed the validity of the Christian religion:

But the Jews who killed him and refused to believe in him, to believe that he had to die and rise again, suffered more wretched devastation at the hands of the Romans, and were utterly uprooted from their kingdom.... They were dispersed all over the world for indeed there is no part of the earth where they are not to be found, and thus by the evidence of their own Scriptures they bear witness for us that we have not fabricated the prophecies about Christ.... About them this prediction was made: 'Even if the number of the sons of Israel shall be like the sand of the sea, it is only a remnant that will be saved.' [Isaiah, 10:20] But the rest of them were blinded.... When the Jews do not believe in our Scriptures, their own Scriptures are fulfilled in them, while they read them with blind eyes.... We recognize that it is in order to give this testimony, which in spite of themselves, they supply for our benefit by their possession and preservation of those books, that they themselves are dispersed among all nations in whatever direction the Christian Church spreads. In fact there is a prophecy before the event on this very point in the book of Psalms, which they also read. It comes in this passage: 'As for my God, his mercy will go before me, my God has shown me this in the case of my enemies. Do not slay them, lest at some time they forget your Law; scatter them by your might.' [Psalm 59:10ff] God has thus shown to the Church the grace of his mercy in the case of her enemies the Jews, since as the Apostle says, 'their failure means salvation for Gentiles.' [Romans 11:11] And this is the reason for his forbearing to slay them – that is for not putting an end to their existence as Jews.[38]

Like Eusebius, Augustine demonstrated that Christians were continuing to counter accusations that their religion was a fraud, and that they needed Jews and their Scriptures to defend it. Jews were not to be slain, but rather preserved alive among Christians, though not in a neutral position. Discussing Genesis 25:23 ("Two nations are in your womb, and two peoples will derive their separate existence from your belly; one of those peoples will overcome the other, and the elder will be servant to the younger"), Augustine wrote:

As for the statement 'The elder will be servant to the younger,' hardly anyone of our people has taken it as meaning anything else but that the older people of the Jews was destined to serve the younger people, the Christians. Now it is true that this prophecy might seem to have been fulfilled in the nation of the Idumeans ... but in fact it is more appropriate to believe that the prophetic statement, 'One of these peoples will overcome the other, and the elder will be servant to the younger,' was intended to convey some more important meaning. And what can this meaning be except a prophecy which is now being clearly fulfilled in the Jews and the Christians?[39]

Augustine continued, "Isaac's two sons, Esau and Jacob, presented a symbol of the two peoples, the Jews and the Christians."[40] Drawing on both the Hebrew Bible and Paul, Augustine created a theological framework for Jewish existence in Christian society, and for an ideal of social order within it. According to that rationale, Jews were to submit to Christian authority and remain subservient to Christians. Christianity faced competing, seemingly contradictory, conclusions that promoted both the despising of Jews, as an obstacle to achieve the pure "one mystical body" of Christendom, and tolerating them within its body.[41]

Roman Imperial legacy also played a part in the shaping of the status of the Jews within Christianity. In the sixth century, Pope Gregory I rephrased the Roman Imperial Law, which the Christian world inherited and which regarded the Jewish religion as *religio licita*, as legal religion. He stated: "Just as one ought not to grant any freedom to the Jews in their synagogues beyond that permitted by law, so should the Jews in no way suffer in those things already conceded to them."[42] Jewish communities could exist legally but limits were set to "what is permitted by law," allowing leeway in defining those limits. With time, the limits came to mean whatever did not obstruct Christianity. As Kenneth Stow pointed out: "Papal policy thus aimed at creating equilibrium between function and presence, making it possible to integrate the Jews into a society structured, at least in theory, according to the tenets of the ideal Christian world order. The maintenance of this equilibrium then became the hallmark of all papal actions involving Jews."[43]

Solomon Grayzel (and Kenneth Stow after him) pointed out that Gregory's stance on the legal position of the Jews was not repeated until the twelfth century, when Pope Calixtus II issued a bull to protect Jews soon after his election in 1119. The bull, which came to be known for its first words, *Sicut Judaeis*, was reissued, sometimes with modifications, by almost every pope up to the sixteenth century.[44] In 1199, the assertive Pope Innocent III reissued the bull, combining Gregory's position with Augustine's theological exposition. With its language of hostility toward Jews, the modified bull exposed the Church's unease about the Jews in its midst. Pope Innocent III wrote, in an influential edict of 1199 on protecting Jews, *Constitutio pro Judaeis*: "Although the Jewish perfidy is in every way worthy of condemnation, nevertheless, because through them the truth of our own Faith is proved, they are not to be severely oppressed by the faithful. Thus the Prophet says, 'Thou shalt not kill them, lest at any time they forget thy law,' or more clearly stated, thou shalt not destroy the Jews completely, so that the Christians should never by any chance be able to forget Thy Law, which, though they [Jews] themselves fail to understand it, they display in their book to those who understand." Innocent III allowed Jews to practice "in their synagogues" what had been permitted to them by law, and, like Gregory I, admonished Christians to refrain from violence as a means of compelling Jews to convert to Christianity.[45] Yet, Jews must live in "perpetual servitude because they crucified the Lord although their prophets had predicted that He would come in the flesh to redeem Israel."[46] Subsequent popes echoed Innocent III's stance, protecting Jews but simultaneously buttressing their status of "servitude."

The Church, by such means, was seeking to impose its ideal of world order on society and, in the process, to protect its own integrity despite the Jewish presence. Thus, the IV Lateran Council of 1215 forbade Jews to mock Christians, and ordered Jews not to walk in public during the last three days of Holy Week and on Easter Sunday. The council sought to reinforce a lower status for Jews by reissuing the by then centuries-old prohibition against Jews' holding of public offices.[47] It also sought to prevent intermixing and sexual interaction between Christians and non-Christians by ordering that "Jews and Saracens" wear distinguishable clothing. Clothing appears to have been seen as an easily perceived means to establish a proper social order. Thus, Canon XVI of the council provided guidelines for making the clergy's clothing distinguishable from that of laity, thereby ensuring that the clergy's "visiting taverns," "playing games of chance," or "attending performances of mimics, buffoons or theatrical representations" would be more conspicuous, and hence less likely to occur.[48]

Despite the Church's efforts to create an order that would correspond to its ideals, the reality proved much more troubling. In 1248, Pope Innocent IV wrote to the Bishop of Maguelonne, Odo of Chateauroux:

Your Fraternity has told us that certain Jews of your diocese and of the surrounding places presume, not without injury to the clerical orders to wear round and wide capes after the manner of clerics and of members of the holy orders. As a result, it often happens that sacerdotal honor and undeserved reverence is paid them by travelers and strangers. Since we do not want them to presume to do anything of this sort, we order that the said Jews, having discarded any such capes, shall wear a habit befitting them, one by which they may be distinguished not only from clergy, but even from laity. This you are to achieve by denying them intercourse with the faithful. Nor are you to delay compelling the nobles, on whose lands these Jews live, to force them to this by temporal powers if necessary.[49]

Although Christianity is thought to have been fairly well established by the thirteenth century, at least among the European elites, the Church continued to face insecurities. Jewish position and proximity to Christians enhanced these anxieties. In seeking to prevent the transgression of religious boundaries, the Church needed the support of the kings and the nobles who held "temporal powers," but who nevertheless, for their part, sometimes gave preference to Jews, "sons of the crucifiers," over Christians in the performance of certain functions. In 1205, Pope Innocent III wrote to the king of France:

Though it does not displease God, but is even acceptable to Him that the Jewish Dispersion should live and serve under Catholic Kings and Christian princes until such time as their remnant shall be saved in those days when "Judah will be saved and Israel will dwell securely," nevertheless, such Princes are exceedingly offensive to the sight of the Divine Majesty who prefer the sons of the crucifiers, against whom to this day the blood cries to the Father's ears, to the heirs of the Crucified Christ, and who prefer the Jewish slavery to the freedom of those whom the Son freed, as though the son of a servant could and ought to be an heir along with the son of the free woman.[50]

In the same letter, the pope complained that Jews employed Christian servants in their homes, and thus that the Kingdom of France tolerated what was a reversed order. The pope asked the king to enforce Church rules.

The Church's sense of confidence in its superiority depended on an ability to control temporal powers beyond the Papal States, in which the Church held, at least in theory, both "spiritual" and political authority. Still, even there, it was not until 1555 that the Church sought to apply that dual authority and establish the order in which the position of the Jews would reflect the Church ideal. In 1555, in the midst of revising Church policies and doctrines challenged by the Reformation,[51] Pope Paul IV issued a bull (*Cum Nimis Absurdum*) declaring Jews "consigned... to perpetual servitude":[52]

Since it is absurd and improper that Jews – whose own guilt has consigned them to perpetual servitude – under the pretext that Christian piety receives them and tolerates their presence should be ingrates [*adeo sint ingrati*] to Christians, so that they attempt to exchange the servitude they owe to Christians for dominion over them; we – to whose notice it has lately come that these Jews, in our dear city and in some other cities, holdings and territories of the Holy Roman Church, have erupted into insolence: they presume not only to dwell side by side with Christians and near their churches, with no distinct habit to separate them, but even to erect homes in the more noble sections and streets of the cities, holdings and territories where they dwell... – sanction.... [53]

Paul IV's bull was a response to the existing disruption of the centuries-old ideal social order of Christianity, an order in which Jews could and should belong but only in a position of subservience or, in Paul IV's words, "perpetual servitude" to the Christian powers.[54] But it was only the increasing transformation of the papacy into a secular "monarchy," as Paolo Prodi argued, that allowed Pope

Paul IV to implement the Church's long-standing theories. Now, for the first time, "the two swords," or the spiritual and temporal powers, were held by one body.[55]

Cum Nimis Absurdum ordered the establishment of a separate, exclusively Jewish quarter in Rome and, subsequently, similar quarters in other papal cities as well, outside of which Jews were not permitted to live and within which Christians were prohibited from living. By the 1590s such a quarter had become known as the "ghetto," after the name of the Venetian Jewish quarter established by the Venetian Republic's government in 1516 – independently of papal sanctions and in response to the local clergy's pressures.[56] By forcing Jews to live in such a quarter the pope intended to "put the Jews in their place" so that "as long as they persist in their errors, they should recognize through experience that they have been made slaves while Christians have been made free through Jesus Christ, God and our Lord and that it is iniquitous that the children of the free woman should serve the children of the maid-servant."[57]

The idea of geographic segregation of Jews from Christians was not new. It first appeared in 1267 when, in the early years of Jewish settlement in the Polish lands, the Church Council of Breslau (Wrocław) in Silesia sought to establish physical segregation of Jews and Christians. It cited as its rationale that "the Polish land was still a new plant in the body of Christianity [*cum adhuc terra Polonica sit in corpore Christianitatis nova plantatio*]."[58] Fearing that these social and religious boundaries were being violated, the Church Council of Breslau insisted that Jews and Christians live in separate areas divided by a moat. It called on the clergy to prevent mixing of Christians and Jews in bathhouses and taverns, and repeated earlier Church canons that prohibited Jews from having more than one synagogue in town, and that forbade them to have Christian servants in their homes, especially overnight, and to engage in sexual relations with Christians. Elaborating on a canon from the IV Lateran Council in 1215, which ordered some kind of marking for Jews and Muslims ("Saracens"), the synod in Breslau ordered Jews to wear a pointed hat so that they could be identified as other than Christian.[59] Some historians have argued that these 1267 laws came as a Church response to the charter issued by Prince Bolesław the Pious of Kalisz in 1264, which afforded Jews extensive privileges of Jewish communal autonomy and economic activity, and which officially recognized Jewish settlements in Poland.[60]

Nonetheless, the policy of the separation of Jews and Christians was not implemented in Poland by the Church or by Polish lay authorities. It was only implemented by the Nazis, when they established Jewish ghettoes during the Second World War.[61] The idea, however, did reemerge in the eighteenth century among Polish Catholic clergy when the bishops, after several centuries during which the policy was not mentioned, turned back to the 1267 laws and reissued them in their synods.[62] But in Poland at that time, as elsewhere outside of the Papal States, the "two swords" were held in different hands.

"ALL HERESIES ARE FORBIDDEN BY BOTH DIVINE AND IMPERIAL LAW"

The anxieties concerning Jews voiced by the Church in the Middle Ages, along with the retaliatory measures against them in the thirteenth century and during the Reformation, coincided with the rise of heretical movements within Christianity itself.[63] The Church was threatened more by heresy than by the Jews, who did not intend to "take away" the Church's spiritual authority, although they did polemicize against it. Heresy came from within; it accepted principles of Christianity but by "perverting them destroy[ed] their value."[64] The threats of heresy became the more acute the more theological orthodoxy developed within the Church itself. Such threats prompted the Church to commit itself more forcefully to ideas the heterodoxy was challenging, thereby solidifying the orthodoxy itself.

In the first centuries of Christianity, and before Christian doctrines were defined, there had existed a fluidity of theological opinions. There was no one true Church. Early Christian theologians wrestled with a number of theological issues before arriving at definite doctrines that began to mark the beginnings of the established Church. One of the first such decisions was the Nicene Creed of 325, which affirmed the dogma of the Trinity. The Creed was issued by the Council of Nicea, which had been convened to respond to the Arian heresy, which was questioning the concept of the divinity of Jesus and thus the doctrine of the Trinity itself.[65]

After Emperor Constantine's conversion in the fourth century, Christianity was embraced by the state and Christian religious leaders received state support to suppress heresy. The first heretic executed by Christian temporal authorities was Priscilian in 383, the leader of a Priscilian sect in Iberia that was professing Gnostic-Manichean beliefs. By 438, the *Theodosian Code*, an Imperial Code of Law, included a section on heretics, declaring that "all heresies are forbidden by both divine and imperial laws and shall forever cease."[66] Heresy had no place in the Christian society and both spiritual and temporal powers were to eliminate it. Yet the same code, in contrast, continued to recognize Judaism as a legal religion within the state, ruling that "it is sufficiently established that the sect of the Jews is prohibited by no law."[67]

The same contrast between legal attitudes toward Jews and toward heretics in Christendom continued for centuries. Although both groups were seen as threats to the authority of the Church, Jews were allowed to exist within Christianity even as their position was restricted; heresy had no such place. But whenever Christian heresies emerged, so did the Church's anxieties about Jews.

In the twelfth and thirteenth centuries, Europe experienced a rise in heretical movements, the Cathars (Cathari) and Waldensians being the most prominent of the groups that challenged doctrines and policies of the Church. The Cathars, a dualistic sect, resembled the ancient Manicheans; they professed that the world consisted of good and evil, and that matter was evil. They saw the Catholic Church "as a false and fraudulent organization which had prostituted itself for power and ill-gotten wealth."[68] The Waldensians sought to reform the Church and return it to its apostolic roots; they promoted apostolic piety and poverty and criticized the opulence of the Catholic Church.[69] "The pope, they say," in the words of a contemporary anonymous author, "is the head of all errors, and they call prelates scribes and religious Pharisees. They say it is a sin that clergy perform no labor. They also say that the clergy are full of avarice, envy and pride . . . and that clerics ought to have no possessions or property."[70]

Already in the thirteenth century, the Waldensians had raised questions of vernacular translations of the Bible, thereby making possible the reading of the Bible without clerical supervision. The thirteenth-century Dominican Etienne de Bourbon wrote:

A certain rich man of the city [Lyons], called Waldo, was curious when he heard the gospel read, since he was not much lettered, to know what was said. Wherefore he made a pact with certain priests, the one, that he should translate the Bible to him and other, that he should write as the first dictated. Which they did; and, in the like manner, many books of the Bible and many authorities of the saints, which they called *Sentences*. Which when the said citizen had often read and learned by heart, he proposed to observe evangelical perfection as the apostles observed it; and he sold all his goods, and despising the world, he gave all his money to the poor, and usurped the apostolic office by preaching the gospel, and those things which he had learned by heart, in the villages and open places, and by calling to him many men and women to do the same thing.[71]

Etienne's contemporary, Anonymous of Passau, considered access to the vernacular Bible one of six causes of heresy: "They have translated the Old and New Testaments into the vulgar tongue, and thus teach and learn them."[72] He went on to state that "men and women, great and lesser, day and night, do not cease to learn and teach."[73]

Until the high Middle Ages, the Church had been "the sole cohesive and unifying body in society, the repository of all knowledge and spirituality."[74] Now education and knowledge of the sacred texts by the laity were confronting this monopoly. With the translation of the Bible and other texts, and with their availability to laity through memorization and teaching, the monopoly of the Church over those texts and the Church's religious authority were at risk.[75] In 1270, David of Augsburg, a Franciscan monk in German lands, noted that "This was their first heresy, contempt of the power of the Church."[76] With the spiritual authority of the Church in question, the Waldensians, the Cathars, and other emerging sects all refused to accept the Church as a mediator.[77]

The impact of the Waldensian heresy was relatively limited, however, because in the pre-print era there were limits to the dissemination of texts. In this context, even the most radical movements had a circumscribed effect, as the movements by John Wyclif in England and Jan Hus in Bohemia demonstrated. For both Wyclif and Hus, preaching and reading the Bible in the vernacular were critical. Both questioned the Church's spiritual authority.[78] Wyclif wrote to Pope Urban VI that "the gospel of Christ [is] the heart of the corps of God's law.... And over this I take it as belief that no man should follow the pope, nor any saint that now is in heaven, but in as much as he follows Christ."[79]

To the Church, Wyclif's teaching was an effort "to subvert and weaken the state of the whole Church and even secular polity."[80] It was unwilling to tolerate these damaging voices within its body; in 1415, the Council of Constance condemned Wyclifian ideas postmortem, and summoned Jan Hus to the Council, condemning him for heresy and executing him.[81] But the ideas themselves were not entirely suppressed. Education, access to sacred texts, and critique of the clergy, of tithing, and of indulgences returned during the Reformation, sounding alarms in the Catholic Church.

The Church needed temporal powers to assist in implementing its policies, whether by eradicating heresy or by forcing Jews into a position of subservience more in line with the Church's social ideal. In 1231, when Pope Gregory X outlined procedures for dealing with heretics, he ordered that those declared heretics by the Inquisition were to be transferred to the temporal powers for execution.[82] "The spiritual sword" was in constant need of "the temporal sword" to maintain its effectiveness throughout the premodern period. And the Church felt doubly uneasy when the temporal powers refused to cooperate and increasingly acted to preserve their own interests – interests that, at times, contradicted the Church's own ideals.

2

The Upset Social Order: Nobles and the Jews in Poland

I N EARLY MODERN POLAND, CATHOLIC CHURCH OFFICIALS DID NOT ASPIRE TO the kind of actual political power held by the Church in the Papal States. They seem to have continued to accept the medieval ideal of Church hierocracy, by which the Church would work together with temporal authorities in the expectation that the temporal powers themselves would act for the good of the Church and "at the will and sufferance of the priest."[1] As late as the eighteenth century, the principle of the two swords of spiritual and temporal powers was still, it seems, of considerable importance in Poland, as the title of the 1731 book by Józef Andrzej Załuski, *Two Swords of Catholic Retaliation against Unrelenting Attacks of Polish Dissidents in the Orthodox Catholic Kingdom*, suggests.[2]

In 1733, after the death of King August II, Bishop Jan Felix Szaniawski urged in a sermon: "Let us plead with God that he will place [the crown] on the head of the one who is able to maintain the Catholic Faith, our Laws and Freedoms, and is able to preserve the Unity of the Kingdom."[3] And in 1753, a preacher, Adam Abramowicz, came close to repeating the idea embodied in bull *Unam Sanctam*: "In the Church of Christ, there is, and has to be, only one highest and visible Shepherd.... And just as there is only one shepherd, there is and has to be only one fold of Christ, outside of which no one will achieve redemption."[4]

But the centuries-old ideal of Church hierocracy was complicated by Poland's fragmented political structure. For one thing, the very interregnum for whose end Bishop Szaniawski prayed in 1733 concluded with the election of a king who, like his father, the previous king of Poland, was a recent convert to Catholicism from Lutheranism. For another, in contrast to the centralization and rise of absolute monarchies in Europe, Poland had moved in the opposite direction. The relatively strong Polish monarchy of the fourteenth and fifteenth centuries had evolved by the eighteenth century into a "republic of the magnates," a state ruled by several extremely wealthy nobles, the magnates, according to their own interests. In this situation, even a most committed Catholic king could do little to implement the Church's ideal of supremacy.[5]

The Polish Catholic clergy needed a strong Catholic king,[6] cooperative and supportive of the Church, as were Sigismund (Zygmunt) I, who went hand in hand with the Church in reaction against the first signs of the Reformation, and his son Sigismund (Zygmunt) August, who issued strong edicts in support of the Church. In 1550 Sigismund August condemned "the heretics," and in 1565 he confirmed the canons of the Council of Trent – twelve years before the Church in Poland itself confirmed them in 1577 at the Synod in Piotrków.[7] So too in the seventeenth century, the political appointments of Sigismund (Zygmunt) III Vasa strengthened the Catholic faction of the nobility and encouraged some others to return to Catholicism for fear of loss of political influence.[8]

This ideal of Church hierocracy was recognized by Polish Protestants. They understood its weight in the politics of religious conflict, and ridiculed it while using it for their own political gains. A sixteenth-century Protestant leader, Marcin Krowicki, stated in a pamphlet in which he sought to appeal to the Polish king and bring him over to the Protestant side: "And the [Catholic] priests do not respect any laws, neither divine nor royal, and so they do whatever they like. And so they invented and wrote down different laws for their own benefit, so that neither you, Your Majesty, nor any other lord, would have any authority over them."[9] Krowicki continued, "And so the pope writes that he has two swords, with which he slashes all Christendom. And he sharpened these swords so much that even emperors, kings, princes and lords have to fall on their knees before him and kiss his smelly feet."[10] Despite such evocative rhetoric, Krowicki was clearly unpersuasive – all Polish kings remained Catholic until the demise of the Polish state in the last decade of the 1700s.[11]

Even after the Reformation, the Catholic Church may have had some hopes for domination in Poland because of its own close historical ties to Polish rulers. It may also have hoped that the historical animosity between Poland and the Holy Roman Empire would discourage Poland from importing from its western neighbor the new religious ideas inspired by Luther. These hopes had their roots in the medieval period, when, in 966, Polish feudal rulers first accepted Christianity from Bohemia in fear of becoming dependent on the Holy Roman Emperor. In the 990s, they had pledged to subject their domains directly to the pope in a move that assured Polish Church independence from the bishoprics within the Holy Roman Empire, especially the bishopric of Magdeburg in Saxony, which was seeking to expand its authority eastward. By taking these steps, Polish rulers in fact had entered into a feudal relationship with the papacy and, as a consequence, were obliged to pay an annual tribute, the *świętopietrze* [Peter's pence].[12]

POLISH TRIANGLE OF POWER: THE KING, THE NOBLES, AND THE CATHOLIC CHURCH

The relationships between principal power players in medieval and post-Reformation Poland – the king, the nobles, and the Catholic Church – were not static. They changed over time with a consequent strong impact on the Polish Catholic Church's sense of stability and confidence. Although in the Middle Ages the Church and the king in Poland engaged in conflicts similar to, and at times bloodier than, those between the pope and the emperor in the West, in the early modern period the Catholic Church in Poland tended to support the king against the Polish nobility, and the increasingly weaker kings generally allied themselves with the Church.[13] Tensions that arose between the nobles, who continuously strove to assert and broaden their rights and freedoms against the royal power, and the king and the Church shaped the political and religious landscape of the Polish state between the sixteenth and eighteenth centuries.

The connection between the monarchy and the Church was reflected in the law, according to which, from 1573, the Polish king had to be a Catholic. According to the same law, the archbishop of Gniezno, who was also the Polish primate, served as the interrex when the king was absent from the country or during interregna.[14] Between the sixteenth and eighteenth centuries, the king's position weakened dramatically to the advantage of the nobility, and Church officials hoped and prayed for a stronger monarch.[15] But even when the king was weak the alliance between monarch and Church continued, and many ecclesiastic careers advanced through the royal court.[16]

The process of the rise of the nobility in Poland at the expense of the royal power had begun in the late fourteenth and in the fifteenth centuries, but not until the sixteenth century did the most significant transformations take place. From the time the Piast dynasty disappeared in the second half of the fourteenth century, Polish monarchs were elected, although at that point not by all nobles but by the most powerful magnates. The electoral process had weakened the monarch's position, for his power was constantly challenged by the magnates. To counterbalance this rise of the magnates, several Polish kings sought the support of the lower nobility, or the gentry; in response, by 1433 the gentry managed to gain royal concessions to protect their property and rights, according to which neither they nor their property were to be touched without due process.[17] Among other political gains, the lower nobility ensured that all governmental positions were to be restricted to the nobility and that nobles' military duty without compensation was to be limited to territories within state borders.[18] The royal alliance with the lower gentry raised their status within the state, balancing it temporarily with that of the magnates and eventually contributing to the development of a notion that all nobles were equal brethren.[19] And although, as Jerzy Lukowski pointed out, on many levels this equality of nobility remained a fiction, the large noble estate (about 8–10 percent of the total population) emerged as a powerful force within the state.[20]

A compelling symptom of this process was the 1505 constitution *Nihil novi*, a reward from King Alexander I to his political supporters in power struggles against the powerful magnates. This constitution decreed that the king could issue no new laws without the consent of the nobles. It gave equal weight, at least in theory, to both chambers of the Polish parliament, the Senate (formerly a royal council) and the lower chamber, the Sejm.[21] The *Nihil novi* constitution significantly weakened the king's power but did not paralyze him entirely, at least not yet. In fact, the first half of the sixteenth century was marked by the rule of a strong monarch, Sigismund I, who appointed his supporters to the highest state positions, including bishoprics, strengthening his own position. He also conducted a policy of territorial expansion.[22] Still, King Sigismund I had to make further concessions to the nobles to ensure that his son would be the next king of Poland. In 1529, when King Sigismund I was still alive and well, his nine-year-old son was crowned king of Poland and became King Sigismund August. The concessions, as historian Józef Gierowski put it, "opened the way for general participation of all nobility in the elections of the future monarch."[23] Both this step and the later "execution of the laws movement" – which began in the 1530s, continued until the 1560s, and aimed to make the monarchy more efficient politically and fiscally – in the short term strengthened the king by bringing in support from the lower nobility against the powerful magnates.[24] In the long term, however, these measures weakened the monarch, as would become obvious after the childless King Sigismund August died in 1572, leaving no guidelines on who his successors were to be. The time for Poland's first free royal elections had arrived.[25]

During this interregnum, which ended in 1573 with the election of Henry of Anjou as king of Poland, the nobles seized the opportunity not only to elect their own ruler but also to ensure that their rights would be respected. They compiled a set of rules the future ruler was to swear to obey, rules that became known as "Henrician articles." These rules laid legal foundations for the "Republic of the Nobles" that Poland became. They obliged the king to call for the general assembly of the Sejm every two years, and prohibited him from imposing new taxes and duties, effectively removing his control over the treasury.[26] They limited the king's powers in conducting foreign policy by forcing him to seek their approval, especially in matters of war or peace. The "Henrician articles" also constrained the king's authority as supreme judge by establishing court tribunals to adjudicate cases among the nobles. In 1578, this judicial body became the Crown Tribunal; it served as a supreme court of appeals in civil and criminal cases involving the nobles.[27] Most important, the 1573 laws stipulated that, should the king violate any of these rules, the nobles had the right to renounce allegiance to him, as they did several times over the next two centuries.[28]

In addition to the "Henrician articles," the elected kings of Poland had to obey the *pacta conventa*, conditions drawn up for each specific king.[29] Increasingly, the main goal of these conditions appeared to be the preservation of the nobility's liberties. The nobles wanted to prevent any attempts by future kings to establish strong monarchial rule.[30] Eventually this led to the collapse of the Polish state. As Lukowski put it, "For most, 'freedom' remained the amassing of 'liberties' rather than Liberty. The extolling of personal privilege came to outweigh collective, or even personal, responsibility."[31]

The strengthening of the lower and middle nobility was not long lasting. Ultimately, the power lay with those who were wealthy, and wealth at the time came from land. The monarch was not only politically but also financially weak. Royal domains were perennially mismanaged and often held in hereditary (albeit not legal) leases by powerful nobles to their own benefit. Even so, the land belonging to the monarch amounted to no more than 15–20 percent of the total land in the Polish-Lithuanian Commonwealth.[32] Most of the land was in the hands of the powerful few.[33]

The nobles, although theoretically equal, were in fact divided into several groups – first, between the land-owning and the landless, and then between the magnates with immense areas under their control and the minor landed nobles.[34] Scholars have shown that some "landed" nobility's possessions were so small as to make these nobles virtually undistinguishable from peasants, except for the nobles' birth and the coat of arms that came with it. The economic crises, crop failures, and especially the wars that ravaged Poland in the seventeenth century had the most devastating impact on the lesser nobility and further widened the gap between the lower nobility and the magnates, who had more resources to weather the crises.[35] By about 1665, land and power distribution had turned the late sixteenth-century "republic of the nobles" into "the magnates' republic."[36] It is estimated that, by the second half of the eighteenth century, in the Lithuanian parts of the Polish-Lithuanian Commonwealth, 1.9 percent of the nobility controlled some 75 percent of the total wealth. Lukowski said that "at the very pinnacle, 16 great magnates (0.7 percent of all nobles) owned 77,000 (63.3 percent) hearths."[37]

This transformation of control resulted in a fragmentation of political power. As a consequence of mid-sixteenth-century laws that gave the nobility control over their own domains and excluded them from royal jurisdiction, the magnates were able to govern their territories almost as independent rulers.[38] Their political influence extended to the Sejm, the noblemen's parliament. Magnate factions ran the country with the help of backers from the lower nobility.[39] The powerful lords dominated the local dietines, the *sejmiki*, which set the policies of a given province for the Sejm. These powerful lords became patrons of the lesser nobles, who, in exchange for support of their magnate, could gain access to offices, magnates' courts, and influence. It was a quid pro quo. Although the magnates held the power, they had to rely on their lesser nobles, who could conceivably switch allegiance. With a weak king, and with most of the vast Commonwealth's territories in the hands of the powerful few, the state became a confederation of principalities controlled by individual magnates. As Antoni Mączak explained, in such a situation, "political life could flourish only at the provincial level," and the magnates' personal interests shaped it greatly.[40]

"WE WERE BORN NOBLES FIRST AND ONLY THEN CATHOLICS"

The transformation of Poland's political life did not bode well for the Catholic Church, for it led to attempts by the nobles to shed the influence over their lives not only of the king, but also of the Church. Tensions between the nobility and the Church were exacerbated during the period of the Reformation, when many nobles embraced new religious trends (mainly Calvinism and, later, more radical anti-Trinitarianism) and temporarily abandoned the Catholic Church. And even when – by the second half of the seventeenth century – most of the nobles had returned to Catholicism, increasingly embracing a Catholic identity, the rift between them and the Church persisted. By then, the nobles, committed to preserving their own liberties, contested anyone who even hinted at encroaching on those liberties. For the nobles, all this outweighed a personal commitment to Catholicism and led them to disobey the teachings of the Church, especially when its goals contradicted the nobles own interests.

As early as 1552, King Sigismund August had noted that at the last Sejm, the nobles had engaged in a fight about the influence of the clergy – "a weed," in the king's words, "which will be difficult to weed out."[41] The king was referring to an attempt by the Sejm to suspend cooperation between ecclesiastical courts and secular courts in matters concerning the laity. That topic, along with the question of tithes, would return to subsequent sessions of the Sejm, in 1562–3, and again in 1573.[42]

The separation between the ecclesiastical and the secular courts resulted in a prohibition against the secular courts' denial of due process to anyone who had earlier been excommunicated by a Church court. Although this process coincided with the Reformation, the authority of ecclesiastical courts over the laity (even if, realistically, this meant over the nobles, because they did not act on behalf of other groups) was questioned not only by those who embraced Protestantism, but also by devoutly Catholic deputies to the Sejm.[43] The nobles, more concerned with their freedoms than with questions of religion, wanted to make certain that the rights they had won against unwarranted arrests and confiscation of property without due process would not be violated by the Church.[44] As an anonymous sixteenth-century writer stated: "It is not about faith, nor about the fact that one who is a Catholic should obey the Church in matters of faith and salvation, but rather – given that we are born nobles first and only then Catholics, and that the Polish kingdom is not a sacerdotal kingdom but a political kingdom – what is owed to God and to the state [ojczyzna] should be given to each of them separately and the holy religion should not be mixed with policing, while the matters of the state should not be dictated by the priests."[45] This was one of the reasons why the Church inquisition in Poland, formally established in 1536, was rather short lived.[46]

Tithes and also the taxing of the Church property were on the nobles' agenda in the 1560s, and continued to be addressed in various forms in the seventeenth century as well. The nobles demanded that tithes received by the Church be taxed and that the revenue be devoted to military expenditures; they questioned also the use of secular power to enforce payment of tithes to the Church.[47] Because for the Church, as Pope Boniface VIII had affirmed in his bull Unam Sanctam, tithes were recognition of the superiority of spiritual power over that of the temporal government, the nobles' attacks on such issues were a strong blow to the very doctrine of Church hierocracy.

The nobles' attacks had double strength because they coincided with the Reformation. Early Protestant synods also had criticized the idea of tithes. In 1555, the Protestant Synod of Koźminki had urged its clergy to find a means of support other than tithes, which "are taken by papists... and hopefully will, with God's help, have no place in our congregation."[48] And in 1558, a Synod in Włodzisław declared that it was not appropriate to give tithes to the "idolatrous papists," who are "false prophets."[49] As a scriptural proof, the synod cited Matthew 15:26: "It is not fair to take the children's food and throw it to the dogs."[50]

For the Protestants this was a matter of doctrine; for the rest of the nobles, the Church was simply another landowner who should live by the laws pertaining to all landowners in Poland and pay its dues. The nobles' attitude was in line with the Execution of the Laws movement. In the years 1562–3, the Sejm of Piotrków demanded that the Church contribute to war efforts from revenues from its lands, "like all other landowners in the Republic."[51] And the 1573 Tax Universal imposed taxes on Church-owned lands in the same way as on that of other landowners, including the king and the nobles themselves.[52] Just as the nobles tried to subject the Church to the laws of the state, so the Church sought to do exactly the opposite – it wanted the state laws to be subject to Church teachings, and to ensure its own privileged political and economic position. The Church was concerned also to prevent secular jurisdiction over clergy.[53]

Catholic synods in Poland frequently ruled that those who took clergy to secular courts deserved to be excommunicated. In this, the Polish clergy simply followed the ruling of the Council of Trent (1545–63): "They are not to be tolerated who by various obstructive devices contrive to withdraw tithes from churches, or who brazenly lay hold of tithes paid by others and annex them, since the payment of tithes is due to God... the holy council orders... that those who either subtract them or obstruct them are to be excommunicated and not absolved from that guilt until they have made full restitution."[54] Each side wanted to impose its authority on the other and neither was willing to submit to the jurisdiction of the other. For the Church it was an issue of a hierarchy of power; for the nobles it was an issue of their liberties.

The nobility frustrated the Church's efforts to implement its ideal order. The nobles in effect tried to equalize "the spiritual power," which, according to Pope Boniface VIII, "surpasses in dignity and in nobility any temporal power," and treated the Church as another landowner. In addition, they blatantly disregarded Church teachings when those teachings did not suit their interests. The nobles were unwilling to permit their own political authority to become dependent on "the will and sufferance of the priest." They carefully guarded their own interests and their relationship with Jews; and their alliance with the Reformation further strained their relationships with the Church and forced the Church in Poland to recognize the limits of its own influence and prestige. The lords' behavior had disrupted the Church's ideal order not only in the domain of politics but also in the realms of religion and social discipline.

JEWS AND THE NOBLES, "THEIR PROTECTORS"

The need for an alliance between the Church and the "temporal powers" to secure the Church's ideal social order was especially intense in Poland, where Jews had begun to settle in the Middle Ages, and where, by the eighteenth century, they constituted the largest Jewish community in the world. As Yosef H. Yerushalmi pointed out, wherever Jews lived they tended to establish liaisons with "the highest governmental power available, whether that of emperor or caliph, count, duke or king, bishop, archbishop or pope."[55] Yerushalmi called it "a direct vertical alliance." In Poland, that alliance shifted with the transformation of the Polish power structure. At the beginning of their settlement in Poland, Jews forged a strong relationship with the monarchs, who issued privileges and assured the Jews' protection. When Poland's balance of power shifted from a strong monarchy to a decentralized nobles' republic, the Jewish relationship with the king was transformed into a symbiotic relationship with the powerful nobles. Jews' reliance on royal protection was transferred to reliance on the nobles. First the king, and then the nobles, often placed Jews in positions that gave them authority over Christians, thus challenging the Church's ideal of Jewish "servitude."

The first centuries of Polish Jewish settlement resembled the legal and economic conditions of Jewish communities in Western Europe, where Jews were mostly urban dwellers, and engaged in trade and banking. As the early charters indicate in Western Europe and in Poland, Jews relied on royal power for privileges and protection.[56] Even the charters of privileges granted to Jews in Poland resembled those granted to Jews in the West. The first known charter of 1264, for example, was modeled on a 1244 charter awarded to Jews of Austria by Duke Frederick.[57]

In the early period of Jewish settlement in Poland and up until the last decades of the sixteenth century, Jews played a prominent role in the royal economy of Poland. They were important economic actors in royal cities – bankers and merchants,[58] and, as the contemporary royal charters suggest, tax and toll collectors, highly positioned administrators, and even lessees of royal salt mines, on which the crown had a monopoly.[59] In the fourteenth century, King Kazimierz the Great is said to have had a Jewish banker, Lewko, who also leased salt mines in Wieliczka and Bochnia, and served as a minter. In the early sixteenth century, the prominent brothers Ezofowicz – Michel, Abram, and Isak – served as royal treasurers [podskarbi], as royal officials [starosta], and as administrators of royal domains.[60] Abram eventually converted to Christianity, assuming the name Jan, and became the administrator of the royal treasury. Michel Ezofowicz was granted nobility and is known to have been the only Jew ever admitted to Polish aristocracy who was not required to convert to Christianity.[61]

Such conspicuous position of some Jews in Poland aroused animosity toward Jews among some Christian burghers and noblemen, who saw them as unwelcome competitors impeding their own social and economic advancement. That sentiment, with an expressly economic twist of competition in the marketplace, is reflected in some anti-Jewish publications of the sixteenth and early seventeenth centuries. Gershon Hundert has said that a particular anti-Jewish work by Sebastian Miczyński portrayed the Jewish role in Cracow's economy in "a fairly accurate, though hostile, and somewhat exaggerated picture."[62] In it, Miczyński sought to discourage Jewish-Christian business relations, warning that "whoever forms partnerships with Jews by selling them goods on credit should know that he will always suffer losses. Do you not know that no one who trades or forms partnerships with Jews can truly make profit? ... If you are taken in by the sincerity of a Jew, only betrayal and fraud await you."[63]

Jewish power sometimes put prominent Jews in vulnerable positions that led to accusations and convictions.[64] Izak Brodawka of Brześć, a royal tax collector, was implicated in, and his servants accused of, two murders, one in Narew in 1564, and the other in Rososz in 1566.[65] In the first case, Brodawka's servant, Biernat Abramovich, also a Jew, was accused of murdering a Christian girl [d'evchina]. He confessed under torture. Biernat's words, as paraphrased by the scribe of the case, implied that the accusations against him were a result of Jews' powerful status. "But," the scribe wrote, "it was the townspeople [meshchane] of Narew who did it [accused him] as a rebellion against his lord [pan] and their arrendator [leaseholder] in Narew, [Izak] Brodawka."[66]

Certain nobles, as well, were unhappy with the prominent role some Jews played in the royal domains. In 1538, the Polish Sejm of Piotrków prohibited Jews from managing the taxes and tolls, and from holding any honorary offices,[67] and the 1565 constitution confirmed the laws against Jews' managing or leasing of taxes, tolls, and salt mines.[68] As long as the king was strong and as long as the nobles were striving to improve their own political and economic condition, Jews' economic role continued to be questioned at the Sejms. But, as Poland's political system changed, so did the Jews' economic and political position; their change in status was reflected in the privileges granted. With the weakening of the king, the royal privileges to Jews, while not entirely displaced, were supplanted by private settlement privileges granted by individual landowners to the Jews who served them. In the noble estates Jews no longer served principally as bankers and merchants but as leaseholders of businesses, like mills and breweries, and sometimes as managers of estates and as nobles' agents.[69]

The change was gradual, and for Jews not immediately beneficial. In 1539 the private owners of towns obtained full jurisdiction over Jews living under their domain,[70] for Jews at the time an ambiguous move because those living in privately owned towns now lost recourse to royal courts and could no longer turn to the king for protection. The ruling established that nobles were to enjoy all profits Jews brought to them [*ex eis fructus omnes et emolumenta percipiant*],[71] a law that benefited the nobles and strengthened the nobles' position.

The interdependent relationship between Jews and nobles was strengthened especially after 1569, when the territories of the Polish Crown expanded to become the vast Polish-Lithuanian Commonwealth. Poland and Lithuania had been united in a dynastic union since 1386, when the Lithuanian Prince, known in Polish as Jagiełło, married the underage Polish queen Jadwiga,[72] but the two states had retained a certain degree of independence. Lithuania prohibited "foreigners," including Polish nobles, from acquiring land within its borders by purchase and even through marriage, and it refused to allow Poles to ascend to high state offices.[73] The Polish throne was elective; the Lithuanian throne remained hereditary.[74] The union, a controversial matter, was not supported by the powerful Lithuanian lords, nor initially by the king, who feared that the hereditary throne in Lithuania would become a subject of elections. But Lithuania was a vulnerable state; its neighbor, Russia, had become stronger and had been challenging its eastern frontier. It had seized some Lithuanian territories, and in 1563 Tsar Ivan the Terrible conquered Polock, a town in the northeastern part of Lithuania.[75] After much negotiation and political manipulations on both sides, union was formalized on July 1, 1569, during Sejm deliberations in Lublin. Poland and Lithuania were declared "an inseparable body," a Republic that "out of two states and nations became one."[76]

The decree of union established that Poland and Lithuania would have a single monarch elected by a joint assembly of Polish and Lithuanian nobles.[77] The Sejm was to serve as a common assembly of nobility from both parts of the new Commonwealth.[78] The currency also was to be common.[79] But, most important, the existing restrictions on land ownership in Lithuania were lifted: "All the statutes and laws issued in Lithuania for whatever reason against the Polish nation concerning acquisition or lease of the land by a Pole [Polish nobleman], whether through marriage [*po żenie*] or as a reward for service, or through purchase . . . will be abolished because they are against law, justice and mutual brotherly love, and against the common Union. And therefore, from now on both a Polish noble [*Polak*] in Lithuania, and a Lithuanian noble [*Litwin*] in Poland will be allowed to hold title to, or lease the land."[80]

Wealthy Polish nobles immediately began to acquire land in the east, and with this new eastward expansion new economic opportunities arose – and not only for the wealthy nobles. With various tax incentives, the nobles encouraged migration and settlement to their newly acquired large estates, which came to be known in Poland as the *latifundia*. Jews also benefited from this process, and increasingly moved eastward.[81] By settling in these underpopulated, noble-owned lands, Jews became ever more central to the economy of the nobles. The Jewish population began to shift from royal cities to private towns and rural estates and, by the mid-eighteenth century, three-quarters of the Jews in the Polish-Lithuanian Commonwealth lived in Polish private towns and villages, which, as Gershon Hundert suggested, amounted to more than half of the Jews in the world.[82] Indeed, the nobles wanted to retain Jews, along with other inhabitants, in their towns. In 1682, the owner of the town of Boćki prohibited Jews and Christians from selling their homes and moving away from his town.[83]

As the king's position weakened to the advantage of the nobility, Jews gained from this once questionably beneficial law of 1539, if at times not without tensions within the Jewish community itself. The lords often protected Jews who lived on their lands from paying taxes to the Crown, an advantage that came at the expense of other Jews. In 1687 the Va'ad Arb'a Arazot, the Council of Four Lands – the Jewish supracommunity – complained to the king that they could not meet their tax payments for the year because "some Jews, living in towns, districts or noble estates have avoided paying that part of their tax obligation because of the protection of their lords."[84]

In another case, Jews living under a certain noble's jurisdiction sought that nobleman's protection against encroachments by the Jewish kahal, the community leaders, in the royal town of Minsk. In 1711, the Lithuanian Tribunal issued a decree against Minsk Jews that compelled Jews who lived in a jurydyka, a part of town excluded from the municipal law and in this case privately owned by a nobleman named Jarosz Mackiewicz, to work on construction of a Jesuit church.[85] The kahal officials of Minsk had borrowed a sum of money from local Jesuits and, to pay off the debt, had agreed to provide labor and perhaps even material for the construction.[86] The coercive methods the kahal used against Mackiewicz's Jews included the threat of expulsion, presumably the retraction of the hezkath ha-yishuv (the permission granted by Jewish officials to other Jews who wanted to settle in town), and even the threat of a more general herem, or ban. Among other measures the kahal employed was overnight imprisonment. As a consequence, the Jews of the nobleman's jurydyka turned to him for help against the kahal. The nobleman went to court, charging an unlawful coercion of the Jews in his jurydyka and, as such, a violation of the judicial boundaries between the royal and the private domain. The kahal was sentenced to pay monetary damages.

This lawsuit reveals as much about the Polish political and juridical distinctions between the private and the royal domains within cities as it does about conflicts among Jews. Jews were willing to turn to Christian authorities for help against other Jews if necessary and to resort to coercion or even to violence to achieve their goals. Nobles, for their part, were willing to support their Jews in court, especially in cases in which their own interests would otherwise suffer.[87]

By the late seventeenth and eighteenth centuries, Polish Jews had become an intrinsic part of the Polish economic landscape and society[88] – not an "alienated minority" relegated to ghettos, as in the Papal States, but living among Christians as neighbors, friends, employers, and even as "lords."[89] Jews and nobles had established a symbiotic relationship. Unlike the petty nobles and the Christian burghers, Jews had no interest in challenging their lords' political power. They were considered most reliable as agents and leaseholders in the nobles' domains and, as Moshe Rosman pointed out, "they played a central role in controlling the distribution of *latifundium* resources" and "were the magnates' most reliable source of cash."[90]

But both the petty nobles who sought contracts from their richer "brethren" and the Christian burghers who sought to monopolize a town's economy perceived Jews as their competitors. Sometimes this competition led to conflicts. On June 13, 1645, Dwora Łazarzowa Leyzerowa Szymczyszowa, a powerful Jewish woman arrendator, or a leaseholder, filed a complaint against a local landowner, Tymoteusz Muraszko, charging him with assaulting her two Jewish servants and inciting peasants to rebel against her.[91] Muraszko's motivation for his actions remains unclear. Because Dwora controlled large tracts of lands, including the town of Pogost (Pohost), and a number of villages, forests, and meadows, with all their inhabitants, perhaps Muraszko had sought to disrupt her business, gain control, and acquire a lease contract. Muraszko is said to have come to one of her estates at Łulin and "prohibited the serfs from working for us and from paying us anything they owed."[92] As with many of these cases, the final outcome is unknown.

From the perspective of the powerful magnates, Jewish loyalty could be assured.[93] Jews needed the magnates for economic, political, and – sometimes – physical protection, and the magnates knew that they did not have to cater to the Jews for their votes and political support, as they had to in establishing relationships with lesser nobles.[94] The nobles supported "their" Jews against incursions of Christian burghers, in courts, and at toll booths, where letters from the lords sometimes helped Jewish merchants avoid paying tolls and dues.[95] Conflicts were more easily resolved in private towns as well because the chain of command there was shorter than in royal towns, and Jews, or anyone else for that matter, could appeal directly to the owner of the town by writing a petition, or a *suplika*.[96] In working with Jews the nobles conducted a politics of self-interest – despite any personal prejudice, as Gershon Hundert has shown;[97] therefore, the Jews could generally count on their noble's backing. Jews did occasionally find themselves in the domain of a cruel nobleman,[98] but they were generally more secure in the private lands than in the royal domains. In royal domains, Jews were more vulnerable, both because by then the king was relatively weak and because he was farther removed, leaving Jews dependent on the attitude of a royal official.

The nobles' close relationship with Jews was doubly problematic for the Church. It challenged the Church's ideal hierarchy of power because the nobles refused to comply with the Church's directives. And Jews, as leaseholders and as employers of Christians, were often in a position of authority over lower-class Christians – a flagrant violation of the Church's ideal social order in which Jews were to be in "perpetual servitude" to Christians, not the other way around.

"A GREAT DANGER ... FROM THE OUTCRY OF THE GENTILES THAT JEWS ... HAVE DOMINION OVER THEM"

The new social context of Jews' working for the nobles in their large *latifundia* and their being in positions of power led to some clashes with the Jewish law, the *halakhah*. In 1590, Rabbi Meshullam Weibesh issued a number of regulations on the observance of Sabbath among Jews who had leased properties, towns, and villages with fields and vineyards, and who appear to have worked on Shabbat in violation of this holiday. The rabbi pointed out that Jews had observed Shabbat even when they were slaves in Egypt; how much more should they do so now when the non-Jews were "under their [Jews'] control [*ha-goi beshi 'avidam shel elu*]"?[99]

Jews had a sense of appreciation – if not unconditional – for Poland as their homeland. In the sixteenth century, Moses Isserles, a rabbi and scholar from Cracow, remarked that in Poland "their [non-Jews'] anger has not risen up against us as in the German states."[100] In a similar vein, an eighteenth-century rabbi, Phinehas of Korzec, testified that "in Poland, exile is less bitter than anywhere else."[101] Hundert, in his polemical article, maintained that the Polish Jews' sense of security can be demonstrated by their failure to produce a messianic movement, in contrast to Jews in Yemen, Spain, or Italy.[102]

And if, as Edward Fram argued, many rabbis still bemoaned the exile,[103] the actions of some Jews in Poland indicated a relative sense of security. Court cases from the entire period indicate that Jews engaged in brawls in which they were not always the only victims. In 1561, three Christian servants of a certain Jan Kowalski filed a complaint against three Jews of Slonim for assault.[104] The Christian men were attending a party [*na besedu*] in the house of a certain Zelmanowa, perhaps a Jewish woman, wife, or a widow of a certain Zelman. According to the Christians' affidavit, the three Jewish men "came to our party [*na besedu nashu*]" and assaulted them. The bailiff reported severe injuries sustained by two of the Christians. The three Christian servants testified that they "did not beat the [Jews], only defended ourselves," whereupon the judge demanded proof that it was the Jews who started the fight. But the accusers had no proof and all they could do was to take an oath. The Jews too had injuries, and they also took an oath, asserting that Kowalski's servants had started the brawl. The Jews were set free. Brawls caused by socializing and drinking between Jews and Christians were not incidents of anti-Jewish violence, but rather incidents of ordinary eastern European life, where alcohol consumption led to violence.[105]

An interesting tit-for-tat comes from the court in Brest in 1644, where the rector of the Jesuit college, Jan Rakowski, and its prefect, Krzysztof Jankowski, filed a complaint against Jews, and in particular against a Pinkas Samuelowicz, accusing him of beating a student, Bartłomiej Nieciecki, and threatening other students on the town's Mostowa street.[106] Just over two months later, Jews in Brest filed a protest against certain Jesuit students and townspeople for attacking them and their market stalls.[107] Unfortunately, we know nothing of the outcome of these cases.

Some Jews felt secure enough to confiscate the goods of Christians or to arrest them (including nobles), and to mete out justice on their own.[108] In 1589, a Jewish toll collector, Shlomo Januszewicz, confiscated two carriages of hops transported by certain townsmen. The court recorded the townsmen's appeal.[109] On October 8, 1615 in Slonim, a nobleman Paweł Masiukiewicz filed a complaint charging that his imprisonment by a Jew, Mayer Shimonivich, for an unpaid debt was illegal. The irate nobleman complained that Shimonivich had disregarded Masiukiewicz's social status [stan moy], treated him like a landless man [gołota],[110] and thrown him into a "dark prison, where only criminals are found."[111] On another occasion, in August 1646, a court beadle recorded that Brest Jews arrested several noblemen who served the aristocrat Jan Andrzejewski.[112] The noblemen were thrown into the "thieves' prison." No reason is given. According to the report, the arrested noblemen complained to the court beadle who came to visit them that "the Brest Jews, having captured us violently among the market stalls with the [help of] castle troops, stripped us of clothing, swords and money, now torment us, honest noblemen, and starve us in this cruel prison."[113] The court beadle and his witnesses, who were also noblemen, met with two Jewish beadles [szkolnicy] and other representatives of the Brest Jewish community and pled for release on bail of the imprisoned noblemen. The Jews rejected their plea and asserted that they would keep the nobles in prison until the trial.[114]

Recent studies have shown that arenda contracts [lease-contracts] sometimes granted Jews significant control over Christians living on their leased estates,[115] especially in the eastern territories of the Polish-Lithuanian Commonwealth, where Jews frequently served as administrators or leaseholders of estates within huge latifundia owned by the powerful aristocratic families.[116] A case in point is the 1638 arenda contract for the latifundium of Raków (which included the town of the same name and surrounding village) between two Jews, Jakub Moyżeszowicz and Moyżesz Rubinowicz, the leaseholders, and Semeon Samuel Kowelski, a voivode (i.e., a palatine) of Vitebsk. Under this contract Kowelski ceded considerable authority to the two Jewish leaseholders,[117] who not only held the right to all revenue from these lands (in cash, produce and animals), but who also had authority over all serfs, free peasants, and boyars in the territories, an authority that stretched so far as imposing even capital punishment. Thus, they had the right to "hold the lease in peace and to enjoy all proceeds they achieve by their entrepreneurship, to judge, govern and punish landed proprietors [ziemianie], boyars, serfs and townspeople [living within that latifundium] with monetary penalties, and should necessity arise, also punish with death [a przyszło li by do tego występnych gardłem karać]. [The leaseholders] have the right to pursue justice for themselves and those who need it."[118] Sometimes the right to mete out capital punishment was moderated by a clause requiring the leaseholder to refer capital cases to the landlord.[119] And the owner of the town of Szczebrzeszyn acknowledged in his 1652 instructions to the administrator of the town that Izrael, the Jewish leaseholder, was given permission to hold six serfs.[120]

Jews could acquire authority over Christians also by lending money to nobles because these lordly borrowers sometimes pledged their serfs as collateral. There is also evidence that some poor Christians even pledged their children to Jews for loans.[121] Moreover, as employers of Christians, Jews wielded power over these employees. These arrangements, all in violation of Church regulations, were a further sign of the Church's inability to execute its own laws and authority – a symbol of its disrupted, or unfulfilled, ideal order.

The power of certain Jews even worried other Jewish leaders, who warned that power in the hands of Jews might lead to abuses and arouse Christian anger against the Jewish community. In his early seventeenth-century responsum, Joel Sirkes of Cracow, who had served as a rabbi in the eastern town of Brest, cited rulings by other Jewish communal leaders in Poland against any Jew who held the lease of the tax on liquor, the *czopowe*. The communal leaders "in some lands in our kingdom," Sirkes wrote, "ruled that under no circumstances Jews shall lease the *czopowe*... because there was in many places a great danger stemming from the outcry of the gentiles that Jews rule and have dominion over them ... like kings and princes." The ruling threatened to impose heavy penalties on Jews who violated this prohibition.[122] In 1653, Nathan Nata Hanover, in his Hebrew chronicle of the Chmielnicki uprising that claimed thousands of Jewish and Christian lives, noted that the Greek Orthodox people in the eastern territories were enslaved not only by Poles but also by Jews. "And even the lowliest among them [Jews] became their overlords," Hannover wrote.[123] He referred to one of the Jews as a "ruler of the town [*moshel ha-ʿir*]."[124] Rabbi Isaiah Horowitz wrote in his book *Shnei Luḥot ha-Brit* (Two Tablets of Commandments) that he "saw sons of Israel [Jews] build houses like fortresses of the princes."[125]

Some Jews did indeed live like nobles. In 1605, a powerful Jewish arrendator, Itzḥak Michelewicz, was murdered by Ivan Soltan, a nobleman.[126] Soltan raided the estate where Michelewicz lived, which Soltan had leased to him and his wife, Esther, two years earlier. Soltan seized a considerable amount of money and property, killed Itzḥak and dumped his body in the river. Soltan and his partners then assaulted Itzḥak's brother and his servants. Itzḥak's widow, Esther, sued Soltan and his wife for violation of the lease-contract, and for theft, assault, and murder.

During the trial, the Soltans brought in a certain man, Jakub Michalovich Ventzkovich, to testify that it was he and not the nobleman Soltan who raided the estate. This only complicated the case and put the Soltans, now accused also of lying in court, at a more disadvantageous position, for the court regarded such behavior as unfitting a nobleman. Itzḥak's brothers, on the other hand, presented as evidence an old privilege granted by King Sigismund I to Itzḥak's ancestor, Michel Ezofowicz. The privilege testified that their ancestor had been admitted to the nobility with all rights and privileges extended to him and his descendants.[127] The case of murder of a Jew by a nobleman thus became a case of murder by a nobleman of another nobleman who happened to be a Jew. And this Jew, Itzḥak Mikhelevich, was portrayed by the court as a model of aristocratic values and way of life: "The deceased Itzḥak Mikhelevich, a Jew, was an honest nobleman who followed nobleman's life, and was not an innkeeper, a craftsman or a merchant, but was engaged and lived according to the aristocratic freedoms. . . . And he sometimes leased estates to provide livelihood."[128] The document declared, "It was thus an attack on a nobleman's house." In 1605 it was still possible to consider Itzḥak a nobleman. After 1673, when the Polish parliament, the Sejm, limited ennoblement to Catholics, such a multireligious and multiethnic definition of nobility could no longer apply.[129]

Ivan Soltan and his wife were sentenced to death, but he fled and the sentence was altered to infamy. His wife's fate is not mentioned. Esther, Mikhelevich's widow, succeeded her husband and became a powerful leaseholder in the area. She became the subject of another lawsuit that same year, accused of raiding the property of and assaulting a nobleman, Jan Dawidowicz Wolkowicz.[130] She appears to have embraced a behavior that was a trademark of the nobles.

Although it could be argued that one cannot be sure that such accusations charging Jews with attacks were not in fact malicious fabrications (and some, much like the blood libels, probably were), the Jews' own trust in Christian courts in Poland-Lithuania suggests that at least some of these charges were true. Despite rabbinic injunctions not to use non-Jewish courts in cases against other Jews, many Jews even sought justice against their own coreligionists in Christian courts.[131] On April 8, 1647, a Jew, Moszko Zelmanowicz, filed a case against another Jew, "Szachna of the town of Krzynek" in a court in Pinsk, a town in the eastern part of Poland-Lithuania, now in Belarus.[132] When Szachna, having divorced his wife, arrived in Pinsk, "allegedly to buy some merchandise,"[133] he stayed in a home of a Jewish woman, Baska Perecewiczowa. There he met a neighbor, Moszko, whom he later visited. Moszko alleged in his affidavit that Szachna, noticing Moszko's affluence, stole a number of valuable objects from his house and fled from the town. Moszko sought Szachna's arrest as soon as he could be found.[134]

Jewish sources also record cases between Jews brought into non-Jewish courts. Moses Isserles noted in one of his responsa a case of a fight between two Jews, in which one filed a complaint against the other in the municipal court and then appealed to the lord of the town.[135] And in 1551, King Sigismund August, seeking to strengthen the authority of rabbis, outlined the responsibilities of the rabbi and admonished Jews to obey his decisions.[136]

Jews even turned at times to the Catholic Church for help and justice. In 1662, when the Augustinian monastery of Brest apparently encroached on Jewish land, the Jews protested to the general of the order. In response, the general of the order enjoined the monastery to return the land to the Jews and prohibited any further encroachment. Jews recorded the general's instruction in the municipal court.[137]

Still, the Jews' sense of security was mixed with a sense of vulnerability. Jewish leaders felt that the well-being of the Jewish community was fragile and endangered, for example, by the behavior of Jewish criminals. Sometime in 1676, Jews of Lithuania requested a royal decree from King John III Sobieski on the responsibility of the Jewish community for crimes committed by Jewish criminals. The king issued such a proclamation in 1679. Fifty-four years later, that same proclamation was confirmed and filed in the Brest court. It was addressed to all royal officers and courts in the Great Duchy of Lithuania:[138]

Senior Jews of different places in the Grand Duchy of Lithuania appealed to me...concerning the burgeoning, among the Jewish nation, of the power of such Jews who harm both nobility and other Christians and because of those there is a fierce rancor against all Jews.... Therefore, we desire that each Jew guilty [of crime] to be punished with the knowledge of the Jewish elders, and after the execution of the punishment [the elders] shall be allowed to exclude the criminal from their community; and if such an excluded individual should commit further damage, no other Jew would be punished for him, but instead [such accused] should be held responsible individually. And, with the knowledge of the [royal] court, all Jewish elders in the Grand Duchy of Lithuania, in cities, towns and areas belonging to us, the Church or secular lords will be allowed to punish dice-players [kosterów], criminals, other malefactors according to their crimes and to exclude them from their community [de suo ordine]; and if such a person were to serve as a witness against Jews, his testimony will not be valid.[139]

The 1723 recording of the decades-old edict in the Brest court was not without a cause. In 1718–19, the court in Brest – and later the royal Lithuanian Tribunal – heard the case of a Wulf Iewłowicz and his son Izrael Wulfowicz of Brest.[140] Wulf and his son had broken into the tomb of the wife of Pociej, the Treasurer of the Grand Duchy of Lithuania, who had been buried in 1717 in the local Bernardine church with some silver and golden ornaments in a coffin fastened by silver nails and draped in an expensive cloth decorated with golden galloons. The two Jews apparently dug under the foundations of the church, broke into the tomb of Lady Pociej, stole the coffin cloth and the ornaments, removed the body, and took the coffin apart to recover the silver nails. They also stole some silver from the church. A year later, the crime was discovered when Wulf's and Izrael's daughters appeared in clothes made from the textile with golden galloons and when Wulf and Izrael tried to sell the silver nails to a local silversmith, who unbeknownst to them had made them for the coffin. Damages were estimated at more than six thousand zloty, including structural damages to the church vaults, which housed the coffin, and court expenses, a huge amount considering that in 1713 one truck-load of hay cost between six and eleven zlotys and that one could buy five chickens for one zloty.[141] Apparently held liable for the costs, the Jewish community elders tried to force the two perpetrators to return the stolen goods, but they refused to return or to pay for the damages, and instead fled. The Lithuanian Tribunal sentenced them in absentia to infamy and death. The Brest Jewish community was forced to pay the damages from "all property mobile and immobile, money deposited, arendas, houses, land, shops and goods."[142]

The limits of Jews' security are apparent also in the evidence of their need of protection from Christian authorities against attacks and accusations filed by other Christians, including for ritual murder and host desecration.[143] In 1577, Nachum Abramovich, a Jew from the small town of Wojnia[144] in the Brest region, was accused by townspeople [*meshchane*] of killing a Christian child,[145] arrested, and taken to the local prison. In an effort to rescue him, local Jews brought to the attention of the court a privilege that had been granted to them by the king. It guaranteed among other things that, in the case of such accusations, four Christian and three Jewish witnesses must be produced to support those accusations. Further, the royal privilege stated that such cases should not be tried in the local courts but should be referred instead to the royal tribunal.[146] The court obeyed the royal privilege and dismissed the case.[147] In other cases, however, when such a defense was dismissed, Jews faced threats and trials.[148]

On September 20, 1741, the rector of the Brest Jesuit academy, Stanislaw Tachanowski, filed a somewhat enigmatic document in the Brest municipal court records:

I order you, Mr. Marek and you, beadles [of the synagogue, *szkolnicy*, Hebr. *shamashim*] not to create any commotion and not to confuse the inhabitants of my *jurydyka* during the upcoming holidays,[149] not to curse against them, since I have inquired and [found out that] they have paid every obligation to Israel; and I forbid other collections and cursing in your synagogue. If not, I will allow them [the inhabitants of the Jesuit *jurydyka*] to fabricate some kind of a rumor against you, so that they may be left in peace.[150]

This brief and ambiguous text implies a business relationship between Jews and Christians who were living in the Jesuit-controlled part of town. The rector, Stanisław Tachanowski, did not say what kind of rumor might be fabricated, but because the threat was to make certain that his Christians be "left in peace," it had to be serious, perhaps a blood libel against the Jews.

In cases of this sort, Jews were often protected by "their" nobles, and the nobles sometimes represented them in court. In one such case in 1700 concerning several Jews accused of robbing a church in Komajce,[151] the court report stated:

These above mentioned Jews, Jakub Salomonowicz, Nochim of Lublin, Izrael of Prze-worsk, Johel of Morawy, who wandered in the various royal towns, especially in the city of Wilno, stealing and causing a lot of damage to people, knowing full well about the miraculous painting of the Most Holy Virgin, decorated in gold, silver, pearls and other gems [and recently generously donated to] the Komayski church, have awakened appetite for these gems, and just before the commencement of the Tribunal began its proceedings, on 26 of April of the current year 1700, somehow in their thievish manner broke into the Komayski church through its strong door, and having broken the ciborium with axes, dared to take the *sacra sacrorum*, a box with forty communion wafers, with their foul hands for the Jews in other kahals, thereby offending the Lord's Sublimity. At the same time they stole two empty chalices, and having stripped from the altar of St. John the painting of the Most Holy Virgin, and pearls, golden rings, silver and other splendors that were attached to this painting, and two silver hanging candelabra, they took [them] with their sacrilegious hands. And not being satisfied with this, they further broke into the sacristy in a thievish way, and stole a large silver monstrance and the parish priest's money, and many other things, which according to the registry of items, are easily worth twelve thousand zloty. So they, in their adamant malice, stripped the Komayski church and God's glory of their silver and splendor.[152]

The accused Jews were helped by the noble Goryszewski, a court official or *podstarosta* and a leaseholder of an estate where one of the Jews, Moszko "the Senator," lived. Goryszewski, described in the court records as a "dissident in religion," released the Jews from their captivity and provided shelter on his estate. In court, the Jews were represented by lords Raweński and Woytkiewicz, who adamantly insisted on their innocence. In the end, however, their efforts proved futile and the Jews were sentenced to death, as other church robbers would have been. Lord Goryszewski and his wife were sentenced to infamy.[153] The court's officials had succumbed to the oaths and pressures of the Catholic clergy.

In some cases nobles rescued their Jews by force from other Jews, or represented their Jews in courts against other Jews. On March 29, 1647, a Jewish woman from Pinsk, Dvora Jakubovna Rubinovichovna Iezeiaszowa, personally filed a case against two noblemen, Kazimierz and Konstanty Kotowski.[154] Dvora Jakubovna's affidavit accused the Kotowskis of coming armed, along with their servants, to the Jewish prison near the synagogue to release by force a Jewish man, Zorokh Symkhovich, whom Dvora Jakubovna had "ordered to be put into the Jewish prison" for unpaid debts of "not a small amount of several thousand zlotys." After she had boldly confronted them about "this lawlessness and violence," the Kotowskis threatened to beat her. As with many of these cases, nothing but her affidavit has survived.

On November 28, 1701, a nobleman, Andrzey Jakób Skalski, filed a case against the Brest *kahal* accusing some Brest Jews of murdering his trusted Jewish factor, Judka Izraelowicz.[155] Skalski had loaned money to the *kahal* and had hired Judka Izraelowicz as his agent. The affidavit called Izraelowicz "honest not only with the lord Skalski but other noblemen as well, in showing them ways to make a fortune."[156] Izraelowicz's job, it appears, was to investigate the borrowers' assets and trade in bills of debt on behalf of the nobles. Some disgruntled debtors had made threats against Izraelowicz's life, and when he was killed, the narrator of the affidavit interpreted it as revenge by Jews "because he was honest with the Christians."[157]

Economic interests of Jews and nobles in Poland frequently converged, leading some to prosperity and others to despair. In the Polish-Lithuanian Commonwealth, Jews were both objects and agents of actions, and their interactions with Christians were close – sometimes intimate and friendly, sometimes hostile and violent. Their proximity to Christians in Poland, their ties to the nobles, the resulting position of power and authority of some Jews over poorer Christians, and the Jews' sense of security, underlined by some Jews' behavior, all contributed to the Catholic Church's own sense of frustration and threat. The centuries-old "enemies of Christianity," the Jews, were often valued and protected in the Polish-Lithuanian Commonwealth. Their ties with the "temporal powers" placed many in a position far from that of the "perpetual servitude" Christian theologians had considered their due.

3

Heresy and the Fleeting "Triumph of the Counter-Reformation"

CATHOLIC CHURCH LEGISLATION AGAINST JEWS OFTEN DID NOT STAND ALONE but coincided with the rise of heretical movements within the Church itself. This was true of the 1215 regulations of the IV Lateran Council promulgated in the midst of the Church's battle against various heresies in Europe, and of the 1555 papal bull *Cum Nimis Absurdum*, which established the Roman ghetto during the crisis of the Reformation.[1] In Poland the Church reacted in similar ways. According to surviving sources, regulations of Jewish-Christian interaction – first promulgated at the Council of Breslau in 1267 and ordering a geographic segregation between Jews and Christians – did not reappear in Poland until the first half of the fifteenth century when, in the wake of the heresy of Jan Hus in Bohemia, Huss's followers moved north into the Polish territories, thereby posing a challenge to the Church in Poland.

Reacting to the Hussite heresy, the 1420 provincial synod held at Kalisz and Wieluń issued a number of decrees against heresy and recommended a number of "remedies" to combat it, requiring, among other things, that secular authorities cooperate with the Church in combating its spread.[2] The "heresy" apparently affected mostly the literate elites. One paragraph of the 1420 synodal laws ordered confiscation of the books of those suspected of heresy when they were captured,[3] but in pre-print culture, only a few could afford to own books. This is perhaps the reason why the Hussite movement did not spread as widely as the Reformation itself would a century later, some decades after the invention of the printing press.

The same 1420 synod also repeated, with only minor changes, most of the laws concerning Jews passed by the Council of Breslau in 1267 and subsequently included in canon law, and added further restrictions that prohibited Christians from eating and drinking with Jews and from dancing at Jewish weddings and New Year celebrations. Again resorting to clothing to identify the Other, the synod ordered Jews to wear a round patch visibly displayed on their outer clothing so that "they may be easily distinguished from Christians."[4]

After Martin Luther and his followers dealt a blow to the legitimacy of the Catholic Church in Europe, the Church in Poland, in tandem with the Polish king, reacted swiftly, punishing disseminators of the new ideas.[5] Simultaneously, Jews became an object of clerical concern. In 1542, the provincial synod, which had gathered to deal with a number of pressing religious issues, including the spreading of new heresies, sought to restrict the number of Jews "who are coming to Poland from the neighboring kingdoms,"[6] and to prevent or to limit social and professional Jewish-Christian relationships. Restrictions on eating together were repeated, along with requirements that Jews wear distinctive clothing. These rulings appear relatively formulaic, and they remained so until approximately the mid-seventeenth century, when synods, bishops, and writing clerics began to pay more sustained attention to the Jews.

The defensive Church rulings concerning Jews reflect the persistent sense of insecurity that the presence of Jews aroused in the Catholic hierarchy. Jews had offered a religious alternative even before the Reformation, but during the Reformation, when the Church's religious supremacy was challenged by other Christians, Judaism could have been attractive to some Christians, who may have seen it as stable and continuous from the biblical times. The 1542 rulings were a response both to the spread of the new religious ideas coming from Wittenberg and to a number of Catholic conversions to Judaism.

CHRISTIANS ON TRIAL FOR "FALLING INTO THE PERFIDIOUS APOSTASY AND THE SUPERSTITIOUS SECT OF THE JEWS"

On a Saturday, April 29, 1539, Katarzyna Malcherowa, a widow in her eighties of a Cracow councilman, Melchior Weigel, was burned at the stake for relapsing into apostasy and falling into the "errors of the Jews."[7] Malcherowa had been brought to the bishop's court first in 1529, under the rule of Bishop Piotr Tomicki.[8] The now missing trial record, as excerpted by the late-nineteenth-century Catholic historian Julian Bukowski, implied that Katarzyna had already been summoned by the Church officials a number of times and had "given up the faith" a number of years before:

Katarzyna Malchurowa [sic], the wife of Melchior Veygyel [sic], a citizen and council-man of Cracow, having accepted the superstitious Jewish sect, rejected the Christian faith, in which she was born from her parents, baptized and brought up, and in which she subsequently was married and brought numerous offspring to the world, several decades ago [od lat kilkudziesięciu], for which [acceptance of Judaism] she has been summoned several times by Mikołaj Bedleński, a scholar and vicar, and admonished to give up these errors.[9]

Katarzyna Malcherowa apparently did not appear in court immediately after the summons, for the next extant record (of July 5, 1530) reported that when Malcherowa was asked why she had failed to come to court, she responded that she had been busy and out of town. During the hearing, she retracted her "Jewish beliefs," which she admitted she had embraced "out of female curiosity, mad-ness, and weakness of her mind [ex mania et cerebri debilitate]."[10] She was asked to abjure these "errors" and affirm her Catholic faith in public.[11] On August 5, 1530, she was released from prison on guarantee from her daughter Anna, and from a Jan Załaszowski, who appears to have been her son. By that time, Malcherowa was already a widow, which explains why her daughter and son were the guarantors present at her release. On August 11, 1530, Katarzyna Malcherowa publicly renounced her apostasy and was reconciled with the Church,[12] her statement recorded in Polish in Acta Episcopalia (vol. 12) and preserved at the Archive of the Archdiocese in Cracow:

I, Catharina Malcherowa, acknowledging the true Christian apostolic faith, openly curse all heresy and unbelief, and especially the squalid Jewish unbelief, of which I was accused and brought [to court] and I agree with the Holy Roman Church and the Apostolic See and I confess with my own lips that I believe and hold this faith, which based on the teachings of the Gospels and holy apostles, the Holy Roman Church teaches to hold, and I swear by the unity of the Holy Trinity and by the Holy Gospels of Lord Christ and I declare that those who are enemies of this faith and its teachings, as well as their enemies deserve eternal damnation, and if I, God forbid, will dare to act or speak against this faith, I want to be subjected to the severity of the spiritual law, so help me God and the holy Gospel.[13]

This retraction, noted by Malcherowa's contemporaries, was quite an event in Cracow. Marcin Biem of Olkusz, a theologian and an astronomer, inscribed on his copy of *Almanach nova plurimis annis venturis in serventia (ab a. 1499–1531)*: "August 11, 1530, Malcherowa *consulissa* of Cracow, who had had fallen into Jewish faith in which she had lived for five years, abjured this infidelity and returned to the Catholic faith in the presence of the bishops of the Curia, prelates, priests and Cracow's councilmen."[14]

Malcherowa did not disappear from the bishop's court; she sued and was sued in business matters, seemingly unburdened by her earlier court experience. In one case dealing with "certain pledges" brought against a cleric, Stanislaw Stanko, the head of a hospital, Malcherowa appealed to the highest ecclesiastical authority in Poland, the Archbishop of Gniezno.[15] But in matters of faith Katarzyna Malcherowa relapsed, and as a result, in accordance with her original abjuration speech, she was subjected to the "severity of the spiritual law." On March 19, 1539, she was back in the bishop's court, not about money but about "apostasy and relapsing [*causa apostasiae et relapsu*]."[16] She was imprisoned, then examined by the Church officials in the "articles of the faith,"[17] and convicted of apostasy and relapse on April 16, 1539. Both records, of the last court proceedings and the sentencing decree, repeatedly stressed that her sentence was a consequence of her return to "Jewish perfidy" after she had renounced the "Jewish errors" and had been reconciled with the Church. Considered a relapsed apostate, and stripped of any "Christian privileges," Malcherowa was released to the secular authorities so that, as the canon law suggests, laws applicable to "perfidious and relapsed heretics" might be applied. In accordance with Church laws, her property was confiscated.[18] The law, based on the

German *Speculum Saxonum* then in use in Cracow, determined that a person who blasphemed against the Christian religion deserved the death penalty.[19] Technically, the Church, while responsible for assessing the heresy and for sentencing, was not responsible for the type of punishment to be applied. It relied on the existing laws of the land in this regard.[20] Thus, according to the provisions of municipal law, Katarzyna Malcherowa was executed by burning at the stake.

The sentence was carried out on a Saturday in April 1539.[21] Marcin Biem of Olkusz, who noted Katarzyna Malcherowa's first public denunciation of apostasy and her reconciliation with the Church, wrote: "April 16, 1539, Malcherowa *consulissa* of Cracow, who had turned to Judaism, was pronounced an apostate by Cracow's Bishop Piotr Gamrat, and her property was confiscated and she was released to secular authorities; April 19, she was burned in Cracow in a place where they collect dead dogs."[22] The symbolism was stark. In the New Testament Jesus is said to have instructed, "Do not give what is holy to dogs" (Matthew 7:6), and to have rebuked a Canaanite woman who asked him for help, saying "It is not fair to take the children's food and throw it to the dogs." (Matthew 15:26). In the second half of the fourth century, John Chrysostom reversed the order and turned Jews into dogs, saying "but see how the order of things has been reversed since then. The Jews have now become dogs and we, children."[23] And in the Middle Ages, beginning with Pope Gregory I, Jewish converts to Christianity who relapsed and returned to Judaism were referred to as "dogs who return to their vomit."[24] Thus, the choice of place for Malcherowa's execution was perhaps not accidental. The execution was even more prominent than her 1530 abjuration. Not only "the bishop of Cracow, all the clergymen of the Cathedral chapter, and the professors of the University [*kollegijaty*]" but also the city's populace came to the event.[25] It left a permanent mark on at least some of its witnesses. Years later, chroniclers noted it. Łukasz Górnicki wrote that Malcherowa went to death defiantly and without fear.[26] Another much-cited sixteenth-century chronicler, Marcin Bielski, said she went to the stake "as if to a wedding."[27]

Malcherowa's death was subsequently embraced by Protestants as the first martyrdom for their faith, and by certain historians as a demonstration of the Catholic Church's intolerance.[28] Until recently, historians had tended to dismiss Malcherowa's acceptance of Judaism as a case of Protestant heresy, perhaps of a proto-anti-Trinitarian in Poland.[29] Yet, in the light of other "heresy cases" found in Church records of this period, her case is different. She became an apostate to Judaism; in other cases the charge was Lutheran heresy. Even some two centuries later some Church writers saw her as a convert to Judaism, as did Stefan Żuchowski of Sandomierz.[30]

Malcherowa's case coincided with other allegations of Jewish proselytizing. In 1539–40, certain Jews in Cracow and in "other royal towns" were accused of circumcising Christians and sending them off to Lithuania to join Jewish communities there. Several letters from the king and other officials claim that certain converts from Christianity to Judaism were transported out of the lands of the Polish Crown and Lithuania to Turkey.[31] On July 22, 1539, the clerics in the cathedral chapter in

Cracow convened in a meeting and voted to establish a committee to investigate and interpret "maledictions of the Jews against Christians, which they utter during their ceremonies."[32] One priest, Trzecieski, was excluded from this committee because he was suspected of having accepted Judaism and of having blasphemed against the Christian religion.

On the same day that the cathedral chapter established the committee to investigate Jewish "maledictions," the chapter exhorted the "Most Reverend Bishop to conduct a diligent investigation concerning circumcised Christians and Jews by whom [these Christians] were induced to be circumcised."[33] The clerics urged that something be done so that the Jews could not multiply "because of their various excesses" – a clause eventually included in the statutes concerning Jews issued at the 1542 synod.[34]

As in the case of Malcherowa's acceptance of Judaism, these reports of "Judaizers," as the converts to Judaism were subsequently called, were regarded as not credible by certain scholars and have been dismissed as mere followers of new religious ideas. Others have claimed that these allegations were entirely fabricated "proselyte libels," as one scholar has labeled them.[35] Considering that Christian converts to Judaism did exist in Poland throughout the post-Reformation period, it would not be surprising to find such converts at the time of the Reformation itself.

BETWEEN "THE PAPISTS" AND "THE ARIANS": THE CHRISTIAN "DISSIDENTES DE RELIGIONE"

The threats against the Church that came from the religious movements of the Reformation, from "apostasy," and from the nobles' political struggle against the Church's political and judicial influence, became doubly daunting when the Polish nobles themselves embraced religious novelties. Although the nobles' adherence to these ideas proved temporary, and sometimes wavering, their religious dissent only exacerbated a rift between them and the Church that was never to be healed, despite the fact that most of the dissenting nobles returned to Catholicism by the second half of the seventeenth century.

The Polish nobles were attracted to the new beliefs, especially to Calvinism – and not to Lutheranism, which was embraced mostly by burghers, a class with whom the nobles considered themselves to have little in common. The nobles found the new beliefs appealing often not because of doctrinal discontent but because the Reformation, by challenging the power of the Church, gave the nobles themselves more control over their communities and parishes. It "abolished all forms of Church hierarchy, established democratic communities and struck at the heart of the Church's wealth and opulence."[36]

Disputing the special status of the Church on a doctrinal level had political and economic ramifications. The Church's own doctrines required an intermediary between God and the lay folk; a priest fulfilled such a function. By attacking the Church rituals, the prime *raison d'être* of the Catholic priesthood, Protestants undermined the legitimacy of the Church and challenged the Church's possession of the "spiritual sword."

Catholic rituals, some Protestants argued, were all about fooling the people and extorting money from them. "Just look," wrote an author of a late sixteenth-century anti-Catholic pamphlet, *False Gods*, "and you will see clearly the unquestionable truth. When the priest blesses salt, butter, wine, eggs and lard [*słonina*], he will get good news too. For on Easter, he will greedily take oats, cheeses, bread, lamb and piglets.... They only bless what they can use."[37] The Antichrist, as the author called the Church,[38] "turns profit because of a tyrannical greed. For there is no end to this greed, deception and lies.... As long as you live, and even when you die, you have to pay, for you buy baptism and confession, and you can buy marriage too."[39] The author exposed what he considered the Church's hypocrisy. On the one hand, he argued, a simple priest, "mumbling something," can turn bread into God. On the other hand, he cannot bless a new church or a new bell; for that a bishop is needed. Only he "has the power to charm [i.e. bless] churches, and in the process he squeezes out quite a bit of silver from poor simple people."[40] "Nowhere," he claimed, "are there more beggars than among [the Catholics], even though the papist church has countless treasures, towns, and estates."[41] The Church "invented this Mass of trickery in order to squeeze money out of simple people," said Marcin Krowicki, a sixteenth-century Protestant polemicist.[42]

Money and power, too, were behind opposition to the Church in Poland. In an effort to unite against the Church, the nobles of three Protestant denominations, Lutherans, Calvinists, and the Bohemian Brethren, formed an alliance and, in 1570, issued the so-called *consensus sandomiriensis*, the consensus of Sandomierz, to "fight together against the followers of the Roman Church, the sectarians, as well as all the enemies of truth and Gospel."[43] The consensus achieved by three principal Protestant denominations – Lutherans, Calvinists, and Bohemian brothers – excluded the Polish anti-Trinitarians, or the Polish Brethren, sometimes referred to as Socinians after Faustus Socinus, a noted anti-Trinitarian who arrived in Poland from Italy at the end of the sixteenth century. Polish anti-Trinitarians were initially strongly opposed to Socinus, and the term "Socinians" was not employed in Poland, where the anti-Trinitarians described themselves as the Polish Brethren, or simply as Christians; their opponents referred to them as Arians.[44] But the term "Socinians" subsequently entered historiography.[45]

Despite the exclusion of the Polish Brethren, the 1570 *consensus* paved the way for the clause guaranteeing religious toleration among "those who differ in matters of religion [*dissidentes in religione*]" in the same 1573 constitution that limited the powers of the monarch. The document, drafted during the interregnum following the death of King Sigismund August, stated:

Since there are quite a few differences in our Kingdom on the account of religion, seeking to prevent any sort of sedition on this account, which we see in other kingdoms, we, who are *dissidentes de religione*, promise each other to maintain peace among ourselves despite differences in faith [and] churches, and [we promise] not to spill blood, nor employ punishment, such as confiscation of property, imprisonment of exile, and [we promise] not to aid any power or office to do so.[46]

The measure of religious toleration was aimed at preventing a future monarch from imposing one religion on all and thus encroaching on the nobles' liberties. "The king must," the document said, "confirm after his election all our rights, privileges and liberties, which exist now and which we will present to him."[47] The confederation text served as a document unifying the nobles, who did not want to allow "the dismemberment of the indivisible Republic."[48] Although hailed by historians as the hallmark of Polish religious toleration, the 1573 constitution had more to do with the nobles' concern with their own liberties than with religious toleration per se.[49] In fact, as historian Józef Siemieński argued, the constitution excluded future sects; it preserved the status quo by recognizing only the existing religious factions.[50]

The mainstream Protestant nobles were opposed to anti-Trinitarians, in part because they saw themselves as Christians, and adamantly affirmed their belief in the Trinity.[51] They were uncomfortable with the anti-Trinitarians' challenge not only to the Trinity but also to other doctrines they considered true and beyond debate, like the Protestant belief that faith is sufficient for salvation, something about which a noted seventeenth-century anti-Trinitarian poet, Wacław Potocki, wrote in a poem, "A Discourse on Good Deeds." He argued that faith was worth little if not accompanied by good deeds, and referred "the Calvinists" to the Gospels in which Jesus fed the hungry.[52]

So too, Protestant nobles, along with Catholics, feared the social radicalism of the anti-Trinitarians, who promoted egalitarianism, pacifism, and abolition of hierarchy, thereby threatening the accepted social order. The nobles sought to be distinguished from them.[53] In 1566 the Protestant synod of Brześć asserted, in a somewhat apologetic manner: "We are not here to learn violence, nor those abominations of Antichrist, nor the crimes of the Münsterites, but rather the teaching of Christ, respect for the magistrate and obedience to him, not only out of fear but also for conscience' sake. We learn also to live a godly life at home with our wives, knowing that God created woman for one husband, and punished bigamists. We learn to supply from our substance means for supporting the worship of God, knowing that the brethren are free to possess property, since even the Apostle Paul collected alms from rich brethren and gave them to the Church."[54]

That same year, after a religious debate with the anti-Trinitarians, the Lutheran, Calvinist, and Bohemian Brethren deputies to the Sejm tried to push the king to ban Anabaptists and anti-Trinitarians from Poland.[55] Catholic nobles also supported that effort, but the plan failed, paradoxically, because of the Catholic bishops' opposition – for them, it did not go far enough. "Two years ago," King

Sigismund August wrote, "we wanted to expel the worst heretics from our Kingdom, that is, anti-Trinitarians, Anabaptists and the Piccardists, but the [Catholic] bishops opposed it unless others also, the Calvinists and the Lutherans, should be expelled. This, of course, was an impossible thing to do."[56] The efforts to expel the anti-Trinitarians altogether would bear fruit some one hundred years later, after a gradual process of their exclusion from the 1573 constitution's guarantees of freedom from religious persecution to the "dissidents in religion" – *dissidentes de religione*.

The Church began to regain political strength among the nobility in the first quarter of the seventeenth century. The process of exclusion, first of the anti-Trinitarians and then of other Protestants as well, came in the form of a linguistic transformation of the 1573 document and reflected a diminishing of Protestant influence against the Catholic forces. The most striking sign came in a 1632 constitution that transformed the general "dissidents in religion" to "dissidents in Christian religion [*dissidentibus in religione Christiana*]," implicitly excluding those who were not deemed Christians.[57] And such was the charge against the anti-Trinitarians, who as early as in 1565 were regarded by other Protestants as "enemies of the Christian faith."[58] In 1573, they were charged with not believing in God.[59] The grammar of the clause changed too, transforming the act's meaning. It was now the Catholics who guaranteed peace *to* the "dissidents in Christian religion,"[60] a symptom of the gradual power shift back to the Catholics. And in 1648, in the *pacta conventa* prepared for newly elected King Jan Kazimierz, the 1632 wording evolved into a further affirmation of Catholic power. "And in matters concerning Christian religion," the king swore, "peace should be among the dissidents in the Christian religion [*inter dissidentes in religione Christiana*], which we pledge to maintain ... provided that the rights of the Roman Catholic Church were not violated [*Salvis Iuribus Ecclesiae Catholicae Romanae integra*] in this peace and security of the dissidents in Christian religion."[61]

So too, minutes of Protestant synods reflect this shift of power back to the Catholics. From the beginning the synods were committed to their anti-Catholicism, but were not quite sure which doctrines to follow. The Polish Protestants were split, and although they sought unity, they were never able to achieve it. Between 1550 and 1632, the Protestants moved from confusion and indecisiveness about which of the new religious ideas to adopt, to defiance in their fight against the "Roman idolatry" or the "Antichrist," to losing their members back to the Catholic Church.[62] At the council of Protestants in 1555 in Koźminek, "all ministers rejected the errors of the Antichrist."[63] But, having done so, they turned to a noted Protestant theologian, Franciszek Stankar, asking "which confessions should we choose?"[64] Stancar suggested Lutheranism; others mulled over other possibilities. Their lack of certainty weakened the movement. Although in 1576 the synods were still listing new members, by the early 1600s signs had emerged of conversions back to Catholicism – as the elders of the Protestant communities saw it, "apostasy" appeared.[65] In 1616, the report of visitation in a parish of Aleksandrowicze noted many "apostates in this community, but not because of the ministry but because of their own wickedness."[66]

Money, too, became an important issue. Funds were desperately needed to oppose the Roman "Antichrist." Although in 1555 the Protestants were still vowing not to take tithes as the "papists" did, soon after they realized that they themselves needed money.[67] In 1560, the general Protestant synod in Książ demanded that "all Protestant lords, who hold anything that belongs to the clergy [tithes and property], return it immediately to the ministers and provide them with further necessary support."[68] And another synod in Poznań, also in 1560, ruled that "all tithes, to which the papists have no rights, should be turned to the advancement of the church, to the allowances for the ministers of God's word, and, if there is anything left over, to the poor."[69] In 1566, a synod protested against the "greed" of some, and asserted that the tithes were needed to "preserve the glory of God [*pro conservandam Gloria Dei*]."[70] In 1578, the synod of Piotrków charged that withholding tithes was a grand sacrilege, for the money was to be used to promote "the ministry of Christ," to build churches, schools, and to help the poor.[71] It was needed also for printing books[72] and, by 1596, for publications against the anti-Trinitarians.[73]

Money was such a problem that some Protestant ministers even served Catholics for pay. A delegation of the Bohemian Brethren at a council in Secemin in 1556 noted, "And after the sermon, persons of the Catholic religion brought their child to be baptized, which is unheard of among us [in Bohemia]. First, they baptize the papists' children, who are not members of their community but are bad, godless and disobedient people, and they do it for some mere pennies, which they charge for this."[74] When confronted with it, the local Protestant minister admitted "with tears that we have to do it against our conscience especially when we take money [for it]."[75] Complaints about the lack of funds continue in the records into the seventeenth century.

Many Catholic churches were seized in that period and transformed into Protestant churches. This in and of itself created problems for those who seized them. The new owners initially did not know what to do with the property, whether they should remove all the Catholic items or not. In 1556, a debate ensued on the question "should the paintings be removed [from churches] before accepting the body and blood of Christ?" One Protestant minister maintained, "I think that the paintings and other church implements should not be thrown out right away, especially if the church is among people who have not yet been taught the word of God and do not know what the reason [for the removal of these items] would be." And, he continued, "I will give you an example from my own experience. After the elders [of the church] sent me to Włodzisław, I realized that there are no people who knew the Truth of God and I let go with them like small children. ... And I suffered the paintings for over half a year. But when they began to see the Truth of God, I threw out the paintings without harmful offence."[76] In 1561, as the Protestant leaders of the Great Poland mulled over ways to "stop idolatry," they pondered whether or not to close down Catholic churches and whether to punish their serfs who attended them.[77]

By 1573, there was more anti-Catholic militancy, perhaps as a result of the 1573 act guaranteeing freedom from religious persecution. The Protestant synod of Cracow ruled that year that "should there be preserved any papist superstitious objects or ceremonies, such as exorcisms, or paintings, organs, unnecessary candles or others in any churches, they should be immediately discarded so that we should not be seen as giving way to this Antichrist."[78] In 1601, the district synod of the Protestants in Kock ordered the lord of Radom to remove an altar from the local church and to replace it with a simple table and an appropriate tablecloth, because people "accuse us of being the pope's mistress."[79]

The confusion over what each religion represented testifies to the fluidity of religious boundaries in this period. In a country without a strong executive lay power no religion could be imposed on everyone. Among the nobility, their identity as members of the noble estate prevailed over religious identity, at least for the moment. Their social contacts continued despite religious differences.

The issue of intermarriage was raised early on. In 1556, the Polish Protestants, still unsure what they should follow, asked a Bohemian pastor whether it was permitted to marry "a person from our church to a papist." They also wondered whether the gender of the spouse mattered, that is, "If the female was from the church of Christ and the male from the papist church, can a minister of Christ bind them in marriage?"[80] The response they received was unequivocally strong against such marriage on the grounds that "a wife must submit to the husband, and would have to suffer his idolatry and blasphemy, and because he would force his wife [to idolatry] by abuse and beatings. And she will have to suffer his mocking and cursing of the faithful. And she will have to submit to his shameful carnal acts.... And should God give offspring to them, she would have to offer it to the Antichrist and idolatry, instead of Christ our Lord."[81] In 1594, the Protestant synod in Lublin ordered Protestant ministers to "admonish Christian lords not to wear sumptuous clothing after foreign fashions, and not to give daughters of Christian parents in marriage to people of other religions without the consent of the elders of the church of the Lord."[82]

It is clear that the forbidden practice of intermarriage continued, because as late as the eighteenth century, several Catholic bishops were forbidding mixed marriages in their rulings. And although intermarriage between Catholics and other Christians was not technically banned, it was eventually explicitly sanctioned by the state at the 1768 Sejm, which provided guidelines on how offspring of such liaisons should be brought up: sons were to follow the religion of their father, daughters that of their mother.[83]

In the area of education, too, laxity was apparent. Protestant leaders understood that the key to success was through education; therefore, they sought to establish schools and to find funding to support them. In 1560 one Protestant synod noted the opening of a school with eighty pupils, but little further evidence suggests that the Protestant schools were a serious resource.[84] It seems that Protestant leaders faced a vicious circle: the lack of money led to lack of schools, and the lack of schools, in turn, led many to send their sons to Catholic schools. For the Protestant nobles, this may not have been a serious concern; they simply sent their children where other nobles did. If the Protestant leadership was unable to create a satisfying school system, the Protestant parents turned where good education was available. After 1565, Jesuits became the prime force behind young noblemen's education. Although by the eighteenth century Jesuit schools were criticized for their backwardness even by Catholics, in the sixteenth and seventeenth centuries Jesuits were offering good education that exposed the youth to a wide range of subjects.[85]

At the end of the sixteenth and at the beginning of the seventeenth centuries, serious competition in education came also from the anti-Trinitarians. Anti-Trinitarian schools were open in Raków, Lewartów, Lucławice (until 1660), and in many other lesser known places.[86] There was relative toleration of different religions in the anti-Trinitarian schools, as in the academy in Raków, where students of different religions studied, each allowed to pray according "to his conscience and the religion in which he has been brought up."[87]

Given the superior education available in either the Jesuit or the anti-Trinitarian academies, some Protestant (mostly Calvinist) nobles sent their sons to these schools. The synods repeatedly complained about it. The 1594 synod in Lublin issued an admonition that "children of Christian parents must not be sent to schools of different faiths because from them the youth absorbs all sorts of depravity."[88] It demanded, too, that the Protestant clergy make certain that their youth did not participate in debates with anti-Trinitarians.[89] A year later, the synod demanded that the ministers make sure that "patrons of our religion removed their children from Lewartów [a school that by then had become anti-Trinitarian] and from the schools run by the papists."[90] In 1614, the synod in Lublin threatened to exclude from the community those who sent their children to "papist or Arian schools," and asked that the Protestant ministers ensure that children not be exposed to erroneous ways.[91] The elders made a special provision for the nobleman Chrząstowski, who had promised that, after the end of the academic year, he would withdraw his children from the anti-Trinitarian school in Raków and send his children to a proper Protestant school.[92] The 1617 synod was even more explicit. Parents should withdraw their children from "Arian and papist schools," both of which provided an opportunity for apostasy.[93] In 1625, the synod in Oksza ruled to excommunicate those who continued to send their children to prohibited schools.[94] And a 1690s' pamphlet, "Discourse concerning a Synod," provided a set of questions for pastoral visitations in Protestant parishes, among which one was to inquire "whether anyone sends their male children to papist schools for learning, or to bishops' or ecclesiastical courts for service, and whether they neglect good upbringing of their daughters by allowing them service opposed to Christian piety, or even allowing them to join convents."[95]

The demands of discipline that the Reformed churches in Poland placed on their members proved too much, especially to those who were not strongly committed to the new doctrines. The nobles, and probably others as well, were not eager to give up their vices and commit to the pious life the Reformers demanded. The 1582 report of a visitation in a community of Lipie, for example, noted that drinking was a serious problem, starting on Saturday and continuing into Sunday.[96] Similar complaint is found in the report from Bełz.[97] And the 1593 synod of Włodzisław expressed a frustration that "various scandals have multiplied: drinking, gluttony, exploitation of serfs, usury, licentiousness, dancing, immodest and lavish clothing, neglect of religious services and communities."[98] A century later, Protestant leaders worried that some members of the Protestant community might "violate the oath given to Lord Christ by engaging in idolatry, such as [attending] processions, masses, placing altars or paintings in their houses or crucifixes on roads."[99]

But it was not only the mainstream Protestants who did not strictly follow the social discipline demanded by their clergy. In the late 1590s, even the radical anti-Trinitarian community, whose members promoted equality and in some cases freed their serfs, also made concessions on social issues. The nobles were assured, as one contemporary chronicler reported, "that they could with clear conscience possess the estates, rights and privileges of nobles, and bear arms, whereupon the Church completely changed, especially among the nobility. They quite ceased to be different in appearance from the rest of their contemporaries, especially the women, who began to dress up, to take part in the wedding feasts of persons from the world and in other festivities.... [The ministers] several times tried to find a remedy for this evil, but to no avail: the longer it went on, the worse it grew."[100]

Without strong doctrinal commitment, education, and cohesiveness among the Polish Protestants, and with the wealth and organizational advantage of the Catholic Church, it was relatively easy for the process of the re-Catholicization of Poland to begin. Some anti-Trinitarians were the exception; in the end, those most committed to anti-Trinitarian beliefs were expelled from Poland because their radicalism challenged the nobles' values and their sense, however utopian, of unity.[101]

"TO ACCEPT ONE TRUE CONFESSION," NOT "SOMEONE ELSE'S ... BUT OUR OWN POLISH AND CHRISTIAN"

The Protestants did seek a unique identity, an identity that would unify them despite their doctrinal and other differences. Like Catholics, they too prayed that there be one pastor and one flock.[102] But faced with choices, all from abroad, they could not fully identify with anyone. The palatine of Cracow put it succinctly at the 1570 synod

of Sandomierz that produced the unified stance of the three Protestant denominations, namely, Lutherans, Calvinists, and Bohemian Brethren: "We have gathered
here not to accept someone else's confession, but to accept one true Confession with
mutual consensus, which would not be Bohemian, Saxon or Helvetian [Swiss], but
our own Polish and Christian [*nasza własna polska, krześcijańska*]."[103] This need for
common "Polish Christian" identity became the key to the re-Catholicization of
the nobility, especially after Poland engaged in wars with non-Catholic powers, that
is, Protestant Sweden, Eastern Orthodox Russia, and Muslim Turkey. The assault
on the state, the "one body," by those non-Catholic powers helped to coalesce
the Catholic identity among those (viz., the nobles) who identified with the state.
And as a result, in the wake of the wars, many mainstream Protestants returned to
Catholicism. That process excluded those whose strong religious commitments did
not allow them to return – the anti-Trinitarians.[104] By 1648, the anti-Trinitarians
were excluded from the framework of the 1573 constitution, which now guaranteed
protection only to those "differing in Christian religion."

Anti-Trinitarians saw themselves as Christians but the political scales had tipped
against them after the first wave of devastating wars with non-Catholic neighbors. In 1648, a destructive uprising began in the southeastern territories of the
Polish-Lithuanian Commonwealth, comprising today's Ukraine, and spread most
widely in the territories most exploited by Polish magnates in colonization. In that
uprising, thousands of Catholics and Jews, many of them administrators of the
magnates' estates, were slaughtered by rebels led by Bohdan Chmielnicki.[105] The
uprising evolved into a war with Russia. So too in 1655, Swedish troops attacked
Poland in the beginning of what became years of the so-called Deluge, a series of
terrorizing and ruinous wars from which Poland was never to recover. Some estimate that the devastation was so great that in population loss it could be compared
to the devastation Europe experienced in the black death of 1348.[106] In these wars,
cities were decimated; the royal cities never returned to their original glory.[107] This
utter disaster was interpreted as a divine punishment against Poles for tolerating
heresy, and that interpretation became an instrument for the coalescing of Polish
Catholic identity among the nobles.

In the 1640s, the Protestant deputies to the Sejm could still take on the Catholics,
who sought to use the wars against Turkey as a unifying element, by saying, "If
the Catholic Lords do not want Christian blood to be spilled and do not want the
kingdom to be destroyed to the delight of the Turks and even the devil himself,
let them stop forcing people to convert to Catholicism. For where do wars in
Christendom come from, if not from this?"[108] Protestants opposed the Catholic
king's attempts to bring Protestant nobles to Catholicism, as he tried to do in 1644
by organizing a religious colloquy.[109] By 1658, such an affront would no longer
be possible. The shock and devastation of the wars was too great. The wars had
become synonymous with an attack not only on Poland but on Catholicism. One
outcome was the expulsion of the anti-Trinitarians.

The first law promulgated by the 1658 Sejm related to "the Arian sect, which has recently began to spread in our territories, at times, causing fatal disaster to the Republic."[110] It ruled that all those who would "dare to profess, disseminate or support" this sect were to be prosecuted and if "legitimately convicted" were to become subject to the death penalty.[111] Those unwilling to renounce "this sect" were given three years to sell their property and leave, after which the severe penalty would apply. Those most committed to their faith packed up and left, settling in Prussia, Transylvania, or Holland, like the noted "Arian" leader and grandson of Faustus Socinus, Andrzej Wiszowaty, who settled in Amsterdam, where he died in 1678.[112] Others chose to convert to Calvinism and stayed, and still others accepted Catholicism.[113] The poet Wacław Potocki was one of those who accepted Catholicism; he remained in Poland after the expulsion decree was promulgated, but his wife remained "Arian," leading to a number of trials. In 1662, she was explicitly accused of Arianism. In 1663, to avoid problems, Potocki had his children baptized Catholic, but the question of his wife's Arianism returned to court in 1675. By 1682 she, too, had converted to Catholicism.[114]

Some of the trials of anti-Trinitarians were related to their property rights. Given the three-year time limit to dispose of their property and leave, the value of their property dropped tremendously. Some anti-Trinitarians chose to cede their property to friends who stayed. As Samuel Przypkowski stated, many "Brethren [were] forced to prefer to entrust our property to the good faith of friends." Wacław Potocki acquired some of his own property this way after he chose to convert rather than leave. Catholics, too, were sometimes penalized by confiscation of their property for associating with "Arians."[115]

Some historians have speculated that the anti-Trinitarians were expelled because they were believed to have sided with Protestant Sweden, but if treason had indeed been the reason, they would not have been allowed to stay upon conversion. Besides, there were large areas in Poland-Lithuania with Catholic and other Protestant leaders who had supported invaders, and conversely, many anti-Trinitarians supported the king.[116] Stanisław Lubieniecki, a prominent seventeenth-century anti-Trinitarian leader and author of a history of anti-Trinitarianism in Poland, admitted that during the chaos of the wars some anti-Trinitarians "subjected themselves and all they had to the protection of the most serene king of Sweden.... But they did this along with the whole Republic... while matters were being settled."[117] Such broad support for the Swedish king among Polish nobles was also noted by the Catholic writer, Samuel Twardowski.[118] In expelling the anti-Trinitarians, religion, therefore, was the primary motive.

That religion and also the rise of Catholic identity among the nobility became factors in the expulsion of the anti-Trinitarians can be seen from the way conversion was treated in the legislation. The 1658 decree of expulsion did not specify to which religion the anti-Trinitarians must convert in order to remain in the Polish-Lithuanian Commonwealth, but a year later the law was amended to stipulate that those who converted to Catholicism were not to be disturbed.[119] Conversions to any religion other than Catholicism were regarded as cases of "crypto-arianism."[120] The anti-Trinitarians understood this well. In 1661, Jonas Sztychling wrote that "we were bidden either to die or to leave our native land, or to forswear the convictions of our hearts and embrace the papal religion. We were prevented from attending the Reformed [Calvinist] or the Augsburg [Lutheran] services as well as our own, that it might be clear that we were punished not for being (as they say) Arians, but for not being or becoming Papists."[121] By such a process, Catholicism gradually became the sole legitimate religion in the kingdom and of the noble estate.

In 1660, the Swedish King Charles X died, and the devastating wars with Protestant Sweden ended with a treaty of Oliwa. Despite the overall disastrous effects of the war with Sweden on Poland, Poland's military successes in this war meant that, in the end, the peace treaty was not disadvantageous.[122] The new peace was viewed as a victory for Poland and as a divine reward for expelling the anti-Trinitarians. In 1661, the Sejm issued another anti-Arian law:

In great gratitude to God, Lord of Hosts, for the blessings of the past year [1660] granted us in the form of our magnificent victories over our enemies [Swedish Protestants], and desiring to induce continuous good fortune from God, we order that the constitutions that we had issued in the Sejm of 1658 expelling from our Kingdom the Enemies of the ever living Son, the Arian sect, and that of 1659 be carried out in all areas of the Polish-Lithuanian Kingdom, in all offices and tribunals, and that this Arian sect may not be concealed in any cunning way anywhere within our State, the Polish Kingdom and the Great Duchy of Lithuania.[123]

Sztychling understood the dynamic and noted that these laws affected the anti-Trinitarian nobles and were a departure from the acts of religious toleration of the earlier days: "God vouchsafes Poland an unhoped-for peace when she was almost subjugated. Great victories were won over her enemies. This is the thanks they now return to him for his great kindnesses. With this service of a grateful heart they endeavor to please and to placate him in turn, so that in spite of guarantees given publicly and repeatedly, in spite of the sworn laws of the Realm they may snatch away both the freedom, the peace and favor of the nation from us, their fellow-citizens and kinsmen, mostly men of the equestrian order."[124]

A year later, the Sejm affirmed that Poland had been rewarded by God for its expulsion of the anti-Trinitarians. The 1662 law "Concerning Arians" stated: "All of the world can see that the Heavens are content with the expulsion of the Arian sect from our State, for after the entire country managed to rid itself of this blasphemy, [the Heavens] provided us with trophies from our enemies. And God, Lord of Hosts, will reward us with the same happiness for further steps [we shall take]."[125] The 1662 laws, in addition to condemning the "Arian sect," condemned any protectors of them, especially husbands, who allowed their wives to remain faithful to their anti-Trinitarian beliefs. The men were liable to the punishment specified in the

1658 constitution against the Arians and their protectors (viz., death), and the women's property – both mobile and immobile – was to be confiscated. As the rulers of the household, husbands who themselves had accepted the Catholic faith were nonetheless guilty of supporting heresy and of furthering it by allowing their children "to be brought up in such blasphemy."[126]

This law applied to the poet Potocki, whose wife remained anti-Trinitarian. In reaction to this law, he wrote a poem in which he insisted that it is the nature of all humans to follow a religion into which they are born, and that to punish them for that is wrong.[127] And although many members of the anti-Trinitarian church recognized their errors, Potocki continued, women, "who have no reason, remain in this faith by virtue of their passions." And should a marriage be destroyed because of that? Should "innocent husbands be brought before law because they continue to live with the [ir wives] as they have for a long time," or because they don't want to use tyrannical force to "convert them out of this sect?"[128] Potocki's poem confirmed the fears of Catholics that anti-Trinitarian women had autonomy within families and influenced the upbringing of their children, under the protection, or at least toleration, of their husbands. This was in contrast to the views expressed earlier by Protestant synods, which emphasized submissiveness of Protestant women married to bullying Catholic husbands.

In 1668, when King Jan Kazimierz abdicated and the nobles gathered for a general electoral Sejm, they again renewed the act protecting the "dissidents in Christian religions" from persecution, but added a clause about the anti-Trinitarians: "Since they are proscribed by the law, no Arians, or apostates from the Roman Catholic religion and from religion of the Uniates,[129] may attempt to be included in this Confederation [which guaranteed peace to the dissidents in Christian religion]. And we confirm the constitutions issued against the Socinians and proclaim them valid in perpetuity."[130] They further affirmed what the 1659 law had established, namely, that anti-Trinitarians were forbidden to accept any other religion than Catholicism. By 1668, the movement between Protestant denominations and Catholicism became a one-way street – it was to lead to Catholicism and Catholicism alone.

As Marek Wajsblum pointed out in his work on the legislation against anti-Trinitarians, the lawmakers, by including apostasy in edict, turned temporary legislation that dealt with a specific transient religious question into a perpetual law aimed at anyone who dared to leave Catholicism.[131] Thus, the following years the law was expanded to include "Judaism" (i.e., conversion to Judaism), sacrilege, and violence and bloodshed in Catholic churches and cemeteries.[132] In 1726, the law added "atheists" and "blasphemers."[133] What started as a law against anti-Trinitarians now applied to anyone who threatened the status quo of the Catholic Church.[134]

In 1733, for the first time, the laws protecting the Catholic Church affected the Protestant nobles the most. Hitherto, the nobles' political rights had not been legally threatened. Although there existed a de facto protectionism of the Catholics and their promotion to various official posts, Protestant nobles' status was legally no different from that of their Catholic "brethren." In 1733, during the interregnum, their situation changed. The document of the general confederation openly stated that "because the foundation and longevity of all states is grounded in the true God and Holy religion, so through our confederation of that year we prohibit anyone from restricting [*derogare*] its rights and privileges of the orthodox Roman Catholic and the Graeco-Uniate churches. And indeed, since in this faithful country we detest strange cults, we pledge and oblige ourselves to stand by the Holy Roman Catholic Church and defend its freedom [*immunitas*]."[135] Paradoxically, the law still included the language of protection of the "dissidents in the Christian religion," as the previous laws had, but in line with its pledge to the Catholic Church, it added a clause that excluded them from any public office and banned them from participation in the Sejm.[136]

The political situation in Poland-Lithuania helped consolidate the Polish Catholic identity of the nobles, and the assaults on their state by the non-Catholic neighbors made it nearly impossible for them to accept non-Catholic denominations. By 1733 the Protestants were, as a whole, deemed to be outside the "Polish nation" as the nobles had perceived and shaped it over the centuries. In the sixteenth century the nobles had assumed the power of admitting new members into their circles. They sought to preserve the purity of "this jewel," as they called their noble status, by setting specific standards of their own.[137] After 1673, the new ennoblements were limited to Catholics only.[138]

That 1733 stance was probably not accidental. After all, the previous king of Poland was August II from Saxony, a Lutheran turned Catholic only after his election to the throne of Poland. He had brought along Lutheran advisors, an act that may have been perceived as threatening.[139] In hindsight, the nobles may have sought to prevent such actions by the next monarch, who happened to be August III of Saxony, the son of August II. Important too was a 1724 incident in Toruń, when several Lutheran officials were executed as a result of a Catholic-Protestant riot. This became an event of notoriety in Europe and the already predatory states surrounding Poland – Prussia, Russia, and Sweden, along with England – became self-proclaimed defenders of non-Catholic Christians in Poland.[140] The 1733 laws may have been a way by which the nobles sought protection of their interests against these non-Catholic powers. The discriminatory laws of 1733 and 1736 against Protestants would remain in effect until 1768, when Prussia, Russia, Sweden, Denmark, and England forced the weak Polish-Lithuanian state to reverse these laws.[141]

Blood and religion began to define Polish nobility and the Polish state, which the nobles thought they embodied. Although Poland-Lithuania continued to be a religiously and ethnically diverse country, in the eyes of the nobles "the nation" was now Catholic. The political backlash affected the Protestant nobles most, for they lost their political rights. But despite the political battering, Protestants in Poland, though weakened, continued to meet for synods, print and import books, and manage their communities.[142]

Other groups, such as Jews, Muslims, and Eastern Orthodox, living on the vast territories of the Polish-Lithuanian Commonwealth, were also not part of the "Polish nation," but their religious identities mattered very little to the nobles as long as they did not threaten the nobles themselves. In fact, during one of the wars with Orthodox Russia, the Jews' resistance to Muscovite attempts to convert them by force into Russian Orthodoxy was interpreted as a sign of their loyalty to the Polish-Lithuanian Commonwealth. In 1664, after the siege of Vitebsk by Muscovite forces, a group of nobles from that region, imprisoned by the aggressors, sent a letter to the Polish king testifying that Jews participated equally in the defense of the city, and as a result, they too were imprisoned and tortured by the Muscovite army. "And they have kept them [in prison] for a long time now," the letter said, "and many of these Jews were being compelled to be baptized by threats and use of force. But as faithful and loyal subjects of His Majesty the King, who love both His Majesty and the Republic, they did not succumb, and awaiting God's mercy they seek to be released from the Muscovite prison."[143]

The Church was soon to discover, however, that the power of the Catholic identity of the nobles had its limits. The nobles remained the nobles, unruly and wary of other powers, striving to preserve their liberties, the value of which they considered higher than anything else, including religion. As far as they were concerned, if something did not threaten the purity of their "nation," and if it benefited them, religion mattered little. Paradoxically, it was their new strong group identity as Catholic Polish nobles that allowed them to defy the Catholic Church and to allow non-Catholics to live and work on their estates. Thus, they accepted the Dutch Mennonites as settlers in their estates, Jews as administrators of their properties and their factors, and even Lutherans as merchants in their towns, and they refrained from forcing Eastern Orthodox peasants to convert to Catholicism. None of these groups threatened the integrity of their nation. The process of excluding non-Catholics from the state applied only to the nobility, who embodied the state.

For the Church, this was a disappointing victory. The Church wanted to impose its control over the broader society, but with unruly (even if Catholic) nobles, it could not go too far. Hence, despite gains in conversions among the nobility, the Church was aware of the continuing religious amalgam in Poland and never felt fully in control. Jews, unruly nobles, "heretics," and other "bad and disobedient" Catholics continued to be perceived as threatening the Church well into the eighteenth century.

4

༕

"Bad and Cruel Catholics": Christian Sins and Social Intimacies Between Jews and Christians

*A*N EIGHTEENTH-CENTURY ANONYMOUS PREACHER LAMENTED IN HIS sermon on "human ingratitude" for the Thursday preceding Easter that "our Savior Jesus" suffered now from "bad and cruel Catholics" just as he had suffered from "malicious Jews" and "heretics":

And so I have been preaching about human ingratitude. And how much more I could say about the horrible ingratitude that our Savior Jesus had experienced in the Most Dear Sacrament, and continues to experience in our times, and is bound to experience until the end of times because of the cruel faithlessness of people who don't believe. Not once was He tortured in the Most Holy Hosts by malicious Jews. Not once was He thrown out of the pyx and trampled, or thrown into fire by blind heretics robbing holy Catholic churches. And not once, was He secretly stolen and desecrated by people possessed by the Devil. And... how much humiliation does he suffer from believing, but bad and cruel, Catholics![1]

The Catholic clergy's frustration with its loss of influence went beyond their frustration with those in power. Many ordinary Catholics, too, ignored the teachings of the Church. The sins and religious ignorance of those the preacher called "bad and cruel Catholics" exposed how far the Church was from its ideal. The Church felt beset on all sides by "malicious Jews," "blind heretics," and disobedient Catholics themselves.

After the Council of Trent (1545–63), the Church throughout Europe began to struggle more aggressively to prevent the infiltration of dangerous ideas among clergy and laity.[2] The concern was not just to re-Catholicize a society "led astray" by the Reformation, but also to connect it more to Catholicism by educating priests and preachers, and by sending them out to small towns and villages.[3] Since the Protestant Reformation, the Catholic leadership in Poland and elsewhere was keenly aware of the low level of education both of its clergy and its laity, especially those from the lower strata of society, the poor and the peasants, and aware also of their lack of social and religious discipline. Numerous sources even from as late as the eighteenth century suggest that Catholics lacked rudimentary knowledge of their religion. In a 1733 polemical book, Jakub Radliński, a priest of Leżajsk, announced that he would not marry anyone who did not know the *Pater noster*. Apparently, even adults did not know this basic Christian prayer.[4]

With the spread of Protestantism, in part a result of regular preaching, the Catholic Church began to emphasize the importance of regular sermons to promote religious doctrines among the people.[5] The Church stressed attendance at weekly masses and at least one annual confession at Easter.[6] Avoiding confessions was seen as one of the causes of heresy.[7] By these and other means, the Church sought to promote tighter and tighter bonds between the laity and the clergy, and the leadership of the Church.

SUNDAY SINS AND JEWISH INNS

In 1689, a noted Jesuit preacher, Jan Krosnowski, complained that Christians were not paying attention to the sermons and did not take the service seriously: "When someone has to talk with an esteemed person, he will behave modestly and cut a dash; but when he has to speak with God in prayer, one yawns in church out of carelessness, another strokes his hair or twiddles his mustache."[8] The preacher warned that one could expect nothing from such prayers but curses.[9]

Total absence from the masses was even worse. The Church could not indoctrinate the "poor sinning folk"[10] if they did not even attend. But church activities had strong competition. In an eighteenth-century sermon at a church in the Cracow suburb of Stradom, one preacher vented his frustration about Sunday "sins of flesh" that tempted Christians:

And the third kind of work that God prohibits on Sundays is committing sins! Oh, my God! When do Christians offend God the most and the hardest? On Sundays and holidays.... All week, a peasant [chłopek] works hard as an ox, and he does not have time to sin, but when Sunday comes, oh, how many sins he commits. When is the best time to get drunk? On Sundays and holidays. When is the best time to go to inns and commit the sins of flesh by these wanton dances? On Sundays and holidays. When [is the best time] to sing coarse [szpetne] songs and to blaspheme with shameless words that scandalize innocent ears? Of course, having gotten drunk on Sunday! When [is the best time] to commit foul deeds [niecnota] with other men's wives in forests and fields? While walking to church on Sunday!... And when [is the best time] to argue with Mother and Father? Having gotten drunk on holidays! When [is the best time] to beat your wife the most, to throw your children out of the house, or to break household items? Having gotten drunk on holidays![11]

The Sunday sins involving sex, alcohol, and violence highlighted the limits of the Church's social and religious influence on its population and further intensified its sense of insecurity at a time of religious crisis.[12]

The preachers' complaints about the behavior of their flock may seem routine.[13] But of the three sources of frustrations voiced by the Stradom preacher, the abuse of alcohol deserves further attention, not only because, as the preacher argued, it led to other transgressions, but also because in early modern Poland alcoholic beverages were often produced and sold in inns or taverns owned or leased by Jews.[14] In his 1737 pastoral letter, Bishop Jan Lipski admonished Polish lords not to allow Jews who held leases [*na arendach siedzących*] to brew beer, vodka, or mead "because it is against God's commandment, *memento: ut diem Sabathi sanctifices*."[15] How brewing violated the commandment to sanctify the Sabbath Lipski did not elaborate, whether it was Jewish work on Sundays, Christian help on the day of worship, Christian drinking, or all of the above. After the usual prohibition to brew alcoholic beverages on Sundays and holidays, the 1733 Synod of Płock, headed by Andrzej Stanisław Załuski, ordered that Jews be informed in advance by a local Catholic about upcoming Christian holidays so that they might avoid violating them through ignorance [*occasio ignorantiae*].[16]

Bishop Załuski shed a bit more light on this issue in his *Edictum contra Iudaeos* of 1751. He forbade Jews to "brew beer and liquor" and to keep their taverns open on Catholic holidays "until the church service ends."[17] Załuski appears not to have objected to Jewish-run inns in principle – they could be open after the mass ended – but he protested the fact that open taverns provided an opportunity for religious negligence.

In these complaints, Jews are a prominent but not the primary cause; they appear as facilitators of Christians' transgressions. Jews, who ran the inns and often held a monopoly to sell liquor, had been granted that right by the aristocratic owner of the estate, who in turn benefited from it by preventing his subjects from getting their alcohol from another source. The monopoly on the production and sale of alcohol could absorb the surplus grain produced on the noble's estate and guaranteed additional income.[18] But the fact that inns were often run by Jews led the bishops to use classic anti-Jewish rhetoric to express frustration with their "faithless flock," who were refusing to submit to the Church's religious authority, ignoring its teachings and rulings. The arrangement between the estate owner and the Jewish innkeeper added one more layer to the already complex conflict between the Church and the nobles, with Jews in the middle.[19]

Many Christians also worked for Jews on Christian festivals, in violation of Church laws. Christian labor for Jews on Sundays and festivals had been legislated against during the Middle Ages in the Carolinian Empire in an early ruling attributed to Charlemagne, according to which the Jews could own Christian slaves as long as they were not compelled to work on Sundays. Early modern Polish bishops repeated similar prohibitions against Christians working in Jewish homes and Jewish-run inns.[20]

Bishop Jan Lipski stated a reason for those prohibitions in his pastoral letter of 1737: "No Jew shall dare to hire a Christian of whatever sex as a servant and [Christian] women as wet nurses. It is because of the danger of not observing holidays and fasts established by the Church."[21] Catholics who did not observe Church holidays removed themselves from direct contact with the clergy, and in some respects perhaps also from the larger Catholic community. Because peasants or other illiterate Christians from the lower strata of the society could not have been expected to be familiar with Church and state laws, the responsibility to inculcate their flock in the doctrines and practices of the Church fell on the priests, who were to maintain close contact with their parishioners in towns and villages through masses, preaching, and regular confession. In synodal decrees, Polish bishops and higher clergy shifted the burden of responsibility for reporting transgressions of Catholics and their contacts with Jews or heretics to local priests.[22]

According to court records, work for Jews on Christian festivals sometimes led to criminal investigation. In 1646, the court in Pinsk, now a town in Belarus, heard a case brought by Łukasz Ludwik Olkowski Kurządka and his wife Anna Dąbrowska Olkowska against a Jew, Dawid Jakubowicz, for beating and killing his Christian servant, Kondrat Szesztelewicz, a son of a serf belonging to the Olkowskis.[23] According to the Olkowskis' accusation, Kondrat Szesztelewicz had been hired by Dawid Jakubowicz as a helper "to make vodka [na robote kurzenia gorzałki]," but Jakubowicz "forgetting the common law and having no fear of God, and consciously tormenting the Christian blood, forced the above mentioned Kondrat Szesztelewicz to work on Sundays."[24] On a fateful January Sunday in 1646, the court report states that Jakubowicz, apparently seriously drunk himself, attacked Szesztelewicz with a bat to compel him to work. Maimed and "half-dead," Kondrat Szesztelewicz was carried home by his father and died a day later. The case was dismissed by the court on the procedural grounds that Jews, in accordance with royal privileges granted to them in royal domains, could not be tried in municipal criminal courts but only by royal representatives or royal courts.[25] It is unclear why the inebriated Dawid Jakubowicz beat Kondrat Szesztelewicz; but the fact that it happened on a Sunday and that the employer was a Jew was used by the prosecution and led the scribe, and perhaps the Olkowskis themselves, to offer a diatribe of anti-Jewish rhetoric that evoked the stereotype of Jewish enmity towards Christianity.

In most cases Christian work on Sundays and holidays did not end with violence and there is some evidence that clergy made concessions to allow Jews, and perhaps also their Christian helpers, to work on minor festivals. In 1667, Franciszek Prażmowski, a scholar and abbot, in a response to local Jews' supplications to priests in the parish church in Brest, admonished the priests to permit Jews to work undisturbed on lesser Christian holidays, specifically to brew beer and to work in bathhouses.[26] Work was prohibited on Christmas, Easter, Pentecost, and the Day of Ascension of Mary. But perhaps by allowing Jews to work "undisturbed" on minor religious occasions, Prażmowski permitted them to go about their normal business also in the employing of Christian servants. Prażmowski understood that the canonical total prohibition of work on Christian holidays was not feasible in Brest. Economic interests outweighed the Church's dogmatic ideal.[27]

On the other hand, the case of Abbot Prażmowski can also be seen as an example of the Catholic clergy's efforts to tighten their control. After all, the Jews still had to turn to a Church official to get permission to go about their business. And although in the end this particular Church official issued restricted permission, the Church had thereby compelled Jews to recognize its authority and their dependence on its will. It was a partial step toward establishing proper social order as the Church defined it.

"DEBAUCHERIES, ADULTERIES AND LEWDNESS": FEMALE SERVANTS IN JEWISH HOMES

If the nobles who profited from business ties with Jews were on one end of the spectrum of those the Church considered "corruptible" Christians,[28] on the other end were poor Christians, especially women, who held jobs in Jewish homes and businesses. Yet, Christian female servants in Jewish homes were a concern not unique to early modern Poland or to the Catholic Church. For centuries, both Christian and Jewish religious authorities had expressed unease about this practice, if sometimes for different reasons. Rabbis struggled to balance their belief that Christianity was a form of idolatry against the ensuing halakhic consequences of the economic reality of Jewish life in Christian lands.[29] For the rabbis, Christian servants posed halakhic questions about the fitness of food cooked by non-Jews for Jewish consumption, about payment for Christians' work around the time of Christian festivals, and about requiring non-Jews to work on Jewish holidays.[30] For the Catholic clergy, the concerns were about the religious negligence of Catholic workers and about sexual relations between Jews and Christian women; both were seen as violations of the social and religious boundaries the Church, and Jewish leaders too, had tried hard to establish.[31]

Because Jewish female servants would pose a different set of halakhic problems to their Jewish employers, and although there is evidence that such Jewish female servants existed,[32] Christian women were most frequently employed in Jewish homes in Poland. As elsewhere in Europe, the majority of domestic servants were poorer women.[33] They were employed not only as domestic servants but also – despite rabbinic misgivings – as wet nurses,[34] living with a Jewish family often in quite intimate settings because, except among the unusually wealthy families, space was quite limited in early modern households. It was a circumstance of Jewish-Christian intimacy Pope Benedict XIV found disturbing.[35]

Although it was a common practice across Europe for wet nurses to live with the family whose children they nursed, in the case of the nursing of Jewish children, a Christian wet nurse may have been even more likely to live with a Jewish family – in part because rabbinic law did not allow non-Jewish women to nurse Jewish infants in a nurse's own home but did reluctantly allow it within a Jewish home.[36] Perhaps the rabbinic law sought to ensure that Jewish families exercised control over their children; perhaps it sought to avoid secret baptism or to ensure that the child was fed with the wet nurse's milk and not something else.[37]

Polish clergy also were troubled by Jewish-Christian domestic arrangements. They feared conversion or loss of faith. In 1685, the synod of the diocese of Wilno stated that "their [Christian] wet nurses can easily become Jewish, and they celebrate their Sabbaths and holidays, neglect going to Church, neglect the Sacraments and Easter Communion and live according to the custom of Atheists."[38] Other synods from the eastern provinces of the Polish-Lithuanian Commonwealth, expressing their concerns about religious negligence and confessional religious purity among Catholics, sought to regulate intimate Jewish-Christian relationships. In 1717 the synod of the Chełm diocese forbade Christian women to nurse Jewish children altogether;[39] and to preserve the purity of the Christian religion and prevent the danger of "perversion," it also issued several rulings that proscribed any other activities involving direct physical Christian-Jewish contact.[40] In 1744, the synod of Wilno, in legislating against Christian service in Jewish homes, singled out Christian youngsters and unmarried women as those most susceptible to "Judaizing."[41] Similarly, in 1741, Bishop Franciszek Kobielski of the diocese of Łuck lamented, in an unusual pastoral letter to Jews of his diocese,[42] that by teaching their own children at home and holding religious services there, Jews "infected" Christian servants to the point that the Christian women serving Jews were able to pray in the "Jewish language" with the Jewish children they cared for.[43] Christian women certainly witnessed and perhaps were occasionally included in family celebrations, thus becoming familiar with Jewish rituals. At the very least, the Jewish calendar, with its day of rest on Saturday, the Shabbat, would have forced Christians to work on Sunday, which was a regular workday for Jews.

"Judaizing" Christians, even as late as the eighteenth century, was not a theoretical matter in Poland, and religious negligence and the abandonment of Catholicism were not small concerns for Church leaders, especially in dioceses with religiously diverse populations, like the diocese of Wilno, where the Church's authority was constantly challenged by Protestants, by the Eastern Orthodox Christians, and also, it seems, by Jews. Court records and other sources demonstrate that a number of Christians abandoned Catholicism for other Christian religions and for Judaism as well.[44]

Among many examples of Christian female conversions to Judaism, we find two criminal cases in the town of Dubno in 1716.[45] After the death of her husband, Dawid Syrowajec, Maryna Dawidowa decided to "accept the Jewish faith."[46] Riding on horseback about fifty miles away from her hometown of Vitebsk, she began to introduce herself to people as a Jewish woman, though she apparently never underwent a formal conversion. As her recorded testimony states, she had received help from Jews along the way until she reached Dubno, where she was arrested for apostasy. Asked whether she was willing to return to the Christian faith, she refused and is reported to have proclaimed: "I do not want [to return to the Christian faith] and I am ready to die in the Jewish religion for the living God, because it is a better religion than your Christian religion, because your religion is false."[47] Even under torture, Dawidowa maintained her stance. She was burned alive at the stake after three pieces of her body had been ripped off, presumably as symbols of the Trinity.

The second woman tried in Dubno, Maryna Wojciechówna (her name indicates that she had been unmarried and was a daughter of a certain Wojciech), was arrested at a Jewish wedding in Dubno at which she was the bride.[48] At her trial on charges of apostasy, she confessed that she had come from Mielec, now a small town in southeastern Poland, where she had served for three years as a maid in the house of a certain Jew. She had then moved to the nearby town of Leżajsk, where according to her testimony she was persuaded to convert to Judaism by a local Jew, Pasternak, and other Jewish men and women.[49] Tortured during her trial, Wojciechówna, unlike Maryna Dawidowa, reverted to Christianity and, so the trial record states, expressed her "disgust with the Jewish religion" and her willingness to die for Christ.[50] She was spared live burning and instead was sentenced to death by beheading. Her body was burned afterwards. Jews involved in the wedding were acquitted on the ground that they were unaware of the fact that she was a (former) Christian.[51] According to the Magdeburg Law, both Jewish proselytism among Christians and marriage between a Jew and a Christian, which was considered adultery, were punishable by death.[52]

The religious and social boundaries in early modern Poland were permeable and were crossed in both directions. Whereas Jewish conversions to Catholicism strengthened the Church, conversions in the reverse direction threatened it. Maryna Wojciechówna's case illustrates that some Christian women serving in Jewish homes indeed developed close relationships with their Jewish employers and converted to Judaism.

The multilayered case of Abram Michelevich, a Jew from Mohilev, and his Christian partner, Paraska Daniłowna, tried in Mohilev in 1748, further illustrates the feared consequence of relations between Christian female servants and Jews.[53] In the trial records, the relationship between Michelevich and Daniłowna was described as "secretly living with each other in marriage."[54] The case had started as a case of infanticide but evolved to include a number of layers of complicated religious and social interaction between Abram and Paraska, in particular, and Jews and Christians, in general. According to his testimony as recorded by the scribe, Abram came from Polock, now a town in the Vitebsk province of Belarus. Around 1743, he had married a Jewish woman, Gisia Jankielewa, but abandoned her the day after their wedding. Soon after, he went to Dubrowek and found a job with a Jewish arrendator, a leaseholder, named Leyba. There he met Paraska, Leyba's Christian servant. About a year and a half later, Paraska became pregnant by Abram. When she was in advanced pregnancy, the couple left Dubrowek and traveled toward a town nearby. In a field near the town, Paraska gave birth to a daughter. Abram later testified that the infant had been born alive and died an hour later. Paraska said that Abram had convinced her to abandon the infant while still alive. After wandering together from town to town, they eventually settled in Wendoroże, in a land-estate leased by a Jew, Hirsch, where Abram found a job as a bathhouse attendant. According to Abram's testimony in Wędoroże,

Paraska accepted our Jewish faith and she observed the Sabbath, in the presence of the Jew, Hirsch, and his wife, who taught her Jewish prayers. And this Hirsch and his wife are the arrendators in Wendoroże [sic], and since then she observed the tenets of Jewish religion and Jewish holidays and she went to synagogue in Kniażyce. And while I initially wanted to become a Catholic, I gave in to her will and remained in my religion, teaching her Jewish prayers. And even though we were not formally married, at the very beginning we took each others' hands and [promised] not to leave each other.[55]

Paraska and Abram were sentenced to death on multiple counts because their relationship violated several social norms of the time: infanticide; adultery, as sexual relation between a Jew and a Christian was defined; apostasy; and Jewish proselytism of Christians. Each of these "crimes" was punishable by death.[56] Paraska was sentenced to death by decapitation and a postmortem burning at the stake, Abram to death by burning. But when after the sentencing Abram accepted baptism, his sentence was commuted to decapitation and postmortem burning.

This case underlines other grounds for the clergy's anxieties – the level of religious understanding among uneducated Christians. Paraska's and Abram's testimonies reveal what they understood of each other's religion. For Abram, Paraska's Christianity involved "mentioning your god's name" and "crossing" oneself.[57] For Paraska, accepting Judaism meant that "Abram himself cut my hair and since then I observed their holidays, and I ate [meat] on Wednesdays and Fridays."[58] She also noted that she had been taught how to bless candles. In the popular minds, it seems, religious precepts were not complicated, and perhaps, therefore, not difficult to transgress.

Similar cases, although with less violent outcomes because the Church had no executive power, can be found in episcopal court records. In 1723, the episcopal court in Cracow recorded two cases of Jews who had had sexual relations with Catholic women. In a case that may be another example of "judaizing," Saul, a Jew from Nowy Korczyn, a village near Cracow, impregnated a certain Magdalena Sewulenka and took her and the child to another village for protection and child rearing [educandam et fovendam tradere]. The language of the document, which casts Saul as the main actor, suggests that, in staying with him, Magdalena probably abandoned her religion and condemned her child to "infidelity." Saul risked his life by moving away with her and their child for protection and "child rearing."[59] If Saul had decided to embrace Christianity, the couple would have had no reason to escape.

The second Jew, Ossior, was a leaseholder of a brewery in Sarnina Zwola, owned by a nobleman, Albert Linowski. Ossior had two Catholic maids, one of whom, Marianna, became pregnant by him, whereupon both the Jew and the nobleman were condemned by the bishop, the latter for permitting such "scandalous" behavior in his domain. The outcome of the case remains unknown.[60] In this case, as well as in the case of Saul and Magdalena, the relations between the Jewish men and the Catholic women were regarded as harmful to the Catholic religion [in grave praejudicium Catholicae religionis].

The Church had voiced concerns about sexual relations between Jews and Christians centuries before.[61] The IV Lateran Council in its 1215 ruling requiring distinctive clothing for Jews and Muslims was intended to prevent sexual relations between Christians and "infidels."[62] With religion as a major defining social category, sexual relations between Jews ("infidels") and their Christian employees (especially women) would have been seen not only as an offence to the spouse or family of the employed woman but also to God, threatening religious purity, as David Nirenberg has shown, and violating religious boundaries.[63]

Although in Poland bishops and other churchmen often complained about sexual relations between Christian women and their Jewish employers, they rarely legislated against it. Bishop Wacław Hieronim Sierakowski of Przemyśl, in his report to Rome of 1743, wrote that Jews' hiring of Christians of both sexes led to various scandals, crimes, adultery, and fornication.[64] A similar complaint came from Bishop Szembek of Chełm.[65] In 1751, Bishop Załuski lamented that the Jews blemished [szpecą] Christian women by lewd relations [nieczysta społeczność, literally "impure relations"] and adultery.[66] He condemned anyone who "God forbid, would have carnal relations [społeczność cielesna] with a Jew or a Jewess."[67] Similarly, Stefan Żuchowski of Sandomierz broke into a diatribe about sexual corruption of Catholic women by Jews. Żuchowski claimed that Jews considered non-Jewish women disposed to sin, and hence were inclined to commit "debaucheries, adulteries and lewdness with Catholic women"[68] and spread "calumnies and suspicion on Catholic women."[69]

Yet few Church synods or bishops' pastoral letters from the early modern period in Poland-Lithuania deal with sexual relations between Jewish men and Christian women in detail. The issue does appear in Church legislation in the codification of Polish synodal decrees, approved by the pope in 1629 and first published in Cracow in 1630.[70] It became a standard code of Polish Church laws and was republished in 1761,[71] stating that a Jew caught with a Christian woman committing the sin of fornication was to be incarcerated until he paid the fine of at least ten marks as reparation. The Christian woman who committed such a crime was to be flogged publicly and expelled from the city without hope of return.[72] Gender appears to have triumphed over religion, for the penalty reserved for the Jewish man was significantly less severe than that to be imposed on the Christian woman. Or, perhaps, sexual relations between a Jewish man and a Christian woman were seen as a more shocking betrayal of the Christian faith and thus as requiring a stronger penalty for the woman.[73] The possibility of sexual relations between a Christian man and a Jewish woman is not even mentioned.[74]

Yet this document cannot be read as representative of Polish Church legislation of the seventeenth and eighteenth centuries. First, it is simply a repetition of an earlier ruling decreed by the Wrocław (Breslau) Council of 1267, retaining even the same monetary value of the fine.[75] Second, despite numerous complaints in the bishops' reports to Rome and in their pastoral letters, the issue of sexual relations between

Jews and Christians was not sanctioned in the rulings of any specific synod in the period under consideration and appeared only in this referential compilation.[76] What is striking about this document and the records from episcopal courts is that the penalties for sexual relations between Jews and Christian women were much more benign than penalties imposed by lay courts. Perhaps the lack of legislation is a consequence of the fact that when cases of Jewish-Christian relationships did find their way to courts they were prosecuted severely, following the Magdeburg Law, which penalized such relations with death.[77]

Nonetheless, Bishop Załuski's rhetoric about the blemishing of Christian women, Żuchowski's complaint about the false representation of Catholic women as being disposed to sexual sins, and the Chełm diocese synod's rhetoric of purity all show how grave were the Church's concerns with religious and sexual purity. The neat boundaries the Church attempted to draw to separate Catholics from Jews and other possible corrupters and create an ideal community, free of religious and sexual pollutions, in real life appear to have been frequently violated, no doubt furthering the Church's sense of insecurity and a sense of disorder blamed especially on Jews.[78]

This sense of disorder stemmed from a broader perception that Catholic immorality resulted from living under Jewish authority. In 1713 the municipal court of Kobryń, a town in the region of Grodno,[79] brought a charge of infanticide against Ulana Romanowna,[80] an unmarried servant hired by Michiel, a Jewish arrendator of a tavern in Głębokie, a small neighboring town.[81] Romanowna became involved with a Christian farmhand, Swiryd Demidowy, a son of the local village leader (*wójt*), and soon became pregnant. The scribe noted that "the Jewish mistress knew about their shameful relationship and deeds, but she did nothing to stop it."[82] Only when Ulana was visibly pregnant did the Jewish mistress throw her out. Ulana wandered about and gave birth to a baby boy, whom she killed. Whereas masters in Germany were held responsible for their servants' out-of-wedlock pregnancies, especially for infanticide, I am not aware of similar laws in early modern Poland. The Jewish mistress in this case was not brought to court.[83] Still, it appears that at least the scribe held her in part responsible for the sins of this Christian couple, an assumption of responsibility that follows the stereotype of Jews as corrupters and enemies of Christianity, a stereotype found in polemical and homiletic works in Poland. It is not surprising that the scribe from Kobryń, and probably others, believed that Jews, "enemies of Christianity," could not be trusted to uphold Christian moral values.[84]

Because of this distrust of Jews and their own insecurity, Church officials sought to restrict activities that would lead to religious negligence, moral corruption, or – worse – to "judaizing." However, on occasion they softened traditional prohibitions in the face of the reality of complex Polish economic and social conditions. In his 1751 *Edictum contra Judaeos*,[85] Andrzej Stanisław Załuski, the bishop of Cracow, modified the canon law prohibition against Christian women's serving as wet nurses to Jewish children. They could not nurse "unless they [i.e., Jewish children] were dying of hunger," in which case Christian women had permission to nurse a Jewish child.[86] In the same document, Załuski modified the old prohibition against assisting Jewish women during labor and against turning for assistance to Jewish women: "It is improper [*nie godzi się*] for Christian women to assist at the birth of Jewish children, unless there should exist such need, that is, unless there should be no Jewish woman to help. [It is improper for Christian women] to use Jewish women for themselves [during their labor]."[87] Again, here the real-life conditions – in remote villages, for example – appear to have outweighed fears of religious negligence or "judaizing" by Christian women. But even these concessions were ways of reinforcing control, even if only nominally; for once allowed under stated conditions, the real-life situations were no longer "violations" of strict laws but sanctioned and approved by Church authority. The bishop, instead of losing control, like Abbot Prażmowski who allowed Jews to work on Christian festivals, had asserted that the situation was under control.

FEASTING, DRINKING, AND DANCING: JEWISH-CHRISTIAN SOCIALIZING

The Church's complaints about sexual sins of which Jews were a part concerned only lower-class Christian women, at least in public. Cases of noblemen or women appear rarely in writing and then only in anecdotes and exempla.[88] Even if it is less likely, if at all, that sexual relationships occurred between Jews and more affluent Christian women, the matter would not find its way to court, and would have been solved secretly behind closed doors. Noblemen and noblewomen did not socialize with Jews; they did business with them.[89] In the lower social strata, it seems that the social boundaries were more permeable, or violations more public.

Given the nature of historical sources from the period it is difficult to find direct descriptions of friendly interpersonal contacts that did not involve some sort of conflict. We find traces of them in prohibitions and in the background of cases that found their way to court. Rabbinic responsa and halakhic glosses sometimes mention them in passing as well.[90] Most descriptive are prohibitions through which several synods and bishops attempted to restrict Jewish-Christian social contacts in contexts of entertainment, dining and drinking, or celebrating holidays together.[91]

The difficulty in using official proscriptive Church documents from this period is that many documents draw heavily on earlier Church rulings, and thus appear very routine. In his *Edictum contra Judaeos*, Bishop Załuski wrote, "We inform everyone that it is not suitable for Christians to sully themselves by close relations with the Jews, to attend their weddings and circumcisions, to visit them at home or in their synagogue, to eat their unleavened bread and their Easter [sic] matzah, to call for their doctors or barbers."[92] Similarly, the synods of Chełm in 1717, following the synodal statutes of Kalisz of 1420 and the synodal constitutions of 1629, ordered "all Christians in this province under the penalty of excommunication not to dare to receive Jewish men or women to live and feast with them [*ad convivandum*], or to eat and drink with them, and also not to dance at their weddings or New Moons. Neither should they eat meat and other foods sold by Jews."[93] The synods of Łuck-Brest in 1726 and of Wilno in 1744, and Bishop Josaphat Michal Karp of Samogitia in his pastoral letter of 1737, forbade Christians to attend feasts or banquets with Jews, or to eat and drink with them, or to eat Jewish matzoth, or to celebrate Jewish weddings or New Moons [*Rosh Ha-Shanah*], or to dance together.[94] But even repetitious rulings from the synods of Chełm and Łuck-Brest, along with the pastoral letter by Bishop Karp, all taken verbatim from the 1630 compilation of synodal legislation[95] (itself based on a canon from the Viennese Council of 1267 and earlier Church legal tradition) are illustrations of the long tradition of the Church's *will* to separate the two communities.

One eighteenth-century preacher unabashedly expressed a keen desire to keep Jews and Christians apart. In a sermon on the celebration of Christian festivals, he wrote, "Remember to sanctify the Holy Day. These are the following reasons why we, Christians, do not celebrate Saturday, as it is commanded in the Old Testament, but Sunday. First because Sabbath was a Jewish ceremony... and it was rejected by Christ, our Lord. And secondly, [it was done] so that we should not socialize with Jews."[96] The seventeenth-century Protestant polemicist Krzysztof Kraiński used the same rationale in his *Postylla*, citing the letter of an early Christian Ignatius of Antioch to the Christians in Magnesia, with a list of reasons for Christians' celebrating Sunday and not Saturday.[97]

Catholic clergy feared religious corruption of their flock from socializing with Jews, a particularly sensitive issue around the time of solemn Catholic festivals. In 1752, Bishop Szembek wrote, "And furthermore, during the Lent and Advent we admonish that Jews dare not organize weddings with music and that they not bring Christians to such celebrations and similar Jewish feasts, and Christians for their part should not attend them."[98] Catholics did not celebrate weddings during periods of fast, but Jews were not bound by such limitations and could celebrate at those times, thereby offending the sensibilities of Church leaders. The offense was all the more conspicuous when Christians themselves attended such feasts in violation of the solemnity of Lent or Advent.

The intentional prevention of Jewish-Christian contacts was not unique for Poland[99] nor limited to Catholic authorities.[100] Church leaders striving for social and religious purity had other, perhaps unwitting, allies – for example, Jewish communal leaders, whose concerns were similar in many ways. But few (if any) voices of protest arose among Catholic clergy about similar contacts between lower-class Catholics and heretics, perhaps reflecting the class nature of the religious divisions among Christians. "Heretics" were predominantly nobles or burghers and they likely did not socialize with lower-class Christians.

"NEITHER MEN NOR WOMEN SHOULD WEAR NON-JEWISH CLOTHES": RESTRICTIONS OF RABBINIC LAW

Laws separating Jews from non-Jews (or "Israelites" from "non-Israelites") appear in the Torah, or the Pentateuch. In the early postbiblical Jewish literature, the Mishnah – and especially the section 'Avodah Zarah – delineated the boundaries and served as a foundation for subsequent rabbinic laws on contacts between Jews and non-Jews.[101] Jewish law concerning non-Jews often parallels Church laws concerning Jews;[102] thus, in the rabbinic law or the halakhah, prohibitions appear against Jews celebrating non-Jewish holidays and attending non-Jewish weddings. There are laws attempting to limit friendly interaction between these two groups and to restrict the use of each other's bathhouses and doctors.[103] Like the leaders of the Church, the rabbis too were trying to set boundaries.

By the early modern period, Jewish law was well established and began to be more available in print. One of the most popular works of Jewish law, which became the standard halakhic compendium, was the Shulḥan 'Aruk, compiled and first published in the sixteenth century.[104] The laws in Shulḥan 'Aruk followed the Tur, a late medieval halakhic compendium by Jacob ben Asher, which reorganized laws included in the Mishnah and the Talmud. The glosses on both the Tur and the Shulḥan 'Aruk by early modern rabbis, most notably the Polish rabbi Moses Isserles, shed some light on local attitudes and practices. Here, as in the Polish Church laws, theory and practice collided. Ideally, Jews were not allowed to celebrate with non-Jews on non-Jewish holidays, but as Rabbi Isserles conceded in his commentary on Shulḥan 'Aruk, Yoreh De'ah 148: "We who live among them and have to do business with them year round" can join in their celebrations out of fear of arousing animosity, but one should do what one can to avoid it.[105]

Jewish dietary laws of kashrut also would have limited contacts, at least to Jewish homes only, something the Catholic Church itself tried to prevent. But Jewish law was often about restricting actual socializing rather than simply about the observance of kashrut. For example, if this issue was limited to the observance of dietary laws alone, one could in theory allow socializing if Jews ate their own food. But this was not in fact the case. According to the halakhah, Jews were not to attend weddings of a non-Jew, even if they ate their own food and were served by their own attendant. If, however, on the occasion of a wedding, the non-Jew sent fowl and fish for a Jew to his house, it was permitted to eat.[106] The prohibition to eat one's own food at a non-Jewish event was probably related to the notion of marit 'ayin, a principle that an action might give the wrong impression even if not inherently wrong; still, it sought to prevent socializing with non-Jews. Indeed, rabbis understood that socializing often led to sexual relations, and accordingly they prohibited the "idolaters'" bread, oil, wine, and daughters. The bread and oil of non-Jews were prohibited on the account of wine, and the wine was prohibited "on the account of the daughters" – food leading to drinking and drinking to relationships, and even intermarriage. All this, the rabbis feared, in turn would lead to idolatry.[107]

From the perspective of Jewish leaders, close contacts like socializing or sexual relations between Jews and Christians could have serious repercussions for the Jewish community. Two responsa from the late sixteenth and early seventeenth centuries can serve as examples. One, by Rabbi Maharam of Lublin, concerns a young Jewish man caught with a Christian prostitute in the town of Opatów. Charged with the "crime" of sexual relations with a Christian woman, he was to be sentenced to death or forced to convert to Christianity to gain commutation of the sentence. The question asked by the community leaders of Opatów was whether the young man should be redeemed by the Jewish community on the basis of the commandment *pidiyon shevuim*, the rescuing of the captives, and, if so, what limits should be set on the amount they should pay. Maharam's response indicated a sense of Jewish vulnerability in such circumstances. He pondered the possible further dangers if they did rescue the young man, among them the risks of further libels against Jews should the Jewish community pay a high price for his release. But, within Maharam's response to the questions, he also indicated that sexual relations between Jewish men and Christian women were not uncommon.[108]

The second case deals with an accusation against a young Jewish girl that she had promised to convert to Christianity and marry a Christian man.[109] Christian authorities would have done all they could to bring about the fulfillment of such a commitment. Whether or not the girl did make such a promise is immaterial here; the responsum indicates the Jewish leaders' sense of fears about the danger that might emerge from contacts between Jews and Christians.

Religious leaders realized that intimacy, though perhaps of a different kind, can result from inadvertent contacts – in bathhouses, for example, and in times of emergencies and life-threatening situations. It is not surprising, therefore, that both Jewish and Christian religious leaders prohibited Jews' and Christians' bathing together and even using each other's services in moments of medical emergencies. Some Polish synods issued prohibitions against Jews attending bathhouses. And these prohibitions are coupled with laws on attending dance halls at the same time, indicating perhaps a broader concern with socializing.[110] The issue of bathhouses is addressed in Rabbi Moses Isserles' annotation in the *Shulḥan 'Aruk* to the section Yoreh De'ah 153.3, which deals with intimate contacts with non-Jews, the *yiḥud*, or being with someone in a private setting. Based on earlier rabbinic rulings, Isserles wrote: "In the place where it is a custom to take trousers off when attending bathhouses, it is prohibited [for a Jew] to go to a bathhouse where naked gentiles wash themselves, but if a Jew is already in the bath house and the gentiles come he need not leave." In his commentary on the same section of the Tur, Isserles allowed this practice, saying that during his time "we are not accustomed to be that strict."[111]

Moses Isserles' words also come in the context of the Mishanic prohibitions that forbid Jews to leave their animals with gentiles, because of the gentiles' alleged inclinations to bestiality, and that disallow Jews from being alone with gentiles because they are suspected of easy bloodshed.[112] These prohibitions present non-Jews as dangerous, as licentious sexual predators or as killers. Perhaps bathhouses were also seen as a place of possible sexual transgressions or of "bloodshed."

Isserles' comment, though based on earlier halakhic sources, may also suggest that many Jews in Poland may have resembled gentiles in appearance, a possibility that troubled both Christian and Jewish religious authorities. In 1607, the Council of Four Lands in Poland, a supracommunal Jewish diet, ruled that "neither men nor women should wear non-Jewish clothes."[113] Indeed, the Jewish leaders desired that Jews dress distinctly in order to prevent any possibility of intimacy; their motivation was similar to that behind the medieval Church rulings about the special marking to be placed on the garments of "Jews and Saracens."[114]

The Jewish reason for not going to Christian bathhouses may have been fear of encountering hostility, although it is noteworthy that Isserles does not mention hostility here as he does elsewhere, and that Shabbatai ha-Cohen, the seventeenth-century author of the commentary on the *Shulhan 'Aruk*, provides the halakhic background for Isserles' annotation by focusing on the discussion of the notions of purity and impurity as the basis for this prohibition. Nevertheless, the question of the parallel Church prohibition remains.[115] Was it because of intimacy? Or, was it because of a fear of pollution by Jews? Whatever the reason, Catholic Church writings illustrate a generalized fear of sexual pollution and of Jews as sexual predators.[116]

A similar tension between vulnerability and intimacy and a fear of religious corruption and pollution is apparent in rulings on midwives, wet nurses, and physicians. Paralleling Church legislation against mutual assistance of Jewish and Christian women at childbirth, the *Shulhan 'Aruk*, in Yoreh De'ah 154.2, prohibited a Jewish woman from helping a gentile woman in childbirth unless she was known to the birthing woman and the help was performed for payment. Isserles added that it was also prohibited to teach a gentile crafts.[117] This prohibition comes from the Mishnah,[118] and as the text states it was intended to prevent a Jewish woman from helping to bring an idolater into the world, a position reiterated by the author of *Turei zahav*, a seventeenth-century commentary on the *Shulhan 'Aruk*.[119] The *Shulhan 'Aruk*, on the other hand, establishes professional boundaries between Jewish and Christian women, discouraging contacts based on friendship. To avoid such intimacy and friendship, rabbinic authorities made a payment part of the relationship.[120]

In a passage that precedes the section on Jewish midwives in the *Shulhan 'Aruk*, the fear of intimacy is meshed with a sense of vulnerability. *Shulhan 'Aruk*, in Yoreh De'ah 154.1, deals with a non-Jewish midwife helping a Jewish woman in childbirth and with a non-Jewish wet nurse hired to nurse a Jewish child. In the case of the non-Jewish midwife, the two women were not permitted to be alone because of possible harm by the gentile woman. Here the specific reason is not stated but in the Tur, which served as the basis for the laws in the *Shulḥan 'Aruk*, the reason, following the Talmud, is murder.[121] So too a non-Jewish wet nurse was not allowed to nurse a Jewish child in her own home or to be left alone with the infant at any time. Moses Isserles noted that although a gentile woman's milk is like that of a Jewish woman, a non-Jewish woman's milk should not be used if a Jewish wet nurse's is available because the gentile woman's milk makes "the child's heart stupid and breeds bad nature in him." The type of food eaten by the wet nurse, even if Jewish, was said also to be important.[122] Like other passages on intimate situations, these illustrate vilification of the other as dangerous, corrupting, and threatening, and highlight certain parallel concerns of the rabbis and the Church.

On the Catholic side, one writer demonized Jewish midwives who were apparently employed by wealthy Catholic women. "And may the grand ladies who commonly use Jewish women in birthing learn how they endanger the life and health of their children.... They sin against Church prohibitions when they use Jewish midwives."[123] The writer accused Jewish women of using magic to harm the children, for "if Christian midwives dare things like that how much more Jewish witches will do it, who out of hatred and devil's advice must practice [such magic]."[124]

Reservations on wet nurses and midwives are to be seen also in the broader context of dangers related to birthing and rearing an infant in premodern Europe, where midwives, wet nurses, and lying-in maids were often accused of witchcraft.[125] Just as birthing women and their infants were vulnerable to potential abuse by the assisting women, so the women hired were vulnerable to accusations when things went wrong.

The tension between intimacy and vulnerability is reflected in laws regarding physicians. Whereas Church laws in Poland and elsewhere prohibited Christians from using Jewish doctors and Pope Paul IV prohibited Jews from healing Christians even when requested and called for,[126] *Shulḥan 'Aruk* in Yoreh De'ah, 155.1 did allow the use of non-Jewish doctors for the sick, but only as a last resort. Isserles, again emphasizing a professionalization of the relationship, ruled that it was allowed but only for a fee, not free of charge.[127] Further, the core text continues, if one knows that the gentile doctor does not mention idols and does not use incantations, one may call on him, but not if he does use the names of idols. Isserles added, based on a medieval rabbinic authority, that it was prohibited to learn gentiles' incantations.[128]

The fear of religious corruption and of idol worship resulting from contacts between Jews and non-Jews in medical emergencies permeates the discussion of non-Jewish physicians in the *Shulḥan 'Aruk*. Rabbis expressed fears of what would happen if someone was cured when a gentile doctor invoked the name of an idol. Isserles' prohibition against learning these "idolatrous" incantations serves as a partial answer to this question because it suggests that people moved between their different systems of beliefs and, further, that in cases of medical emergencies, anything that worked was accepted.

Isserles' fear is illustrated by an early eighteenth-century Catholic sermon delivered in Cracow and preserved in manuscript in the archive of the Reformed Franciscans in Cracow.[129] Based on a medieval tale, it tells the story of a Jewish woman giving birth while her husband was away. When complications began, Christian women who were there to help convinced her to invoke Mary. Both she and the infant survived, whereupon the women urged her to accept Christianity, attributing her survival to her invocation of Mary. She became a Christian along with her newborn child. When her husband returned home and learned what had happened, he killed the infant in a rage, an act typical for these tales. The wife screamed and wailed, leading him to try to escape, but the city gates were already locked. He managed to find shelter in a church, and there he experienced visions of Mary; and when the crowd of people caught him, he too was ready to accept Christianity. At that moment the son he had killed miraculously came back to life. And thus they lived happily ever after as a Christian family.[130] Clearly, this is a fictitious, typological story to promote Marian devotion; but it is also a story that illustrates the dynamic between the two groups and their mutual fears and hopes.

The mutual anxieties and mutually promoted attitudes of animosity added a level of distrust and suspicion of the Other and, therefore, a sense of vulnerability that such intimate contacts might bring.[131] Yet, both Jewish and Christian sources suggest often friendly on-going relationships. In his article on the process of halakhic decision making, Edward Fram discussed a seventeenth-century responsum by Polish rabbi Joel Sirkes on the adultery and sexual promiscuity of a certain Jewish woman. It appears that she maintained friendly, and maybe even sexual, relations with non-Jews in town.[132] Another Polish rabbi, Benjamin Slonik, responding to a question whether Jews were allowed to lend clothes to Christians to be worn on Christian festivals, focused on whether Christianity was idolatry or not and whether lending clothes to Christians made Jews contribute to idolatrous worship.[133] In the end, he allowed Jews to lend clothes to Christians, arguing that even though Christians wore such clothes to church, elegant clothing was not required by their worship and, therefore, Jews were not contributing to idolatry.[134] Christians felt comfortable turning to Jews to borrow clothes, and Jews apparently felt comfortable lending them, though it provoked reservations among their religious leaders.

Because socializing and eating together could lead to simple friendships, then to emotional closeness, and eventually also to sexual relations, neither Jewish nor Church authorities wanted to encourage the crossing of boundaries. Both clearly saw contacts between Jews and Christians more as opportunities for corruption within their communities and as threats to religious loyalty among their co-religionists than as opportunities to gain converts. Thus, Catholic leaders did not consider such contacts a means of converting Jews – and therefore of strengthening the Church – but seemed rather to perceive such contacts as threats of further erosion of the Church's social influence, as another symptom of the Church's sense of embattlement and weakness, and of its attempts to regain prestige and influence by issuing rulings to create a more cohesive and more easily controlled society.

"EVEN JEWS AND TURKS OBSERVE HOLIDAYS BETTER": THE CHURCH REBUKES SINNING CHRISTIANS

Despite the anxieties experienced by both rabbinic and Church authorities about relationships, the social and economic reality did not allow for a strict separation, and Jews and Christians continued to live side by side. Poorer Christians continued to take up jobs in Jewish homes and businesses. The Church turned to rhetorical consolation and attack.

The story of the "fallen" Agnieszka exemplifies one of those paths.[135] In it the Catholic preacher turned an activity that violated Church law into a positive action. The story supposedly took place after a war, when convents for "young ladies had to release them back to their homes," perhaps a reference to the religious wars of the sixteenth and seventeenth centuries, though such conflicts did not greatly affect Poland. Agnieszka had been forced to leave the convent and return to her father. Upon her return, her father raped and impregnated her. As she was about to give birth, the devil, disguised as a monk, advised her to drown the newborn. Struggling against her maternal feelings, she threw the baby into a lake and traveled to a town where she was hired as a wet nurse by a Jewish woman. She moved in with the Jewish family and lived there for five years, befriending her Jewish mistress, Sara. Agnieszka told Sara of "the Virgin Mother of Christ" and Mary's motherly qualities, and taught her the *Pater Noster* and the Hail Mary. After years of inner struggle and depression, Agnieszka confessed her "sins" to a Dominican friar, who sent her to the pope for absolution.

Upon Agnieszka's return from Rome, Sara welcomed her warmly, infuriating her husband "since he already suspected that she had led his wife astray." In his fury, he killed Agnieszka as Sara, terrified, hid in a closet until midnight, when he went to the synagogue. When Sara left the closet, she saw Mary and two other virgins attending Agnieszka's body and anointing her wounds. By morning Agnieszka's body was gone. When the husband came home and found no corpse, he assumed that his wife had buried the body, whereas Sara assumed he had but was afraid to ask. Forty days later, a woman appeared bearing Agnieszka's greetings for Sara and her husband.[136] Sara said that the mighty Christ had resurrected the murdered servant; enraged, her husband replied, "I was always afraid that she had led you into error," and locked her up for two years. When he left for a business trip, Sara took their three children and departed. Inspired by the miracle she had witnessed, she became a Christian.

This story turns a situation that violated multiple Church laws – incest, infanticide, and, perhaps most important, Agnieszka's role as a wet nurse and a live-in servant in a Jewish household – into a positive story of conversion and reassurance. Instead of the often-feared judaizing, Agnieszka did the opposite, converting her Jewish mistress and her children to Christianity. The narrator seems to have accepted the economic reality and crafted it to encourage Christian servants to convert Jews (and, conceivably, to raise the confidence of these servants in Catholicism) and to discourage judaizing.[137] Agnieszka's story works in the same way the tale of the Jewish woman giving birth in the assistance of Christian women does. It turns a violation of Church laws into a positive situation that brings Jews to Christianity. The resulting conversion becomes a justification for problematic Jewish-Christian interaction. The end here justifies the means.

In some sermons, the discussion of Christian sins acquired a different twist. Jews were not presented as corruptors of Christians; rather, the preachers argued that the questionable behavior of Catholics prevented Jewish conversions to Catholicism. Catholic sins and lack of religious observance made even Jews and heretics seem pious. Jan Krosnowski, the late seventeenth-century preacher, contrasted Christians' behavior with that of "Turks and pagans who are used to staying in their temples [bóżnicach][138] and mosques, while praying with great honesty." He continued, "And in our Christian churches we see enough laughing, joking and gamboling every day. Oh, how such ungrateful dissonance instead of pleading must insult God's ears."[139] Krosnowski sought to emphasize the seriousness of Catholics' transgressions. The enemies of the Church – as Turks, Jews, and pagans were viewed – were a better example of piety than disobedient Catholics, and that, according to Krosnowski, was insulting to God.

Similarly, Jan Choynacki, an early eighteenth-century preacher, complained in a series of sermons on the Ten Commandments at the St. Mary's Church in Cracow that "even Jews and Turks observe holidays better than Catholics."[140] Another eighteenth-century preacher complained about the lax observance of Catholics on Sundays. His sermon used the rhetorical device of personal confession of sins. "And we [poor] craftsmen," he impersonated, "regret that we worked till the dawn and, therefore, we often skipped the mass entirely or parts of it. And [we regret] that we rarely listened to the sermons, but instead went to the fairs. Or sometimes, instead of going to church, we chose to stay at home, or wander around the house and barns, or go to pick nuts, pears, mushrooms or berries in the forests. Oh, how much better Lutherans, Calvinists, and Jews celebrate their holy days in their churches [zbory] and synagogues [bóżnice], where they sit almost all day praying, singing and listening to the sermons."[141]

The churches are not houses of piety, so an eighteenth-century preacher said, but appear to be places of games and play. "And was there any laughter, any jokes, when naked Jesus stood by the pillory?" he asked. "But today in Catholic churches we can hear and see laughter and jokes in front of the Holy Sacrament! What would a Turk, not familiar with our faith, think if he entered a church when there were people in it? He would rather believe that he was in a place of games, comedies and laughter and not in a place of religious worship. Muscovite churches [Eastern Orthodox, *cerkwie*], Lutheran ones [*zbory*], Turkish mosques, and Jewish synagogues are not profaned as much as our churches with the Holiest Sacrament inside them."[142] Catholics' behavior was considered worse than that of all the enemies the Church tried to combat. "Jews committed a great sacrilege when they cruelly killed the True Messiah Lord Christ, God and King.... They deserved punishment for killing Christ, and they carry it on till today.... But aren't Catholics who kill Christ every day even more deserving of punishment? [Jews] tortured Christ before he had suffered for them, [Catholics] kill him, after he had already suffered [for their sins]. [Jews] killed him once, [Catholics] kill him with frequency. [Jews] killed him without recognizing that he was God and their Lord, but [Catholics] cruelly murder him after they already recognized and accepted him."[143] The juxtaposition of the contemporary behavior of Catholics with that of Jews at the crucifixion exaggerated Catholic transgressions by implying that they were worse than the behavior of Jews during the crucifixion. Such Catholic behavior, preachers argued, discouraged Jews and dissidents from accepting Catholicism. Indeed, as one preacher stated, "While you call yourself a Christian, you offend God more than infidels, and thereby heretics are confirmed in their errors."[144]

Another preacher who burst out against Catholic moral laxity and sinful behavior at Catholic festivals stressed that Jews and Lutherans, instead of taking Catholic piety as a model inspiring conversion to "the Holy Catholic Faith," were scandalized at seeing Catholics drunk or working or blaspheming on a holy day.[145] On the controversial issue of indulgencies, which had triggered the Reformation, and the indulgence celebrations by Catholics, the noted Franciscan preacher Antoni Zapartowicz argued that drinking on such occasions was "an evil example for the Jews and dissidents, for is it not possible that in witnessing such godless devotions of Catholics they would be disgusted? The indulgence festivities present themselves to them as monstrosities, instead of what they are, true devotions."[146] Not that indulgences were inherently wrong, as the Protestants claimed, but that Catholics celebrated them in a way that made them appear "ungodly" and corrupt. The behavior of Catholics themselves confirmed both Jews and "heretics" in their errors. In a strange twist, Jews and heretics were turned from the corruptors of Catholics into those corrupted by Catholic behavior.

So, too, Catholics were described as a terrible model of piety in their failure to perform acts of charity.[147] An early eighteenth-century preacher, Jakub Filipowicz, wrote: "We read in the Gospels *beati misercordi quoniam ipsi misericordiam consequentur. Misericordiam volo.*[148] But who believes that? Here live corpses walk, wretched people die of cold and hunger, and where is this [Christian] mercy?... Jews and pagans do not have Gospels but has anyone ever seen a Jew dying in muck? Christians have the Gospels but they do not believe in them. They hear them many times, but they do not listen to them."[149]

And in a 1731 sermon, an anonymous preacher lamented that at the beginning of Christianity the Church was perfect and there was not a single Christian poor or a beggar, but "now it is quite different. . . . You don't find crowds of wandering beggars among Turks or Jews, or among dissidents, but they are found among us."[150] Such behavior, which some claimed was worse than what Jews did to Jesus,[151] did not help the cause of the Church.

The churchmen faced a vicious circle. On the one hand, Jews were seen as obstacles and often as corrupters of Christians, both rich and poor. On the other hand, it was the Catholics' own behavior that prevented Jews, and other non-Catholics, from being brought into the fold. The Church was striving for an ideal difficult to achieve. The realities of everyday life made the Catholic clergy feel insecure, leading to increasingly hostile rhetoric and consequently contributing to the division of the society and the eventual exclusion of some from that society in the name of religious purity, verity, and unity.

5

∾

"A Shameful Offence": The Nobles and Their Jews

$\mathscr{A}$T THE END OF THE SEVENTEENTH CENTURY, A NOTED FRANCISCAN preacher, Antoni Węgrzynowicz, in a sermon addressed to an audience of nobles, lamented the nobles' blatant disobedience to Church teachings, their questionable daily behavior, their assaults on the Church during political gatherings, and their relationships with Jews. To appeal to the nobles' own fears, Węgrzynowicz claimed the political crises Poland faced, including the destructive wars with its neighbors, were a consequence of the nobles' reckless conduct. He urged that they return to the right path, one more in line with Church teachings:

You will not hear during the sessions of the Sejm and the Sejmiks [regional diets] anything but screaming against priests, and servants of God.... The sins of the Poles led to the collapse of the integrity of the [territories] of the Polish Crown, so our motherland has shrunk as it lost so many provinces.... O Poles! Bring your sins to an end.... Stop violating the laws, privileges and freedoms of the Church, give to God what belongs to God, to the Church what belongs to the Church and to the King what belongs to [him]. End all injustice in courts, and judge the cases of the poor the same way you would those of the rich, don't be corrupted. Stop giving special and undeserved favors to the Jews, [these favors] are a sign of great contempt for the Christian religion. Stop the drunkenness, adulteries and all kinds of lewdness. Refrain, Ladies and Lords, from luxurious sophisticated clothes![1]

In this, Węgrzynowicz represented his contemporaries in desiring more social and political influence over, and more obedience from, the Polish political elites, who, as the Church recognized, were essential in enforcing the Church's doctrines and laws.

By the seventeenth century, the Polish king was weak, if relatively cooperative with the Church, whereas the nobles followed their own self-interest, often in open defiance of Church teachings, especially in their own dealings with Jews. Their defiance of the Church's teachings on relations between Jews and Christians, and on the position of Jews in Christian society, was a reminder of how tenuous the Church's influence really was and where the limits of Church power lay. Jews had become a token of the power conflict between the Church and the nobles. An eighteenth-century priest, Jakub Radliński, wrote in his book published in 1733: "Jews are allowed more in our Kingdom than monarchs and senators, because when they organize their weddings during Advent or Lent, or other days during which celebrations are prohibited by the Church, they do not have to answer to the Authority of the Church, and they. . . . do whatever they feel like, with music, and play, and other things they fancy, trusting that they will receive protection from the secular authorities, and they succeed more in this regard than the priests [succeed] in their zealous faith."[2] The priest further complained that when the local priest intervened and prohibited the Christian servants from participating, Jews "run directly to the manor [to the lord]" to complain. The lord then intervened on behalf of Jews against "the law and conscience."[3]

The Polish clergy's impatience with both the nobles and the Jews was expressed in standard sounding anti-Jewish rhetoric, in polemical works and sermons, and in legislation, all an inseparable part of the Church's ongoing contest with the powerful Polish lords. But churchmen used anti-Jewish language even when Jews themselves were not the direct cause of their frustrations, and even when the Church itself engaged in business relations with them,[4] drawing profit from its own business ties with Jews. What troubled the Church was not business contacts between Jews and Christians per se, but the fact that it was unable to shape and control such relationships.[5] In fact, the Church itself often supported the Jews and judged fairly when Jews turned to the Church for help or when they were brought to Church courts in business matters,[6] because this and the Church's business relations with Jews made Jews dependent on the Church and allowed the Church to remain in control. But the relationships that fell outside of the Church's sphere of influence troubled the Polish clergymen. A mid-eighteenth-century Jesuit preacher, Kasper Balsam, provided a catalogue of Christian relationships with Jews that were considered mortal, or at least grave, sins, from nursing Jewish infants to friendships with Jews:

[He], who loves the enemy of the Cross, is himself an enemy of the cross; that is why all of those Catholics who serve the Jews, and even more, those who could prevent this but do not prevent it, mortally sin; Christian wet nurses who nurse Jewish children in their [Jewish] homes [mortally sin]. Those gravely sin who place Jews in offices where they are in high esteem or where they have authority over Catholics. Those gravely sin who attend their [Jewish] dinners, weddings, Sabbaths or religious services, who socialize with them, put extraordinary trust in them or maintain friendships with them. Those gravely sin who do not stand up against Jewish abuses of and wrongdoings against Christians, or who help Jews to the detriment of Christians.[7]

Balsam declared that such persons "deserved anathema," which, according to Church law, "can only be issued in case of mortal sin." He further proclaimed that "such persons who through familiarity with the enemies of Christ profane His blood, are similar to Judas," and they "act against God's decree: God decided that this ungrateful nation [Jews] be in disdain of the whole world; they [Christians who have contact with Jews], on the other hand, give them [Jews] esteem through their affairs and deeds, and thus [they cause] their [Jews'] impudence towards Christians."[8]

Church frustration extended to powerful Christians who condoned or facilitated what the Church regarded as sins, when the nobles, in violation of Church laws, placed Jews in positions of authority over Christians. The clerics claimed that such symbiotic relation between Jews and the nobles, and the protection lords afforded Jews who lived in their domains, led to an abuse of justice; hence, "Jewish crimes" against Christians were not being prosecuted. Questions of competency of Church and secular jurisdiction were at issue. What the Church regarded as a transgression or even as a "crime" deserving prosecution, the nobles may have considered harmless, or trivial, or not worth opening procedures for economic or political reasons.[9]

In religious arguments and rhetoric, Balsam and other Church authors addressed such issues of authority and obedience. Jews were enemies of "the Cross" or "enemies of Christ"; thus, lay Catholics who engaged in business or social relations with Jews were profaning Jesus' blood. By linking Church laws with "God's own decrees," Balsam reinforced the notion that the Church was the transmitter of divine will.

"IMPOVERISHED AND DESTROYED": CHURCH REVENUES AND THE JEWS

In 1717, the archbishop of Lwów, Jan Skarbek, opened his "Edictum contra Judaeos" with these words: "We hear with great grief in our heart and we see with our own eyes that the unfaithful Jewish nation increases daily in our archdiocese, uprooting Christians and bringing them to ruin."[10] Jews became rich and Christians impoverished as a result of the nobles' protection of Jews: "Everywhere these enemies of Christ get rich because of the lords' protection and consideration; and His faithful become impoverished and destroyed with mockery and abuses by Jewry itself. *Facti sunt hostes eius in capite, inimici completati sunt.*[11] Even Christ Himself becomes impoverished because of them, for His churches...now have become empty because Christians retreat and Jews are not their ornament.... The priests, monasteries and convents deteriorate causing the impoverishment of Christians, when their provisions, rents and alms do not arrive."[12]

Like Balsam, the archbishop characteristically interwove politics and theology. Jews, the predictable "enemies of Christ," were juxtaposed to "His faithful," with secular lords somewhere in between, subverting the Church's desired social order. "Therefore," Skarbek wrote, "with the help of the Love of Jesus Christ Our Savior, we demand of all faithful [to remember] His blood and suffering and not to allow His enemies, who have had an innate hatred of Him since His suffering and His death on the Cross, to increase, and [we demand of the faithful] not to give them [Jews] any protection.... It is indeed a great offence to God to take land, plots and houses away from poor Christians and to give them to Jews."[13]

The bishops' frustration with the lords' defiance of Church teachings pervades their reports to Rome. In his report of 1666, Bishop Stanisław Sarnowski of Przemyśl asserted that Jews had support from the "secular lords and also magnates," who derived benefit from them, a situation he could do nothing to prevent. Sarnowski maintained that Jews could not prosper without support of Christians, but he could do little to discourage such support. He exaggerated that as a result, the towns had few Christian inhabitants and were filled with Jews.[14] Almost a century later, Bishop Wackan Sierakowski, also of Przemyśl, voiced similar complaints about Jews and the nobles.[15] And in 1751, Bishop Załuski of Cracow wrote in his report to Rome, "I frankly confess that neither I nor other bishops in Poland can find any remedy to this evil." The laws of the land are established by the nobles and "all our efforts are destroyed."[16] After Załuski pleaded for a papal constitution and support from Rome, Pope Benedict XIV issued a bull *A Quo Primum*,[17] urging the Polish bishops to try to enforce synodal laws among the clergy and also among the laity: "The essence of the difficulty, however, is that either the sanctions of the synods are forgotten or they are not put into effect. To you then, Venerable Brothers, passes the task of renewing those sanctions. The nature of your office requires that you carefully encourage their implementation. In this matter begin with the clergy, as is fair and reasonable. These will have to show others the right way to act, and light the way for the rest by their example. For in God's mercy, we hope that the good example of the clergy will lead the straying laity back to the straight path."[18]

Despite the Church's complaints about impoverishment, the Church was in fact one of the largest land owners in Poland.[19] Real-estate ownership influenced patterns of residence of the local population, which in turn affected levels of the Church's influence and power that came from the revenue and recognition of its authority by the population. Catholics were more likely to accept the Church's authority than were Jews or Protestants, but Jews did accept it reluctantly in certain matters. Still, from the clergy's various discussions of real-estate ownership and dwelling patterns of Catholics, Jews, and other non-Catholic Christians, one senses the Church's lack of full control.[20]

In his polemical work, *Prawda chrześcijańska*, Jakub Radliński, like Bishop Sarnowski of Przemyśl, complained about Jewish real estate and the Jews' apparent increasing prominence in towns at the expense of local Christians: "By acquiring Christian homes, Jews slowly and imperceptibly spread and in the end [*tandem*] they buy out all public houses and the ones convenient for trade, and they settle in town's market squares and push the Christians back [*zatyłki*]."[21] Similar complaints were voiced by townspeople against Armenians in towns in eastern territories of Poland-Lithuania.[22]

The 1751 report from the Cracow diocese to Rome informed the pope darkly that it was increasingly difficult to conduct Catholic processions through town on

Corpus Christi or to take the Eucharist to a sick person because of the presence of this "blaspheming people" everywhere. It was not that Jews physically prevented such processions but that their presence was perceived by Christians as offensive and perhaps even as polluting. Beyond that, Jews were inviting Catholics to their taverns to play music and dance, and Catholics were responding.[23]

In 1737, the then bishop of Cracow, Jan Alexander Lipski, elaborated on the causes of the Church's objections to a growing number of Jewish residences by focusing on the link between Jews and the Church's own economic well-being. "Because Jews settle in many places in cities and towns," he wrote, "from which *the Church could have a certain benefit*, and in order to *prevent a significant decrease of Church revenues* [my emphasis], we fully confirm old synodal rulings and constitutions."[24] The synodal constitutions sought to regulate and limit the Jewish population and its perceived impact on Christian society, including the financial losses for the Church. It was clearly Bishop Lipski's hope that if the Jews moved or were removed, Catholics would come to live there, and therefore that the Church would benefit from the revenue, now lost, from tithes and, more important, from fees for baptisms, weddings, and funerals.[25] Allowing Jews to expand their communities, on the other hand, would rupture the Church's authority by loss of revenues and by defiance of Church decrees.

The bishops' concern with such loss of revenues was somewhat disingenuous, because the Church itself found a way to regain from Jews what it may have lost. As Judith Kalik's work and other sources suggest, the Church engaged in business relations with Jews and extorted certain fees for "toleration" of Jews in the Christian territories.[26] Henryk Samsonowicz points to a 1721 case from Ostrów Mazowiecki, a small town in today's central Poland, in which Jews were required to pay three Polish zloty to the local parish Church and provide meat (beef), spices (cumin, cloves, nutmeg, and cinnamon), and "good vodka" to the local parish priest on the occasion of both Christian and Jewish holidays in exchange for protection from disturbances by local Christians, including parish students.[27]

Similar demands for compensation for lost revenue were applied to Protestants. Sometimes the specific sum was defined as a part of formal legal privileges granted by the municipal authorities or the nobles who were a town's owners.[28] Sometimes it was described as "a gift" that Protestants were to pay for protection.[29] In the eastern parts of the Polish-Lithuanian Commonwealth, where a large population of Eastern Orthodox believers lived, the issue of tithing became a burning concern. The Catholic Church demanded revenues from the Eastern Orthodox population, and sometimes employed the royal authority to enforce its demands. The Eastern Orthodox protested against this move as an unjust assertion of Church authority over them, an authority they refused to recognize.[30] Archives provide many cases of such refusals, sometimes also of confiscations of tithes by town owners, especially during the Reformation when lords who had become Protestant refused to pay tithes to local Catholic churches.[31] As for Jews, Judith Kalik has described a case of a Jewish leaseholder of a grain mill who refused to pay tithes from grain and flour he processed in his mill, despite claims from the local priest that such tithes belonged to him.[32]

And yet many other Catholic clergy welcomed Jews living on Church lands, indicating that economic interests outweighed the ideal of religious homogeneity and purity. This circumstance outraged Pope Benedict XIV.[33] Many synods ruled against leasing Church properties to Jews, and internal Church correspondence reflects irritation at ongoing economic ties between some Church institutions and Jews. In 1668, the synod of Wilno issued a ruling against the leasing of Church property to Jews, its language suggesting that such a prohibition had been issued before but had been ignored.[34] Some decades later, in 1711, the synod of Cracow issued a similar protest against business relations between Jews and the clergy.[35]

A puzzling complaint appeared in the legislation of the 1684 synod of Łuck and Brest: "It is rare that Jews become Christians because of contacts with priests [*ex conversatione sacerdotum*] but we are rightly afraid lest the priests, God forbid, judaize."[36] Whether these Church leaders actually meant that priests had apostatized because of their contacts with Jews, or whether they used the term "judaize" more figuratively, as Bernard of Clairvaux did, to mean that those who engage in usury "judaize," is unclear here.[37] But it does show the Church concern with possible religious "contamination" of Catholics from business contacts with Jews.

In 1740 Bishop Jan Lipski wrote to the cathedral chapter in Cracow that "So many times I have suggested to this venerable chapter to get rid of the Jews from the chapter's *praestimonia* [benefices]. However, my advice seems to have been in vain, as ... these infidel Jews remain with their *arenda* [lease] not without devastation of ecclesiastical property and disgust from the laity. The Church laws and Royal laws prohibit leasing properties and breweries to the Jews, for because of their [the Jews'] treachery and cunning the faithful become poor and devastated [*wniwecz obracaja sie*]."[38] Lipski urged that Jews be removed from ecclesiastical properties. His demands must have gone unheeded because a year later he wrote again: "Not without sorrow did I receive the news that my demands made so many times to remove Jews from some ecclesiastical properties[39] have been in vain and that the decrees you passed generally have not been effective, as these Jews are stubbornly tolerated in ecclesiastical properties by some chapter priests [*capitulares*]."[40]

Bishop Lipski's "sorrow" stemmed from realization of the inefficacy of his rulings. The order was disrupted, for he had displayed weaknesses as the head of the archdiocese, a weakness highlighted by the Jewish lease of ecclesiastical properties. Through a lease contract, the landowners had ceded their rights to the land and revenue and to authority over it in exchange for a regular fee. Because a lease gave autonomy to the leaseholder, the Church in the case of ecclesiastical property had relinquished some of its power and may have put Jews in a position of authority over Christians living there. Perhaps this was what prompted the statement that such arrangements aroused "disgust from laity," who saw the Church in this practice violating its own laws.

Many documents in the *Acta Episcopalia*, which record proceedings of episcopal courts in the Archdiocesan Archive in Cracow, deal with cases of conflict resulting from Jews' leasing of ecclesiastical properties in Poland.[41] A decree of December 3, 1749, punished a parish priest in the small town of Gawłuszowice, near Mielec in Małopolska, for failure to expel a Jewish leaseholder of a Church-owned brewery in the village of Niekurza, despite previous orders to do so.[42] Another case tells of a Jew from Nowy Korczyn, a town near Cracow, who held the lease of a brewery in the nearby village of Chańcza, a brewery belonging to the Cistercian monastery. The bishop's decree admonished the Jew, Abram Józefowicz, under penalty of arrest not to take future leases of ecclesiastical properties or anything else prohibited by canon law.[43] It ordered him to give up his lease of the brewery in Chańcza.[44] Whether Abram obeyed or not is unknown. Notably, although this case involved a Cistercian monastery, the Jew – not the monastery – had given the lease that was sanctioned and subjected to canon law. This case not only highlights Church efforts to extend its authority over non-Catholics but also points to the limits to the episcopal authority since the bishop had narrow formal powers over religious orders, often directly under Papal control, a difficulty of executing episcopal authority that even Pope Benedict XIV acknowledged in his 1751 encyclical.[45] Sanctioning the Jew may have been his only recourse.

The pattern of involvement of the clergy and of Church institutions in business affairs with Jews is further corroborated by Polish court records and Jewish sources.[46] After a 1701 plague in the town of Szawel, Prince Jakub Ludwik issued a privilege to the Jews of the town: "When almost no townspeople were left, and seeking to prevent further collapse of the town, so that the empty houses would not go to ruin," Jews were invited to settle. Szawel resembled "a village more than a town" and few Christian merchants ever settled there, by which Ludwik must have meant "Catholic" because he had mentioned also Greeks and Armenians among those who came to live in the town. When Jews were threatened by a bad administrator and sought to leave the town, the decree explained, the townspeople themselves, "having seen the [Jews'] kindness toward the city," pleaded that they stay. The prince said that Jews now lived in Szawel "with the permission and protection" of the local parish priests, even in the Church's *jurydyka*, with the approbation of the bishop.[47]

A memoir by an eighteenth-century Jewish merchant, Ber of Bolechow, gave many examples of business ties to rich Polish lords and Catholic clergy. On one occasion, Ber mentioned in passing his friendly contacts with a certain priest: "We then went to the house of the inspector, Kegler, who knew that my brother was friendly with the priest, and we said: 'We want to buy some wines from the Crown cellars for the priest Wieniawski, who is a friend of yours.' Kegler then made an arrangement with the other officials, according to which we were to choose our wines – 200 casks – and to seal them with our seal. In two months we were to send 100 ducats with an agreement signed by us and by the priest for 200 casks of wine for the sum of 1000 ducats."[48]

Ber stored his wine with the Carmelite friars.[49] "The other wines, which we had bought," he explained, "were afterwards stored in cellars of the aforesaid brick house of the Carmelite friars, opposite the gate of Halicz, where it was proposed that they should be brought for sale as in previous years. The friars let us also have an apartment for ourselves, so that we could live in the same building, at the second entrance to the right of the general entrance."[50] Ber and his partner not only had business ties with the clergy but they lived on the premises of the Carmelite monastery. Boundaries of space had, therefore, been transgressed.

Other Jewish sources show business ties between the Jews and the clergy. The *takkanot va'ad arb'a arazot*, or minutes of the Council of Four Lands, listed communal expenses and included payments of debts owed by Jews to the Jesuits and Dominicans, debts Pope Benedict XIV condemned in his encyclical *A Quo Primum*.[51]

Just as the clearly exaggerated statements of Polish bishops that Jews outnumbered Christians in Polish towns are not supported by the actual demography, so the clergy's rhetoric about the loss of revenue seems less related to actual financial distress than to the Church's sense of lost influence and power, and also to a broader sense of insecurity.[52] That so many Catholics, including some clergy, ignored Church laws and teachings outlined the actual bounds of the Church's social and religious control.

The nobles had political power and could use it against the Church, and their own interests were often at odds with the Church's aggressive ideology and political posture. The nobles' adherence to their own interests further upset the ideal order the Church was striving to achieve by preventing the Church from acting where it wished. In 1658, the cathedral chapter in Cracow evidently tried to put these boundaries of power to the test, intervening in the affairs of Jews in the dominion of a prominent nobleman, Stanisław Potocki. Potocki protested the cathedral chapter's intervention, arguing that the Jews were not under ecclesiastical jurisdiction.[53] This case underlines the Church's intent to extend its influence into areas where it technically had no jurisdiction, in this case, on the nobleman's land.

The list of transgressions that the Church claimed deserved excommunication further highlights the sharpness of its conflict with the secular lords. Among those wrongdoings were infringements on the freedoms of the Catholic Church, lawsuits brought by laity against Church officials in secular courts, usurpation of Church property and refusal to pay tithes, and protection and defense of "heretics, schismatics," and all who disobeyed "the Most High Apostolic See."[54] Indeed, a refusal to pay tithes and rents "belonging" to the Church was considered by some as sacrilegious.[55] All these measures were intended to set limits to secular powers and regain moral authority for the Church.

In 1694, the synod of Chelm resorted to spiritual sanctions against lords who entrusted their estates to Jews. It threatened to deny absolution to such lords unless they compensated the Christian population for these *injuria*.[56] Because the consequences for not receiving absolution could lead to social stigmatization – such persons would not be allowed to take communion and to participate in those rites of which a communion is a part, such as serving as a godparent or a witness in a wedding – establishing religious sanctions was a strategy of reasserting authority over the nobles. It was a significant step considering that, technically, the nobility had been exempt from Church legal jurisdiction from the mid-sixteenth century.[57]

Jews, caught in the middle of this conflict between lay and religious authority, gradually became a symbol of the nobles' defiance of Church proscriptions. That defiance further threatened the Church's authority and influence over lower-class Christians because it was the nobles who had placed Jews in a position of authority over poorer Christians, turning both the Church's decrees and its ideals upside down.

"THE JEWS AS THEIR LORD SQUIRE": A WAVE OF PROHIBITIONS TO RESTORE THE CHURCH IDEAL OF SOCIAL HIERARCHY

In his pastoral letter of 1737, Bishop Josaphat Michał Karp of Samogitia (Żmudź) lamented that "not a few" Christians shamelessly appointed Jews to collect taxes, permitted them to build synagogues, leased taverns and even their hereditary estates to Jews, or hired Jews to administer estates, and "all this against Royal statutes." Bishop Karp was dismayed that such persons had no qualms about subjecting "free sons" (i.e., Christians) to "the sons of Hagar the maid,"[58] a phrase sometimes applied to Jews by churchmen and taken from Paul's Epistle to the Galatians (4:21–26), later elaborated by Augustine in a Christological exegesis on Genesis (25:23ff), and subsequently inserted in numerous papal rulings.[59] Bishop Karp's use of this ancient phrase implicitly held powerful Catholics responsible for a social order the clergy saw as contrary to the Church's long-standing doctrines about Jews.

In that same year, an *Epistola Pastoralis* of Bishop Jan Lipski of Cracow warned "all lords and squires, and whosoever holds estates in our diocese" against leasing any villages, domains, or serfs to the Jews and against granting Jews "power and authority" at all. Lipski supported his interdiction with reference to a ruling forbidding Jews to hold public office or any other post of authority over Christians.[60]

Polish bishops complained to Rome about Jewish authority over Christians. Bishop Sierakowski of Przemyśl wrote in his report of 1743 that Jews caused him "great pain of his soul [*non minore afflictione spiritus*]": "not only do they hold breweries and taverns everywhere on annual or three-year contracts from lords of whatever status, but they also cultivate fields and they obtain whole villages with full jurisdiction in them."[61] Jewish control of arable land meant for the Church potential problems with extraction of tithes, an issue of concern since the Middle Ages.[62] Jewish jurisdiction over villages meant authority over their Christian inhabitants and therefore a serious theological and practical problem for the Church.

There had long been Jews in positions of power – for example, the tax collector Izak Brodawka, or the prominent royal factor Michel Ezofowicz in the first half of the sixteenth century. But not until the late seventeenth and especially in the eighteenth centuries was frequent and blunt opposition to such power voiced by Polish Church leaders,[63] an escalation that reflected the Church's sense of threat from all sides and its frustration with its incapacity to discipline the laity in full conformity to Church teachings. This perception intensified in the late 1600s and 1700s.

In 1751, frustrated Polish bishops obtained an encyclical, *A Quo Primum*, from Pope Benedict XIV on the Jews in Poland. Circulating in two versions, one in the original Latin and the other in Polish, it praised "faithful Poles" for withstanding pressures from various non-Catholic sects, including the Lutherans.[64] But the Pope did express concern with the position of Jews, who "posed another threat to Christians." The Latin text said that because a number of Jews in Poland held authority over Christians, "Those unhappy people depend on the authority of a Jewish man, as if subdued by the will and power of a lord."[65] The Polish text sent an even blunter message; in the Polish text the above passage read: "these unhappy Christians regard the Jew as their lord and squire, on whose beck and call, will and orders they appear to be dependent," and it sharply emphasized the power of Jews over Christians:[66]

And although the Jews use Christian executioners to apply punishments of flogging and beating other Christians, nonetheless this Christian executioner is forced to do this cruelty, which the Jew orders, and to obey the orders of his lord Jew [*Żyda Pana swego*], lest he will lose his job and his daily bread. And aside from these public posts, which as we have mentioned are held by Jews, they also lease inns, villages, manors with surrounding lands and Christian serfs, and because of this a lot of lawlessness takes place. For what can be worse than Jews ruling the manors in place of the lords-of-the-manor, managing and governing according to their will, and subduing Christians by forcing them to obey their orders?[67]

The pope asserted that "all those activities that are now allowed in Poland are forbidden" by the centuries of papal rulings. Benedict XIV argued that, regrettably, the situation in Poland was not a result of the lack of Church rulings, but was because "the sanctions of the synods are forgotten or they are not put into effect."[68]

Generally, Polish bishops opposed arrangements that would subordinate Christians to Jews who were their employers, as did Pope Benedict XIV, who wrote in *A Quo Primum* that Jews "ceaselessly exhibit and flaunt authority over the Christians they are living with. It is now even commonplace for Christians and Jews to intermingle anywhere. But what is even less comprehensible is that Jews fearlessly keep Christians of both sexes in their houses as their domestics, bound to their service."[69]

Nevertheless, even some of the most militant bishops in pursuit of religious hege-mony (like the zealous Bishop Andrzej Stanisław Załuski) understood, or at least took into consideration, the socioeconomic conditions of life in Poland-Lithuania that caused the continuation of practices that sometimes conflicted with canon law. Although canon law prohibited Jews from hiring Christian servants,[70] Polish bishops, as noted, tended to reserve opposition only to long-term service in Jewish homes or businesses, allowing temporary employment.[71] Bishop Załuski's "Edic-tum contra Judaeos," in its typically controlling manner, ruled that no Christian who served Jews on a one-year contract could be absolved by a regular priest. Still, he seems to have accepted a shorter-term employment.[72] When Bishop Franciszek Antoni Kobielski lamented that some Christians "were growing old while serving Jews," he may have implied that these Catholics had been serving Jews on a per-manent basis. Nonetheless, Bishop Kobielski permitted Christians without other means of making a living to take up jobs with Jewish employers on a short-term contract – usually for a period of less than one year.[73] Other bishops agreed. In his 1737 pastoral letter, Bishop Josaphat Karp of Samogitia refused to permit Christians to accept jobs from Jews on a yearly contract but apparently condoned short-term jobs.[74]

Some jobs Christians took on under Jewish employers were seen as more humil-iating and problematic than others. The episcopal prohibitions against Christians working for Jews singled out some such jobs. Bishop Szembek pronounced: "We prohibit the commoners and all faithful who are living members in Christ, to hire themselves out to Jews as coach-drivers, as farmhands, guards, helpers, or bath-house assistants [winniki] to Jews; whereas we prohibit the women from hiring themselves as maids, laundresses, wet nurses, nannies of Jewish children, innkeep-ers or from taking up any work with Jews on a yearly contract [myto]."[75] Bishop Załuski prohibited Christians from serving Jews on Jewish holidays, and in par-ticular from trimming candles on Yom Kippur or serving in synagogues.[76] Jews hired Christians to restore damaged synagogues, in simultaneous violation of two Church prohibitions: against hiring Christian workers and against restoring dam-aged synagogues.[77]

One curious job assumed by some Christians infuriated a number of bishops. Jan Alexander Lipski, Franciszek Antoni Kobielski, Józef Eustachy Szembek, Josaphat Michał Karp, and Stefan Bogusław Rupniewski forbade Christians to accept the role of Haman at Purim, the wicked biblical character in the Book of Esther who planned to destroy the Jews but failed and was punished by hanging.[78] As Bishop Kobielski described the ritual, "and on the day of Haman, having dressed the Christian as Haman, they drag him through streets, tousle him and beat him."[79] This ritual symbolized not only the worrisome, for the clergy, Jewish authority over Christians but also the religious triumph of Jews over non-Jews, a total reversal of the order the Catholic leaders sought.[80]

"THE MONEY, THE PEPPER, THE SAFFRON, AND THE CHRISTIAN BLOOD"

Polish Church writers turned to religious arguments and medieval anti-Jewish myths in their assaults on the powerful Polish nobles. In 1602, Szymon Hubicki, in a short pamphlet on "Jewish cruelties against the Most Holy Sacrament and Christian children," denounced Christian lords who leased mills, inns, and rights to collect various taxes and tolls, and "even towns and villages owned by the nobles [miasteczka i wsi ślacheckie]" to the Jews.[81] Later writers would draw from this pamphlet, elaborating on its themes. Przecław Mojecki followed soon with an almost identical work under the same title, "Jewish Cruelties." In the eighteenth century, Stefan Żuchowski accused Jews – in a manner similar to Mojecki's – of blood libel and implied that secular lords were complicit in this "Jewish crime":

That's why they sprinkle the money, the pepper, and the saffron which they give to Christians with [Christian] blood, partly to make them partners in this murder and partly to win their [other Christians'] favor. And, while it is not fitting for good Christians to believe such superstitions, we can clearly see that those who once chummed up to the Jews and are avid for their money or a pound or two of spices, become so friendly that they allow Jews to lead them by the nose; those who earlier could not look at the stinking [smrodliwy] Jew without disgust, afterwards they entrust all their fortune and almost their soul and heart.... And even though Jews are God's and our main enemies, they appear to be the most faithful, most kind-hearted and the most needed to bring profit from breweries, to administer farms [folwarki], to [receive] dispensations on the roads and to make rooms comfortable.[82] We do not want to listen to the Holy Doctors warning us that we should avoid this nation as a snake in a pocket [węża w zanadrzu] and a fire in the bosom.[83]

Exploiting the myth of the Jewish taste for Christian blood, Żuchowski condemned Polish noblemen who entered into business dealings with Jews. Relationships developed, the text implied, because the lords desired income from the estates, and Jews, as their leaseholders, could provide that income. The lords also wanted imported goods – spices, at the time – that Jewish merchants could supply. This symbiosis, which benefited both nobles and Jews, was a sore point for Polish Catholic clergy. Żuchowski suggested, somewhat indirectly, that the noblemen were accomplices in "Jewish crimes," referring to Jews who "sprinkled" Christian blood on the luxury goods they delivered to the nobles. It was a clever manipulation: what appears to be anti-Jewish rhetoric was at the same time an attack against upper-class Christians who were on good terms with Jews and happy to accept their services.

All the profits the lords received from business dealings with Jews were "tainted" by the sweat and blood of Christians who were under Jewish authority.

Jews are depicted in texts as tempters for offering profits and goods that tied Jews to the nobles, or rather, as the clergymen saw it, that tied the nobles to the Jews. These writers claimed that the Church had been losing influence over the lay lords, for the lords preferred "to chum with Jews," despite their being "God's and our main enemies."[84] Jews were crafty enemies of Christians who, when driven by self-interest, might appear most friendly. Through such deception, Żuchowski argued, Jews gained the trust and support of the nobles – and, as such, Jews represented a temptation that thwarted the Church's attempts to gain influence and control. "Christians do the Jews unmerited favors," Żuchowski wrote, "and especially the lords who lease their properties, mills and inns to the Jews. This used to lead to great and lewd sins of Christian women, as [the Jews] use them to steal the Eucharist [sakramentów], to give Christian children away for slaughter and they [also] use them for obscenities. And rarely are they justly punished, since Christians let themselves be tempted by presents [Chrześcianie im dopuszczaią łapać upominkami], which causes Jews to laugh and turn away from the Holy Faith for [they see] that Christians respect their Faith and Christian blood so little, that their justice is venal and corruptible."[85]

To Żuchowski, this chaos and these "sins" were a result of the nobles' disobedience of Church teachings, caused by their desire for profit and luxury goods. "For this desecration of our religion," Żuchowski wrote, "we will soon not be able to avoid God's hard vengeance and all this because of the enemies of our religion about which we care so little. I do not know whom to believe, whether the pious preachers or the Jewish Christians [żydochrześcianie], who have such flimsy consciences that for Judas' money they solve, defend and deny the worst Jewish crimes."[86] God would punish those who defied the Church and reward those who obeyed its teachings, promoted Catholicism, and did not succumb to the "temptations" offered by Jews. Some claimed that the punishment for the nobles' favorable treatment of the Jews "and their crimes," in disobedience to the Church, was the wars and political crises that plagued Poland from the middle of the seventeenth century.[87]

Żuchowski, drawing again from Mojecki, included in his book a chapter entitled "That the Lord God blesses those who hate Jews and punishes their protectors, just as he has also punished Poland."[88] He cited several examples of punishments that had afflicted Poland and the supporters of Jews, whom he compared to "Satans, that is, enemies of God."[89] As one of these "divine punishments" he listed the 1648 uprising in the eastern territories of the country, headed by Bohdan Chmielnicki, that precipitated a period of incessant conflicts and wars that lasted well into the eighteenth century, destroying the economy and political well-being of the country. Jewish communities too suffered from it.[90] Żuchowski attributed this disorder to God's revenge for murders of Christians in the towns of Chwastów and Pruszczyce by Jews never prosecuted for these "crimes."[91] It was also, he added, ultimately a punishment for the avarice of the Polish lords and for their relationship with Jews. "In the year 1648," Żuchowski wrote, "using the Cossacks, Lord God avenged innocent blood spilt but not prosecuted in Chwastów and Pruszczyce. What was the reason for Cossack war with the cruel Chmielnicki if not that Rus' could not bear its slavery under Jews? It was caused by the lords' avarice who leased even baptisms, weddings, and churches to the Jews."[92]

This rather unusual explanation of the causes of the uprising is in line with Żuchowski's overall strategy to present Jews and other non-Catholics as dangerous to the unity and security of Catholicism.[93] In the same chapter, Żuchowski provided examples of rewards for those who did not befriend Jews, singling out "the Denhoffs, the Potockis, the Radziwiłłs and the Sapiehas," some of whom had only relatively recently gained affluence and influence. Yet, these generally large and influential aristocratic families' dealings with Jews were less clear-cut than Żuchowski wanted to see them.[94] Still, he considered their fortune and "splendor" part of God's rewards "because they gravely punish Jews for their excesses."[95] He praised by name members of those families who deserved "God's rewards" but he did not provide names of specific "supporters" of the Jews who conversely were, or ought to be, punished for their actions. Perhaps many of those supporters were of high status, "too high for [him] to repudiate" freely.[96]

Żuchowski was not alone. His contemporary, Jakub Radliński, in his *Prawda Chrześciańska* [Christian Truth], also identified "praiseworthy" persons, while conferring anonymity on those he criticized. "May God bless him," Radliński wrote of Wojewoda Potocki, "and his home *superabundanter* now on earth, and after *post sera fata*, may He make him immortal."[97] And he elaborated on Potocki's deeds:

And it has to be said that when in 1732 a new house of the Starosta [*dom starościński*] was built near the Church [in Leżajsk], and the Jews wanted greatly to lease it and open an inn there [*arendować i w nim szynkować*], the Woiewoda [Potocki] did not allow that and ordered that a Christian settle in this house. I wish that future Starostas would imitate this Senator who is so zealous in the Holy faith. Give, O God, inspiration of the Holy Spirit to the town's people so that they will not sell or rent their houses secretly to the Jews.[98]

Recognizing the importance of patterns of real-estate ownership, Radliński had characteristically woven religious rhetoric into a call of despair to prevent the transfer of houses to Jews.

In an edict, Bishop Szembek of Chekm employed the rhetoric of divine rewards and punishments, expressing both dismay and desperation at specific relations between lords and Jews:

And we expect of all those who at any point have given protection to the Jews, with great harm to their conscience and a shameful offence [z *niegodziwą ochydą* (sic)] to the Christian name, to remember God and their own consciences and not to extend any further protection to the Jews and not to continue their actions prohibited by Spiritual and Canon Laws,[99] the Royal Statutes and Constitutions for the sake of their fleeting and illusory profits. And we prohibit leasing taxes, tolls, inns, estates, and villages to the Jews; and we oblige them for the sake of God's love and the salvation of the Christian name and soul not to give them, under any circumstances, authority and jurisdiction over the faithful serfs [*nad poddaństwem prawowiernym*]. And we assure them that should they fulfill this obligation they will receive God's blessing and avoid just divine punishments.[100]

The strictest state laws against Jews had been enacted by the nobles in the Sejm in the sixteenth century, when Jews were more aligned with the monarch; when Jews became more tied to the nobles, state laws were moderated. By appealing for enforcement of state laws, although only the strict laws of earlier days, Bishop Szembek sought to engage the nobility who had taken part in the enactment of some of them. Here, as elsewhere, the argument was at its core about discipline and obedience to the Church, with a tangible tension between the language of helplessness and the language of power. On the one hand, the sense of frustration with the lords whose economic benefits derived from their relationships with Jews forced the clergy to appeal to "higher values" to bring the lords under the Church's control. On the other hand, the Church's language, with expressions such as "we prohibit" or "we oblige," reflects Church efforts to assert authority over the lords. A number of bishops – Jan Skarbek of Lwów, Andrzej Stanisław Kostka Załuski, Jan Aleksander Lipski, and Franciszek Antoni Kobielski among them – seconded Szembek's stricture.[101] Bishop Skarbek, for example, lamented that Christians supported Jews for short-term benefits and "small returns," thereby forfeiting God's grace and eternal happiness.[102]

Those who disobeyed the Church for "small returns" were compared to Jews and their actions to "Jewish cruelties and crimes." An eighteenth-century Franciscan preacher, Fortunat Łosiewski, considered leasing or selling property to Jews an act of sacrilege similar to the desecration of the Host itself:

I pass by so many perpetrators of sacrilege [*świętokradca*] who have sold the Most Holy Hosts for a penny or a piece of bread! Just recall the story – Oh! How sacrilegious – from Poznań in 1399, when a godless Catholic woman sold three Hosts stolen from the Church of the Dominican fathers to the Jews rather cheaply. Not to mention that once Jesus revealed Himself to the resting St. Woyciech and complained that he was again being sold (as he was sold by Judas) to the Jews in Prague, *and also now* some Catholics lease, others sell farms, breweries, market stalls, shops, cellars, sometimes estates, offices [*starostwa*], houses, manors, and stone townhouses [*kamienice*] to [Jews].[103]

Żuchowski said of the sale of houses and land to Jews by townspeople: "[S]ome of the townspeople got the idea into their heads that they cannot make a fortune unless they sell or rent their homes to the Jews. But they are mistaken because Jewish money disappears in Christian hands like smoke in the air.... God does not bless those who sell their houses blessed with the presence of the Eucharist and other sacraments to be profaned by the Jews."[104] Żuchowski had extended the sacredness of Christian space from churches into homes, sanctifying them in an effort to exclude Jews from Polish towns altogether. Jews were to have no place in Christian space, a big shift from earlier Church attitudes toward Jews, which reluctantly tolerated the Jews' presence.

Mikołaj Popławski, the archbishop of Lwów, who lived and worked at the end of the seventeenth and the beginning of the eighteenth centuries, included in his published collection of stories and exempla for preaching and Catholic education a medieval story about a Jew desecrating a picture of Jesus.[105] In that story, a Jew bought a house from a Christian, who had left behind a picture of Jesus by mistake. Predictably for such a tale, the Jewish owner and other local Jews "did the greatest harm they could to the picture, they blasphemed, reviled it, and through the picture of Lord Jesus, they held us in contempt, by whipping and tearing it."[106] Such tales, when told in the context of earlier iconoclastic conflicts within Christianity, usually ended with a miracle, but here no miracle occurred and Popławski ended with a strong statement that Jews deserve no "favors from Christians." This tale appears at first as yet another medieval Christian story of Jewish blasphemies against Jesus, but because of the modification, it may have been intended to discourage the rental or sale of real estate to Jews. Here as elsewhere, medieval anti-Jewish tales were employed to address contemporary issues.[107]

But beyond that, religious symbols describing the transfer of real estate from Christian to Jewish hands were convenient rhetorical tools to divide people and spaces into sacred and profane or even evil. The sacred body of Christianity was desecrated by the presence of the Jews. And so was Poland.[108]

THE LORDS' DEFIANCE OF THE CHURCH AND
THE CONSEQUENCES THEREOF

The Catholic clergy argued that not only did the nobles' blatant rejection of Church laws and teachings about Jews contribute to the toleration and spread of Jewish "crimes" but it also led to the hardening of the hearts of Jews against the Christian religion and discouraged them from converting to Catholicism. And this, in turn, had an even more profound meaning, for if Jews did not convert and if they continued as a conspicuous non-Catholic element in society constantly challenging the legitimacy of Christianity, the Church could achieve neither full religious hegemony nor political or social control. Theologically, if this argument were taken to its conclusion, the lords' favorable treatment of Jews, which discouraged Jewish conversions, delayed the Second Coming of Christ and, therefore, the final redemption, for it was believed that Jews would convert to Christianity/Catholicism at the Second Coming.[109]

In 1729, an anonymous author published a pamphlet under the name of a supposed convert to Catholicism, Jan Krzysztof Lewek, seeking financial support after his conversion. But the content of the pamphlet, peppered with references to Christian theologians, the author's strong criticism of Catholic morality, and the absence of the criticism of Jews that characteristically mark works by true Jewish converts, all raise questions about Lewek's real identity.[110] The anonymous author claimed that Jews did not convert to Catholicism because the efforts by "pious" and "zealous" preachers to convert them were fruitless "for they do not have any support from the secular arm [*a brachio saeculari*], from the lords and secular officials."[111] Rather, "some powerful lords and people of high status do not hesitate to converse in a familiar manner [*poufale*] with [Jews], to say nothing of keeping company or even fraternizing with them; they even give [Jews] access to their estates more easily than to Christians, and they entrust them with their affairs and show them respect by addressing them with respectable titles."[112]

Against such benevolent treatment of Jews, "Lewek" proposed measures that closely resembled the post-Tridentine policies toward Jews in the Papal States, designed to bring Jews into the Catholic fold through a worsening of their status. Jews needed to feel "the taste" of the exile, Lewek argued. Favoring them over Christians would have had a contrary effect.[113] A decline in their status would have placed Jews in their proper theologically assigned position, from which they could free themselves only by accepting Christianity.[114]

If favoring Jews disrupted the ideal social order and frustrated the clergy, the nobles' favoring of the Jews over the clergy was a blow to Church prestige and a sign of the Church's profound theological and political failure. One anonymous eighteenth-century preacher complained in a holiday sermon that the lords treated Jews more favorably than Catholic priests: "[I]t is bad, and un-Christian and un-Catholic what the Lords and Ladies in our Poland do, by giving protection to this nation – the enemies of God, killers of and blasphemers against Jesus Christ – damned by God. A Jewish *parch* now has better access and more respect from Lords and Ladies than a Catholic or even a Catholic priest has."[115]

Another eighteenth-century preacher, Eugeni of St. Matthew, elaborated on the clergy's frustration with the political situation in Poland and the insubordination of the nobles. In a homily based on the book of Esther, Eugeni transposed his frustration onto Jews and their presumed political influence, arguing that Haman's motivation was vengeance because Jews did not honor him. "This was the reason," Eugeni wrote, "for this decree against the Jews, for the arrogance of their hearts gave them away! And to whom would they bow today, when they almost occupy the senate and have moved to the noblemen's estates? They almost are equal with the lords [*ledwo na równy ckwałnie idą z panami*], having taken possession of cities, towns, and royal estates."[116]

But the most explicit, and at the same time most revealing, example of the clergy's frustration with the nobles and their problematic relationship with the Catholic

Church, as vented through anti-Jewish complaints, comes from Stefan Żuchowski's book, *Process kryminalny*. Żuchowski, like "Lewek," maintained that the Jews were better off than not only poor Christians and "heretics" but also better off than the nobles and the clergy:

Finally, I wish that God would open our eyes, for great harm is done to the Republic [*Rzeczpospolita*], and that He would not punish us. The measly poll-tax, of which the Jews pay merely two *grosze* and have the most liberties of all estates, is not enough. As for the gentry, not only do they pay the taxes, serve in the government, fight in wars but they also die [in wars] and are taken prisoner; they also have to provide their sons with education and their daughters with dowries.... The clergy, aside from the common taxes, pay the increased *hiberna*[117] ... and they serve human souls, without provisions [*prowenty*]. All serfs work hard tilling the soil, the common people sit in their workshops on dry bread and they [also have to] pay everyone. Jews serve neither in war nor at the altar, nor do they till the soil, they only make money by swindling [*machlarstwo*][118] and deceit, [look] what dowries they give their detestable [*przemierzłe*] kids [*bachory*],[119] what purchases they make, in order to sustain and cling to their Protectors in Sejms, Conventions and Tribunals.... And what is [most] annoying is that they [the nobles] defend the Jews but they attack the clergy.[120]

Here, Żuchowski follows the common cliché that Poland was a Purgatory for the clergy, a Hell for the peasants, and a Paradise for the Jews [*Polonia Purgatorium Clericorum, Infernus Rusticorum, Paradisus Iudeorum*].[121] Żuchowski tried to appeal to poorer and less influential nobles, who often considered Jews their competitors for leases, by arguing that even they were worse off than the Jews. But the key, and most telling, point is Żuchowski's statement about lords attacking clergy while defending Jews. The attacks, Żuchowski argued, came in the form of unfair taxation – a serious bone of contention between secular and ecclesiastical power. Imposition of taxes, after all, is a function of political authority and power. Fiscal subordination frustrated the Church officials, who ruled on a number of occasions that imposing new taxes on the clergy and the Church was a sin that merited excommunication. And, although claims by Żuchowski and others that Jews were better treated by secular lords than were the clergy and the Catholic Church were undoubtedly exaggerated, they did reflect the Polish clergy's frustration with their failure to achieve political and social dominance, and indicate poignantly their sense of a loss of prestige.

In a sermon by an anonymous preacher, found in a manuscript now in the Czartoryski Library of Cracow, the preacher concentrated on superstitions, beliefs unapproved by the Church. In a passage about good and bad luck, he explained, "There is a third kind of [popular] superstitions...for instance, when a rabbit crosses the road in front of someone that means bad luck, when a wolf – good luck (that's probably because he has not eaten you!). When a Jew, that means good luck, but when a priest [crosses the road] – bad luck!"[122] Such clerical protests against popular beliefs and practices may be seen as resistance to a religious independence among those the Church sought to bring under its control. After all, deciding which beliefs are valid and which ones are "superstitions" is part of such a process; and as Guido Ruggiero pointed out in his study *Binding Passions*, the prosecution of "superstitions" was about control and authority.[123] The reported positive perception of Jews in the popular mind,[124] in tandem with a negative perception of Catholic priests, must have seemed clear evidence of the Church's loss of prestige, thus only furthering its sense of insecurity and heightening its need for reassurance. The clergy's frustration extended from those with political power in Poland to the poorer members of society, all of whom the Church saw as slipping out from under its influence.

6

꙰

"Countless Books Against Common Faith": Catholic Insularity and Anti-Jewish Polemic

*I*N WESTERN EUROPE DURING THE POST-REFORMATION PERIOD, CATHOLIC and Protestant scholars engaged in a scholarly, often ethnographic study of the Jewish religion, and produced competent, if still polemical, works grounded in Jewish sources. But in Poland in the eighteenth century, despite its brief Renaissance of the early sixteenth century, some Catholic clergy were still writing of Jewish thirst for Christian blood in a manner reminiscent of medieval works. In religious rhetoric, as in the ideas of Church hierocracy, Poland froze in time while the outside world moved on. The Polish Catholic Church's reaction to the new religious ideas of the Reformation, including its control of the dissemination of knowledge through restrictions on printing and education, contributed to the cultural insularity of Poland and the Polish Catholic Church, and prevented its clergy, and others, from benefiting from, and participating in, western European Christian scholarship.

Polish clergy's writings continued to raise ritual murder accusations and blood libels against Jews as late as the eighteenth century. Whereas the early ritual murder accusations against Jews in twelfth-and thirteenth-century Western Europe were associated with Passover, when Jews were accused of reenacting the crucifixion of Jesus on a small boy, the blood motif was later added to the charges, according to which Jews were said to seek Christian blood in order to make *matzah*, the unleavened bread eaten during the Passover holiday. These accusations, no longer confined to a specific Jewish festival, evolved into blood libels, claiming that Jews needed Christian blood for other purposes, such as healing or magic, and accordingly might kill a Christian child at any time in the year.[1]

The second medieval accusation against Jews that found its way to Polish Catholic writings concerned the desecration of the host. It emerged in Europe in the thirteenth century, contemporaneously with the Catholic doctrine of transubstantiation, according to which the communion wafer was transformed into the body of Jesus upon the priest's blessing during each mass. Catholics believed that they "witnessed" Jesus' recurrent suffering and resurrection at every mass, and that each time they took communion, they consumed his actual body in the consecrated host.[2] The claim of desecration of even a small piece of host by Jews was seen not only as desecration of the bread but as an act of cruelty against Jesus himself.[3] The element of what Gavin Langmuir called cannibalism in Catholic doctrine made the blood libel and ritual murder charges more believable to Catholics.[4]

In Western Europe the Christian belief that Jews used Christian blood for their own religious purposes gradually disappeared after the rise of the Reformation, but it continued among some Catholic scholars, such as the Bollandists of Catholic Antwerp.[5] The new Protestant theology could not support myths of ritual murder or host desecration by Jews. For Protestants, who denied the doctrine of transubstantiation, a wafer was a wafer, not the flesh and blood of Christ. They believed that Jesus suffered only once, in his crucifixion, that he was resurrected on the third day, and ascended to heaven. Protestant doctrine could thus not accept the idea that Jesus could be harmed by Jews or anyone else because he was no longer physically present on earth.[6]

Protestant Hebraism contributed further to the demise of these medieval myths. Protestant scholars of Jewish texts and Jewish rituals found little there to reinforce such claims. But, in Poland, the cultural isolationism and the strenuous efforts by the Catholic clergy to shield their flock from "contaminating" contacts with "corrupting elements" from the West contributed to continuing the propagation of anti-Jewish blood accusations well into the eighteenth century.

The dissemination and popularization of religious myths and accusations against Jews in Poland were, in part, a consequence of the development of printing in the West and of the consequent book trade in the late fifteenth and in the sixteenth centuries. With the rise of Protestantism, the Catholic Church became increasingly concerned with the production and dissemination of books. Protestant books were banned in Poland and people who sold them were often punished. The printing and selling of books by Catholic authors were not banned, and along with earlier Christian classics, anti-Jewish medieval tales written by Catholic writers were published and disseminated. Before the dawn of the print age, few anti-Jewish works seem to have found their way to Poland, and those that did had limited impact because of the difficulty in disseminating works in manuscript. It was a costly and time-consuming process because only one copy could be produced at a time. With the invention of movable type, many medieval books, among them anti-Jewish works, hitherto available in manuscript only and accessible to few, could now be published relatively quickly and in quantity and disseminated much more widely. Works like the thirteenth-century *Historia Maior* (or *Chronica maior*) written by Mathew Paris, and the fifteenth-century *Fortalitium fidei* by Alfonso de Espina, the bishop of Orense,[7] reached Poland and were cited by Polish clerics in their own published books over the next several centuries.[8]

"SO, IS IT INAPPROPRIATE FOR US TO HAVE BOOKS?":
CONTROL OF PRINTING AND SCHOLARSHIP

In Poland, the first official Church moves against dissemination of books that challenged Church doctrines came even before the Council of Trent (1545–63) and its *Index Librorum Prohibitorum*, first issued in 1559, itself not the first attempt by the Church to control scholarship and books. Even before printing was introduced in the West, Church leaders had understood the potential of books for spreading dangerous ideas. As early as the fifth century, in the context of combating Acacian schism, Pope Gelasius I (492–6), at the Roman synod of 494, had issued a catalogue of authentic patristic writings, a list of permitted apocrypha, and a list of prohibited heretical books.[9]

In Poland, trials for disseminating "heretical" works (i.e., Lutheran) were held in episcopal courts already in the 1520s. In 1526, in Cracow, two unrelated booksellers, one named Michał and another Marek Bawarczyk, were summoned to the bishop's court, Michał accused of importing from Germany works by heretics, and Marek "and other booksellers" ordered not to disseminate those works in the diocese or face a steep fine of 300 złoty and expulsion from the territory.[10] Considering that an average annual salary of a municipal scribe was 40 złoty at the time, the fine was high.[11] In February 1530, Peter, another bookseller, was summoned to the bishop's court in Cracow for disseminating Lutheran books, especially a children's catechism.[12] And in 1536, Hieronim Vietor, a noted printer and bookseller in Cracow, was charged with heresy and with contributing to its spread in violation of Church and royal decrees.[13]

The first such laws in Poland had been promulgated by Church officials and the king decades before the Council of Trent. As early as 1520 and in 1521, King Sigismund I issued decrees against importing Lutheran books into Poland.[14] His 1521 edict was subsequently republished and incorporated into the legislation of the Church. In 1526 a papal bull against "the errors of Martin Luther" was published in Poland together with that royal decree.[15] And in 1542, the provincial synod of Piotrków listed books it considered legitimate and others that were banned from parishes. Among approved books were the Bible, books by Church fathers, such as Augustine, John Chrysostom, Origen, and Gregory the Great, and Catholic works that attacked Luther.[16] The synod ordered books suspected of promoting heresy to be burned; it prohibited the printing of new books it considered dangerous, and recalled to Poland all scholars who were studying at Luther's university at Wittenberg.[17] In 1557, the synod of Piotrków called for restriction of access to "heretical books" and "elimination [*propellere et exterminare*] of heresy from the kingdom of Poland."[18] In the seventeenth century, books continued to be sentenced to be burned, as Bishop Marcin Szyszkowski of Cracow recounted in his 1625 report to Rome. Bishop Szyszkowski made a concerted effort to control book printing and trade in his diocese, including Jewish books in Hebrew, "which," he complained, "contain numerous falsities."[19] Synods continued to express concern with books into the eighteenth century; as late as 1717 the synod of Chełm ruled against reading books unapproved by the Church, including the Bible in the vernacular.

Preachers and Church polemicists expressed similar apprehension. A sixteenth-century clergyman, Benedict Herbest, sought to turn people away from reading books and toward the authority of the churchmen. In his own polemical book, written in a form of dialogue between a burgher and a Catholic priest, "the burgher asked: So, is it inappropriate for us to have books?" The priest responded, "It would be far better to listen to the word of God directly from the priests, so that there were no difference within the Church and so that the heretics [*kacyrze*] would not infect these books with their venom. But we have come to an unfortunate age, when even ladies discuss religion. Would that someone wrote one book explaining the teachings of the Catholic Church, and would that only this book be read in homes, this way the word of God would not be defiled by contempt and dishonesty."[20]

Any unsupervised discussion of religious ideas alarmed the Church. Herbest sought to resolve the tension between the transmission of ideas in books and oral debates and church teachings. He hoped to find a single book that could explain Church doctrines to people, "even ladies" in "that unfortunate age" of public controversy over religion. Such a single book might well make it easier for the Church to control what people read and talked about. His wish was to come true soon, at least in part. Just two years later, in 1568, the first catechism was published in Poland.[21] The translator of the catechism into Polish advertised its virtues: "everyone can trust that this catechism is written so well that it would be hard to do it better. All Christian teachings are enclosed here and it shows everything from the fundamentals that a Christian man should know, so much that this book can replace a large library. And I don't know of anything more perfect than this book."[22] But even this 1568 edition was not for everyone, printed in a large size (duo) with beautiful woodcuts throughout, it must have been expensive, nor was it an easy text. It explained Catholic doctrines with references to multiple sources and terms familiar to scholars.[23] But many, more accessible, catechisms followed.[24] In 1600, a short catechism in small format (octavo) appeared. It was cheap and, as the title page claimed, intended for "simple folk and children."[25] In 1603, a new, smaller, Polish rendition of a Roman Catholic Tridentine catechism was published in quarto, with less elaborate ornamentation so that "each, even the simplest, priest could have this book at hand."[26] A number of other editions followed, the last in 1762.[27]

The Church continued to warn against printed books that could contribute to the spread of heresy. Bishop Stanisław Karnkowski's introduction to the 1603 edition of the catechism pointed out that "where Satan could not lead people astray from the true faith by talk, he did it through writings and infected books published in order to infect people."[28] For those who might skip his introduction, the catechism reiterated the point at the beginning of the text proper:

Q: How do Heretics lead so many people away from the true faith?
A: Mostly through writings and books. Because they consider it impossible to disseminate their false and poor teachings among all people by mouth, what they can't do orally, they do through writing. And that's why they print countless books against the common faith, so that they could fool more people faster.[29]

Even as late as the eighteenth century, the Jesuit polemicist, Poszakowski, echoing the sixteenth-century churchman Stanisław Sarnicki, continued to blame printing for the spread of heresy. He accused Protestants, whom he called "apostates and fugitives," for popularizing the Bible:

Before there were only three copies of the Bible in all of Poland, that is one in the Royal library, second in the Office of the Primate and the third in the house of the Ostrorog, and yet the Holy Catholic faith flourished beautifully without any blemish of heresy for more than five hundred years, based on the oral telling of the Christ's Gospel by the parish priests and preachers, and always adhering to the teachings and decisions of the Church of God, that is the successors of the Apostles. But now who knows how many versions of the Bible in how many languages have been multiplied through print by these apostates and fugitives from the Church. And all the time, they forge new dogmas and from them a weapon against the Church.[30]

Sarnicki and Poszakowski were right. Protestants understood the importance of printing. An anonymous early seventeenth-century Protestant author of a pamphlet on the importance of synods wrote that Protestant synods should support establishment of presses, *typographiae*, "without which we cannot do and whose expense cannot be put on the shoulders of one man."[31] Yet Protestants, much as the Catholic Church, feared that certain books would spread unauthorized ideas. Therefore, most Protestant synods in Poland between 1550 and 1632 that discussed printing included a requirement that the printer's work be supervised by community leaders so that no books with ideas that contradicted Protestant teachings would be published.[32] And a Protestant pamphlet from the 1690s recommended that all books about to be printed be censored in order to prevent sin.[33]

Books could, indeed, cause harm to religious dogma and lead to heresy, but there was no escape from books in the new era of print. Resigned, the authors of the catechism opted to employ the new medium to their own advantage to propagate the Catholic litany of questions and correct answers to "heretical" teachings and to promote a uniform faith.[34] A catechism would replace a "whole library."[35] The 1643 catechism explained: "The Council of Trent wished that a book like that be published, so that, because there is only one God and one unchangeable Faith, people around the world would learn properly Christian Faith and Christian duties, described in one form."[36] Yet, although both Karnkowski and also those who published subsequent editions of the Roman catechism intended – as the 1643 edition's title page indicated – that it be used by "poor parish priests and the heads of Catholic households," it clearly was not widely known. In the early eighteenth century, Bishop Jan Krzysztof Szembek, concerned with the low level of education among his flock and the parish priests in his dioceses, published his own catechism and, on his required visitations, left a copy in each parish and extra copies for "different other people" for the salvation of their souls.[37] The use of catechism and religious instruction did not go as well as the bishops had wished. The synods of Poznań in 1720 and of Płock in 1733 threatened to fine priests who neglected religious instruction of their parishioners.[38] The 1762 edition of the Roman catechism was intended for all: priests, lay people, missionaries, teachers, heads of households, and even women, who "desirous of debates and knowledge will find this book more beneficial than any other book."[39] By the late eighteenth century, although the Catholic Church accepted the fact that the laity was becoming literate and was now reading books, it continued to seek to control what they read and their access to books.

The same effort at controlling ideas carried over to education. In 1556, the provincial synod of Łowicz forbade Catholics to study in "heretical" schools,[40] and, in 1557, so did the synod of Piotrków.[41] In 1625, Bishop Szyszkowski of Cracow, reporting to Rome on his efforts to eliminate "heretical schools" from the town of Lublin, wrote that he had marshaled royal support in Poland and obtained a royal decree banning the establishment of such schools under the threat of capital penalty and confiscation of property.[42] More than a century later, in 1745, Bishop Załuski ruled against sending one's sons to "heretical schools," that is, by then, certain mainstream Protestant schools in Poland and abroad.[43] Polish youth were to be schooled only in Catholic doctrine and in schools approved by the Church. Many were, indeed, trained at Jesuit academies and colleges established throughout the Polish-Lithuanian Commonwealth.[44]

In the eighteenth century Polish Protestants experienced a mild renaissance. A number of Protestant books in Polish were published just outside the state's borders, in Królewiec (Königsberg), Berlin, and Leipzig, and imported into Poland. Some sons of the Protestant nobility were sent to schools abroad, and some of the Protestants remaining in Poland received help and support from Protestants abroad.[45] The surge of anti-Protestant legislation and polemic within the Catholic Church in the eighteenth century coincided thus with this modest Protestant revival. An eighteenth-century Jesuit polemicist, Jan Poszakowski, explicitly stated in the title page of his book that he was refuting a book by Wojciech Węgierski, "just freshly republished in Królewiec."[46] But the Church's efforts to control books and education – to keep doctrinal "impurities" out of the country and, consequently, to prevent the "corruption" of Poles – had only mixed results. On the one hand, by the eighteenth century it had succeeded in closing Protestant presses in Poland. On the other hand, it had been unable to prevent the publication of Protestant books in the Polish language outside of Poland and their spread into Poland.

The Polish Protestant books that directly challenged Catholic doctrines based their assaults on the Bible, prompting a swift polemical response from the Church in tandem with legal measures enacted at synods. Poszakowski's book refuted Protestant emphasis on *sola scriptura*, arguing that the Bible would become a tool of the Devil if its reading was unaccompanied by proper Catholic interpretation: "How will you escape to the Bible, if Satan produces numerous texts from the Scripture against [your arguments]? Accepting only the proof [from the Scripture] you will become an Arian, a Nestorian, a Jew or even an atheist. But a Catholic [who is] well-grounded in the Word of God, as understood and explained by the Church, assisted by the Holy Spirit, will strongly counter your faith."[47] Poszakowski argued that studying without Church supervision led to Protestant heresy, then to Arianism (anti-Trinitarianism), to Judaism, and, worst of all, to atheism. To prevent such a fall into heresy, the "Word of God" had to be explained and interpreted by the Church alone; *sola scriptura* was not enough.

JEWISH INSTRUCTION OF CHRISTIAN SCHOLARS, IN POLAND AND ABROAD

In the first half of the sixteenth century, Polish scholars were still traveling abroad, foreigners still came to Poland to teach, books were imported into Poland from the West, and the biblical languages – Hebrew and Greek – were taught at Polish universities and colleges.[48] But by the end of that century, instruction and publication of works based on Hebrew and Greek had virtually ceased in Poland. Such scholarship was not renewed until the coming of the Enlightenment in the second half of the eighteenth century. An exception was the Braunsberg's Jesuit College near Protestant East Prussia.[49]

But, on the whole, in the wake of the Reformation, Poland and its Catholic Church welcomed neither the study of the Hebrew language nor new Western scholarship based on Jewish sources, thought, and customs. This was because such scholarship, with few exceptions, came from German Protestants, and was thus a potential source for "heresy." The Church was not entirely wrong in its suspicion. Hebrew scholarship and Protestant "heresy" did sometimes go hand in hand. So, for example, Francesco Stancaro, known in Poland as Franciszek Stankar, a professor of Hebrew for a short while at Cracow's Catholic Academy and author of a handbook of Hebrew grammar published first in Basel in 1547 and then in Cracow in 1548, became an active member of Poland's fledgling Protestant community.[50]

Works by Protestant scholars that challenged Jews, their beliefs, and rituals differed from most medieval Christian works against Jews. Unlike the earlier works, these were written by scholars competent in the Hebrew language and familiar with original Jewish sources and Jewish customs.[51] Polish writers, in contrast to western Christian Hebraists like Johannes Buxtorf, were seldom, if at all, familiar with Hebrew or with the Talmud, which remained an object of ridicule by Polish clergymen. A survey of library catalogues of religious orders from Poland, including a 1698 catalogue of the Jesuit library in Cracow, shows no Hebrew books at all. The same is true of the eighteenth-century catalogue of the Capuchin library in Cracow.[52]

Stephen Burnett has said, "Christian Hebraism in early modern Europe was a step-child of theology. Born of humanist ideals on the eve of the Reformation, it was nurtured and institutionally supported by both Protestants and Catholics."[53]

What Burnett wrote was true for Western Europe but not for Poland. Poland lacked the intellectual foundations humanism introduced in the West. The Renaissance came to Poland rather late, coinciding with the Reformation, and as a result, new learning seemed darkly dangerous in the eyes of the Church in Poland.

An anonymous seventeenth-century Dominican preacher claimed that "heresies and schisms arise from excessive curiosity."[54] The prolific eighteenth-century Jesuit polemicist Jan Poszakowski related a story of a noble woman who read the Bible on her own without the assistance from "the Catholic Church that is assisted by the Holy Spirit," fell into heresy, and eventually converted to Judaism.[55] Church officials, fearful of independent Bible study, doubtless would have resisted even more rigorously if Catholics were to study with Jews, or read publications about Jews and Jewish customs written by Protestant scholars or by Jews themselves.[56] After all, even though competent Protestant works by Christian Hebraists undermined Judaism, they also, implicitly, promoted the Protestant version of Christianity.

The Polish clergy's lack of familiarity with Jewish beliefs and customs may seem surprising given the numerous Jews in Poland and their unavoidable proximity to Christians.[57] Yet, this proximity and Jewish preeminence in early modern Polish society, along with the Polish Catholic Church's persistent sense of its unstable authority, may in part explain the continued use of old demonizing rhetoric. The Church resisted its clergy's studying with Jews to acquire the knowledge of Hebrew and Jewish customs and resisted sending them abroad to do the same. Its goal was prevention of undue intermixing and the outcome of such intermixing. In Poland, the use of medieval-style anti-Jewish rhetoric was a part of the early modern process of defining confessional boundaries and of distinguishing Catholic Christians from others. It was a consequence of Catholic Poland's intellectual separation from, and efforts to defend itself against, new and potentially dangerous ideas coming from the Protestant West.

Polish Jews themselves did not seek to remedy the Christians' ignorance of Judaism. Indeed, certain Polish rabbis, Rabbi Eliyahu ben Samuel of Lublin among them, prohibited teaching a non-Jew about the Jewish religion. Asked if a Jew might study the Torah with a gentile, "on the account of fear, or a little danger or income," he said "no" and, following the Talmudic dictum and citing a long tradition of rabbinic teachings, allowed only the study of the seven Noaḥide commandments that non-Jews were expected to follow:[58] prohibitions against idolatry, blasphemy, murder, adultery, robbery, eating of the flesh cut from a still-living animal, and the commandment to establish courts of justice. Like most rabbis, he too prohibited more advanced instruction of non-Jews.[59]

By contrast, Jews in Italy taught and studied with Catholics from the Renaissance through the late seventeenth century, though not without ambivalence in light of the Talmudic prohibitions. Elias Levita, a noted Jewish scholar in early sixteenth-century Italy, wrote, in the introduction to his book on Hebrew grammar, *Masoret ha-Masoret*: "[Now] I swear, by my Creator, that a certain Christian encouraged it [writing the book] and brought me thus far.[60] He was my pupil ten years uninterruptedly, I resided at his house and instructed him [in Hebrew], for which there was a great outcry against me, and it was not considered right of me. And several Rabbis would not approve of me, and pronounced woe to my soul because I taught the law to a Christian."[61] Other Italian Jews who taught Christians from the fifteenth through the seventeenth centuries included Johanan be Isaac Allemanno and Elia del Medigo, who were teachers of Pico della Mirandola; Abraham de Balmes, teacher of Cardinal Grimani; and Leon Modena, who taught several Italian Christians of lesser stature. Modena also reported that Christians came to listen to his sermons.[62]

Initially, it was the scholarly humanism of the Renaissance that encouraged such study. But, one may speculate that later on, the existence of ghettoes in Italy – a segregated, specifically Jewish space within a Christian community and one meant to be permanent – may paradoxically have given both Italian Jews and Christians a greater sense of security of their separate identities.[63] Ghettoes, based on isolating Jewish life from the wider Christian society, were a result of a social policy that emerged during the Counter-Reformation. They set geographic and religious boundaries, and for the Church established a dependable order of the Christian world, as they enforced the inferior status of Jews within Christianity according to the Church's ideal. Contacts between Jews and Christians in such clearly delineated space may, perversely, have seemed to the Church less threatening than in Poland, where there were no ghettoes and where Jews and Christians lived intermixed, and in close proximity.

"THE RABID AND CRUEL SYNAGOGUE": ACCUSATIONS BY CATHOLIC CLERGY IN POLAND

Discouraged from studying with and about Jews, and with restricted access to new works on Jewish religion published in the West, Polish Catholic clergy first turned to earlier Christian anti-Jewish works, and, from the late seventeenth century on, to writings by late sixteenth-and early seventeenth-century Polish burghers hostile to Jews. Two such burghers, Sebastyan Miczyński and Sebastyan Śleszkowski, emphasized the role of Jews in the crucifixion of Jesus and evoked myths of ritual murder in the course of condemning Jewish economic activities in Poland.[64] This kind of rhetoric, along with Catholic devotional sermons and works based on the New Testament, sought to consolidate the cohesiveness of the Catholic community by promoting Catholic piety and, at the same time, by separating Catholics from Jews – by accentuating Jews' otherness – and from other non-Catholics, as well.

Anti-Jewish rhetoric served another rhetorical purpose: to underscore the severity of Catholic *and* Protestant transgressions. Paradoxically, the hated Jews were sometimes cited by the Catholic clergy as examples of piety in contrast to "sinning" Catholics and Protestants. Thus, Catholic priests compared disobedience to its

teachings to "Jewish crimes": the crucifixion, murder of Christian children, desecration of the host.[65] Those continually exposed to such language and imagery,
D. L. d'Avray argued, might come to accept such accusations as true.[66]

The persistent adherence of Jews to their religion was itself a continuous challenge
to the legitimacy of Christianity, an adherence most threatening to the Church in
times of religious upheavals. In early modern Poland, it became a symbol of the
Catholic Church's own vulnerability. Its diatribes against Jews, both biblical and
contemporary, and against their religion served, in the Church's view, as a validation
of Christianity itself.

The Polish clergy had a treasure trove of old sources to draw from for this effort.
Evocative stories, some from the Gospels themselves, were used to portray Jews
as killers of Jesus, a claim not officially excised from Church teachings until the
Second Vatican Council of 1965.[67] Nor did all Jews deny this accusation. Several
medieval Jewish leaders and polemicists – Maimonides, for example – declared
that Jewish "sages" acted properly in punishing Jesus for his provocative actions.[68]

In Poland, most Catholic sermons for Easter, centering around the Passion –
the suffering, death, and resurrection of Jesus – were devotional only and made no
mention of the role of the Jews in the crucifixion. They focused on the meaning
of Jesus' suffering and resurrection in the context of individual salvation.[69] But
other Catholic preachers used the Gospels as evidence of Jewish cruelty and contrasted Jews with Pontius Pilate, who, in their view, acknowledged Jesus' innocence.
One seventeenth-century Jesuit preacher, Wojciech Tylkowski, wrote in a typical
narrative:[70] "And seeing the innocent Lord, he [Pilate] did not want to kill him on
his own, and therefore he told them [the Jews]: If you want, you can kill the innocent [man] as you wish, here I put him at your disposal. Seeing that Pilate did not
want to kill the Lord, the Jews blamed Him in front of Pilate . . . complaining that
Christ damaged their law, as he made Himself the Son of God, for which according
to their laws, he deserved death."[71]

A 1704 collection of devotional "teachings, stories and examples" by Mikołaj
Popławski, the one-time archbishop of Lwów, however, did not hold Jews responsible for the crucifixion. Jesus was sentenced, the archbishop said, in accordance
with Roman tradition and Roman law. Had Jesus been tried according to Jewish
law, "they would have torn his body apart after death, or they would have treated
him in the most insulting way, just as they did with Jeremiah or others. But the
Roman judge, Pontius Pilate, upon Jewish urging, followed through with the execution, hard and cruel, as it was on the cross, but he, nonetheless, ordered that
his most holy body be treated properly after death and be buried in a known and
new tomb."[72] This absolution of Jews for Jesus' death had, ironically, led to an even
stronger indictment of Jews as particularly cruel. But Popławski was inconsistent.
There were, he said, three Jerusalems: Jewish Jerusalem, where Jews "slash, whip,
crown and crucify Lord Jesus"; Christian Jerusalem, where people show remorse
and pray; and Heavenly Jerusalem, where people love, worship, and exalt Jesus as

the Messiah and as God.[73] The undoubted intent of Popławski's book was to foster Catholic piety and to encourage Catholics to recognize and obey the religious authority of the Church.

In France at the time, an intensive debate was underway on the fidelity of art representations of the biblical stories but, in Poland, Catholic authors shaped these tales in ways that met their own needs.[74] The Polish historian, Mieczysław Brzozowski, has offered examples of Polonization of Jesus and Mary, in which Jesus was represented as the king of the nation of the nobles [*król narodu szlacheckiego*] and Mary as "the queen of Poland."[75] Even Catholic theology was explained through the prism of Polishness. A seventeenth-century Jesuit preacher, Tomasz Młodzianowski, declared that the "third proof of the immaculate conception [of Mary] is that the Most Holy Virgin is not only *Serenissima*, Most Exalted, not only *Regina*, the Queen, but the Queen of Poland, *Regina Poloniae*."[76] He cited Polish law, which specified that nobility came from the father, as proof that Mary was free of the original sin of Adam and Eve. Mary, he said, is "*filia aeterni patris*, of the eternal father, she falls under the laws of her father and she is not defiled by the original sin. She is decorated with the nobility of the original grace."[77] And so, Catholicism was neatly blended with Polishness.

Catholic manipulation of biblical stories was not difficult because many Catholics were unfamiliar with biblical texts. A sermon in an eighteenth-century collection of missionary sermons, "Pro Dominica infra Octavam epiphanae," by a Franciscan, Bernard, focused on the story in Luke 2:41–51, which tells of Mary and Joseph finding the young Jesus, preaching in the Temple. Bernard wrote, "An unspeakable sorrow fell on the most Holy Mary and Joseph. The Lord Jesus, their beloved Son disappeared somewhere along the way, they did not know where. They ran into Jerusalem and in tears they asked about him. They inquired whether the Jews caught him somewhere and killed him."[78] But the original text in Luke emphasized Jesus' genius and wisdom, while Mary expressed her anxiety about his disappearance by saying to Jesus, "Child, why have you treated us like this? Look, your father and I have been searching for you in great anxiety."[79] But Bernard's rhetoric that "Jews caught him somewhere and killed him" cast Jews as dangerous murderers. In his retelling, Mary, Joseph, and Jesus appeared not to be Jews at all, while Jews embodied their enemies. Also, in his focus on Jesus as a child, Bernard conflated the notion of Jews as "Christ killers" with stories of Jews as potential child-killers. Bernard's passage alludes to the beginning of many stories of ritual murder, most of which began with a child's disappearance and with the child's desperate parents or a mother searching for that missing child.[80] With actual accusations of ritual murder and blood libels against Jews and the dissemination of stories of Jews' killing Christian children persisting in Poland throughout the eighteenth century, Bernard may have even intended to evoke them.

Bernard's parallel between the images of hostility of biblical Jews toward Jesus, the Christian God, and of contemporary Jews, the neighbors of Polish Catholics, led

to the transposition of Jewish enmity toward Jesus and of Jewish rejection of him as
the Messiah and God, to Jewish hostility toward all who accepted Jesus. To Bernard,
cruelty and enmity toward Christians were inherent Jewish traits. If Jews could kill
God, how much more willing would they be to kill ordinary Christians?[81] Piotr
Hyacynth (Jacek) Pruszcz, a seventeenth-century writer, cited Jesus' love of children
and juxtaposed it to "smelly" Jews who kill children to get their blood.[82] Still, certain
churchmen resisted such accusations. In 1680, the general of the Carmelite order
denied that Jews sought Christian blood, and admonished all members of his order
[religiosis nostris] to strive to correct this common opinion.[83]

Nevertheless, many anecdotes and exempla evoked in Poland continued to vilify
Jews. In his sermon for the fourth Sunday after the Epiphany, Archbishop Mikołaj
Popławski of Lwów incorporated a parable about Danaam, a Jewish administrator
of a town in Arabia, who was said to find pleasure in persecuting Christians, and
especially Catholics, with children his favorite victims. Popławski concluded that
"it seems that given the Jewish malice toward Catholics, if they could, they would
be happy to bring [all Catholics] to ruin, and because of their blasphemies they
are not worthy of our affection [afektów]."[84] Though the tale is set in "Arabia,"
Popławski clearly intended it as a parable of Poland. Like many Jewish leaseholders
or administrators of the nobles' estates, the Jew in this tale as a town administrator
held authority over Catholics.

Another version of the same story, from a slightly later collection of sermons, is
set (historically incorrectly) in 1522 "under the rule of Emperor Justinian." There
the Jew is named "Dunaas of Arabia."[85] This Dunaas was "a great persecutor of
Christians, whose blood he spilled numerous times over many cities."[86] The tale is
longer and much more pointed than Popławski's on Jews' ruthlessness, which, the
author claimed, was "Jewish nature."[87] Because exempla are by definition timeless
and ahistorical, the focus here is not historicity or accuracy but the message to be
conveyed – both the tale told by Popławski and that by the anonymous preacher
were intended to convey Jewish cruelty and to warn Catholics against Jews who
had power.[88]

New Testament stories and exempla, epithets describing Jews as "malicious,"
"ungrateful," "fierce" [zawzięty], and "rabid" [zajadły], and the contrast of such
alleged traits with Jesus' kindness and love, all helped to set up rigid boundaries
between Jews and Catholics.[89] As late as the seventeenth and eighteenth centuries
Catholic clergy in Poland were maligning the Jews, biblical, fictitious, or contemporary, and undermining Judaism to validate Christianity. A passage from a Passion
sermon delivered during Easter by an anonymous Polish Dominican depicts Jews,
who do not accept the Church, as malicious and the synagogue, meaning Judaism,
as "cruel and rabid":

And Jewish malice arises, Jewish diabolic cruelty rages over Jesus even more. . . . Oh,
rabid and cruel Jewish Synagogue, you lashed your God and mine. You godless, stubborn
Jewish Synagogue, having become a disciple of Moses' perfidious teachings, accepted

Moses' scripture not because you wanted to respect God, but because you wanted to insult my Christ, not because you wanted to serve your Creator, but because you wanted to beat, cudgel and lash my Savior, tyrannically repeating the blows again and again as if [He were] a slave.[90]

Here the negative portrait of Jews served the preacher in asserting both Christianity's and the Church's own legitimacy. Jews' "stubborn" adherence to Jewish law and Jewish scripture ("Moses' scripture"), this preacher claimed, was not intended to serve God but to affront Jesus. As in Bernard's passage on Jews' attack on the young Jesus, this writer (as many others) sought to estrange Jews from God. In Bernard's sermon, Jews assaulted God physically; here, Jews are seen as insulting God through adherence to "Moses' scripture," an adherence that was the foundation of the centuries-old Christian sense of insecurity.

Many Polish preachers, following medieval tradition, told stories of Jews encountering the devil.[91] On occasion, the Jew defeated the devil or the demons by accepting Catholicism. One exemplum, with roots in the sixth century, tells of a Jew who was stranded overnight in a country church.[92] Frightened when he encountered demons, the Jew remembered that Christians crossed themselves to fend off the devil. He did the same, and the demons could not reach him. In the morning he converted to Catholicism at the next town. "What do you say, dear Christians?" the preacher asked rhetorically. "If God fended off the enemies away from the infidel Jew, how much more will he help those with living faith?"[93] Although the tale is of medieval origin and Protestants are not mentioned here, the tale seems a covert response to a Protestant challenge. Protestants, including a noted Protestant preacher, Krzysztof Kraiński, mocked the Catholic belief that the devil feared the holy water and escaped when a person made a sign of the cross. If the devil did fear the holy water Catholics used in their churches, then "why is it that the devil appears in Papists' churches and frightens the people there?"[94]

The promise of Jews' acceptance of Christianity was the only reason, some Polish Catholic clergy argued, for any friendly interaction or expression of neighborly love. "Do you understand?" an eighteenth-century Jesuit preacher, Kasper Balsam, commanded. "It is not required to love a Jew, because he who is a friend of an enemy of the Cross, he himself is an enemy of the Cross. But it is said that each infidel is our neighbor, and God commands neighborly love. Yes, it is true that one should love an infidel, but as far as he is one's neighbor, one should wish him a revelation by the Most Holy Ghost, so that he may accept the Catholic Faith.... Otherwise to love an infidel is not neighborly love, but a mortal sin."[95] A Jew unwilling to convert and to accept the authority of the Church was an enemy of Christ and, thereby, of the Church itself.

"According to the faith," the polemicist Poszakowski wrote in one of his many works against Protestants, "it is definite that the Antichrist is supposed to be one certain man.... He is to be a Son of the Doom, and Jew by birth, unbaptized and thus not a member of the Church of Christ."[96] Refuting a Protestant argument that the Pope was the Antichrist,[97] Poszakowski explained, the "Antichrist is supposed to be an unbaptized Jew, and which Pope was ever unbaptized? Can he be a head of the Church of God not being his member? . . . the Antichrist will pose as a Jewish Messiah, he will first attract the Jews and will build them the Temple in Jerusalem [Kościół w Jerozolimie], for which the Jews long so much even today."[98] With one stroke Poszakowski had turned the Jewish religion upside down, presenting Jews and their messianic hopes as the exact opposite of the "Christian truth." He had affirmed the divine legitimacy of the Catholic Church and the pope as its head. Jews recruited by the Antichrist were unbaptized outsiders excluded from the Church; once baptized they would "become one body with Christ, of which He is the head."[99]

Archbishop Popławski, too, emphasized Jewish enmity of Christianity in his variation of a medieval parable about Jews destroying Catholic images. "How great is the Jewish enmity [złość żydowska] of Christ," Popławski wrote:

A Jew moved to a house [where a picture of Christ was], but he did not notice it. When other Jews came to visit him, they saw the picture and they began to scold him. Later they informed on the Jew to their elders, who ran into the house and began to do greatest harm to the picture by offending it and blaspheming [against Christ]. They spat on it, they whipped it and tore it into pieces. That's how strong the Jewish cruelty is against Lord Jesus even today. And that's why the Jews do not deserve any favors from Christians, who should be rewarded for all these Jewish offenses with love and respect.[100]

Through this medieval-style tale, Popławski extended Jewish "enmity" against Jesus to the contemporary context and to a familiar Polish setting of Jews' rental or purchase of houses from Christians. He accused Jews of cruelty and admonished Christians not to engage with Jews in a friendly manner, for Jews did not deserve such favorable treatment and Christians deserved not to be offended by them. The vilification of Jews – biblical and, by extension, contemporary – was a defensive strategy of the Church at a time of religious crisis and political struggles, and of challenges to its authority in Poland.[101]

In Protestant communities clerical manipulation of biblical texts similar to that by Catholic priests would have been more difficult because the Protestant laity was more familiar with the Bible itself, or at least it was permitted to be. A Polish Protestant catechism published around 1600 explicitly instructed the head of a household to read the Bible daily to his family and servants [czeladka].[102] Its authors underscored the importance of literacy and familiarity with the Bible:

Q: Can images, which are used by the simple folk instead of books, be tolerated in churches?
A: No, they cannot. Because we cannot outwit God, who wants his Church to be strengthened not by mute images but by a living word.[103]

This Protestant catechism contained fewer claims of Jewish hostility to Jesus than found in Catholic writings. Yet, Protestants too used Jews in polemics against Catholics, usually by comparing Catholic practices to Jewish. The prominent Protestant writer and preacher, Krzysztof Kraiński, in pointing to Catholic insistence that the miracles proved Catholic doctrines, argued that if miracles were indeed proofs of sainthood, then "witches, pagan priests, Jews, false prophets, and heretics should have been saints and [constitute] the True Church of God, for they also produced miracles."[104] And, in rebutting the Catholic emphasis on works in contrast to grace alone as a road to salvation, Kraiński contended that "Turks, Tatars, and Jews, who give generous alms, rescue the poor and perform other good deeds" would also be saved by such logic.[105] Just as Catholics denied salvation to those outside the Church, so did the Protestants deny salvation to non-Christians in their anti-Catholic polemic.

THE HOST AND THE BLOOD: THE MEDIEVALISM OF POLISH ANTI-JEWISH POLEMIC

Catholic allegations that Jews used actual Christian blood to their own ends dehumanized and estranged Jews from the larger Christian society.[106] No new stories of the bleeding host or of baby Jesus emerging from the host said to have been mutilated by Jews appeared in late seventeenth- and eighteenth-century Polish polemical works, and the accusations about Jewish desecration of the host diminished and eventually ceased.[107] In Polish anti-Jewish literature, even the writers who continued to promote the blood accusation had by then shifted their focus from desecration of the host, and the miracles that followed it, to a charge that Jews stole or traded in Church ritual objects. But this absence of new tales of miracles can perhaps be traced to a broader cultural shift in which miracles appear increasingly to have had little place. Even in tales of blood accusation, it was Jewish hostility and not the miracles cited in the medieval period that received primary attention.[108] Anti-Protestant polemic by Catholic writers, too, was devoid of miracles associated with host desecration.[109]

Stefan Żuchowski's notorious anti-Jewish work, *Process kryminalny o niewinne dziecię Jerzego Krasnowskiego iuż to trzecie, roku 1710 dnia 18 sierpnia w Sendomirzu okrutnie od Żydów zamordowane* (A criminal trial concerning an innocent child Jerzy Krasnowski cruelly killed in Sandomierz by Jews on August 18, 1710) demonstrates the contrast between the use of legends of ritual murder, blood libel, and desecration of the host. Żuchowski had instigated blood libels against Jews in Sandomierz but, in discussing "Jewish crimes," once a typical occasion for stories of host desecration, he emphasized instead stolen silver:

In Kościelec near Cracow, an *arendarz* [here synonymous with a Jew] bought a Eucharist tin.[110] Father I. Opacki, Archdeacon of Cracow made sure that the Jew was executed and all others from the brewery in this parish were expelled.... In Sienna[111] a Jew was executed because of the Church silver and the relic of St. Anthony.... In 1697 in Ćmielów a jeweler took the silver from the Altar of St. Anna, [the silver] reached the Jews. Only the jeweler was executed. In 1697 in Volhynia, Jews had a Thieves Guild that stole more than twenty silver objects from the churches around Łuck.... In 1700 in Szczeglice, Opatów Jews bought silver objects stolen from churches.... In 1711 Woyciech Floryk and other criminals burgled a Church in Ulanów. It is written that they sold the silver to the Jews, some in Biłgoraj, some to Leyb the Butcher in Goraiec.[112]

So, too, in court records from the same period, Jews appear as liquidators of stolen Church objects and as thieves. There is little, if any, mention of the Eucharist. In 1750, in Mohilev, when a Christian was accused of stealing Church property, Jews appeared in the background as receivers of the stolen goods.[113] Elsewhere, when Jews were charged with theft of Church objects, it was the value of the property that received most attention. Jews were sentenced to death for such thefts, the usual penalty for robbing churches or for any robbery for that matter, the same sentence that applied to Christian thieves.[114] One could call this process de-theologizing of the host desecration stories, with a shift from theft and abuse of the Eucharist to theft of the Church's precious silver. With no miracles, perhaps many ordinary Catholics no longer considered Jewish "hostility toward the host" of serious concern because some of them had used the wafer for purposes other than communion, like a woman in Przemyśl in 1664 who stole the Eucharist because she believed that pouring milk through the host would magically prevent its fermentation.[115]

This shift away from the host desecration stories was accompanied by an increasing stress on stories of Jews murdering Christian children. Such tales, certain to emphasize personal danger and to fan hatred of Jews and thus to hasten the desired Jewish-Christian separation, persisted in anti-Jewish literature and court documents throughout the eighteenth century. A number of anti-Jewish works chronicled "Jewish crimes" said to have occurred throughout Poland and Europe. Polish writers repeated tales of ritual murder out of medieval chronicles; thus, Jakub Radliński described a case in Lincoln, England, that had appeared in a thirteenth-century chronicle of Matthew Paris.[116] Matthew had written: "They scourged him till the blood flowed, they crowned him with thorns, mocked him, and spat upon him; each of them also pierced him with a knife, and they made him drink gall, and scoffed at him with blasphemous insults, kept gnashing their teeth and calling him Jesus.... When the boy was dead, they took the body down from the cross and for some reason disemboweled it."[117] Radliński echoed, "In England in a town of Lincoln, Jews caught an eight-year old child and having beaten him, they crowned him with thorns, crucified, gave him gall to drink, cut his side, ripped his intestines for magic and buried his body."[118]

So, too, Stefan Żuchowski repeated Alfonso de Espina's description of a case in the Italian city of Ancona:

In 1456 in Ancona, Emmanuel [who was baptized] gave two examples of Jewish cruelties. The first, that Simon the Physician from Ancona, having cut the head off a servant boy (to drain the blood from the trunk of the body), left. A dog, having stolen the head, took it into the town and left the trace of blood on the ground, but the Jew escaped overseas with the Turks, this he heard only from his Father. But this he saw himself: "When I was in Saona [sic], my father took me to a house of a certain Jew, where eight Jews, having closed themselves inside, obliged each other under oath not to reveal the secret of a Christian Sacrifice even under torture. Then three Jews spread a child of three on the Cross by head and hands over a vessel used for circumcision, the fourth stabbed [the child] into heart with a knife and then continued stabbing frequently and rapidly. The body was thrown into the sewer. Then they mixed the blood with apples and pears, and nuts and other fruit, and they ate it, [I ate] too but with disgust.[119]

This author sought not only to emphasize Jewish cruelty but also Jews' alliance with the other "enemy" of Christendom, the Turks. Both passages reflect a religious, Christological perspective, with the victim's torture described in vocabulary reminiscent of crucifixion. Of course, in medieval stories of ritual murder, the crucifixion had indeed been the focus.[120]

Lest his medieval stories be discounted as foreign, related simply to Jews from distant lands and times, Żuchowski offered examples of more contemporary and local Jewish "crimes." "In Pińczów, fifteen years ago [ca. 1698]," Żuchowski wrote, "a Jew was apprehended when mangling a child, having spread [the child] over a trough [*koryto*] in a sheet, [he] ripped his veins out like from a sheep [or a ram]."[121] In contrast to earlier, overtly Christological images, this imagery resembled the act of a Jewish ritual slaughter of an animal. It reflects some familiarity with Jewish practices because the removal of veins is a part of the preparation of kosher meat. So does an incidental statement in a sermon on Catholic sins by an eighteenth-century preacher, Woyciech Józef Barański: "If the stinking Jews reject cattle [meat] when they see something unhealthy inside, how much more should the Divine Wisdom reject whatever depraved emerges from within us."[122]

Jews sold to Christians meat considered unfit for their own consumption, thus arousing suspicion and irking the Church, which saw selling of "rejects" to Christians as offensive. Jews required a special permission to sell meat to non-Jews, a permission sometimes granted by civil authorities in the privileges granted to Jews upon settlement. In 1208, Pope Innocent III wrote to Count of Nevers: "Another scandal of no mean consequence is created by them in the Church of Christ, in that, while they themselves shrink from eating, as unclean, the meat of animals killed by Christians, yet they obtain it as a privilege from the favor of the princes to give the slaughtering of the animal over to such who cut the animals according to the Jewish rite, and then take of them as much as they desire and offer the leavings to the Christians."[123]

Selling cheaper non-kosher meat to Christians would arouse animosity from Christian butchers, too, though some Jewish and Christian butchers cooperated in this practice. The medieval rabbinic authority Rabbi Meshullam was asked if it was legitimate for a Christian butcher to assist a Jewish slaughterer, who as soon as the Jew completed the ritual slaughter, symbolically "applied his knife to the neck of the cow," assuring that non-Jews would buy meat that Jews found unfit for their own consumption. The rabbi responded that such practice was allowed.[124] In Poland, too, such cooperation was to be found. In 1728, the owner of the city of Rzeszów issued a privilege to a joint Christian-Jewish guild of butchers.[125]

The setting of Żuchowski's passage included other familiar elements – a manger and trough – both of which would have been recognizable to Polish Catholics who lived in rural settings. Żuchowski was bringing the imagery of Jewish "cruelty and crimes" closer to home. It was perhaps a de-theologization of the ritual murder story, with the Christological elements of earlier ritual murder tales replaced by familiar practical references to local customs, much as the stories of desecration of the host were being replaced by stories of stolen Church property.

Still, identification of a Christian child with a sheep to be slaughtered may have had a symbolic resonance. Although the Polish word *koryto* (a trough or a manger), which Żuchowski used, is not the same as *żłób*, a manger, used to describe the nativity scene, still in this setting many might have associated this scene with nativity. The child here is represented as a lamb ritually slaughtered by Jews, which is also an allusion to Jesus, who is often likened in Christian thought to a lamb.[126] In another place Żuchowski asserted that "the blood of many Christian children was shed by Jews... like that of innocent lambs."[127] Here, it seems, the transposing of the practice of ritual animal slaughter onto a scene of a murder of a Christian child with a mixture of symbols and familiar elements may well have been intended to evoke religious and social associations in readers or listeners, or at least to arouse a sense of danger. Such descriptions, in works by Żuchowski, Radliński, and earlier writers like Mojecki, Miczyński, or Hubicki, were both an expression of the writers' anti-Jewish sentiments and also a reflection of intent to discourage intimate Jewish-Christian interaction by presenting Jews as inhumane and dangerous.

Żuchowski was blunt about his goal and his anti-Jewish sentiments. In his earlier work on a ritual murder trial of Jews in Sandomierz in 1698, the title page declared that he had written the book for the benefit of the public. At the end appears this verse (rhymed in Polish): "I brought you this trial and described it truthfully, but I am not sure whether I will gain appreciation. And if you don't have faith and don't trust me, it is because you see it through Jewish spectacles."[128]

Joshua Trachtenberg, in his classic study of medieval anti-Jewish sentiments, *The Devil and the Jew*, offered medieval Christian explanations for why Jews needed Christian blood: to counter what they believed to be a Jewish odor, to cure blindness or leprosy, to heal the circumcision wound, and other physical maladies, such as the persistent bleeding (menstruation) Christians said was experienced by Jewish women *and* men.[129] According to Żuchowski, Christian blood could also annul the curse Jews had taken on themselves during Jesus' crucifixion, which led to the birth of Jewish infants with a closed fist filled with blood (the fist could not be opened, so it was said, unless sprinkled with Christian blood). Sometimes, Żuchowski claimed, Jewish infants were born with two fingers affixed to their body.[130] He also said that Christian blood cleansed Jews of skin diseases [parchy, świerzb],[131] eased the pain of circumcision and of postpartum, and remedied "menstrual" bleeding in Jewish men. Żuchowski claimed Jewish men bled monthly and "that is why they do not have a good complexion but are pale and sickly."[132] Christian blood given in an egg to a bride and groom at the wedding ceremony was supposed to promote fertility.[133] Furthermore, Christian blood was used to bring salvation to Jewish dead, so Żuchowski said; Jews smeared the eyelids of the dead with Christian blood because they knew that the True Messiah had already come.[134]

Christian blood was said also to ensure good fortune in business and, given in food or drink, made Christians inclined to help and support Jews. To enjoy these benefits, Jews had to solicit from a rabbi a letter that contained a drop of Christian blood. The letter then had to be buried under the doorstep of a Christian home.[135] All of these "explanations" from Żuchowski's book are repeated almost verbatim from an earlier anti-Jewish book by Przecław Moiecki, published in 1589, subsequently somewhat reworked by Szymon Hubicki and republished in 1602.[136]

All such images of Jews – menstruating men, children born with closed fists filled with blood, women bleeding incessantly after postpartum – were not images of ordinary human beings but of scary and "diabolical" freaks to be avoided.[137] If desecrating the host no longer created an immediate danger, these vivid descriptions of murder to harvest Christian blood could have the intended powerful effect of alienating Christians from Jews. Perhaps this in part explains the shift away from accusations of desecration of the host.

"IS IT PERMISSIBLE TO KILL A PAGAN OR A JEW . . . ?"

In the West, post-Reformation writings by both Protestant and Catholic authors did not dehumanize Jews and, therefore, did not make it rhetorically impossible for potential Jewish converts to Christianity to be accepted. But, in Poland, to the contrary, the goal seemed to be not to bring Jews to Christianity through theological polemic but to repudiate Jewish beliefs through demonizing Jews.[138] Jewish beliefs were portrayed not simply as erroneous but as absurd and alien. Such texts assaulted not only the beliefs but the very nature of Jews.

Following medieval anti-Jewish rhetoric again, many Catholic writers in Poland claimed that Jewish hostility toward Christians had its roots in the Jewish religion and in the Talmud.[139] Polish clerics repeated old claims that in their rituals and prayers, Jews cursed and blasphemed against Christianity.[140] Jan Poszakowski, following the notorious Jewish convert to Christianity in German lands, Johannes Pfefferkorn, singled out two prayers as examples of such Jewish blasphemies. He called these prayers *Selam szamudin anicho* and *Batel mahe szefos zonnenu*.[141] *Selam szamudim anicho* is a corrupted version of *ve-la-meshumadim al tehi tikva* and stems from the daily 'Amidah prayer, which, however, has this verse in a slightly different version, *ve-la-malshinim al tehi tikva*, while *Batel mahe sefos zonnenu* is a corrupted version in Ashkenazic pronounciation of the verse *batel maḥshevot sonenu* [annul intentions of our enemies] from the prayer *Avinu Malkenu* said on Jewish fast days and during the days of repentance.[142] Earlier Polish writers, Szymon Hubicki and Przecław Moiecki, had cited Jewish festivals as occasions when Jews blasphemed against Christianity: Sabbath, Passover (called Easter in Hubicki's book), Sukkot, Rosh ha-Shanah (New Year), and fast days [*mięsopust*], presumably Yom Kippur, the Day of Atonement, and perhaps Tish 'a be-Av, a day commemorating the destruction of the Temple and other catastrophes of Jewish history.[143] Hubicki employed the Catholic term *mięsopust*, a meat-free day, to mean a Jewish fast day. Entailing a prohibition against eating meat, the selective fasting practiced by Catholics on Fridays and during Lent differed from fasting as understood in the Jewish tradition, in which, with few exceptions, neither food nor drink are taken from one sunset to the next.

Catholic writers were not entirely wrong in their claims about Jewish writings on Christians. Jews did express in prayers strong negative views of Christianity and of Jesus and Mary, sometimes even calls for vengeance.[144] Although passages offensive to Christianity were later removed from Jewish prayers, an early sixteenth-century collection of penitential prayers published in Cracow still contained a few references to Christianity as a religion of the "hung-one," an expression to denote the crucified Jesus, and references to a "menstruating woman." According to medieval Jewish counternarrative of the Gospels, Jesus was born of a menstruating woman, in Jewish tradition a powerful and insulting denotation of impurity. Such prayers played on the contrast between Christian impurity and defilement and the ritual purity of the Jews. Christians were portrayed as the impure uncircumcised.[145]

Still, the majority of Polish clergy who left written evidence seem to have been ignorant of Jewish religious practices. In his *Process kryminalny* published after 1718, Stefan Żuchowski reported on testimonies in the 1710 case of blood libel in Sandomierz, which he himself had instigated.[146] He referred to what he considered Jewish rituals: "The beadle [said] this blatantly lying [*in caput suum mentitus*]: 'It is not true, and it is not known to me that we use Christian blood, *evicomen* means *Peysak* but we don't use blood for it.' (This should be noted that he came up with another falsehood, since *Peysak* among Jews is not the matzah, but curls of hair left around the ears)."[147] Żuchowski confused the term *peysak* (*Pesaḥ*, Passover) with *peysy* (as *peyyot* or *peyes*, side-locks, were known in Polish). His text betrays confusion, too, about the meaning of *evicomen* (or *afikoman*, the piece of *matzah*, unleavened bread, eaten at the conclusion of the Passover meal). Nor was Żuchowski the only Catholic author who was ignorant, or deliberately misleading, about this Jewish term. One seventeenth-century Polish writer, Hyacynth (Jacek) Pruszcz, wrote that *evicomen* (afikoman) was a drink used at Passover: "This blood, which this venomous nation uses in their drink during Easter [*Wielkieynocy*], as well as in other needs, is called *evicomen*. That is why when you say to a Jew 'Have you drunk *evicomen* this Easter?' he runs away scared; some interpret this word *Evae peccatum* [Eve's sin]."[148]

Pruszcz's claim that Jews drank blood during Passover concerned the red wine drunk during the Passover Seder, subject to Christian suspicion because in color it resembled blood.[149] The Christian belief that Jews drank blood has relevance in the light of Catholic belief in the transformation at mass of the wine into Christ's blood,[150] with Christ's blood seen as atonement for humankind's sins, including the original sin of Adam and Eve. Pruszcz's explanation illustrates how Christian beliefs shaped the myth of blood libel, or what Alan Dundes called "projective inversion," and ultimately also Pruszcz's own ignorance of the Jewish religion.[151]

Alexander Dowgiało, an early eighteenth-century Dominican preacher, exhorted his audience in a funerary sermon for Stefan Moroz, a town official in Wilno: "Read the Talmud, in it the Rabbis teach that God cries every day,[152] mourning Jewish servitude and two tears fall into the great sea which we call the ocean, [he also] roars like a lion and hits his legs on the sky three times a day in grief... He prays to himself everyday, so that his own mercy may alleviate his wrath."[153] Following earlier writers, Dowgiało claimed that the Talmud prescribed that: "Each Jew should curse the Christian nation thrice a day, wishing it destruction, in contempt for Jesus of Nazareth, God ordered that the Jew take property away from Christians by means of usury or theft, that the Jews regard Christians as beasts. The Jew should not do anything good or bad to the pagan, but he should make an effort to kill or at least to harm a Christian. The Christian churches are places of idolatry and Jews should ruin them."[154] Ignorance is revealed also in the Dominican preacher's reference to the direction Jews face during prayer. According to Jewish tradition, in synagogues Jews face the eastern wall, which contains the Torah scroll (in the direction of the Jerusalem Temple).[155] Dowgiało wrote that Jews believed that if they prayed facing south, they would receive wisdom from God and if they prayed facing north, they would receive riches.

Still, it would be wrong to say that all Polish Catholic preachers promoted hatred of Jews. There were preachers, for example, who, in the tradition of St. Bernard of Clairvaux, considered violence unbecoming to Christians and sought to avert violence against Jews while assuring a victorious end for Catholicism.[156] One anonymous preacher discussing a theft remarked, "It is a sin to harm the rich or the poor, the Christians or the Jews."[157] And another said of a crime committed against one's neighbor that Christian moral obligations extended to Jews, and heretics and pagans, too:

Is it permissible to kill a pagan or a Jew because he was not baptized and take all his belongings? How about a heretic, who is not united with the Church? Can one steal, cheat someone because he is a Lutheran? Or a Calvinist? How about an adversary who wishes us bad things, is it permissible to thrust oneself on him, beat him up, wish him vengeance from God or to be content from his misfortunes? Without any exception whether he is a good or a bad man, a Jew or a pagan, faithful or an infidel, Catholic or heretic, servant, lord or a serf, relative or kinsman, rich or poor, he is our neighbor and therefore, he must be loved, *albeit not equally* [my emphasis, *choc nie iednakowo*].[158]

In one collection of exempla, a tale intended for use in a sermon against homicide[159] portrays a Christian who wanted to kill a Jew and steal his possessions (corresponding to one of the questions in the sermon cited above). The Jew begged the Christian not to "commit this sin," warning that it would be revealed. But the Christian asked sneeringly, "Who would reveal it? We are in such a remote place," whereupon the Jew pointed out a covey of partridges. The Christian ignored the Jew's warning, killed him, and took his possessions. Some time later, the partridges revealed the crime (unfortunately, the author does not tell us how), and the Christian was hanged.

A similar warning about violence against Jews appears in a discussion of the validity of baptism in a manuscript collection of various Catholic teachings:

Q: Is the following christening valid? A student crossing the Vistula river with a Jew, stopped in the middle and forced the Jew to be baptized, threatening him with death. The Jew fearful that the student would drown him, agreed. The student took water from the Vistula, asked the Jew whether he wanted to be baptized, the Jew responded that he did, [the student] then poured the water over the Jew, said the required formula. But then [the student] was afraid that the Jew would leave the holy Faith and therefore he killed him with a paddle and threw his body into the river.
A: If the Jew had sincere intention [to be baptized] not prompted by fear, [the student] baptized him properly, but it was not appropriate for the student to kill the Jew, he sinned mortally, because the student had no right or power to baptize the Jew and then to kill him. If the Jew said that he wanted to be baptized only with his mouth but in his heart he had no will or intention, the baptism was illegal.[160]

Although Jews were to be converted, violence, so some Catholic clergy argued, was an inappropriate means to that end, and sometimes illegal.[161] Genuine voluntary conversions of Jews, on the other hand, would strengthen the Church in numbers, and reassure Catholics of Catholicism's validity and ultimately represent "a triumph for the Church," to use the words of St. Bernard of Clairvaux, repeated by Pope Benedict XIV in his 1751 encyclical to the bishops in Poland.[162] In tales included in sermons, Jews often converted because of miracles caused by divine intervention mediated through a saint or Mary. In polemical works, Jews were said to convert in response to convincing debates with Catholic priests.[163] Such tales, most of medieval origin, appear to have been carefully selected to resonate in contemporary Poland, to be useful in homiletic works in the promotion of Catholicism, and, at times, in the denigration of non-Catholic practices.[164]

Yet, Polish Catholic churchmen were more likely to vilify Jews than to engage seriously with the tenets of Judaism, for unlike their Western counterparts, their principal goal was not conversion but a staving off of intimate Jewish-Christian relationships. The Church in Poland felt too vulnerable to allow scholarly pursuits about Jews and personal contacts with the Jews because such pursuits challenged the truth and the validity of Catholicism. Emphasizing Jews' dangerous "otherness" was perhaps more effective in countering such threats than was furthering knowledge about Jewish religion. There was a relationship among the state of Catholic scholarship in Poland, Jews, and the Polish Church's continuing sense of insecurity.

7

ॐ

"Warding Off Heretical Depravity": "Whom Does the Catholic Church Reject, Condemn, and Curse?"

*A*FTER THE REFORMATION, THE CATHOLIC CLERGY IN POLAND SOUGHT to combat the spread of heretical ideas and, simultaneously, to promote Catholic doctrines, the one abetting the other. Catholic piety and dogma were promoted through devotional works and artwork in newly built or renovated baroque churches, serving as indirect religious polemic against Protestants. In more overt and more direct polemic, the Church provided Catholics with explicit counterarguments to Protestant ideas and and sought to discourage contacts between Catholics and heretics and others who did not submit to the authority of the Church.

PROMOTING MARY AND THE SAINTS

The vast majority of books written and published by the Catholic clergy in post-Reformation Poland were devotional.[1] Still, even in these works, elements of polemic appeared in the promotion of baroque piety in the form of the cults of Mary, Jesus, and the saints, all figures the Protestants were challenging. The Church offered constructive responses to Protestant claims that Mary was Jesus' mother but not an object of veneration, that the cult of saints was a form of idolatry, and, as the anti-Trinitarians insisted, that Jesus was not divine. Protestants, for their part, acknowledged no intermediaries in the people's relationship with God. Wojciech Węgierski, a seventeenth-century Polish Protestant leader, wrote, "The Holy Scripture says that we should pray concerning our spiritual and bodily needs only to the true God, Father, Son and the Holy Spirit, who knows our hearts and human thoughts."[2]

From the late sixteenth century on, the Church and its supporters set up multiple new altars in sanctuaries and encouraged veneration of paintings of Mary and saints, sometimes "crowned" in special masses, and accompanied by publication of works celebrating these events. Ostensibly purely devotional art was an effort, in part, to counter attacks against Catholic doctrines. A Polish art historian, Lidia Kwiatkowska-Frejlich, has shown that newly founded Catholic churches or churches regained from the Protestants were depositories for devotionally polemical art, especially in towns in Małopolska, a center of anti-Trinitarian activity.[3] In Tarłów, for instance, a church was founded in 1655 by the Oleśnicki family, earlier at the forefront of the Protestant and the anti-Trinitarian movement, as expiation for the family's "heretical" past.[4] In the church's two chapels, one devoted to Mary, "God's Mother," the second to "Lord Jesus," the art addressed the anti-Trinitarian challenges.

Anti-Trinitarians considered Jesus a human, not a deity, and contested any dogma that claimed his divinity. Jesus' mother was a starting point. Catholics believed in the immaculate conception of Mary, a dogma not officially sanctioned by the Church until 1854 but one whose elements appeared among the Church fathers in late antiquity and in the early Middle Ages,[5] gradually entering the Church teachings by the early modern period.[6] According to this dogma, Mary, as a future mother of God, was herself conceived untainted by the original sin of Adam and Eve, and thus, unlike the souls of all humans, her soul and her body were pure. This evolving dogma of Mary's nearly divine purity was questioned not only by anti-Trinitarians but also by less radical Protestants who did accept Jesus' divinity. Krzysztof Kraiński, a noted late sixteenth-century Calvinist polemicist, explicitly criticized this Catholic dogma in his *Postylla*, a collection of homiletic materials that followed the Catholic liturgical calendar.[7] Kraiński's sermons, or perhaps counter-sermons, for the day of "the Immaculate Conception of Mary," stated that the day had been a holiday unknown to Christians for more than 1,200 years from the earliest days of Christianity, with a disagreement about it even among the "papists." To highlight how contemporary Catholics erred, Kraiński produced textual proofs from earlier Catholic writers against this dogma, and addressed a number of other Catholic teachings about Mary and the saints with which he and other Protestants disagreed.[8] The various holidays devoted to Mary, he said, were a papal and thus a human and unnecessary appendage to Christianity.[9]

The Catholic feast of the Assumption, celebrated each August 15, honored Mary's final ascension to heaven, and accentuated her sainthood. But for Protestants, Mary was simply the mother of Jesus, and for Socinians, even more radically, the human mother of a merely human Jesus, in no way divine.[10] Protestants, including the Socinians, were appalled that Catholics "ascribe[d] more to Mary the Virgin than to the Lord God."[11] Marian devotion, the art in the Marian chapel in the church in Tarłów, such as the frescoes depicting Mary's life from immaculate conception to ascension to heaven, were a specific strategy to oppose anti-Trinitarians and a broader strategy against all Protestants.

The second chapel in the church in Tarłów was devoted to "the Lord Jesus," a theme that represented devotional and polemical streams in contemporary Catholic religiosity. The Church's focus on the meaning of Jesus' death and suffering, omnipresent in devotional works, sermons, and church art from the period, was a response to anti-Trinitarian questioning of the salvatory significance of Jesus' death.[12] His death and his spilled blood saved humanity, so the Catholics argued. Jesus' suffering for humanity's sins, emphasized in Catholic art, literature, and sermons, reaffirmed these dogmas.[13] A book dedicated to Jesus' suffering by the eighteenth-century Catholic preacher Alexander Dowgiało provided countless

examples of saints or holy people who had suffered voluntarily in commemora-
tion of Jesus' own pain.[14] Dowgiało called on Catholics to remember Jesus and
weep for him: "The most merciful Jesus, you have said to the Blessed Veronique, a
maiden from the order of St. Augustine, 'I wish that all people would suffer with
me suffering by remembering my torment.'"[15]

The rejuvenated cults of saints, Marian devotion, and devotion to the suffering
Christ became, in turn, subjects of further condemnation by Protestants. Kraiński
bemoaned that Catholics worshipped Mary more than God and cited eight holidays
devoted to Mary as a proof. "The papists," Kraiński wrote, "celebrate more holidays
in honor of Mary than in honor of God, for they only celebrate one holiday devoted
to God, who is one in Trinity."[16] In a book outlining Calvinist doctrines and worship,
also written by Kraiński and published in three editions in the seventeenth century,[17]
the elders of Calvinist congregations in Małopolska, Little Poland, offered a critique
of the newly established Gregorian, Catholic calendar: "And they added so many
holidays to this calendar that even the situation of the Jews is better, for they – as
Erasmus tells us – had a reasonable number of holidays and now there is no end to
them.... In this Calendar they put one saint above the next, they build churches
and altars to some, paint paintings and give offerings, but to some they will even
light a candle.... They put the holiday of St. John and St. Peter etc. above the
holiday of the Holy Trinity or the Lord's circumcision."[18]

Protestants had reason to feel uncomfortable with Catholic holidays because the
Church, in an effort to achieve uniformity of festivals, often (and especially in the
seventeenth and eighteenth centuries) tried to compel them to attend these festivals. In 1689, the bishop of Cracow, Jan Małachowski, reported to Rome that he had
ordered "all heretics, Calvinists and Lutherans alike" in his diocese, notably in the
cities of Cracow and Lublin, to participate in the public processions during celebrations of Corpus Christi under "severe penalty" should they absent themselves.[19] In
1716, Bishop Kazimierz Łubieński of Cracow reported similar measures, in line with
the synodal legislation enacted in the diocese five years before, according to which
Protestants were to "help diligently" during the celebrations of Corpus Christi and
its Octave.[20] Bishop Konstantyn Felicjan Szaniawski, in 1725, dispatched a pastoral
letter to his flock of the diocese of Cracow that said Protestants "should apply
themselves diligently and observe feasts and holidays according to the Roman calendar. And they should not compel Christian families or those under their power
[subditos] to violate them or to violate fasts."[21] Szaniawski was referring to Catholic
servants in Protestant homes.

Protestant criticisms of the Catholic calendar were a form of self-defense against
the imposition of Catholic worship.[22] Kraiński's *Postylla*, a prime example, provided
counter-sermons pointing to the human origins of Catholic holidays and their
"idolatrous" nature. Protestants sometimes, if somewhat less frequently, employed
references to Jews to underline the impropriety of Catholic worship, criticizing
practices by some Catholics, who stopped working on Saturday afternoon, or who

refused to perform certain types of work, "in honor of Mary the Virgin. . . . And so the Papists profess dead Jewish religion [*żydowstwo pogrzebione*] and total heresy on the account of Saturday."[23]

The Protestant polemicist Woyciech Węgierski spoke against Catholicism in a spirit reminiscent of Christian ripostes to Jewish post-biblical tradition: "Oh, how greatly mislead themselves and others those who replaced the Holy Scripture with traditions, customs and human decrees under a grand name of the *verbum Dei non scriptum*, the unwritten word of God." He continued, "And not only do they equate it with the Holy Scripture but they even favor it over the Word of God and base their faith on it."[24] Perhaps Węgierski tried to imply, as some other Protestant polemicists did more explicitly, that Catholicism with its rituals was like Judaism.[25] Jews were, indeed, an oft-employed tool in Christian religious polemic.

CHALLENGING THE PROTESTANTS BY UNDERMINING THE JEWS

Among some Catholic works that at first glance appear to be defending Catholic doctrines against Jewish challenges may, in fact, have also been rebuttals of Protestant beliefs.[26] Religious arguments aimed ostensibly at Jews, who did not accept Christian dogmas such as the Trinity, the messiahship and divinity of Jesus, or worship of saints and Mary, coincidentally addressed issues at the core of the battle between Catholics and Protestants.[27] These polemical works were reminiscent of pre-thirteenth-century Christian polemic against Jews, which was based solely on the Bible, and, unlike other anti-Jewish works in Poland and elsewhere,[28] ignored post-biblical Jewish literature, which would have been useless in combat against Protestants.[29] This roundabout strategy of using anti-Jewish religious polemic in defense of Catholic beliefs against Protestants was characteristic of the Church's assaults against anti-Trinitarians, whose doctrines the Church sometimes construed as "judaizing."

Even after the eventual expulsion of anti-Trinitarians from Poland in 1658, Catholics continued to feel compelled to affirm the dogma of the Trinity, which both anti-Trinitarians and Jews had disputed. As late as the 1700s, decades after the expulsion of the anti-Trinitarians, at least one bishop reported that certain "Arians" were still in Poland.[30] The clergy considered a continued polemic against them still relevant. So too the laws *ex regestro arianismi*, which by the eighteenth century embraced different kinds of transgressions against the hegemony of the Catholic Church, assured that even if the "Arians" were no longer present in person in Poland, their ideas remained part of the religious discourse.[31] In June 1691, Bishop Andrzej Chryzostom Załuski delivered a sermon in Warsaw in which he felt compelled to affirm the dual nature of Jesus, his divinity and humanity. "And [the apostles] want[ed] to convert Jews, a stubborn people constantly rebelling against God. [A people] that did not believe Jesus himself. They want[ed] to persuade them that the crucified one, while a human, was also God."[32]

Debate over the validity of the Bible and its prophecies had been central to
the Jewish-Christian polemic for centuries, and had also appeared in polemics
within Islam.[33] Yet, at least until the thirteenth century, Jews were regarded by
Christians as guardians of the Scripture and as witnesses, albeit blind, to the truth
of Christianity.[34] And it was this assumption that, at least theoretically, allotted Jews
a place within Christianity, despite differences of biblical interpretations between
Jews and Christians. In the thirteenth century, however, questions were raised
about the reliability of the Jewish Bible, some Christian scholars charging that
Jews had falsified the scriptures in order to conceal their prophecies about Jesus
and his messiahship.[35] The Jewish response to the Christian accusation of falsi-
fication of the Scriptures was a counterclaim that some of the conflict of interpretations stemmed from Latin mistranslations of the Hebrew Bible by Christian
scholars.[36]

One Latin translation of the Bible, the Vulgate, completed at the turn of the
fourth and fifth centuries by Jerome and accepted by the Catholic Church, became
most vulnerable to the challenges. Its validity was not questioned by Jews alone;
in the Middle Ages certain Christian scholars also criticized it.[37] But not until the
spread of humanism, the coming of the Reformation, and the discovery of printing
did the Vulgate's problematic nature present a serious threat to the validity of the
Church's religious authority, for it was not a matter of the translation only but
was also of the Church's reliance on a flawed version of the Bible for its teachings,
doctrines, and exegesis.

With the humanist, and subsequently also the Protestant, revival of the doctrine
hebraica veritas, asserting the validity and reliability of the Hebrew Scriptures as
preserved by Jews, and with a growing Christian interest in the Hebrew language
in Western Europe, the Church was forced to defend the version it had been relying
on for centuries.[38] It did so at the Council of Trent by asserting the authenticity of
the Latin Vulgate:

Moreover, the same sacred and holy Synod – considering that no small utility may
accrue to the Church of God, if it be made known which out of all the Latin editions,
now in circulation, of the sacred books, is to be held as authentic – ordains and declares,
that the said old and vulgate edition, which, by the lengthened usage of so many years,
has been approved of in the Church, be, in public lectures, disputations, sermons and
expositions, held as authentic; and that no one is to dare, or presume to reject it under
any pretext whatever.[39]

In Poland, this canon on the authenticity of the Latin Vulgate was accepted
with other Tridentine canons in 1577 and reaffirmed in Polish synods in the first
half of the eighteenth century, coinciding with the brief renaissance of Polish-
language Protestant publications.[40] In this canon, the Church was responding to
new biblical scholarship. Humanists, and Protestants later, published their revised
editions, placing the validity of the Vulgate at issue. Protestants criticized too the

Church's restrictions on reading and interpreting the Bible as a ruse to lead "simple people away from the Holy Scriptures."[41] In this context of newly emerging biblical criticism based on the Hebrew Bible and the Protestant emphasis on the biblical text, the medieval Christian accusations, incorporated into early modern Polish polemical literature, that Jews corrupted the Bible may have been a conscious choice of arguments as ammunition against Protestant challenges to the validity of Catholic doctrines. By challenging the validity of the Hebrew Scriptures as preserved by Jews, Catholic polemicists sought to remove the very source on which Protestants based some of their own attacks on Catholicism and its version of the Scriptures.[42] What might appear as a traditional medieval anti-Jewish argument also represented in this context a voice in the Catholic contest with Protestants.

"THE HERETICS ARE TRULY WORSE"

The most explicit, and complex, example of the double use of religious polemic against both Jews and Protestants appears in Marek Korona's 1645 work, written in a popular form of a dialogue between a Catholic theologian, a rabbi, and, on the sidelines, an anti-Trinitarian. In it, Korona, a prolific Franciscan writer,[43] argued that Catholics alone should be trusted with the veracity of the Bible. With biblical textual criticism still in its infancy, Korona contended that the Church had received the original texts of the Bible, both "Old and New Testament," from Jewish sages right after the destruction of the Temple in 70 CE. These original texts, Korona asserted, were now securely guarded by the distinguished prelates in the Vatican.[44] Only false versions were in the hands of Jews, who were not careful to guard the text but stored it "near stoves and children."[45] This peculiar explanation probably referred to the instruction of small Jewish boys in the Torah, which often took place in the house of the teacher. Whatever the meaning, Korona managed to remove the claims of *hebraica veritas* and, thereby – at one stroke – to undermine the Protestant argument against the Vulgate, at the same time asserting the validity of the Catholic Scriptures and the religious authority of the Church and its "distinguished prelates." Korona's explanation also underscored the direct link between the era of the Temple in Jerusalem and Rome. Still, the Franciscan writer was unique in making this claim: his book referred to the Hebrew language, enhancing its value as *lingua sacra et casta*, holy and pure language, which, so Korona claimed, was spoken by Jesus in Paradise.[46]

The Trinity and the nature of Christ, like the validity of the Catholic Bible, were subjects of disagreement between Catholics and Jews, and between Catholics and radical Protestants. An anonymous late-sixteenth-century Polish author asserted decisively, "We only have one God the Father."[47] He mocked the Catholic belief in Trinity, "and the priests fool simple people, claiming that there is only one God they call him a Trinity. Just as one coin will not be four,[48] nor will our one God be three."[49] In addressing such questions the Catholic apologists had multiple strategies: anti-Jewish polemic, anti-Protestant polemic, and, with a successful refutation of arguments that challenged the Catholic teaching, reassurance for Catholics themselves. Here too Korona can serve as an interesting example. He employed the tetragrammaton, YHWH, as a proof of the Trinity:

It is not without reason that God's name is made of three letters, because the first letter, Y, which is at the beginning, signifies the first Divine Person, that is, the Father from whom the other two Persons [in the Trinity] stem. The second letter, H, signifies the second Person, for it means *respirationis* [resting, breathing], and it is the Person of the eternal word, about whom St. John says: *quod omne factum est, in ipso vita erat.*[50] The third letter, W, means unity, and this is the expression of the third Person, the Holy Spirit that comes from the Father and Son and ties them together and is *nexus Patris et Filii.*[51]

In Korona's book, the rabbi agreed with the above explanation of the meaning of the tetragrammaton but pointed out that there were four, not three, elements in this name of God. Korona's Catholic theologian, not surprisingly, had an answer, responding that the second occurrence of the letter H symbolized the Son's two appearances: first, through a timeless birth without a Mother, only with a Father; and second, on earth, without a Father and with a Mother.[52] All this was accepted by Korona's rabbi, who, in turn, offered his own proof of the Trinity, using the first word from the Hebrew Bible in a slightly corrupted form, *beresit* [Hebr. *be-r'eshit*, at the beginning]. The Hebrew letter *bet*, he stated, signified *ben* (Son), *resh* meant *ruaḥ* (Spirit), *'aleph* stood for *'ab* (Father) and is also the first letter of the alphabet – the beginning of everything – and *sit*, like in Latin, "indicates *factum est.*" And, he concluded, all that meant that these personages were indivisible.[53] The explanations by Korona's rabbi would not have worked had he maintained the actual structure of the word – *be-r'eshit*, not *beresit.*

   This was not the first time a Christian polemicist had used the first word in the Hebrew Bible, *be-r'eshit*, to prove the Trinity, ignoring the remaining three letters that do not support that argument. Indeed, Korona's argument is of medieval roots; in the Middle Ages, this word was a source of disagreement. In a thirteenth-century work against Christianity, a Jewish polemicist challenged this very interpretation of the Hebrew word *be-r'eshit*. "A Gentile defiantly asked a Jew: Why did the Holy One, blessed be he, begin his Torah with the word *Bereshit* [in the beginning]? The reason is that by doing so he referred to the son [*ben*], the holy spirit [*ruaḥ*], and the father [*'ab*]. The Jew answered him: You have expounded the *bet, resh*, and *aleph*, as you wished. Now finish the word and you will find *shin, yod, tav*; these too constitute an acrostic."[54] Korona's rabbi, unlike the actual Jewish polemicists, ignored the Hebrew spelling and used the Latin to solve the problem of extra letters. Not many people would have recognized such manipulation, for not many Polish Catholics knew Hebrew. Instead, Korona, as the author, presented himself as an authority in the Hebrew Scriptures, thereby managing to reclaim the Scriptures from both

Protestants and Jews, who claimed the same. Korona sought, simultaneously, to validate Catholic interpretation. His Catholic theologian enlisted the rabbi as his ally, underscoring his own competency but also affirming his, and thereby the generally Catholic, correct understanding of the divine message concealed in the Scriptures. After all, it is through this ostensibly competent argument that he was successful in convincing the Jew – a member of the people who for centuries had challenged the validity of Christianity and of Christian interpretation of the biblical prophecies.

Another use of this method was in the debate over the nature of Jesus. Although the rabbi embraced the idea of the Trinity he could not understand the Catholic claim for the divinity of Jesus, who was born in flesh. Korona's anti-Trinitarian seconded the Jew's doubt, only to be dismissed – ironically by a Catholic – for not knowing his Bible.[55] To convince the Jew, and to refute the anti-Trinitarian claims, Korona turned to the *gematria*, a system of calculation employed in Jewish mysticism that attaches numerical values to Hebrew words based on the numerical values of the letters in the Hebrew alphabet. Korona argued that according to the *gematria*, the numerical value of YHWH is 26, that of Miriam [Mary] is 290, and that of Jesus [*Yeshu*] is 316. It is clear, Korona concluded, that Jesus' numerical value (316) is a sum of YHWH (26) and Miriam (290) – of the God and the human mother,[56] and hence one has a proof of Jesus' dual nature. The Catholic writer had skillfully crafted an attack on Polish anti-Trinitarians by using Jews and arguments taken from anti-Jewish polemics. At the end, Korona's rabbi is converted to Catholicism while the anti-Trinitarian remains unmoved.[57]

The failure to convert the anti-Trinitarian was not a sign of the Catholic theologian's failure or lack of polemical skills, but a careful rhetorical construct that judged heretics worse even than Jews. At least Jews in Catholic works of religious polemic and reassurance, despite their errors and sins, potentially could be converted if appropriately approached. Heretics, on the other hand, were obstinate and unwilling to see religious truths even in the face of a convincing argument.

Depending on the purpose of a particular polemical work, Polish Catholic writers created a twofold, but interdependent, picture of a Jew. On the one hand, as we have seen, in writings on social and political issues, they perpetuated an image of the Jew as a dangerous enemy of Christians and Christianity – an enemy to be avoided. On the other hand, in Catholic works pertaining to religious polemics against Protestants, Catholic writers asserted that the Jew, despite his sins and initial rejection of Christianity, became a possible convert to Catholicism, and his conversion proved the validity of the doctrines of "the only True Christian Church."[58]

In this way, rhetorically constructed Jews who came to accept the Catholic interpretation of the Bible served both as a refutation of Protestant anti-Catholic arguments and as a reassurance of the truth of Christianity. Such books, to be sure, were intended for Catholic audiences, for it is unlikely that many Protestants, or Jews, would purchase and read books hostile to them and their beliefs. These works were intended to preempt the questions Catholics themselves might have had about their own religion and to reassure them that their religion was true because, as Roch Trucki claimed, that religion "was transmitted by the Holy Spirit through the Church."[59]

In preaching and other homiletic works, which had no room for elaborate religious arguments, Jews were converted not necessarily through intellectual reasoning but through witnessing miracles performed by the saints or by Mary, another area of dispute between Catholics and Protestants. Catholic preachers used books of lives of saints or collections of exempla as illustrations to underscore their message.

The tale of the "fallen Agnieszka," related earlier, represents a group of exempla in which a conversion of a Jew occurs because of Mary's intercession.[60] Agnieszka, a servant and a wet nurse in a Jewish home, was visited by Mary and resurrected, which in turn led to the conversion of her Jewish mistress and her children. Another tale from the same collection tells of a Jewish girl, Rachel, who, "inspired" by Mary, converted to Catholicism and, though still a child under the canonical age of twelve, became a nun, assuming the name Mary. Rachel's parents tried to take her back, but she persisted because she could feel "Mary's presence."[61]

Some stories are of conversions that resulted from the intervention of a saint. One, explicit in its use of Jewish conversion to buttress Catholic doctrine against Protestant challenges, appears in a collection of sermons by a Jesuit preacher, Stanisław Bielicki. It tells the story of a Jew said to have been converted in Cracow during the Northern War with Protestant Sweden (1700–21).[62] The Polish Royal Army was building a bridge over a river in the presence of the Polish king Augustus II, his generals, two Catholic bishops,[63] and a prominent Jew, "an agent of the General Commissar Bliwernicz." The Swedes cut the bridge's ropes, and the Jew, who was standing nearby, fell into the water and began to drown, whereupon the Catholic bishops prayed to St. Stanislaus, who was said to have crossed that very river with dry feet. This legend evoked mockery among the Protestant royal generals in Augustus II's Saxon army. Why, the Protestant generals asked, if the saint had crossed the river with dry feet, did he not save the Jew? The bishops continued to pray intensely, and the Jew miraculously did survive. The Protestants had been proven wrong and the Jew was converted, taking a new name, Stanislaus, acknowledging the power of saints and the efficacy of prayers to them. Such stories of conversions to Catholicism consoled the Church and "proved" that it held the key to the divine truth.[64] This particular tale also significantly illustrates the anxiety of the Church about the prominence of Lutherans within the royal court under Augustus II.

Protestants, understanding the propagandistic nature of Catholic use of Jewish converts, fought back. Krzysztof Kraiński stated bluntly: "It is an appropriate thing to teach Christian faith to an adult infidel before he is baptized. Not as the Papists do, they don't teach the faith to the Jew, or the Turk, or Tatar, and that we can see with a bare eye. Instead they prepare a great spectacle with splendor in order to affirm their idolatry and to fool [dla zmamienia] simple people."[65]

For Catholics, real or imagined Jewish converts served to underline the obstinacy of the Protestants. For that reason, Catholic writers described Protestants as worse than Jews.[66] And Jews, this time not as potential converts but as a highly pejorative construct created in anti-Jewish rhetoric, highlighted the gravity of Protestant errors. An early eighteenth-century Dominican preacher, Woyciech Ochabowicz, argued in a sermon that although Jewish infidelity was worse than the nonbelief of the pagans, the heretics were the worst of all.[67] Another eighteenth-century preacher – the Franciscan Marceli Dziewulski – evoked in a sermon "the crucified" Simon of Trent[68] and turned to New Testament imagery to maintain that, although Jews had killed Jesus, they had left Mary in peace. "The heretics are truly worse," he continued, as if speaking to Mary herself, "because they treaded not only on [your] Son's but also on your honor: they reviled, mangled, gashed and burnt your holy images."[69] Here, Dziewulski not only portrayed Jews as better, so to speak, than Protestants, but, in referring to Protestant iconoclasm, depicted Protestants in a manner that evoked the stereotypes of Jews as desecrators of Catholic images and as killers of Christian children from premodern anti-Jewish rhetoric.[70]

"BLINDNESS," "OBSTINACY," AND "BLASPHEMIES": ANTI-JEWISH SOURCES OF ANTI-PROTESTANT ASSAULTS

Dziewulski was not alone in evoking anti-Jewish stereotypes and accusations as means of combating Protestants. In a sermon for the Thursday before Easter, an anonymous eighteenth-century preacher turned to the theme of the suffering of Jesus in the Eucharist as a way of underscoring Protestant sins, evoking imagery of the desecration of the host familiar from anti-Jewish works: "And what should I say about the hideous ingratitude from which our Savior Jesus suffered in the most precious Eucharist, and still suffers, and will suffer until the end of the world because of the cruel godlessness of the infidel people? He has suffered in the holy host many times from the vicious Jews. And not once was He thrown out of the pyx, trampled by their feet or thrown into the fire to be burnt by blind heretics pillaging holy Catholic churches."[71]

By evoking medieval images of Jewish desecration of the host, the preacher was underlining the doctrinal conflict between the Church and the Protestants, and at the same time, managing to compare Protestants to Jews as enemies of God and Christianity.[72] As a result of Protestant challenges to the Catholic doctrine of transubstantiation (among other things), one can notice an increased Catholic interest in stories of host desecration performed by both Jews and Protestants in the sixteenth century and also a revival of Eucharistic cult among Catholics.[73] This parallels in some ways the developments of such stories in the Middle Ages, when the Church sought to convince society of the validity of this newly sanctioned doctrine.[74] The stories of miracles were "a proof" that the Church's teachings on transubstantiation were true. But Protestants openly challenged this doctrine. One such author noted that the priests were like witches, using magic to fool people: "And the priest, dressed up and [equipped] with all kinds of instruments in front of him – candles, bells, crosses, and wine – huffs and puffs, turns around, then eats and drinks himself without sharing, and fools people in charming the wafer."[75] He also noted that the Catholics were willing to do anything to defend this doctrine against Protestant challenges, including fabricating stories of miracles. "And as for this bread they worship during mass as God. . . . They killed many people over it. [They say] when Jews allegedly secretly receive it, they prick it, pick it and drain blood from it. (As it happened in Sochaczew some time ago, for which several Jews lost their heads.) And female tavern-keepers and witches also use it in their magic, and sometimes they feed it to cows."[76]

At the height of the Reformation in Poland, the Polish polemicist Benedict Herbest cited miracle stories of the Eucharist to buttress Church doctrines about the Eucharist and to emphasize Protestant blindness – another parallel with a common description of Jews. Following a story about a Calvinist woman who had desecrated the host, Herbest invoked the image of Jewish blindness, implying that Protestants too did not "see" the miracles, just as Jews in their blindness "did not want to accept the miracles and the teachings of the Lord."[77] He followed with another story in which a blind girl was cured by witnessing the Eucharist during celebrations of Corpus Christi. Herbest argued that accepting "God's Most Holy Body" and, thereby, Church doctrines about it, had removed the blindness from her eyes, a metaphor that referred to both Jews and Protestants.[78]

By the late seventeenth and eighteenth centuries, as noted earlier, stories of desecration of the host by Jews had lost their appeal in explicitly anti-Jewish literature in Poland, but their symbolism remained powerful in disputes with the Protestants. Bishop Mikołaj Popławski, whose writings did not hide his feelings against Jews,[79] summarized the Church's attitudes toward Protestant challenges on the Eucharist without even mentioning Jews. "In the current age," he wrote, "we no longer live among idolaters, but we live among heretics who concoct various false opinions about the Most Holy Sacrament. Some [claim] that there is no real body [of Christ in the Eucharist], that it is only a symbol [*figura*], [some claim] that it is only bread etc., etc.; let's fend off these idols with our faith, let us condemn the heretical errors, let us profess that here is the real flesh and blood of Jesus and let us give thanks for all this grace."[80] In this context earlier anti-Jewish polemic offered a great deal of material. The Eucharist served as a conduit to show the enmity against the Church of those who fell outside of it. It came to be seen as one more example of what divided "true Christians" from the rest.[81]

The topic of the Eucharist illustrates a tendency of the Polish clergy to assault the Protestants directly and indirectly with methods and with a tone familiar from the anti-Jewish polemic: by pairing Jews and heretics or drawing on imagery found in anti-Jewish works to apply to heretics, or by enacting laws that paralleled those enacted against Jews. And this should not be surprising because both were perceived as threats to Catholic purity and Church authority, and both, therefore, needed to be controlled.

The Catholic clergy's anti-Protestant sentiments, and the legal steps taken against Protestants, are reminders that the Church was fighting a larger battle to eliminate or neutralize by all feasible means any group perceived as a challenge to its hegemony. To prevent the spread of heresy, the Church had resorted to dehumanizing rhetoric that resembled its own earlier and continuing rhetoric against Jews, though sometimes without even mentioning Jews. As the Jews were earlier, heretics were sometimes linked to the devil or described as united with "the powers of the fiends from hell," as one anonymous preacher stated.[82] Another anonymous preacher discussing the Eucharist evoked a medieval tale of a heretic who tried to show Christ, Mary, and the saints to a Dominican friar. The friar did not trust him and, suspecting "a devil's" trick, took the Eucharist with him. The two went to a splendid palace with all kinds of marvels, and apparent saints, and angels. There the heretic fell on his knees and bowed down before what he thought was God. The friar remained standing. The heretic was shocked at the friar's arrogance, but the friar took the Eucharist and turned to the "Queen Mary." If she indeed was Mary, he said, then the wafer was her son. As a result of this the palace crumbled, demonstrating that the heretic was seduced by the devil. Predictably, the heretic accepted Catholicism.[83]

This complex story links the heretic to the devil but in an intricate way. The palace seems to resemble a Catholic, perhaps even a baroque, church, in which there would have been statues of saints, angels, God, Jesus, and Mary the Queen. Yet, it was an illusory or even false church, not the real *Domus Dei* – as churches were viewed in early modern Catholicism – for God neither founded it nor was present there.[84] When confronted with the true God, Christ, represented by the Eucharist, this fake church crumbled. The tale emphasized the verity of the Catholic Eucharistic doctrine of divine presence in the wafer itself. So, though Catholics might be seduced by what appeared to be the true religion, they must resist "a devil's trick," and rely instead on the Church.

Like Jews in anti-Jewish rhetoric,[85] heretics were sometimes depicted as even worse than the devil. One anonymous preacher raged over the Lutheran and Calvinist attitudes to fasting. "As we come to the point, let's listen first how heretical obstinacy [*zawziętość*] attacks the prescribed fast ... [according to heretical teachings] all fasting is ugly and detestable in the eyes of God, and gluttony, drunkenness, voracity are more pleasing to God than observing fasts, that is the heresiarch's reasoning about fasts, he believes it because he himself gorges worse than a beast ... and he blasphemed with his wicked tongue, even the devil would be ashamed to say what this blasphemer said of the fasts."[86] Further on, reverting to the more common comparison, the preacher compared Lutherans and

Calvinists to the devil, who – according to the Gospels of Mark, Matthew, and Luke – tempted Jesus during his retreat in the desert.[87] In its rhetorical application of the devil, notions of obstinacy and carnality, and dehumanizing language, this anti-Protestant passage closely resembles Catholic anti-Jewish rhetoric, in which carnality and the devil were favorite themes for combating religious enemies.

Protestants paid the Catholics back in kind. Krainski wrote a series of powerful sermons for the Sunday before Ash Wednesday, condemning Catholic fasts and arguing that fasts led to sin and served the devil because they were preceded by feasts of food, drinking, and dancing until the merrymakers vomited and dropped.[88] Krainski branded gluttony a Catholic practice. "It is no surprise," he wrote, "that the seduced Christians stuff their stomachs up with meat and eat it voraciously. The priests forbid them to eat meat during the fast, so they want to eat as much as they can during those crazy days, in order to make up for the upcoming fast."[89] He warned "the true Christians who call themselves Evangelicals" to avoid such celebrations and especially feasting, since they would not share the fasting.[90]

In 1616, a Protestant synod noted that one of its ministers, Reverend Grzegorz Jankowski, had returned to Catholicism, "a Roman Babylon, from which God led him away."[91] His move was explained by his inability to live a simple life; "he was seduced by gluttony [and greed] and he could not think of anything else but property and bread and other earthly things."[92] Carnality had led him back to Catholicism. In 1637, a Protestant synod ruled that fasting was refraining not only from some foods, as Catholics held, but also "from all foods and drinks, from sleeping and all carnal pleasures, such as drunkenness, dance, gambling, hunting. . . . And these are to be observed not to earn something with God, nor as a part of divine worship, but as a method of mortifying the body, [arousing] humbleness . . . so that one can contemplate divine matters more peacefully."[93]

In Christian anti-Jewish polemics, Jews had long been represented as "carnal" in contrast to "spiritual" Christians. Beginning with Paul's statement in I Corinthians (10:18), referring to "Israel of the flesh," and through Augustinian interpretation of this and other biblical passages, "carnality" had become associated with Jews.[94] But Jewish carnality was mostly sexual, in part as a consequence of the Jewish observance of the circumcision.[95] In Christian rhetoric, carnality was associated more generally with lack of control over all passions of the flesh, sexual or otherwise. According to Paul, "the passions of the flesh wage war against [the] soul" (I Peter 2:11). And, after all, gluttony was one of the seven deadly sins.[96] Because of the Protestant rejection of fasts established by the Catholic Church as "works," Catholic preachers exaggerated rejection of fasting as a sign of "carnality" and of inability to control bodily passions.

Protestants themselves called Catholic fasts passions of the flesh that led to promiscuity and to uncontrollable eating and drinking before the fasts began. Indeed, Catholic fasts were even worse than the Jews' rejection of certain foods because Jews did not follow orders of bishops or priests but rather followed the order of God himself, and did so with conviction.[97] As for Jews, it seems that, in Poland, their "passions of the flesh" could not be associated with gluttony because Jews did observe fasts (albeit, as the Christians argued, fasts rejected by God),[98] and refrained from certain foods. It was sexuality instead that highlighted Jewish carnality in anti-Jewish rhetoric, represented in Poland by discussion of the corruption of Christian women.[99] As for Protestants, because they did not observe circumcision, their carnality was frequently represented as indulgence in food.[100]

It was a battle between the spirit and the flesh, the divine and the corporeal, the true and the false. The late seventeenth-century Polish Catholic preacher Alexander Lorencowic cited a lack of self-discipline among Protestants,[101] and another quoted John Chrysostom as stating that honoring fasts was not about abstaining from food but about fleeing from sins, therefore not carnal and earthly, but spiritual.[102] A popular Catholic catechism stated openly that carnality was the root of heresy.[103] The Polish word used for carnality in the catechism, *cielesność*, has sexual undertones, bringing the rhetoric perhaps a step closer to the sexualization of Jewish carnality.[104]

In the late seventeenth and in the eighteenth centuries, again despite the apparent decline of Protestantism, the language of anti-Protestant polemic became even more inflammatory and dehumanizing. In one example, Luther and Lutherans were referred to as gorging beasts.[105] In others, Protestants were called larvae and vermin. Jan Krosnowski, in his 1689 collection of sermons, said that because of the works of Jesuits, "this pestilence [Protestant heresy] ebbed away significantly and by God's grace, now we cannot see a single heretic in the senate, and the cities purified themselves greatly from this heretical vermin."[106] Despite the Jesuit's self-proclaimed victory over heresy in Poland, which most historians have accepted, Catholic clergy persisted with a rhetoric of siege. The eighteenth-century preacher Marceli Dziewulski referred to Lutherans and Calvinists as "ungrateful rabble full of carion and venom," and an anonymous eighteenth-century preacher compared Poland to Egypt and Protestants to "the larvae of heretics that are spreading, threatening to destroy [us], while we sit in the darkness."[107]

Heretics were often represented as an internal threat, as a sickness that attacked the holy body of the Church from within. One preacher compared the new religious denominations to leprosy,[108] while the popular catechism stated that these "heretics" were more dangerous than those infected with the plague.[109] The 1745 synod of Chełmno and Pomerania, in the northern territories of Poland, exhorted the nobles not to "infect their towns and villages" by employing heretics, and urged them to preserve these places in their Catholic purity.[110] The language of sickness predominated.

Jews, by contrast, were commonly perceived by the Church as external enemies, who threatened the morality of the Christians and corrupted them through material temptations and power. But Jews were not "wolves in sheep's clothing," as the 1744 synod of Wilno had said of Protestant clergy,[111] corrupting from within the Church.

Protestants claimed they too were Christians, celebrated similar major holidays, and came from within the Church; hence, they were especially threatening and to be avoided at all costs. To be sure, Jews threatened religious purity by leading some Christians to apostasy, but they were outsiders who identified themselves as such and were also more easily distinguishable because they celebrated different holidays and ate different foods, even if they sometimes dressed similarly and perhaps even spoke the same language.

In a 1718 sermon delivered in the cloister of the Franciscan order in Cracow, one apparently Carmelite preacher expressed his angst about intermixing between Catholics and "heretics." "It is no one else," he wrote, "but Heretics – Lutherans, Calvinists, Atheists – who have mixed with Christ's Faithful [*pomieszali się między wiernemi Chrystusowemi*]. It is they who disrupt and break peace among Christians, who tear off Polish adornment. It is they who violate the true faith among true Catholics [*prawowierni*]."[112] Clearly addressing the powerful lords and illustrating the complexity of the conflict between the lords and the Church, the preacher continued:

These enemies of the Republic [i.e. Poland] hide and secretly teach the Machiavellian treason of their sects. They have mixed with the faithful, and who shall recognize them? There are plenty of atheists, Lutheran heretics at the manorial estates [*po dworach pańskich*], there are many Lutherans in royal offices, Lutherans not only hold but rather forcefully take [*zdzierają*] starosties, tolls, leases of estates. There are many Lutherans in our camp, many Lutherans and Calvinists are now presidents, councilors, burghers and merchants in Polish towns.... Where are all [the laws] passed by the Sejms, Councils and Royal Constitutions? This lawlessness brings the latest destruction to the Polish Crown.[113]

This preacher's voice clearly contradicted the self-congratulatory tone of Jan Krosnowski, and reflected the Church anxiety about the continuing presence of Protestants in Poland. Reminiscent of the Catholic preachers' accusations against Jews of political influence through their connections to nobles,[114] it emphasized heretics' infiltration of Poland and their threat to Poland's purity, leading the country to ruin, leasing estates and "controlling" Polish towns. Those who allowed heretics to flourish were blamed for Poland's dire political and economic conditions. They would be punished by finding a place of "eternal cohabitation [in hell] with your Jews and heretics, with whom you now meet and enter into business relations."[115] It was not "the Republic" that was at risk but rather the ideal Republic that would rid itself of non-Catholic enemies and, by extension, submit to the rule of the Church.[116] That submission was not easy to attain, and the Church found that out as it confronted Polish nobles who maintained business relationships with Jews.

Sometimes without even mention of Jews, anti-Protestant statements drew deeply from anti-Jewish writings. Salient parallels with anti-Jewish works are apparent in the language and topics used by the Church to combat Protestants, whom Catholic writers portrayed as blind, obstinate, and dehumanized, and from whom Catholics should separate at any cost. Anti-Protestant rhetoric demonstrates that the Jews had no monopoly as objects of the vehemence and aversion of Catholic clergy.

In his collection of Catholic teachings, published in 1719, Bishop Krzysztof Szembek wrote,

Q: And whom does the Catholic Church reject, condemn, and curse?
A: The Catholic Church rejects, condemns and curses all pagan errors . . . heresies, and all schisms. It condemns and excludes from the community of the faithful all pagans, Jews, heretics, schismatics, and bad and disobedient Catholics.[117]

This text reiterates more specifically the medieval doctrine of the unity of the Church "without which there is neither salvation nor remission of sins."[118] The Church displayed antipathy for anyone who challenged its claims to divine truth, its claims to authority and, ultimately, to power. Because Jews were the oldest challengers, the Church could draw on their legacy of multilayered pronouncements and actions. In doing so, it further spread anti-Jewish sentiment.

"THEY ARE OBLIGED TO BE SUBORDINATE TO THE DOMINANT RELIGION": LEGISLATIVE MEASURES CONCERNING HERETICS

Like the printers and booksellers, those who were suspected of sympathizing with the new ideas were tried in Cracow at the bishop's court as early as the 1520s and 1530s. In 1522 a priest in a small town of Bienarow near Cracow was accused of sympathizing with Martin Luther.[119] In 1525, Gregier Wójtowicz of Garbarzów, also a small town near Cracow, was accused of Lutheran sympathies because he denied the existence of purgatory and the efficacy of confession.[120] Eating meat during Catholic fast days, too, led to trials of a few. In 1525, the bishop's court heard several cases of persons suspected of sympathizing with the "Lutheran schism" by eating meat during Lent. That same year, a widow, Dorothea Laslowa, was accused of eating meat in the company of a cleric from the Church of the Holy Spirit in Cracow.[121]

Because there were in the first half of the sixteenth century no clear definitions of separate Christian denominations nor laws protecting religious differences, the Church claimed judicial authority over such cases, treating them as cases of Catholics who had fallen into heresy. Thus, in 1530, the synod of Piotrków ordered the clergy to investigate diligently any suspicion of "Lutheran heresy" and any other "perverse doctrine."[122] As late as the seventeenth century, a Polish version of the Roman catechism explained the basis for this claim of authority over "those who fell out of the Church," asserting that the "heretics and schismatics, who fell out of Church because they had broken with it, still belong to the Church, and just as deserters belong to the army from which they fled, so does the Church have authority over them to judge and to punish them."[123]

And if such claims would have been unsurprising in the early sixteenth century, when no defined boundaries between confessions existed, they would have been less so by the eighteenth century, when the Church became even more assertive. Despite then-existing de facto religious divisions, the Church continued to claim authority over non-Catholics. In his *Edictum contra Dissidents*, published in 1725, Bishop Konstantyn Felicjan Szaniawski stressed: "Although because of the connivance of the public laws, the Protestants [*Acatholici*] claim that they are allowed to exercise their religion, nonetheless, in a Catholic kingdom the unworthy [*degentes*] are obliged to be subordinate to the dominant religion and follow its principles."[124]

The Church, in its broad desire to establish control over all those who lived in Poland, issued laws that tried to assert its authority over Protestants by forcing them to observe Catholic holidays or, more specifically, Corpus Christi, a holiday that celebrated the "Holy Eucharist" as the body of Christ, one of the most contentious Catholic doctrines rejected by the Protestants. The law was meant to subjugate Protestants to the rule of the Church, as Bishop Szaniawski wished could be done in his *Edictum contra Dissidents*.[125] But, to be effective, assertions of power were not enough; a set of judicial mechanisms to enforce them would be needed and none existed.[126] Yet, assertions of authority do illustrate the Church's conviction that its authority extended over everyone who lived in its dioceses, while also underlining the constant need for cooperation from the secular arm.

In 1741, Bishop Franciszek Kobielski, of the Łuck and Brest diocese, wrote in a pastoral letter to the Jews of his diocese:

Out of our Pastoral obligation and the authority given to us by God over all neighbors, and regarding you also as our neighbors and desiring your conversion, we commanded the superiors of the Churches in our diocese, having advised you about the time, to demonstrate at least once every four months to you, gathered in your synagogues or schools, the proofs about the Messiah and Incarnated God, from your Prophets and Scriptures, clearly described by Patriarchs, Prophets, and St. David your King of Israel, by the Prophet Jeremiah in your Psalms and other books. [Now] we command you to receive with respect the priests who come to you with God's word and teachings in your schools, and to listen to them.[127]

Like Pope Gregory XIII's overtures to Jews in Rome in 1584, Kobielski's pastoral letter to Jews asserts his "God-given" authority. Jews, Protestants, and all others were to submit to the authority of the Church.

There are a number of parallels in the Church's legal and rhetorical treatment of Protestants and Jews. Ancient Christian laws that had limited the number of Jewish synagogues in towns resurfaced in 1555, in Paul IV's bull *Cum Nimis Absurdum*, and again almost two centuries later, in the early eighteenth century, when Polish Church leaders began to issue similar measures against Protestant churches.[128] In

1711, Bishop Łubieński of Cracow prohibited the construction of new Protestant houses of worship, and in 1720, the synod of the archdiocese of Gniezno ordered demolition of illegal Calvinist and Lutheran churches and full implementation of the 1717 Sejm law that called for a demolition of Protestant churches built after 1674.[129] Aside from the ruling issued in 1542 by Bishop Piotr Gamrat of Cracow concerning synagogues there, apparently none of the rulings by the Church in early modern Poland advocated the destruction of synagogues. Church laws ranged from a prohibition against building new synagogues and restoring the old ones to the same prohibition "without an explicit permission and consent" of the bishop to a blanket permission to rebuild old synagogues.[130] Jews, unlike Protestants, usually received such permissions, if for a fee, a fact that illustrates that the Church was set to eradicate "heresy" but intended to put Jews under their authority, restoring its ideal social and political order and benefiting from it.[131] In fact, in several cases, Protestant churches were turned into synagogues, as it was the case of the originally Calvinist, and then anti-Trinitarian (Arian), church in Wodzisław near Pinczów, or in Orla near Białystok.[132]

Ber of Bolechów, the eighteenth-century Jewish merchant, recounted an event from around 1759 about a permission to reopen a closed synagogue: "And after my brother had proceeded to Brody," Ber wrote in his memoir, "an order came from the new bishop of Lwów, Sierakowski,[133] to close the Holy Synagogue, which remained closed from the Passover to the Feast of Weeks [Shavuot]. I settled this affair for a sum of 20 ducats paid out of my own pocket, after which I procured a license to open the synagogue, written and signed by the bishop; this license is still in my hands."[134] For the price of four casks of wine, Ber secured a permit to reopen a synagogue. The Church had asserted its authority over Jews and profited from it, and Jews were allowed to continue their worship.

Church law treated questions of Protestant ownership and occupancy of real estate in a manner similar to its treatment of questions of Jewish ownership. In 1733, the synod of Płock ruled that "since heretics in the Duchy of Masovia are restrained from dwelling there under a criminal penalty, we prohibit all Catholics from renting their houses, apartment houses [kamienice], cellars, ovens, unless it is limited to the times during fairs or to those traveling."[135] In a similar manner, Church laws had banned the sale or rental of properties to Jews.[136]

In efforts to limit the Catholics' exposure to and contact with Jews or Protestants, Church law in Poland banned public display of religious worship. The 1717 synod of Wilno prohibited both Jews and Protestants from engaging in public processions. Jews were forbidden to wail loudly on their way to cemeteries, and Protestants were forbidden to flaunt their religion publicly in any form, especially to orga- nize processions with singing.[137] Instructions for such processions were included in a seventeenth-century Calvinist manual, or catechism, intended for ministers. The guidelines referred specifically to singing during a funeral on the way to the cemetery.[138] Public display of non-Catholic religious worship and contacts with

either group raised fears of potential heresy among Catholics and of further dete-
rioration in the Church's social and religious control. The Church hoped, by a
full-fledged campaign, to eradicate Protestant religious services altogether. Along
with bans on new places of worship and public processions, several synods and
bishops ruled against any organizing of private worship.[139] Protestant books and
education in "heretical schools" continued to be a target of Church bans.[140] In
its defensive efforts, the Church followed the harshest model available from the
existing Jewry laws enacted by the Church, which in Poland were often ignored or
softened in regard to Jews themselves.

Guarding social and religious purity, some Polish clergy also opposed social
contacts between Catholics and "heretics"[141] lest they lead to feared intermarriage
between Catholics and non-Catholic Christians. Unlike marriages between Jews
and Christians, such marriages were technically not outlawed by Polish law or
canon law,[142] and they must have occurred, since both Protestant and Catholic
sources refer to them.[143]

One preacher compared Catholics whose children married "heretics" to "those
Herods who offer their children to Moloch as a burnt offering."[144] Several diocesan
synods forbade these marriages for fear that the children of such unions would not
be reared as Catholics.[145] Bishop Felicjan Szaniawski of Cracow did permit mixed
marriages *if* the goal was to strengthen Catholicism, that is, "if the offspring coming
from such marriage, male or female, is to follow the matters of the religion of the
Catholic Father or Mother."[146] To lose Catholics to the "heretics" meant, as one
of the preachers put it, "leaving the Church of God" and, for the Church, loss of
religious and social hegemony.[147]

The low level of religious education and doctrinal understanding among the
people no doubt further blurred religious boundaries and exacerbated the Catholic
clergy's anxieties, as an eighteenth-century catechism written and published by
Bishop Szembek testifies:

Q: Is it allowed to join in marriage those who do not know *Pater Noster* and the
basic secrets of the Holy Catholic Faith?

A: No, it is not allowed to join in marriage those who don't know *Pater Noster* or
the basic tenets of the Holy Catholic Faith. Even the banns should not take place
until they learn first the *Pater Noster* and then the secrets of the Holy Catholic
Faith.[148]

The marriage question related another anxiety of the Church – competition
for priestly authority. In his *Edictum contra Dissitentes*, Bishop Szaniawski wrote
that "we severely prohibit marriages to Protestants [*akatolicy*] performed by their
ministers in non-Catholic churches and we order that marriages be contracted
instead in Catholic churches, assisted by appropriate and legitimate priests [*sed
ea in Ecclessiis Catholicis in assistentia proprii et legitimi parochi contrahi debere*

volumus et mandamus]."[149] A similar warning appeared in a Catholic catechism written in a form of questions and answers:

Q: Does a Catholic sin when he is married by a Calvinist minister?
A: Yes, he does. He sins against the Faith because [by engaging in a ceremony led by a Calvinist minister] he regards the minister as a legitimate Canon and shepherd. And that is why children born out of such marriage are not to be eligible for inheritance because they were conceived out of wedlock [*z łoża nieobyczaynego*, lit. in an indecent/immoral bed].[150]

The competition for priestly authority may indicate how permeable the boundaries of religions actually were and how sensitive the Church was about maintaining its religious authority. Like Pope Innocent IV, who in 1248 wrote to the bishop of Maguelonne complaining that Jews wore similar clothes to the clergy, the Catholic synod of Wilno in 1744 prohibited Protestant ministers from wearing outfits similar to those worn by Catholic clergy, lest they be "like wolves in sheep's clothing."[151] The Church appears to have feared that "illegitimate" priests would infiltrate and indoctrinate Catholics in "heretical" teachings. Almost all synodal proceedings from this period include references to priests' garb. At the same time, the Protestant ministers, by wearing clothing similar to Catholic priests, may have been seeking to claim legitimacy for themselves.[152]

The 1711 synod of Cracow admonished Catholics to stay out of Protestant houses of worship; they were not to attend their celebrations and not to listen to their sermons.[153] Protestants, for their part, were forbidden to entice Catholic priests to join Protestant ceremonies.[154] Post-Reformation religious boundaries were clearly still permeable, enhancing the Catholic Church's sense of danger.

In 1733 Bishop Andrzej Stanisław Załuski and the synod of the Płock diocese, of which he was the head, writing about the Protestants, sought to "banish the worst wild beast from among our flock," and "to ward off heretical depravity . . . lest they corrupt even a single heart."[155] The continuation of such pronouncements against Protestantism in the late seventeenth and in the eighteenth centuries demonstrates that the Church still felt under siege, despite the decreasing numbers of Protestants in Poland, a decline many bishops admitted in their reports to Rome,[156] and despite what many scholars have since dubbed "the triumph of the Counter-Reformation."[157] The Church continued to live in the era of the "Counter Reformation," and did not seem to notice its "triumph."[158]

Conclusion: Did the Counter-Reformation Triumph in Poland?

G ENERATIONS OF HISTORIANS FROM THE EARLY TWENTIETH CENTURY TO the present have agreed on the common view that the Counter-Reformation triumphed in Poland. If there has been a debate about these matters, it has usually been limited to the timing.[1] Did the Counter-Reformation triumph before or after mid-seventeenth century, when wars with non-Catholic neighbors plagued Poland-Lithuania and the anti-Trinitarians were expelled? A number of events and trends have been cited as evidence: the decline of the number of Protestants in Poland, including the decline in their Senate representation, in students of Protestant schools, in church membership and number of churches, and in the number of Protestant books published.[2] Also taken as evidence of the Catholic triumph were the 1658 expulsion of the anti-Trinitarians, who dispersed throughout Western and Central Europe, and the anti-Protestant laws – peaking in the first half of the eighteenth century – that prohibited the building of new Protestant churches and restricted political rights by banning Protestants from political posts. Scholars of culture have pointed also to the increased number of new Catholic churches built in the baroque era and to the dominance of Catholic devotional works in the numbers of books published in Poland after the end of the sixteenth century.

This view of the "triumph of the Counter-Reformation" has been accepted both by the Catholic historians who cherished the "victory of Catholicism" and by historians who saw the period between the end of the sixteenth century and the end of the eighteenth century as a period of dark ages between the brightness of the Renaissance and the Enlightenment. The latter blamed the "triumph of the Counter-Reformation" for the overall cultural and political decline of Poland, leading ultimately to the final collapse of the Polish-Lithuanian state at the end of the eighteenth century.

The "triumphalist" views from either group are true in part, but only in part. Scholars were right about what one may call a medievalism of Polish Catholicism, reflected in the polemical and homiletic works, which they saw as evidence of cultural decline. They were also right in noting the process of relatively rapid re-Catholicization among the nobility, as they funded new churches and promulgated anti-Protestant legislation against their fellow noblemen. Among nobility the numbers of Protestants dwindled the most. The nobles were also the group most influenced by Jesuit education, although not by Jesuit missions, which involved preaching, hearing confessions, and baptisms and were aimed at a broader, non-aristocratic society. The nobles did come to embrace a Catholic identity, identifying their state and their nation increasingly with the Catholic Church. By the end of the eighteenth century aristocratic lineage and Catholicism defined the Polish nation. But the "Polish nation," as defined by the nobles in premodern Poland, excluded nearly ninety percent of the population in the Polish-Lithuanian Commonwealth and, among that ninety percent, Catholics were not a majority. The Catholic Church was well aware of that, for its perception of itself was as something more than the Church of the nobility. But even among Catholic nobles, the Church could not have been satisfied with its level of influence. Though now Catholic, the nobles remained insubordinate, as usual, and continued to follow their own interests, frequently in defiance of Church teachings. The Catholic clergy felt threatened even by those nobles who had embraced it. It did not have a sense of triumph.

Norman Davies was one of the first historians to question the common view of the triumph of the Counter-Reformation. In four or so paragraphs of his two-volume history of Poland, *God's Playground* (1982), Davies wrote: "The 'Triumph of the Counter-Reformation' in Poland is sometimes cited as the only instance of a country where the Roman Catholic Church successfully attacked and reversed the gains of the Reformation. Yet, the Roman Triumph is a deceptive, not to say an illusory phenomenon; and is largely attributable to arbitrary or external factors."[3] Davies pointed out that the Lutherans of the northern provinces of Poland-Lithuania were never converted to Catholicism, that Orthodox Christianity persisted in the eastern territories as long as those territories belonged to Poland, and had disappeared only with the Russian annexation of the eastern parts of Poland-Lithuania in 1772, 1793, and 1795. He attributed the conversion of Protestant nobles back to Catholicism in post-Reformation Poland more to the mid-seventeenth-century wars with Protestant Sweden than to the Counter-Reformation efforts by the Church itself, including the educational work of Jesuits. Davies concentrated primarily on the demographic and political aspects of the re-Catholicization of Poland, but his intuition went in the right direction, as Church sources, studied in depth, confirm.

It is necessary to look beyond the noble estate to discover that the notion of the "triumph of the Counter-Reformation" in Poland is less firmly grounded than historians have maintained. Such a broader look conforms to the Church's own perception of its universal role, a role that stretched beyond the noble estate to correspond to its claim of spiritual authority over all members of the society. As late as the eighteenth century, the Polish Church clung to the Church's medieval ideal that "there was only one Church" and that its authority surpassed any temporal power. As outlined in Pope Boniface VIII's bull *Unam Sanctam*, "[I]t belongs to spiritual power to establish the terrestrial power and to pass judgment if it has not been good. . . . 'Therefore whoever resists this power thus ordained by God, resists the ordinance of God' [Rom 13:2]."[4]

In early modern Poland many forces resisted the Church's claim of dual power, the spiritual and the temporal, reminding the Church that it was far from achieving its ideal. The Church, well aware of falling short, felt insecure, even threatened, and demonstrated that sense of danger in its proclamations and polemic. The insubordinate nobles, other "bad and disobedient Catholics," heretics, and Jews continued to remind the Polish Catholic Church of the real limits to its authority and influence.

Jews became the symbol of the Church's failures. Their symbiotic relationship with the nobles frustrated the Church, as nobles often placed Jews in positions of power over lower-class Christians, thus upsetting the ideal social and religious order the Church sought to establish, in which Jews were to be subservient to Christians, and the Church hegemonic over all earthly and spiritual power. Jews, by their existence, also continued to remind the Church of the religious competition they had posed, for some Polish Christians embraced Judaism throughout this period, especially poorer and lower-status women, who served in Jewish homes.

Jews were viewed by the Church as corruptors of both the nobles and the poor – of the nobles because they "tempted" them with profits, of lower-class Christians because they employed them and made them work on days of Christian festivals, and tempted them to skip the mass by opening their taverns on Sunday. Such Christians preferred a drink to a mass, did not know their basic prayers, and ignored Church teachings about observance of Church holidays and about living a righteous and pious life.

Heretics too continued to threaten the Church's sense of security in Poland well into the eighteenth century, by which time Protestant dissidents were supposed to have left or become impotent. Politically the Protestants may, indeed, have been impotent, but religiously their presence continued to trouble the Church, as is evident in the Catholic clergy's continuing anti-Protestant polemic and in the Catholic synods' renewed anti-Protestant legislation in that period.

In all these contexts, Jews were both liminal and central to the Church's principal concerns. Jews were only one of many perceived threats but their presence allowed the Church to open its treasure trove of medieval anti-Jewish polemic to combat not only the threat of Jews but of Protestants as well.[5] Jewish presence was salient in the very areas that caused the Church's sense of insecurity: they had ties to the nobles and they employed lower-class Christians, sometimes leading them to heresy and apostasy. The clergy turned to medieval anti-Jewish rhetoric as the prime instrument of defense and offense; anti-Jewish rhetoric intensified with the intensification of the Church's response to its perceived multiple threats. In the eighteenth century, when western Church and societies moved toward the era of the Enlightenment, the Polish Church was still waging battles of the medieval and Counter-Reformation kind. Those larger struggles shaped and perpetuated the Church's anti-Jewish attitudes.

A wide variety of the Church's own sources and a broader scope of investigation, including but extending beyond the nobles, suggest that the era of the "triumph of the Counter-Reformation" in Poland did not occur in the manner in which it has been commonly perceived. The Church in Poland continued to feel threatened despite its alliance with the monarch and its gains among the nobles. Poland continued to be a multicultural and multireligious country up until the Second World War, when it lost its non-Catholics either through genocide, as with the Jews, or through territorial losses, as with the Eastern Orthodox denominations and German Protestants. But not even then, after the war, could it claim a triumph. Poland had become subordinate to the Communist rule. It did seem that, at the end of the twentieth century, the Church in Poland had begun to enjoy a triumph of sorts, with a Polish pope, an ethnically Polish nation, and the Communists gone. But the Church in Poland faced other problems of modernity, among them secularization, consumerism, social liberalism – and, as evidenced by debate concerning Poland's membership in the European Union, perhaps reluctantly it has begun to admit that it never had and never will truly triumph.

Glossary

Arenda – a lease on an estate, tavern, mill, etc.

Arrendator – a lease-holder; a holder of the *arenda*.

Council of Four Lands, *Va'ad Arb'a Arazot* – a supra-communal organization of Polish Jews active from the late sixteenth century until 1764.

Ciborium – see "pyx."

Halakhah – Jewish law; adj. *halakhic*.

Jurydyka (pl. *jurydyki*) – a privately owned district in a town or city, excluded from the municipal jurisdiction and subject to the jurisdiction of the owner.

Kahal – a local Jewish self-government, community leaders.

Latifundium (pl. *latifundia*) – large plots of land, encompassing numerous (sometimes hundreds of) towns and villages.

Pater Noster – Christian prayer known also as the Lord's Prayer or the Our Father.

Pyx or *ciborium* – a container in which the consecrated wafer is held in church.

Rosh ha-Shanah – Jewish New Year, which occurs usually in September or October.

Sejm – Polish parliament (a diet) of the nobles; *sejmik* – a local dietine.

Shulḥan 'Aruk – a sixteenth-century code of Jewish law compiled by Joseph Caro (d. 1575) and annotated by Moshe Isserles (d. 1572).

Starosta – a regional royal official, with administrative and judicial responsibilities.

Tur – the *Arba'ah Turim*, a code of Jewish law written by Jacob ben Asher (d. 1340), a basis for *Shulḥan 'Aruk*.

Notes

INTRODUCTION

1. Amiram Barkat, "2 ha-rabanim ha-roshiim nifgashu le-rishona 'im apifior be-vatikan," *Ha'aretz*, January 18, 2004, 4A.
2. E.g. Robert Jarocki, "Biskup pada…" *Rzeczpospolita* 258, November 4, 2000; Teresa Torańska, "Sąd nad sądem," Dodatek do *Gazety Wyborczej* no. 3, January 16, 2003; Teresa Torańska, "Sąd nad obrazem," *Gazeta Wyborcza* 252, October 27, 2000; Jakub Sito, "Czy usuwać obrazy z kościołów?" *Gazeta Wyborcza* 206, September 4, 2000. Bishop Stanisław Gądowski issued a statement in which he emphasized that "Jews did not murder" children. *Gazeta Wyborcza*, August 18, 2000, 5.
3. Stefan Żuchowski, *Process kryminalny o niewinne dziecię Jerzego Krasnowskiego iuż to trzecie, roku 1710 dnia 18 sierpnia w Sendomirzu okrutnie od Żydów zamordowane* (no place: 1713). Żuchowski, *Odgłos processów kryminalnych na Żydach o różne excessy, także morderstwo dzieci. Osobliwie w Sandomierzu roku 1698 przeświadczone* (Sandomierz, 1700).
4. Melchior Buliński, *Monografia miasta Sandomierza* (Warsaw, 1879), 220–35. Jerzy Łozinski and Barbara Wolff, eds., *Województwo kieleckie: Powiat sandomierski*, Katalog zabytków sztuki w Polsce, 3/11 (Warsaw: Instytut Sztuki PAN, 1962), 59.
5. By premodern I mean medieval and early modern.
6. The series was inspired by the Counter-Reformation liturgical calendar also entitled "Martyrologium Romanum," which focused on the cult of the saints and Catholic martyrdom. The notable exception is Waldemar Kowalski, who has pointed out the complexity of Żuchowski's religious motivations in his article. See Waldemar Kowalski, "'W obronie wiary': Ks. Stefan Żuchowski – Między wzniosłością a okrucieństwem," in *Żydzi wśród chrześcijan w dobie szlacheckiej rzeczypospolitej* (Kielce: KTN, 1996).
7. As Sara Lipton has shown, in the medieval art Jews were also not the only threats to the Church. Sara Lipton, *Images of Intolerance: The Representation of Jews and Judaism in the Bible Moralisée* (Berkeley: University of California Press, 1999).
8. For examples of this view see Wacław Sobieski, *Nienawiść wyznaniowa tłumów za rządów Zygmunta III-go* (Warsaw: Nakładem S. Dembego, 1902); Jerema Maciszewski, "Mechanizmy kształtowania się opinii publicznej w Polsce doby kontrreformacji," in *Wiek XVIII-kontrreformacja-barok: prace z historii kultury*, ed. Janusz Tazbir (Warsaw, Wrocław, Cracow: Zakład Narodowy im. Ossolińskich, 1970), 68; Janusz Tazbir, *Szlachta i teologowie: studia z dziejów polskiej kontrreformacji* (Warsaw: Wiedza Powszechna, 1987), especially chapter 13; Gershon David Hundert, *Jews in Poland-Lithuania in the Eighteenth Century: A Genealogy of Modernity* (Berkeley: University of California Press, 2004), chapter 3; Jerzy Kłoczowski, *History of Polish Christianity*, trans. Małgorzata Sady (Cambridge: Cambridge University Press, 2000), 108–16.

9. Jakob Wujek, *Postilla katholicka mneysza, to iest krótkie kazania abo wykłady świętych ewangeliey, na każda niedziele y na każde święto, przez cały rok według nauki prawdziwej kościoła chrześcijańskiego powszechnego* (Cracow: 1870–1 <1617>), 175.

10. Jacob Marchand, *Katechizm abo nauka chrześcijańska* (Cracow: Typis Societatis Iesu, 1682 <Kupisz, 1648>), 50–2.

11. Marchand, *Katechizm abo nauka chrześcijańska*, 50–2.

12. For example, Paweł Misiakiewicz, *Korona braterska* (n.p.: n.p., 1724), 216–17.

13. Jan Felix Szaniawski, *Kazanie na solenney wotywie o duchu świętym przy zaczynaiącey się elekcyi roku 1733 dnia 25 Augusta w kollegiacie warszawskiey świętego Jana miane* (Warsaw: 1733), b2 ff.

14. Ronald Asch argued that in the early modern period there was little distinction between the "state" and the "estate." Ronald G. Asch, *The Thirty Years War: The Holy Roman Empire and Europe, 1618–1648*, European History in Perspective (New York: St. Martin's Press, 1997), 4–5.

15. For an example of portraying Jews and heretics and other non-Catholics as "foreign elements," see Mikołaj Popławski, *Stół duchowny, rozlicznemi nauk zbawiennych historyi y przykładów, przy reflexyach na całego roku tygodnie, niedziele y święta, nie tylko dla nabożnych dusz ale y kaznodzieyów spowiedników potrawkami zastawiony* (Warsaw: Krzysztof Domański, 1704), 1420. For an example of the discussion of the impact of religious discord on the unity of the state and all of the society, see G. Wylie Sypher, "'Faisant Ce Qu'il a Plaisir': The Image of Protestantism in French Catholic Polemic on the Eve of the Religious Wars," *Sixteenth Century Journal* 11, no. 2 (1980): 70.

16. On different messages transmitted by Catholic preachers to different strata of early modern society, see, for instance, Louis Châtellier, "Rinnovamento della pastorale e società dopo il concilio di Trento," in *Il concilio di Trento e il moderno*, ed. Paolo Prodi and Wolfgang Reinhard (Bologna: Il Mulino, 1996).

17. Kasper Balsam, *Kazanie pobudzaiące do modlitwy, na uproszeni szczęśliwego powodzenia seymowi walnemu w roku 1754* (Cracow, 1754), A2-A2verso.

18. Krzysztof Jan Szembek, *Krótkie zebranie nauki chrześciańskiey zlecenia nayprzelewiebneyszego w Chrystusie panu jaśnie wielmożnego i. mc. Krzysztofa Jana Szembeka, biskupa przemyskiego, proboszcza y generała miechowskiego etc. dziatkom chrześciańskim przez pytanie y odpowiedź według porządku y podzielenia catech: S. concil: Trinden:* (Cracow: Drukarnia Franciszka Cezarego, 1719), 54.

19. Woyciech Tylkowski, *Problemata święte abo pytania około wyrozumienia świętey ewangeliey* (Poznań: 1688), Zz3verso.

20. Stefan Wielowieyski, *Nabożeństwo dla ludzi zabawnych, którzy czasu nie maią, dla tych, którzy nie mogą, dla niedbałych, którym się nie chce modlić* (Poznań, 1693), M3v–M4r.

21. Daniel Tollet summarized the wars that Poland was engaged in in the seventeenth century; see Daniel Tollet, "La Pologne au XVIIe siècle: une puissance en cours de marginalisation," *Dix-septième siècle [France]* 41, no. 1 (1990).

22. There is ample literature now about the process of confessionalization that took place in early modern Europe. See, e.g., Robert Bireley, *The Refashioning of Catholicism, 1450–1700: A Reassessment of the Counter Reformation* (Washington, D.C.: Catholic University of America Press, 1999); R. Po-chia Hsia, *Social Discipline in the Reformation: Central Europe, 1550–1750*, Christianity and Society in the Modern World (London; New York: Routledge, 1989); R. Po-chia Hsia, *The World of Catholic Renewal, 1540–1770* (New York: Cambridge University Press, 1998); Patrick Ferry, "Confessionalization and

Popular Preaching: Sermons against Synergism in Reformation Saxony," *Sixteenth Century Journal* 28, no. 4 (1997); Joel Harrington and Helmut Walser Smith, "Confessionalization, Community, and State Building in Germany, 1555–1870," *Journal of Modern History* 69, no. 1 (1997).

23. See, e.g., Ferry, "Confessionalization and Popular Preaching"; Hsia, *Social Discipline in the Reformation*; Paolo Prodi and Carla Penuti, eds., *Disciplina dell'anima, disciplina del corpo e disciplina della società tra medioevo ed età moderna* (Bologna: Il Mulino, 1994).

24. In Poland the most prominent example of this was Jeske-Choiński, whose book *Neofici polscy* did just that – exposed the Jewish roots of Polish Christians of Jewish origins. Teodor Jeske-Choiński, *Neofici polscy: materyały historyczne* (Warszawa: Druk P. Laskauera, 1904).

25. However, this is exactly what happened in the Iberian Peninsula following mass conversions of Jews in the fourteenth and fifteenth centuries. See most recently on this David Nirenberg, "Mass Conversion and Genealogical Mentalities: Jews and Christians in Fifteenth-Century Spain," *Past and Present* 174 (2002).

CHAPTER 1: "ONE MYSTICAL BODY ... ONLY ONE SHEPHERD": THE CHURCH IDEALS OF SOCIAL ORDER

1. Richard J. Plantinga, ed., *Christianity and Plurality: Classic and Contemporary Readings* (Oxford: Blackwell, 1999), 124–5.

2. The bull *Unam Sanctam* by Pope Boniface VIII is published in Plantinga, ed., *Christianity and Plurality*, 124–5.

3. Plantinga, ed., *Christianity and Plurality*, 124–5.

4. Salo Wittmayer Baron, "'Plenitude of Apostolic Powers' and Medieval 'Jewish Serfdom'," in *Ancient and Medieval Jewish History*, ed. David M. Feldman (New Brunswick, NJ: Rutgers University Press, 1972), 287. D. William McCready, "Papal Plenitudo Potestatis and the Source of Temporal Authority in Late Medieval Papal Hierocratic Theory," *Speculum* 48, no. 4 (1973): 656.

5. Plantinga, ed., *Christianity and Plurality*, 124–5.

6. Plantinga, ed., *Christianity and Plurality*, 124–5.

7. Steven E. Ozment, *The Age of Reform (1250–1550): An Intellectual and Religious History of Late Medieval and Reformation Europe* (New Haven: Yale University Press, 1980), 145–7.

8. J. A. Watt, "The Papacy," in *The New Cambridge Medieval History*. Vol. 5, *C.1198–C.1300*, ed. David Abulafia (Cambridge: Cambridge University Press, 1999), 158–63. William Chester Jordan, "The Capetians from the Death of Phillip II to Phillip IV," in *The New Cambridge Medieval History*, 5: 305–8. Norman F. Cantor, *Medieval History: The Life and Death of a Civilization* (New York: Macmillan, 1969), 524–5. William J. Courtenay, "Between Pope and King: The Parisian Letters of Adhesion of 1303," *Speculum* 71, no. 3 (1996).

9. Gordon Leff, "Heresy and the Decline of the Medieval Church," *Past and Present* 20 (1961): 37.

10. See, for example, Ozment, *The Age of Reform*, 143.

11. See, for example, James Given, "The Inquisitors of Languedoc and the Medieval Technology of Power," *American Historical Review* 94, no. 2 (1989); Bernard Hamilton, "The Albigesian Crusade and Heresy," in *The New Cambridge Medieval History*. Vol. 5; Malcolm Lambert, *Medieval Heresy: Popular Movements from the Gregorian Reform to*

the Reformation (Oxford: Blackwell, 1992); Leff, "Heresy and the Decline of the Medieval Church"; Edward Peters, *Heresy and Authority in Medieval Europe: Documents in Translation* (Philadelphia: University of Pennsylvania Press, 1980); Watt, "The Papacy."

12. See, for example, Ozment, *The Age of Reform*, "The Ecclesiopolitical Traditions."

13. See, for example, R. A. Markus, "The Latin Fathers," in *The Cambridge History of Medieval Political Thought C. 350–C. 1450*, ed. J. H. Burns (New York: Cambridge University Press, 1988), 93–4, 101–2, 116–22. D. M. Nicol, "Byzantium," in *The Cambridge History of Medieval Political Thought C. 350–C. 1450*, 63–73.

14. On these developments, see, for example, R. A. Markus, "Introduction: The West," in *The Cambridge History of Medieval Political Thought C. 350–C. 1450*, 83–9, 90–1, Nicol, "Byzantium," 52, 58, 63–72.

15. Cantor, *The Medieval History*, 199. See also Rosamond McKitterick, ed., *The New Cambridge Medieval History*. Vol. 2, *C. 700–C. 900* (New York: Cambridge University Press, 1995), 105. See also Matthew Innes, "Charlemagne's Will: Piety, Politics and the Imperial Succession," *The English Historical Review* 112, no. 448 (1997). On the coronation of the Byzantine emperors by the Church patriarchs, see Nicol, "Byzantium," 63–4.

16. Cantor, *The Medieval History*, 191–201. McKitterick, ed., *The New Cambridge Medieval History*, 2: 97–9, 105.

17. For example, Baron, "'Plenitude of Apostolic Powers' and Medieval 'Jewish Serfdom'"; Kenneth R. Stow, "The Church and the Jews," in *The New Cambridge Medieval History*, 5: 218; John Howe, "The Nobility's Reform of the Medieval Church," *American Historical Review* 93, no. 2 (1988); McCready, "Papal Plenitudo Potestatis."

18. Cited in Paolo Prodi, "Il 'Sovrano Pontifice'," *Storia d'Italia: Annali* 9: La chiesa e il potere politico dal medioevo all'età contemporanea (1995):197.

19. Paolo Prodi, *The Papal Prince: One Body and Two Souls: The Papal Monarchy in Early Modern Europe* (New York: Cambridge University Press, 1987).

20. Norman P. Tanner, ed., *Decrees of the Ecumenical Councils* (Washington, DC: Georgetown University Press, 1990), 630–1, 784.

21. On the Second Temple Judaisms, see for example Shaye J. D. Cohen, *From the Maccabees to the Mishnah* (Philadelphia: Westminster Press, 1987); Lawrence H. Schiffman, *From Text to Tradition: A History of Second Temple and Rabbinic Judaism* (Hoboken, NJ: Ktav Pub. House, 1991); Lawrence H. Schiffman, *Reclaiming the Dead Sea Scrolls: The History of Judaism, the Background of Christianity, the Lost Library of Qumran* (Philadelphia: Jewish Publication Society, 1994); Lawrence H. Schiffman, *Understanding Second Temple and Rabbinic Judaism* (Jersey City, NJ: Ktav Pub. House, 2003).

22. There is extensive literature on this subject. See, for example, Jostein Ådna and Hans Kvalbein, *The Mission of the Early Church to Jews and Gentiles*, Wissenschaftliche Untersuchungen Zum Neuen Testament 127 (Tübingen: Mohr Siebeck, 2000); M. J. Edwards et al., *Apologetics in the Roman Empire: Pagans, Jews, and Christians* (Oxford: New York, 1999); John M. G. Barclay, Morna Dorothy Hooker, and J. P. M. Sweet, *Early Christian Thought in Its Jewish Context* (Cambridge: Cambridge University Press, 1996); Robert S. MacLennan, *Early Christian Texts on Jews and Judaism*, Brown Judaic Studies 194 (Atlanta, GA: Scholars Press, 1990); Justin the Martyr, *Justin Martyr, the Dialogue with Trypho*, trans. A. Lukyn Williams, Translations of Christian Literature (London S.P.C.K.: New York, 1930); David Rokeah, *Jews, Pagans, and Christians in Conflict*, Studia Post-Biblica 33 (Jerusalem: Magnes Press, 1982); David Rokeah, *Justin Martyr and the Jews*, Jewish and Christian Perspectives Series 5 (Leiden: E. J. Brill, 2002); David Rokeah,

Yustinus Martir veha-yehudim, kuntresim, mekorot u-meḥkarim, (Jerusalem: Merkaz Dinur, 1998); Jeffrey S. Siker, *Disinheriting the Jews: Abraham in Early Christian Controversy* (Louisville, KY: Westminster/John Knox Press, 1991); H. Gregory Snyder, *Teachers and Texts in the Ancient World: Philosophers, Jews, and Christians, Religion in the First Christian Centuries* (New York: Routledge, 2000); Tertullian and Immacolata Aulisa, *Polemica con i giudei, collana di testi patristici* (Roma: Città nuova, 1998); James C. Walters, *Ethnic Issues in Paul's Letter to the Romans: Changing Self-Definitions in Earliest Roman Christianity* (Valley Forge, PA: Trinity Press International, 1993); Robert Louis Wilken, *John Chrysostom and the Jews: Rhetoric and Reality in the Late 4th Century,* The Transformation of the Classical Heritage 4 (Berkeley: University of California Press, 1983).

23. Justin the Martyr lived from 100 to 165.
24. Justin the Martyr, *Justin Martyr's Dialogue with Trypho the Jew,* trans. Henry Brown (London: Macmillan Barclay and Macmillan, 1846), 38–9, section X.
25. The literature on early Christianity is abundant; see, for example, G. W. Bowersock, *Martyrdom and Rome, The Wiles Lectures Given at the Queen's University of Belfast; Variation: Wiles Lectures* (New York: Cambridge University Press, 1995); W. H. C. Frend, *Martyrdom and Persecution in the Early Church: A Study of a Conflict from the Maccabees to Donatus* (New York: New York University Press, 1967 <1965 >); Simeon L. Guterman, *Religious Toleration and Persecution in Ancient Rome* (Westport, CT: Greenwood Press, 1971 <1951 >); Herbert Musurillo, *The Acts of the Christian Martyrs,* Oxford Early Christian Texts (Oxford: Clarendon Press, 1972); Judith Perkins, *The Suffering Self: Pain and Narrative Representation in Early Christian Era* (New York: Routledge, 1995); Giuseppe Ricciotti, *The Age of Martyrs: Christianity from Diocletian to Constantine* (Milwaukee: Bruce Pub. Co., 1959); Herbert B. Workman, *Persecution in the Early Church* (Oxford: Oxford University Press, 1980); Douglas R. A. Hare, *The Theme of Jewish Persecution of Christians in the Gospel According to St. Matthew,* Society for New Testament Studies 6 (Cambridge: Cambridge University Press, 1967).
26. *Justin Martyr's Dialogue with Trypho,* 51, section XVII.
27. *Justin Martyr's Dialogue with Trypho,* 93, section XXXIX.
28. Eusebius, *Ecclesiastical History,* II.1.
29. See, for instance, Augustine, *The City of God,* trans. Henry Bettenson (New York: Penguin Books, 1984). Books XV–XVI, especially XV.1, 7, 26; XVI.23–5, 31–3, 35–7, 42.
30. John Chrysostom lived from 347 to 407.
31. John Chrysostom and Mervyn Maxwell, "Chrysostom's Homilies against the Jews: An English Translation" (Ph.D. diss., University of Chicago, 1966), 4, sermon I:1.
32. "Chrysostom's Homilies against the Jews," 10, sermon I:3.
33. In English, Jacob Rader Marcus and Marc Saperstein, *The Jew in the Medieval World: A Source Book, 315–1791* (Cincinnati: Hebrew Union College Press, 1999), Section II, chapter 19.
34. Augustine lived from 354 to 430.
35. Paula Fredriksen, "Divine Justice and Human Freedom: Augustine on Jews and Judaism, 392–398," in *From Witness to Witchcraft: Jews and Judaism in Medieval Christian Thought,* ed. Jeremy Cohen (Wiesbaden: Harrassowitz Verlag, 1996).
36. "Chrysostom's Homilies against Jews," 10, sermon I:3.
37. "Chrysostom's Homilies against Jews," 26, sermon I:6.
38. Augustine, *The City of God,* Book XVIII, chapter 46.

39. Augustine, *The City of God*, Book XVI, chapter 35.
40. Augustine, *The City of God*, Book XVI, chapter 42.
41. Israel Yuval, "Jews and Christians in the Middle Ages: Shared Myths, Common Language," in *Demonizing the Other*, ed. Robert Wistrich (Amsterdam: Harwood Academic Publishers, 1999), 88.
42. For an English translation, see Marcus and Saperstein, *The Jew in the Medieval World*, 125–6. See also Edward A. Synan, *The Popes and the Jews* (New York: Macmillan, 1965), 46.
43. Kenneth R. Stow, *The "1007 Anonymous" and Papal Sovereignty: Jewish Perceptions of the Papacy and Papal Policy in the High Middle Ages* (Cincinnati: Hebrew Union College–Jewish Institute of Religion, 1984), 2.
44. Solomon Grayzel, "The Papal Bull *Sicut Judaeis*," in *Essential Papers on Judaism and Christianity in Crisis*, ed. Jeremy Cohen (New York: New York University Press, 1991 <1962>); Stow, *The "1007 Anonymous" and Papal Sovereignty*, 9, 12–20. Calixtus II's issuance of the bull is thought to be related to the persecution of Jews during the First Crusade in 1096–9.
45. For the text of the constitution, see Solomon Grayzel, *The Church and the Jews in the VIIIth Century* (Philadelphia: The Dropsie College, 1933), 92–5, doc. 5.
46. Letter to Archbishop of Sens of July 15, 1205. Grayzel, *The Church and the Jews*, 114–17, doc. 18.
47. Grayzel, *The Church and the Jews*, 306–13.
48. For the text of Canons 15–16 in English, see Henry Joseph Schroeder, *Disciplinary Decrees of the General Councils, Text, Translation, and Commentary* (St. Louis: B. Herder Book Co., 1937), 256–7. For the Latin text, see Schroeder, *Disciplinary Decrees*, 568–9.
49. Grayzel, *The Church and the Jews*, 280–1.
50. Grayzel, *The Church and the Jews*, 104–7.
51. For papal reactions during the Counter-Reformation, see for example Kenneth R. Stow, "The Burning of the Talmud in 1553 in the Light of Sixteenth Century Catholic Attitudes toward the Talmud," *Bibliotheque d'humanisme et renaissance* 34 (1972); Stow, *Catholic Thought and Papal Jewry Policy, 1555–1593* (New York: Jewish Theological Seminary of America, 1977); and Stow, "The Papacy and the Jews: Catholic Reformation and Beyond," *Jewish History* 6, no. 1–2 (1992).
52. The text of the bull and its translation can be found in Stow, *Catholic Thought*, 291–8.
53. Stow, *Catholic Thought*, Latin: 291; English: 294–5.
54. The term "perpetual servitude" was first used by Pope Innocent III. Before then the term "subservience" was used. Stow, "The Church and the Jews," 206–7.
55. Prodi, "Il 'Sovrano Pontifice'"; Prodi, *The Papal Prince*. Prodi also argues that this transformation of papacy into a political monarchy represents a decline of papal universalism on the eve of the modern era.
56. Kenneth R. Stow, "The Consciousness of Closure: Roman Jewry and Its *Ghet*," in *Essential Papers on Jewish Culture in Renaissance and Baroque Italy*, ed. David Ruderman (New York: New York University Press, 1992). On the establishment of the Venetian ghetto, see for example Benjamin Ravid, "The Venetian Government and the Jews," in *The Jews of Early Modern Venice*, ed. Benjamin Ravid and Robert Davis (Baltimore: Johns Hopkins University Press, 2001). On the use and misuse of the term "ghetto," see Benjamin Ravid, "From Geographical Realia to Historiographical Symbol: The Odyssey of the Word Ghetto," in *Essential Papers on Jewish Culture in Renaissance and Baroque Italy*, ed. Ruderman.

57. Stow, *Catholic Thought*, 295.
58. Solomon Grayzel and Kenneth R. Stow, *The Church and the Jews in the XIIIth Century*, Vol. 2, *1254–1314* (Detroit: Wayne State University Press, 1989), 245.
59. For the Latin text and English summary see Grayzel and Stow, *The Church and the Jews*, 244–6. For the 1215 canon, see Grayzel, *The Church and the Jews*, 308–9.
60. The English translation of the text can be found in Robert Chazan, *Church, State, and Jew in the Middle Ages*, Library of Jewish Studies (New York: Behrman House, 1980), 88–93. On the relation between the 1264 charter and the 1267 laws of the Breslau synod see for example Simon Dubnow, *History of the Jews in Russia and Poland*, trans. I. Friedlander (Bergenfield, NJ: Avotaynu, 2000), 16–17; Bernard D. Weinryb, *The Jews of Poland: A Social and Economic History of the Jewish Community in Poland from 1100 to 1800* (Philadelphia: Jewish Publication Society of America, 1973), 43.
61. The city of Poznań may have been one exception. There the authorities sought to build a wall separating the Jewish section of the city from the rest of town. See MS. D 580 "Rescriptum SS. Augusti III Varsaviae 16 mensis Octobris 1756 ratione transmurationis Judaeorum Posnaniae" in Archiwum Państwowe w Poznaniu.
62. Synods of Chełm (1717), Płock (1733) repeated the 1267 rulings. *Constitutiones et Decreta Synodi Dioecesana Plocensi sub Illustrissimo Excellentissimo Reverendissimo Domino D. Andrea Stanislao Kostka in Zaluskie Zaluski Dei et Apostolicae Sedis Gratia Episcopo Plocensi Pultoviae Anno Domini M.D. CC.XXXIII Die 4 Augusti Celebratae*, (Warsaw: Typis Societatis Jesu, 1735); *Synodus Diaecesana Chelmensis ab Illustrissimo et Reverendissimo Domino D. Christophoro Ioanne in Slupow Szembek, Dei et S. Sedis Apostolicae Graita Episcopo Chelmensi, Nominato Premislensi etc, Crasnostaviae in Ecclesia Cathedrali Praesente Universo Dioecesis Clero Celebrata Die Decima Mensis Julii et Aliis Duobus Sequentibus Diebus, Anno Domini M.D.CC.XVII* (Zamość: 1717).
63. Jews were sometimes accused of luring Christians to heresy. An image depicting this is found in the *Bible Moralisée*, Paris 1225. I am indebted to a presentation by Sara Lipton of SUNY (Stony Brook), "Sight of the People: Jews as Sign and Witness in Medieval Christian Art," presented at the Institute of Advanced Studies, Hebrew University in Jerusalem, May 5, 2004. See also her *Images of Intolerance: The Representation of Jews and Judaism in the Bible Moralisée* (Berkeley: University of California Press, 1999), especially chapters 4–5.
64. Steven Runciman, *The Medieval Manichee: A Study of the Christian Dualist Heresy* (New York: Viking Press, 1961), 1–2.
65. Peters, *Heresy and Authority*, 38–42.
66. Peters, *Heresy and Authority*, 45.
67. Amnon Linder, *The Jews in Roman Imperial Legislation* (Detroit: Wayne State University Press, 1987), 190, see also 202.
68. Malcolm Barber, *The Cathars, the Medieval World* (Harlow, UK: Longman, 2000), 1. Also, Peters, *Heresy and Authority*, 103–37; Lambert, *Medieval Heresy*, 44–61.
69. For a recent study of the movement, see Gabriel Audisio, *The Waldensian Dissent: Persecution and Survival, C. 1170–C. 1570*, (New York: Cambridge University Press, 1999). Also, Lambert, *Medieval Heresy*, 62–87. For Waldensian texts in English, see, for example, Peters, *Heresy and Authority*, 139–63.
70. Peters, *Heresy and Authority*, 157.
71. Peters, *Heresy and Authority*, 144.
72. Peters, *Heresy and Authority*, 151.

73. Peters, *Heresy and Authority*, 150.
74. Leff, "Heresy and the Decline of the Medieval Church," 45.
75. In 1199, Pope Innocent III responded to a controversy in Metz, where a group of people obtained a vernacular translation of parts of the Bible and inspired by it, engaged in unauthorized preaching. Leonard Boyle, "Innocent III and Vernacular Versions of Scripture," in *The Bible in the Medieval World: Essays in Honor of Beryl Smalley*, ed. Katherine Walsh and Diana Wood (Oxford: Blackwell, 1985).
76. Peters, *Heresy and Authority*, 149.
77. Leff, "Heresy and the Decline of the Medieval Church," 40.
78. See for example Lambert, *Medieval Heresy*, 225–42, 284–326. František Šmahel, "Literacy and Heresy in Hussite Bohemia," in *Heresy and Literacy, 1000–1530*, ed. Peter Biller and Ann Hudson, Cambridge Studies in Medieval Literature (New York: Cambridge University Press, 1996), especially 251–2.
79. Peters, *Heresy and Authority*, 271.
80. Peters, *Heresy and Authority*, 269.
81. Peters, *Heresy and Authority*, 265–6, 274–7, 286–97.
82. Given, "The Inquisitors of Languedoc and the Medieval Technology of Power," 339 (on Gregory X) and 356–7 (on reliance on temporal powers); Leff, "Heresy and the Decline of the Medieval Church," 49.

CHAPTER 2: THE UPSET SOCIAL ORDER: NOBLES AND THE JEWS IN POLAND

1. Richard J. Plantinga, ed., *Christianity and Plurality: Classic and Contemporary Readings* (Oxford: Blackwell, 1999), 124–5.
2. Józef Andrzej Załuski, *Dwa miecze katolickiej w królestwie ortodoksyjnym odsieczy przeciwko natarczywym pp. dysydentów polskich zamachom* (Warsaw: n.p., 1731).
3. Jan Felix Szaniawski, *Kazanie na solenney wotywie o duchu świetym przy zaczynaiacey się elekcyi roku 1733 dnia 25 Augusta w kollegiacie warszawskiey Świetego Jana miane* (Warsaw: 1733), b2 ff.
4. Adam Abramowicz, *Kazania niedzielne jaśniewielmożnemu Bogu nayprzewielebnieyszemu jego mości x. hrabi na Zasławiu, Bychowie, Dabrowie etc. Józefowi Sapieże* (Wilno: Typis Societatis Jesu, 1753), 463.
5. This can be contrasted by the fate of the Counter-Reformation in the Habsburg Monarchy; see for example Robert John Weston Evans, *The Making of the Habsburg Monarchy, 1550–1700* (Oxford: Clarendon Press, 1979).
6. Władysław Czapliński, "Myśl polityczna w Polsce w dobie kontrreformacji (1573–1655)," in *Wiek XVII – kontrreformacja – barok: prace z historii kultury*, ed. Janusz Pelc (Wrocław: Zakład Narodowy im. Ossolińskich, 1970), especially 42–5.
7. Janusz Tazbir, "Problemy Wyznaniowe," in *Polska XVII wieku: państwo, społeczeństwo, kultura*, ed. Janusz Tazbir (Warsaw: Wiedza Powszechna, 1969), 189. Sigismund August is often seen as a ruler sympathetic to the Reformation, and these strong endorsements of Church policies are overlooked.
8. Daniel Stone, *The Polish-Lithuanian State, 1386–1795*, History of East Central Europe 4 (Seattle: University of Washington Press, 2001), 44, 56, 136–7.
9. Marcin Krowicki, *Chrzescijańskie a żałobliwe napominanie*, ed. Zbigniew Ogonowski, Lech Szczucki, and Janusz Tazbir, Biblioteka Pisarzy Reformacyjnych 7 (Warsaw: Polska Akademia Nauk, 1969), 12.

10. Krowicki, *Chrześcijańskie a żałobliwe napominanie*, 12.
11. This can be contrasted with the developments in the Habsburg Monarchy in Austria. On this see Evans, *The Making of the Habsburg Monarchy*.
12. Kazimierz Tymieniecki, *Polska w średniowieczu* (Warsaw: Państwowe Wydawnictwo Naukowe, 1961), 53–60. Jerzy Wyrozumski, *Historia Polski do roku 1505* (Warsaw: Państwowe Wydawnictwo Naukowe, 1978), 120–1. Norman Davies, *God's Playground: A History of Poland*. vol. 1, *The Origins to 1795* (New York: Columbia University Press, 1982), 67. Aleksander Gieysztor, ed., *History of Poland*, 2nd ed. (Warsaw: PWN, 1979), 51. For the text of the donation of the Polish lands to the papacy, *Dagome Iudex*, see for example Jakub Sawicki, ed., *Wybór tekstów źródłowych z historii państwa i prawa polskiego* (Warsaw: PWN, 1952), 11.
13. See for example the conflict between King Bolesław II (Szczodry) and Bishop Stanisław of Cracow in 1079, which ended with the execution of the bishop and the eventual fall of the king. Davies, *God's Playground: A History of Poland*, 1 : 70. Wyrozumski, *Historia Polski do Roku 1505*, 134–7.
14. Andrzej Sulima Kamiński, *Republic vs. Autocracy: Poland-Lithuania and Russia 1686–1697*, Harvard Series in Ukrainian Studies, ed. George Grabowicz (Cambridge, Massachusetts: Harvard Ukrainian Research Institute, 1993), 18. Jan Dzięgielewski, "Biskupi rzymskokatoliccy końca XVI-pierwszej połowy XVII wieku i ich udział w kształtowaniu stosunków wyznaniowych w Rzeczypospolitej," in *Między monarchią a demokracją: studia z dziejów Polski XV–XVIII wieku*, ed. Anna Sucheni-Grabowska and Małgorzata Zaryń (Warsaw: Wydawnictwa Sejmowe, 1994), 191.
15. See, for example, Czapliński, "Myśl polityczna w Polsce w dobie kontrreformacji (1573–1655)."
16. Dzięgielewski, "Biskupi rzymskokatoliccy," 197–200.
17. For a good overview of this process in English, see Antoni Mączak, "The Structure of Power in the Commonwealth of the Sixteenth and Seventeenth Centuries" and Andrzej Wyczański, "The Problem of Authority in Sixteenth-Century Poland: An Essay of Reinterpretation," both in *A Republic of Nobles: Studies in Polish History to 1864*, ed. J. K. Fedorowicz (New York: Cambridge University Press, 1982); Davies, *God's Playground: A History of Poland*, vol. 1.
18. Jerema Maciszewski, *Szlachta i jej państwo* (Warsaw: PWN, 1984), 61–2.
19. For an alternative view see James Miller, "The Origins of Polish Arianism," *Sixteenth Century Journal* 16, no. 2 (1985).
20. Jerzy Lukowski, *Liberty's Folly: The Polish-Lithuanian Commonwealth in the Eighteenth Century, 1697–1795* (New York: Routledge, 1991), 9–10.
21. Stone, *The Polish-Lithuanian State*, 34–5.
22. Stone, *The Polish-Lithuanian State*, 37.
23. Józef Andrzej Gierowski, *Historia Polski, 1505–1864* (Warsaw: Państwowy Instytut Wydawniczy, 1978), 1 : 137.
24. This is argued by Andrzej Wyczański against a general perception that the "execution of the law movement" was in fact a movement weakening the monarch. Wyczański, "Problem of Authority." For the opposite view, see for example Anna Sucheni-Grabowska, *Spory królów ze szlachtą w złotym wieku. Wokół egzekucji praw*, Dzieje narodu i państwa polskiego, ed. Feliks Kiryk et al. (Cracow: Krajowa Agencja Wydawnicza, 1988). A useful overview of the problem is presented in Mączak, "Problem of Authority." See also Gierowski, *Historia Polski, 1505–1864*, 138–43.

25. Gierowski, *Historia Polski, 1505–1864*, 150–1. In 1550, while King Sigismund August was still alive he confirmed the law that stipulated that kings could only be officially crowned if they were willingly elected by the nobility. *Volumina Legum: przedruk zbioru praw staraniem xx. pijarów w Warszawie od roku 1732 do roku 1782 wydanego*, 2nd ed., 10 vols. (Petersburg: Jozafat Ohryzka, 1859; reprint, 1980), 2: 6.

26. Józef Andrzej Gierowski, *The Polish-Lithuanian Commonweath in the Eighteenth Century: From Anarchy to Well-Organised State*, trans. Henry Leeming, Rozprawy Wydziału Historyczno-Filozowicznego 82 (Cracow: Polska Akademia Umiejętności, 1996), 22. For the text see *Volumina Legum*, 3: 131–7.

27. Sucheni-Grabowska, *Spory królów ze szlachtą*, 38. Gierowski, *The Polish-Lithuanian Commonwealth*, 22.

28. Gierowski, *The Polish-Lithuanian Commonwealth*, 22.

29. Lukowski, *Liberty's Folly*, 10. Gierowski, *Historia Polski, 1505–1864*, 152–3. Henryk Olszewski, "Ustrój polityczny Rzeczypospolitej," in *Polska XVII wieku*, ed. Janusz Tazbir (Warsaw: Wiedza Powszechna, 1969), 58.

30. Most prominent examples are those of King Sigismund III Vasa (1587–1632) and the Saxon monarchs, August II and his son August III (1697–1764). Mączak, "Problem of Authority," 132.

31. Lukowski, *Liberty's Folly*, 11.

32. Lukowski, *Liberty's Folly*, 12.

33. Stone, *The Polish-Lithuanian State*, 294–5, 298–9.

34. Maciszewski, *Szlachta i jej państwo*, 20–1, 31–6. Kamiński, *Republic vs. Autocracy*, 30. Lukowski, *Liberty's Folly*, 14. Gierowski, *The Polish-Lithuanian Commonwealth*, 17–18.

35. Maciszewski, *Szlachta i jej państwo*, 248.

36. Gierowski, *The Polish-Lithuanian Commonwealth*, 36.

37. Lukowski has an overview of the wealth of Polish nobles, including their comparison to western aristocracy. Lukowski, *Liberty's Folly*, 11–25.

38. Stone, *The Polish-Lithuanian State*, 199.

39. Olszewski, "Ustrój polityczny Rzeczypospolitej," 70.

40. Mączak, "Problem of Authority," 122, 124.

41. Sucheni-Grabowska, *Spory królów ze szlachtą*, 22.

42. *Volumina Legum*, 2: 21, 52. On taxing Church property along with others see *Volumina Legum*, 2: 126.

43. Janusz Tazbir, "Społeczeństwo wobec Reformacji," in *Polska w epoce Odrodzenia: Państwo, społeczenstwo, kultura*, ed. Andrzej Wyczański (Warsaw: Wiedza Powszechna, 1986), 337. Sucheni-Grabowska, *Spory królów ze szlachtą*, 25, 39.

44. Sucheni-Grabowska, *Spory królów ze szlachtą*, 39.

45. Cited in Maciszewski, *Szlachta i jej państwo*, 161–2.

46. MS. Acta Actorum Rmi Capituli Cathedrali Ecclesiae Cracoviensis Liber III (a. d. 3 Februarii 1524–ad d. 16 Julii 1543), in AKW, fol. 156v. For the establishment of a salaried office of the inquisitor, see MS. Libri Privilegiorum 7/2, AKW, 278–80.

47. Sucheni-Grabowska, *Spory królów ze szlachtą*, 23, 26. Maciszewski, *Szlachta i jej państwo*, 172. For examples of cases concerning tithes in the court of the bishop of Cracow, see MS. AEp 13, AKM in Cracow, case of 19 March 1532, fol. 49v; AEp 16, AKM in Cracow, cases of 26 August 1536, fol. 31; 1 September 1536, fol. 36. AEp 18, 333v. AEp 16 is particularly rich in cases concerning tithes.

48. Maria Sipayłło, ed., *Acta Synodalia Ecclesiarum Poloniae Reformatarum, 1550–1559*. Vol. 1, *Akta synodów różnowierczych w Polsce* (Warsaw: Wydawnictwa Uniwersytetu Warszawskiego, 1966), 42. A sixteenth-century anti-Trinitarian poet, Erazm Otwinowski, argued the same in his poem "Dziesięcina"; see Jan Dürr-Durski, ed., *Arianie polscy w świetle własnej poezji: zarys ideologii i wybór wierszy* (Warsaw: Państwowe Zakłady Wydawnictw Szkolnych, 1948), 90.

49. Sipayłło, *Acta Synodalia*, 1: 275.

50. Sipayłło, *Acta Synodalia*, 1: 275.

51. *Volumina Legum*, 2: 20.

52. *Volumina Legum*, 2: 126–7.

53. Maciszewski, *Szlachta i jej państwo*, 120–1.

54. Session 25, canon 12. Norman P. Tanner, *Decrees of the Ecumenical Councils* (Washington, DC: Georgetown University Press, 1990), 792.

55. Yosef Hayim Yerushalmi, *The Lisbon Massacre of 1506 and the Royal Image in the Shebet Yehudah*. Hebrew Union College Annual. Supplements 1 (Cincinnati: Hebrew Union College /Jewish Institute of Religion, 1976), xi.

56. Lack of documents and other evidence make the beginnings of the Jewish settlement in Poland unclear. The early history of the Jews in Poland is surrounded by speculations and, sometimes, politically motivated debates. In the nineteenth and early twentieth century, when struggling for citizenship in Eastern Europe, Jews sought to show their rootedness in the country and often sought to prove that their settlement preceded even the official Christianization of the territory. Simon Dubnow is one of the most prominent, if not the only, examples of scholars who espouse this view. Simon Dubnow, *History of the Jews in Russia and Poland*, trans. I. Friedlander (Bergenfield, NJ: Avotaynu, 2000), 1–16. Eleventh-and twelfth-century coins with Hebrew inscriptions may be the earliest verifiable evidence, and the 1264 charter of privileges granted by Prince Bolesław the Pious to Jews of Silesia is the other later confirmation. Although the charter itself did not survive, its text is known from its confirmations by later rulers of Poland. For the discussion of early Jewish settlements, see Edward Fram, *Ideals Face Reality: Jewish Law and Life in Poland, 1550–1655*, Monographs of the Hebrew Union College 21 (Cincinnati: Hebrew Union College Press, 1997), 15–16; Jerzy Wyrozumski, "Jews in Medieval Poland," in *The Jews in Old Poland, 1000–1795*, ed. Antony Polonsky, Jakub Basista, and Andrzej Link-Lenczowski (New York: I. B. Tauris / Institute for Polish-Jewish Studies, 1993), 13–17; Omelijan Pritsak, "The Pre-Ashkenazic Jews of Eastern Europe in Relation to the Khazars, the Rus' and the Lithuanians," in *Ukrainian-Jewish Relations in Historical Perspective*, ed. Peter Potichnyi and Howard Aster (Edmonton: Canadian Institute of Ukrainian Studies, 1988); Bernard D. Weinryb, *The Jews of Poland: A Social and Economic History of the Jewish Community in Poland from 1100 to 1800* (Philadelphia: Jewish Publication Society of America, 1973), 17–27; Israel Ta-Shma, "On the History of the Jews in Twelfth and Thirteenth-Century Poland," *Polin* 10 (1997). For the 1264 decree, see Robert Chazan, *Church, State, and Jew in the Middle Ages*, Library of Jewish Studies (New York: Behrman House, 1980), 88–93, and Israel Halpern, ed., *Bet israel be-Polin* (Tel-Aviv: Youth Department of the Zionist Organization, 1953), 231–3. For a charter modeled on the 1264 charter given to Jews by Bolesław the Pious, see the 1388 charter by Duke Vitold Alexander of Lithuania, published in Mathias Bersohn, *Dyplomataryusz dotyczacąy Żydów w dawnej Polsce, na źródłach archiwalnych osnuty (1388–1782)* (Warsaw: Druk E. Nicz i s-ka, 1910), 15–18.

57. For the 1244 charter in English, see Chazan, *Church, State, and Jew in the Middle Ages*, 84–8; Marcus, *The Jew in the Medieval World*, 27–30.

58. The role of Jews in Cracow's economy until the end of the fifteenth century can be surmised from the municipal records published in Bożena Wyrozumska, ed., *The Jews in Mediaeval Cracow: Selected Records from Cracow Municipal Books* (Cracow: Polska Akademia Umiejętności, 1995). For the sixteenth and seventeenth centuries, see Jan Małecki, ed., *Jewish Trade in Cracow at the End of the Sixteenth Century and in the Seventeenth Century: Selected Records from Cracow Customs Registers, 1593–1683* (Cracow: Polska Akademia Umiejętności, 1995).

59. Majer Bałaban, *Historja Żydów w Krakowie i na Kazimierzu: 1304–1868* (Cracow: Krajowa Agencja Wydawnicza, 1991), 1: 16–23. See also Majer Bałaban, *Historja i literatura żydowska, ze szczególnem uwzglednieniem historji Żydów w Polsce* (Lwów, Warsaw, Cracow: Zakład Narodowy imienia Ossolińskich, 1924), 2: 327–71.

60. See, for example, Sergei Aleksandrovich Bershadskii, ed., *Dokumenty i regesty k istorii litovskikh evreev* (St. Petersburg: A. E. Landau, 1882), 1:65–7, 76, and also 3: 63, 76–7. S. A. Bershadskii, *Avram Ezofovich Rebichkovich, podskarbii zemskii, chlen rady Velikago Kniazhestva Litovskago: otryvok iz istorii vnutrennikh otnoshenii Litvy v nachalie XVI veka* (Kiev: Tip. G. T. Korchak-Novitskago, 1888). On Michel Ezofowicz, see Władysław Pociecha, "Ezofowicz, Rabinkowicz Michel," in *Polski słownik biograficzny*, ed. Władysław Konopczyński (Cracow: Polska Akademia Umiejetności, 1948), 6:331–3.

61. For the text of the ennoblement decree, see S. A. Bershadskii, *Russko-evreiskii arkhiv* (1882), 1: 125–6.

62. Gershon D. Hundert, "Jews, Money and Society in Seventeenth-Century Polish Commonwealth: The Case of Cracow," *Jewish Social Studies* 43, no. 3–4 (1981): 264.

63. Hundert, "Jews, Money and Society," 264. Hundert cites an extensive passage from Miczyński's book, 264–5.

64. See Rubin, *Gentile Tales*, 72.

65. I. D. Kuzmin, *Materialy k voprosu ob obvineniakh evreev v ritualnykh prestupleniakh* (St. Petersburg: Tip. Smolinskago, 1913), 28–32. Also in Bershadskii, *Dokumenty i regesty*, 2: 129–31, 169–74.

66. Kuzmin, *Materialy k voprosu*, 28. Bershadskii, *Dokumenty i regesty*, 2: 131.

67. *Volumina Legum*, 2: 258–9, par. "De Judaeis," col. 525.

68. *Volumina Legum*, 2: 51–2, col. 691.

69. See, for example, Jacob Goldberg, *Jewish Privileges in the Polish Commonwealth: Charters of Rights Granted to Jewish Communities in Poland-Lithuania in the Sixteenth to Eighteenth Centuries* (Jerusalem: The Israel Academy of Sciences and Humanities, 1985); Gershon David Hundert, *The Jews in a Polish Private Town: The Case of Opatów in the Eighteenth Century*, Johns Hopkins Jewish Studies (Baltimore: Johns Hopkins University Press, 1992), where the privilege to Jews in Opatów is discussed in the appendix.

70. *Volumina Legum*, 1: 270, par. "Qui nobiles," col. 550.

71. "Qui nobiles in oppidis aut in villis suis idaeos habent: per not licet, ut soli ex eis fructus omnes et emolumenta percipient: iusque illis, arbitratu suo dicant: verum ex quibus iudaeis, nullum ad Nos commodum pervenit, eos uti iudaeorum iure non permittimus, per Nos et Antecessores nostros concesso: neque de injuriis eorum deferri ad Nos volumes. Ut ex quibus nullum commodum sentimus: hi eiram nullum in Nobis praesidium habeant collocatum." *Volumina Legum*, 1: 270, par. "Qui nobiles," col. 550.

72. Stone, *The Polish-Lithuanian State*, 7–11.

73. Stone, *The Polish-Lithuanian State*, 11–14, 45.
74. Stone, *The Polish-Lithuanian State*, 60.
75. Stone, *The Polish-Lithuanian State*, 60–1.
76. *Volumina Legum*, 2: 89, col. 770, par. 3. Daniel Stone cites this passage in Stone, *The Polish-Lithuanian State*, 62.
77. *Volumina Legum*, 2:89–90, par. 4.
78. *Volumina Legum*, 2:90, par. 8.
79. *Volumina Legum*, 2:90, par. 12.
80. *Volumina Legum*, 2:90–1, par. 14.
81. Salo Wittmayer Baron, *Poland-Lithuania 1500–1650*. Vol. 16, *A Social and Religious History of the Jews* (New York: Columbia University Press and Jewish Publication Society of America, 1976), 164–213: "Expansion" (henceforth cited as *SRHJ vol. 16*). See also, Weinryb, *Jews of Poland*, 108–9.
82. Hundert, *The Jews in a Polish Private Town*, xi. It is estimated that there were about 750 thousand Jews in Poland in 1764.
83. Bohdan Baranowski, ed., *Instrukcje gospodarcze dla dóbr magnackich i szlacheckich z XVII–XIX wieku, źródła do historii kultury materialnej* (Wrocław: Zakład Narodowy im. Ossolińskich; PAN, 1958), 1 : 342–43.
84. Israel Halpern and Israel Bartal, eds., *Pinkas va'ad arb'a araẓot* (Jerusalem: Mosad Bialik, 1989), 208, no. 438. Cited in English in Gershon D. Hundert, "The *Kehilla* and the Municipality in Private Towns at the End of the Early Modern Period," in *The Jews in Old Poland, 1000–1795*, ed. Antony Polonsky, Jakub Basista, and Andrzej Link-Lenczowski (New York: I. B. Tauris / Institute for Polish-Jewish Studies, 1993), 184. On nobles' protection of their Jews from royal tax burden see also Adam Teller, "The Magnates' Attitude to Jewish Regional Autonomy in the Eighteenth Century," in *Studies in the History of the Jews in Old Poland*, ed. Adam Teller (Jerusalem: Magnes Press, 1998), 251–2, and Murray Jay Rosman, *The Lords' Jews: Magnate-Jewish Relations in the Polish-Lithuanian Commonwealth During the Eighteenth Century* (Cambridge, Mass.: Harvard University Press, 1990), 188.
85. AIVAK, vol. XXIX, 356–9.
86. AIVAK, vol. XXIX, 356.
87. This example also illustrates a phenomenon of movement across the social *and* religious boundaries within premodern east European society. The employment of Jews in building a Jesuit church went against Jewish law, which prohibited Jews to build gentile houses of worship. See for example *Shulḥan 'Aruk*, Yoreh De'ah, 143.2.
88. For Jewish economic activity in the sixteenth and seventeenth centuries, see Baron, "Socioeconomic Restratification," *SRHJ Vol. 16*, 214–312, and Fram, *Ideals Face Reality*, especially 67–163. For the eighteenth century see for example Hundert, *The Jews in a Polish Private Town* and Rosman, *The Lords' Jews*. For examples of the variety of roles see the two volumes of instructions sent by the nobles to their administrators concerning their estates, Baranowski, ed., *Instrukcje gospodarcze*.
89. The phrase "alienated minority" comes from Kenneth R. Stow, *Alienated Minority: The Jews of Medieval Latin Europe* (Cambridge, Mass.: Harvard University Press, 1992).
90. Rosman, *The Lords' Jews*, 207.
91. For the case see *Akty o evreiakh*, vol. XXVIII, *Akty izdavaemye vilenskoiu kommisieiu dla razbora drevnikj aktov* (Vilna: Russkii pochin, 1901), 215–16, no. 175. For the document on the extent of her lease contract see AIVAK, vol. XXVIII, 217–18, no. 176.

92. AIVAK, vol. XXVIII, 215–16.
93. Sometimes they were swayed by money. See a case in the late sixteenth century, where a Jewish leaseholder was outbid by a non-Jew. The non-Jew, however, had outbid the Jew only to obtain the lease but was not sincere and was, in fact, unwilling to pay the higher price. Benjamin Aaron ben Abraham Slonik, *Mas'at Binyamin: ve-hem she'elot u-teshuvot* (Cracow: M. N. Meisels, 1632), no. 27.
94. Rosman, *The Lords' Jews*, 207. On the magnates' relationship with the lesser nobles, see Maczak, "Problem of Authority," 121–3.
95. On some aspects of this protection, see Hundert, *The Jews in a Polish Private Town*, and Rosman, *The Lords' Jews*.
96. See also Hundert, *The Jews in a Polish Private Town*, 20; Rosman, *The Lords' Jews*, 38; Teller, "The Magnates' Attitude to Jewish Regional Autonomy in the Eighteenth Century," 255. For examples of the petitions by peasants in the eighteenth century, see Janina Leskiewiczowa and Jerzy Michalski, eds., *Supliki chłopskie XVIII wieku. Z archiwum prymasa Michała Poniatowskiego: Materiały do dziejów wsi polskiej* (Warszawa: Książka i Wiedza, 1954).
97. Hundert, *The Jews in a Polish Private Town*, 141.
98. Such was apparently the fate of Solomon Maimon's grandfather; see Solomon Maimon, *An Autobiography* (New York: Schocken Books, 1947), 3–8. See also the critique of this traditional view by Gershon Hundert in Hundert, "The *Kehilla* and the Municipality in Private Towns at the End of the Early Modern Period," 174–5.
99. Israel Halpern, ed., *Pinkas va'ad arb'a arazot* (Jerusalem: Mosad Bialik, 1945), 486, par. 11.
100. Moses Isserles, *Shu"T*, no. 63, cited in Fram, *Ideals Face Reality*, 33–4.
101. As cited in Gershon D. Hundert, "Poland: Paradissus Judaeorum," *Journal of Jewish Studies [Great Britain]* 48, no. 2 (1997): 333.
102. Hundert, "Poland: Paradissus Judaeorum," 341. Edward Fram, on the other hand, suggested that the prayers for the coming of the Messiah may be an indication of a sense of insecurity. Fram, *Ideals Face Reality*, 33–4, and note 89.
103. Fram, *Ideals Face Reality*, 32–6. Especially page 35, where he discusses Shlomo Luria.
104. AIVAK, vol. XXVIII, 8, no. 11.
105. For example AIVAK, vol. XXVIII, 104–95, no. 88; 130–1, no. 110; 188, nos. 151–2; 201, no. 164.
106. AIVAK, vol. XXVIII, 179–80, no. 43.
107. AIVAK, vol. XXVIII, 181–3, no. 146.
108. Teller, "The Legal Status of the Jews on the Magnate Estates," 50–1.
109. AIVAK, vol. VI, 89–90, no. 59.
110. The word used here is *gołota*, which means a landless nobleman, but in the eastern territories of the Polish-Lithuanian Commonwealth it would have been pronounced *hołota*, which, in turn, also means "riff raff" or "rabble." Either of the two words would have been offensive for a nobleman.
111. AIVAK, vol. XXVIII, 112–13.
112. AIVAK, vol. V, 19–20.
113. AIVAK, vol. V, 19.
114. AIVAK, vol. V, 20: "And on my and the nobles' behalf, Gałemski asked the Jews, who captured the prisoners to release them on bail, promising that they will all come to stand the trial.... But the Jewish beadles and other Jews who were with them said, 'we

will not allow any bail from you or even the lord himself and we will not release them from prison and we will keep them imprisoned until the trial because that's the order we received from the elders and the whole kahal.'"

115. For example, Jacob Goldberg, "Władza dominalna Żydow-arendarzy dóbr ziemskich nad chłopami w XVII–XVIII w.," *Przeglad Historyczny* 81 (1990). Rosman, *The Lords' Jews*.

116. Rosman, *The Lords' Jews*. See also Adam Teller, "Tafkidam ha-kalkali u-me'amadam ha-hevrati shel yehudim be-ahuzot bet Radziwil be-Lita ba-meah 18" (Ph.D. dissertation, Hebrew University, 1997).

117. AIVAK, vol. XXVIII, 166–7.

118. AIVAK, vol. XXVIII, 166–7. Goldberg, "Władza dominalna," 194–5. For a Christian complaint about abuses by Jewish leaseholders, see also *Arkhiv iugo-zapadnoi Rossii,* ed. Komissiia dlia razbora drevnikh aktov (Kiev: 1869), 1: 325–7.

119. See AIVAK, vol. XXVIII, 170.

120. Baranowski, ed., *Instrukcje gospodarcze,* 2:4. Judith Kalik found a case concerning an Eastern Orthodox priest and a Jewish arrendator who had monopoly rights to sell vodka in the town of Pupowiec. In order to prevent the violation of his rights and illegal production of alcohol, he searched local homes, including that of the local parish priest, sometimes confiscating property. In this case, the parish priest appealed to the bishop, who in turn appealed on behalf of the priest to the magnate-owner of the town. Yehudit Kalik, "Ha-knesiyyah ha-katolit ve-ha-yehudim be-mamlekhet Polin-Lita ba-meot ha-17–18." (Ph.D. dissertation, Hebrew University, 1998), 179–80.

121. For example, AIVAK, vol. XXVIII, 10. Also *Akty izdavaemye vilenskoiu kommisieiu dla razbora drevnikj aktov,* vol. XVII (Vilna: Tipografia A. G. Syrkina, 1890), 194, 333, 397. For examples of transactions involving serfs, see Janusz Deresiewicz, *Transakcje chłopami w rzeczypospolitej szlacheckiej w w. XVI–XVIII* (Warsaw: Książka i Wiedza, 1959).

122. Joel Sirkes, *Bait hadash (yashanot),* no. 61.

123. In Hebrew: "ve-afilu otah uma ha-yerudah bein kol ha-umot haiu moshlim behem." Nathan Nata Hannover, *Sefer yeven mezulah: gezerot tah-tat* (Kibbuz ha-meuhad: Ha-histadrut ha-kalkalit shel 'ovadim ha-'ivriim be-erez Israel, 1945), 20–1. The English translation is from Nathan Nata Hannover, *Abyss of Despair (Yeven Metzulah),* trans. Abraham J. Mesch, Judaica Series (New Brunswick, NJ: Transaction, 1983).

124. Hannover, *Sefer yeven mezulah: gezerot tah-tat,* 25.

125. Cited in Hayyim Hillel Ben-Sasson, *Hagut ve-hanhagah: hashkafotehem ha-hevratiyot shel yehudei Polin be-shilhe yeme ha-beynayim* (Jerusalem: Mosad Bialik, 1959), 124.

126. Izhak Michelewicz' property was valuable and the recorded list of things stolen is long and impressive. AIVAK, vol. XXVIII, 60–72. See also Nadav's discussion of the case in Modekhai Nadav, "Ma'aseh alimut ha-dadiyyim bein yehudim le-lo-yehudim be-Lita lifney 1648," *Gal-Ed* 7–8 (1985): 54–5.

127. AIVAK, vol. XXVIII, 70. On Michel Ezofowicz, see note 60.

128. AIVAK, vol. XXVIII, 70. Moshe Rosman discussed the difference between a Jewish lease and a noble lease in Rosman, *The Lords' Jews,* 110–13. The 1588 Lithuanian Statute specified that living in a town, "brewing and selling alcohol," "engaging in crafts" or usury, or selling merchandise were not befitting for a nobleman, and if some-one was to be regarded a nobleman he had to give up such activities and engage in "nobleman's and knightly works," otherwise he risked the loss of a nobleman's status.

Statut Velikago Kniazhestva Litovskago: s podvedeniem v nadlezhashchikh mestakh ssylki na konstitutsii, prilichnyia soderzhaniiu pnago: perevod s polskago (Sankt Petersburg: Pravitelstvuiushchii Senat, 1811), 1 :156, chapter 3, article XX, par.2, also 1 :161, chapter 3, art. XXV, art. 1–2.

129. *Prawa konstytucye y przywileie Królestwa Polskiego y Wielkiego Xięstwa Litewskiego y wszystkich prowincyi należących: na walnych seymiech koronnych od seymu wiślickiego roku pańskiego 1347 aż do ostatniego seymu uchwalone* (Warsaw, 1737–8), 5: 133. Also *Volumina Legum*, 5: 79. See also Janusz Tazbir, *Reformacja w Polsce* (Warsaw: Książka i Wiedza, 1993), 9.

130. AIVAK, vol. XXXVIII, 76–80, no. 69.

131. For an example of prohibitions to sue Jews in non-Jewish courts, see the takkanah of the Council of Lithuania, *Va'ad medinat Lita*, from 1628, no. 168. For a discussion on the prohibitions to bring cases into non-Jewish courts see Jacob Katz, *Exclusiveness and Tolerance: Studies in Jewish-Gentile Relations in Medieval and Modern Time* (Oxford: Oxford University Press, 1961), especially the chapter titled "Juridical and Moral Controls."

132. AIVAK, vol. XXVIII, 336, no. 274.

133. AIVAK, vol. XXVIII, 336.

134. AIVAK, vol. XXVIII, 336.

135. Isserles, *Shu"T* no. 88; a short fragment of this responsum is reprinted in Ben-Zion Katz, *Le-korot ha-yehudim be-Rusya, Polin ve-Lita* (1899), 10. Also Maharam Lublin, *Shu"T* (Venice: Pietro & Lorenzo Bragadin, 1618), no. 120, a short fragment is reprinted in Katz, *Le-korot ha-yehudim*, 11–12. For a call for a comparison of Jewish and non-Jewish court records see Fram, *Ideals Face Reality*, 10. See also Hundert, *The Jews in a Polish Private Town*, 20, 137.

136. "Vobis etiam iudaeis nostris in terris majoris Poloniae et ducatus Masoviae consistentibus severe percipimus et mandamus ut doctori, qui pro tempore constitutus fuerit, authoritatem illius agnoscatis, ei in hiis quae legis sunt, hoc est in spiritualibus, obedientiam debitam exhibeatis." Bersohn, *Dyplomatariusz*, 51. For a discussion of the King's role in shaping the rabbi's responsibilities, see Adam Teller, "The Laicization of Early Modern Jewish Society: The Development of Polish Communal Rabbinate in the Sixteenth Century," in *Schöpferische Momente des europäischen Judentums: In der frühen Neuzeit*, ed. Michael Graetz (Heidelberg: Winter, 2000).

137. AIVAK, vol. V, 24–5, no. 431. See also discussion in the following chapters, and Kalik, "Ha-knesiyyah ha-katolit ve-ha-yehudim be-mamlekhet Polin-Lita ba-meot ha-17–18," 136–7.

138. AIVAK, vol. XXIX, 211–12.

139. AIVAK, vol. XXIX, 211–12.

140. AIVAK, vol. XXIX, 409–11.

141. *Istoriko-iuridicheskie materialy*, vol. 24, 70–1.

142. AIVAK, vol. XXIX, 411.

143. Zenon Guldon and Jacek Wijaczka counted sixty-seven accusations of ritual murder in Poland-Lithuania during the sixteenth through the eighteenth centuries, with the majority ending in trials, and some in deaths of the accused. Zenon Guldon and Jacek Wijaczka, *Procesy o mordy rytualne w Polsce w XVI–XVIII wieku* (Kielce: DCF, 1995). Zenon Guldon and Jacek Wijaczka, "The Accusation of Ritual Murder in Poland, 1500–1800," *Polin* 10 (1997). See also Hundert, "Poland: Paradissus Judaeorum," 339.

144. The town is referred to as Wojnia in the text, but *Słownik geograficzny Królestwa Polskiego* (Warsaw: Wydawnictwa Artystyczne i Filmowe, 1977 <1893>), vol. 13, does not list such a town in the Brest region. The only towns with names related to that in the area are Wojnicz and Wojnówka, a small village. S. A. Bershadskii claims that there were only two Jewish homeowners in Wojnia, or Wojnicz, in 1566, yet he also gives names of two Jewish butchers in town, one of whom was a woman. It is unlikely that there would be two Jewish butchers with virtually no Jewish families. Either there were more Jews settled by 1566 and they were simply not homeowners, or there is a mistake in his assumption that these two butchers were kosher butchers. Bershadski, *Dokumenty i regesty*, 2: 155–6. Without explanation of the different possibilities, Hanna Węgrzynek identifies this town as Wohyń. Hanna Węgrzynek *"Czarna legenda" Żydów*, 101, 186.

145. AIVAK, vol. V, 4–6.

146. AIVAK, vol. V, 4–5.

147. On the use of these privileges by Jews see also Nadav, "Ma'aseh alimut," 3.

148. In fact one eighteenth-century anti-Jewish writer, Stefan Żuchowski, himself an instigator of a blood-libel trial in Sandomierz, questioned the authenticity of a papal bull condemning such accusations, saying that the popes believed in the blood libel as it is testified by their canonization of four victims. See Stefan Żuchowski, *Process kryminalny o niewinne dziecię Jerzego Krasnowskiego iuż to trzecie, roku 1710 dnia 18 sierpnia w Sendomirzu okrutnie od Żydów zamordowane* (Sandomierz after 1718), 191. See also Magdalena Teter, "Jews in the Legislation and Teachings of the Catholic Church in Poland 1648–1772" (Ph.D. dissertation, Columbia University, 2000) 161–2.

149. The complaint was written on September 17, 1741 and filed in the court records on September 20, 1741. Yom Kippur that year fell on September 20, the Holiday Tachanowski may therefore have been Yom Kippur, or Sukkot, which started at sundown on September 24.

150. AIVAK, vol. V, 267.

151. *Akty izdavaemye vilenskoiu kommisieiu dla razbora drevnikh aktov*, vol. XXIX: "Akty o evreiakh" (Vilna: Russkii Pochin', 1902), 244–53, no. 153.

152. AIVAK, vol. XXIX, 244–5.

153. AIVAK, vol. XXIX, 252–3.

154. AIVAK, vol. XXVIII, 333, no. 272.

155. AIVAK, vol. VI, 472–4, no. 150.

156. AIVAK, vol. VI, 473.

157. AIVAK, vol. VI, 473.

CHAPTER 3: HERESY AND THE FLEETING "TRIUMPH OF THE
COUNTER-REFORMATION"

1. For an overview of the thirteenth-century heresies, see for example Bernard Hamilton, "The Albigesian Crusade and Heresy," in *The New Cambridge Medieval History*, vol. 5, *C. 1198–C. 1300*, ed. David Abulafia (Cambridge, UK: Cambridge University Press, 1999). On the thirteenth-century change in Church attitudes, see for example Robert Chazan, *Barcelona and Beyond: The Disputation of 1263 and Its Aftermath* (Berkeley: University of California Press, 1992); Robert Chazan, *Daggers of Faith: Thirteenth-Century Christian Missionizing and Jewish Response* (Berkeley: University of California Press, 1989); Robert Chazan, *The New Christian Missionizing of the Thirteenth Century*

(Cambridge, Mass.: Harvard University Library, 1988); Robert Chazan, "Twelfth-Century Perceptions of the Jews: A Case Study of Bernard of Clairvaux and Peter the Venerable," in *From Witness to Witchcraft: Jews and Judaism in Medieval Christian Thought*, ed. Jeremy Cohen (Wiesbaden: Harrassowitz Verlag, 1996); Jeremy Cohen, *The Friars and the Jews: A Study in the Development of Medieval Anti-Judaism* (Ithaca: Cornell University Press, 1982); Solomon Grayzel, "The Papal Bull *Sicut Judaeis*," in *Essential Papers on Judaism and Christianity in Crisis*, ed. Jeremy Cohen (New York: New York University Press, 1991 <1962>); Kenneth R. Stow, "The Church and the Jews," in *The New Cambridge Medieval History*, vol. 5, *C. 1198–C. 1300*, ed. David Abulafia (Cambridge, UK: Cambridge University Press, 1999).

2. Bolesław Ulanowski, Jan Fijałek, and Adam Vetulani, eds., *Statuty synodalne wielunsko-kaliskie Mikołaja Trąby z r. 1420*, Studia i materiały do historii ustawodawstwa synodalnego w Polsce 4 (Cracow: Polska Akademia Umiejętności, 1915–1951), 94–7, "De Hereticis" and "Remedia contra hereticos."

3. *Statuty synodalne wieluńsko-kaliskie Mikołaja Trąby*, 94–7.

4. *Statuty synodalne wieluńsko-kaliskie Mikołaja Trąby*, 91–3, "De Judaeis."

5. See infra.

6. *Constitutiones Synodorum Matropolitanae Ecclesiae Gnesnensis Provincialium*, (Cracow: 1761 <1636>), 269.

7. MS. AEp 18: Volumen Primum Actorum Reverendissimi in Christo Patris et Domini Petri de Gamratis Episcopi Cracoviensis a Die 1ma Mensis Novembris Anni 1538-ui ad Finem Eiusdem Anni et Successive per Annos 1539num et 1540mum, in AKM in Cracow, 91–92v, report of execution 96v. Apparently the proceedings of the case were also recorded in AEp 2, now reported missing. Julian Bukowski, *Dzieje Reformacyi w Polsce: Od jej wejscia do Polski aż do jej upadku* (Cracow: Nakładem Autora, 1883), 176–9.

8. Bukowski, *Dzieje Reformacyi w Polsce*, 175–6. It was initially found in the now missing AEp 2.

9. Bukowski, *Dzieje Reformacyi w Polsce*, 176.

10. Bukowski, *Dzieje Reformacyi w Polsce*, 177.

11. Bukowski, *Dzieje Reformacyi w Polsce*, 177. See also AEp 12 in AKM in Cracow, fols. 48–48v.

12. AEp 12, fols. 48–48v.

13. AEp 12, fols. 50v–51: "Ja Catharina Malcherowa znayącz prawdzia chrzesczianska y appostolska wyara, przeklynam tho yaneni kazde caczersthwo y niedowyarstwo a zwlaszcza sprosthynorz y nyedowyarstwo zydowskie, o ktorych thich czaszow yesthem pomowyona y ostawyona, y przyswalam swyetemu Rzymskemu Cosciolowy y apostolskiy stoliczi a usti y berczem wiznawam, ysz wyerza y tha wyara dzierza kthora swiethii Rzimski Cosciol, z nauky evangelyey y apostllow swyantich dzerzecz naucza y tho poprzysyenfawam przezz yednoscz troycze svyanthey przesz sviethe evangelie pana cristusove, a ty kthorzy naprzeciw tey wyerze są, z ych naukami y naslawniki wyecznego pothepuenia dusthyne bycz obyawyam, a gthy ya sama czego panie boze uchoway przeczwiko they wyerze przyswalacz albo mowicz gde kowlwyck banda smiala srogoszczy prawa duchownego chcza bycz poddana tak my bog pomoczy y thy svyante evangelye."

14. Biblioteka Uniwersystetu Jagiellońskiego, MS. 5358 II: Notaty z kalendarzy dawnych krakowskich XV, XVII, XVII w., 14v: "1530 d. 11 Augusti Malchrowa consulissa Crac. per apostasiam prolapsa ad fidem judaicam in qua multo 5 annos fuit illam infideliatem

abjuravit et fidem Catholicam prosequita est in Curia episcopali praesentibus omnibus praelatii, plebanii et consulibus Crac."

15. The case lasted from March 28, 1531, till at least July 4, 1532, with numerous court appearances. See AKM in Cracow: MSS. AEp 12, fols. 130, 143, 152v, 154, 194v, 196v, 233, 238v; AEp 13, fol. 130v. See also AEp 13, 3v.

16. AEp 18, fols. 88v–91. For the reference to March 19, 1539, in Marcin Biem's of Olkusz notes, see MS. 5358 II in Biblioteka Uniwersytetu Jagiellońskiego in Cracow, fol. 27v.

17. AKM w Krakowie, AEp 18, fol. 90.

18. According to Canon 18 of the IV Lateran Council, Church officials have no authority to employ the death penalty: "sententiam sanguinis nullus clericus dictet aut proferat." But according to Church law, people sentenced by Church court were to be released to secular authorities for punishment applicable to such crimes in a given state. See note 20. See Gregory IX's decree "Damnati vero per ecclesiam saeculari iudicio relinquatur, animadversione debita puniendi." On the basis of these laws, Jerzy Waldemar Syryjczyk argues that whether or not a convict was executed depended on the local laws. Jerzy Waldemar Syryjczyk, *Apostazja od wiary w świetle przepisów kanonicznego prawa karnego: studium prawno-historyczne* (Warsaw: Akademia Teologii Katolickiej, 1984), 194.

19. Although it was published in Polish by Bartłomiej Groicki only in the second half of the sixteenth century, the Magdeburg law had been in place in Polish towns for a long while. Bartłomiej Groicki, *Artykuły prawa majdeburskiego. Postępek sądow około karania na gardle. Ustawa płacej u sądów* (Warszawa: Wydawnictwa Prawnicze, 1954 <1558, 1559>), 149. See the strong assertion by Janusz Tazbir that "if she had withdrawn her declarations he would have undoubtedly been released, but since she was obdurate, it was decided to punish her, in accordance with the law, for repeated heresy." Janusz Tazbir, *A State without Stakes: Polish Religious Toleration in the Sixteenth and Seventeenth Centuries* (Warsaw: Państwowy Instytut Wydawniczy, 1973), 47.

20. Canon 18 of the IV Lateran Council in 1215 established that "No cleric may pronounce a sentence of death, or execute such a sentence, or be present at its execution. If anyone in consequence of this prohibition should presume to inflict damage on churches or injury on ecclesiastical persons, let him be restrained by ecclesiastical censure. Nor may any cleric write or dictate letters destined for the execution of such a sentence. Wherefore, in the chanceries of the princes let this matter be committed to laymen and not to clerics. Neither may a cleric act as judge in the case of the rotarii [bands of robbers], archers, or other men of this kind devoted to the shedding of blood. No subdeacon, deacon or priest shall practice that part of surgery involving burning and cutting. Neither shall anyone in judicial tests or ordeals by hot or cold water, or hot iron bestow any blessing." Henry Joseph Schroeder, *Disciplinary Decrees of the General Councils, Text, Translation, and Commentary* (St. Louis: B. Herder Book Co., 1937), English, 258, Latin, 569.

21. The sentencing decree is found in AEp 18, fols. 91v–92. For a note on execution, see AEp 18, 96v.

22. Biblioteka Uniwersystetu Jagiellońskiego, MS. 5358 II: Notaty z kalendarzy dawnych krakowskich XV, XVII, XVII w., 27v: "1539 d. 19 Martii Citata fuit Malcherowa iterum ratione Judaismi quem abjuraverat 1530 d. 11 Augusti; d. 16 Aprilis Malcherowa consulissa Craco. Quod transiverat ad Iudaismum, pronunciat est apostata a Petro Gamrat episc. Crac. bona eius confiscata et ipsa potestati saeculari tradita in curia episcopali crac. et d. 19 Aprilis igne cremata est in circulo Crac. in eo loco ubi canes ucisi per canicidam colliguntur." A sixteenth-century chronicler, however, noted that she was burned to

death on the market square in front of the stone houses known as *Krupkowskie*, near the Church of Mary the Virgin, with her ashes thrown into the Vistula. "Kronika od r. 1507 do 1541 spisana (z rękopismu 1549)," in *Biblioteka starożytna pisarzy polskich* (Warsaw: n.p., 1854), vol. 4: 35.

23. Sermon I. 2. verses 40–53. C. Mervyn Maxwell, "Chrysostom's Homilies against the Jews: An English Translation" (Ph.D. dissertation, University of Chicago, 1966), 6. I am grateful to Prof. Kenneth Stow of Haifa University, Israel, for allowing me to read his forthcoming book on the concept of "Jewish dogs" in Christian thought based on the Bollandists and their discussion of the blood accusations against Jews in their *Acta Sanctorum* published in 1643.

24. This phrase comes from Proverbs 26:11. In June 591, Pope Gregory I wrote a letter to Bishop of Arles admonishing him not to force Jews to accept Christianity: "For when anyone is brought to the font of baptism not by sweetness of preaching but by compulsion, he returns to his former superstition.... For so our purpose is rightly accomplished and the mind of the convert returns not again to his former vomit." The English text is in Jacob Rader Marcus and Marc Saperstein, *The Jew in the Medieval World: A Source Book, 315–1791*, rev. ed. (Cincinnati: Hebrew Union College Press, 1999), 124–5. This phrase became a stock phrase in Church writings. See for example the Council of Tours in 1236: "Bishops shall take care that new converts in their diocese are instructed in the Faith, and that they are supported liberally, by such means as the bishops deem proper, lest under pretext of poverty the converts return to their vomit." Solomon Grayzel, *The Church and the Jews in the XIIIth Century: A Study of Their Relations During the Years 1198–1254* (Philadelphia: The Dropsie College, 1933), 328–9. See also Magdalena Teter, "Jewish Conversions to Catholicism in the Polish-Lithuanian Commonwealth of the Seventeenth and Eighteenth Centuries," *Jewish History* 17, no. 3 (2003): 277–8, note 48. Also Kenneth Stow's forthcoming book on "Jewish dogs."

25. Roman Pollak, Stanisław Drewniak, and Marian Kaczmarek, eds., *Antologia pamiętników polskich XVI wieku* (Wrocław: Zakład Narodowy im. Ossolińskich, 1966), 235.

26. Bukowski, *Dzieje Reformacyi w Polsce*, 178. Pollak, Drewniak, and Kaczmarek, eds., *Antologia pamiętników polskich XVI wieku*, 234–5.

27. Marcin Bielski, *Kronika* (Sanok: Karol Pollak, 1856), vol. 2: 1081. In the sixteenth-century edition of 1597, *Kronika polska Marcina Bielskiego* (Cracow: Jakób Siebeneicher, 1597), 590.

28. Wacław Sobieski, "Modlitewnik arjanski," *Reformacja w Polsce* 1, no. 1 (1921). Simon Dubnow, *History of the Jews in Russia and Poland*, trans. I. Friedlander (Bergenfield, NJ: Avotaynu, 2000), 34. Notably, Majer Bałaban acknowledged that there were those "who sympathized with the dogmas of Jewish religion." However, Bałaban still saw this case as an example of Church intolerance. Majer Bałaban, *Historja Żydów w Krakowie i na Kazimierzu: 1304–1868.* (Cracow: Krajowa Agencja Wydawnicza, 1991), vol. 1: 125. For the Protestant claims see for example Stanislaw Lubieniecki, *History of the Polish Reformation: And Nine Related Documents*, trans. George Huntston Williams (Minneapolis: Fortress Press, 1995), 93; and Wojciech Węgierski, *Kronika zboru ewangelickiego krakowskiego* (Cracow: n.p., 1817 <1651>), 3–4.

29. For example, Shmuel Ettinger, "The Council of Four Lands," in *The Jews in Old Poland, 1000–1795*, ed. Antony Polonsky, Jakub Basista, and Andrzej Link-Lenczowski

(New York: I.B. Tauris / Institute for Polish-Jewish Studies, 1993), 103; James Miller, "The Origins of Polish Arianism," *Sixteenth Century Journal* 16, no. 2 (1985): 235. In *A State without Stakes* (47), Janusz Tazbir acknowledged that she indeed converted to Judaism. However, in another book (*Reformacja w Polsce* [Warsaw: Książka i Wiedza, 1993], 15), Tazbir is less explicit about it.

30. Stefan Żuchowski, *Process kryminalny of niewinne dziecie Jerzego Krasnowskiego* (Sandomierz: n.p., after 1718), 29.

31. Eric Zivier, "Jüdische Bekehrungsversuche im Jahrhundert," in *Beiträge zur Geschichte der deutschen Juden: Festschrift zum ziebzigsten Geburstage Martin Philipsons*, Schriften herausgegeben von der Gesellschaft zur Förderung der Wissenschaft des Judentums (Leipzig: Gustav Fock, G.m.b.H., 1916), 96–113.

32. July 22, 1539, AKW (Cracow), Acta Actorum R[e]v[erendissi]mi Capituli, vol. III, fol. 228v. This at first glance formulaic charge of Jewish "maledictions" may be connected with the printing of a contemporary Hebrew book of penitential prayers around that time that was filled with anti-Christian invectives. See infra, and Edward Fram and Magdalena Teter, "Matai hithil ha-defus ha-ʿivri be-Krakov [When Did the Hebrew Printing Start in Cracow]," *Gal-Ed* 20 (2005).

33. Acta Actorum Rvmi Capituli, vol. III, AKW (Cracow), fol. 229.

34. Acta Actorum Rvmi Capituli, vol. III, AKW (Cracow), fol. 229.

35. Shmuel Ettinger, dismissing documents that suggest that such conversions took place, called them "ʿalilat ha-gerim" – the libel of proselytes. Shmuel Ettinger, "Maʿamadam ha-mishpati ve-ha-ḥevrati shel yehudei Ukraina ba-meot ha-15–17," *Zion* 20 (1955): 131. For examples of treatment of the "judaizers" as early Protestants see Sobieski, "Modlitewnik arjanski," 58. Bałaban, *Historia żydów w Krakowie*, 1: 125–30. Dubnow, *History of the Jews in Russia and Poland*, 34–6. See also Żuchowski, *Process kryminalny*, 29.

36. Jerema Maciszewski, *Szlachta i jej państwo* (Warsaw: Państwowe Wydawnictwo Naukowe, 1984), 122–3.

37. Alodia Kawecka-Gryczowa, ed., *Bogowie fałszywi: nieznany pamflet antykatolicki z XVI wieku* (Warsaw: Biblioteka Narodowa, 1983), 46.

38. See also Marcin Krowicki, who called the Catholic Church the Antichrist, or Roman Antichrist, and Catholic priests "God's and our enemies." Marcin Krowicki, *Obraz a kontrefet własny Antykrystów z Pisma Świętego dostatecznie wymalowany y wystrychniony przez sługę słowa Pana Krystusowego, Marcina Krowickiego, dla przestrogi ludziom krześcianskim*, Biblioteka pisarzy reformacyjnych 7, ed. Zbigniew Ogonowski, Lech Szczucki, and Janusz Tazbir (Warsaw: Polska Akademia Nauk, 1969). Marcin Krowicki, *Chrześcijańskie a żałobliwe napominanie*, Biblioteka pisarzy reformacyjnych 7, ed. Zbigniew Ogonowski, Lech Szczucki, and Janusz Tazbir (Warsaw: Polska Akademia Nauk, 1969).

39. Kawecka-Gryczowa, ed., *Bogowie fałszywi*, 47.

40. Kawecka-Gryczowa, ed., *Bogowie fałszywi*, 68.

41. The pamphlet was discovered in 1979 in a binding of another book by librarian Elemér Lakó of the Rumanian Academy of Sciences in Cluj-Napoca, and was published in Kawecka-Gryczowa, ed., *Bogowie fałszywi*, 34. This point was also made by Catholic preachers in moralistic sermons. See infra.

42. Krowicki, *Chrześcijańskie a żałobliwe napominanie*, 7. See also Krowicki, *Chrzescijańkie a żałobliwe napominanie*, 22–3, 24, 25. The anti-Trinitarian poet Wacław Potocki wrote

a poem mocking the wealth of Catholic bishops. See Potocki, "Biskup krakowski ze skotakiem," in *Arianie polscy w świetle własnej poezji: zarys ideologii i wybór wierszy*, ed. Jan Dürr-Durski (Warsaw: Państwowe Zakłady Wydawnictw Szkolnych, 1948), 109.

43. Cited in English after Valerian Krasiński, *Historical Sketch of the Rise, Progress and Decline of the Reformation in Poland* (London: Murray, 1838–1840), 1:385.

44. For a discussion of the name used by and ascribed to the Polish anti-Trinitarians, see Benedict Wiszowaty, Jr., "An Epistle Setting Forth a Brief History of the Life and Death of Andrew Wiszowaty and of the Unitarian Churches of His Time" (1684), published in English in George Huntston Williams, *The Polish Brethren: Documentation of the History and Thought of Unitarianism in the Polish-Lithuanian Commonwealth and in the Diaspora, 1601–1685* (Missoula, MT: Scholars Press for Harvard Theological Review, 1980), 1: 21–2, 27, 40.

45. Stanisław Kot, *Socinianism in Poland* (Boston: Starr King Press, 1957), xix–xxii.

46. *Volumina Legum: Przedruk zbioru praw staraniem XX. Pijarów w Warszawie od roku 1732 do roku 1782 wydanego*, 2nd ed., 10 vols. (Petersburg: Jozafat Ohryzka, 1859; reprint, 1980), 2:124.

47. *Volumina Legum*, 2: 124.

48. *Volumina Legum*, 2: 124.

49. Janusz Tazbir is one of the greatest proponents of the idea of Polish toleration. Most of his works argue that Poland was a very tolerant country and juxtapose Poland to western states, where, as he claims, the situation of religious dissidents was much worse. For example, see Janusz Tazbir, *Dzieje polskiej tolerancji* (Warsaw: Interpress, 1973); Janusz Tazbir, *Reformacja, kontrreformacja, tolerancja, a to Polska właśnie* (Wrocław: Wydawnictwo Dolnośląskie, 1996), 57–107; and Janusz Tazbir, *A State without Stakes*.

50. Józef Siemieński, "Dysydenci w ustawodawstwie," *Reformacja w Polsce* 20 (1928): 81–9.

51. See for example the minutes of the Sandomierz synod, in Maria Sipayłło, ed., *Acta Synodalia Ecclesiarum Poloniae Reformatarum, 1560–1570*, vol. 2, *Akta synodów różnowierczych w Polsce* (Warsaw: Wydawnictwa Uniwersytetu Warszawskiego, 1972), 251–304.

52. Dürr-Durski, ed., *Arianie polscy*, 77–8.

53. See for example Miller, "The Origins of Polish Arianism," especially 248 ff. See also Kot, *Socinianism in Poland*, and Faustus Socinus, "Epitome of a Colloquium Held in Raków in the Year 1601," in Williams, *The Polish Brethren*, 1: 125–6. Socinus opposed participation in wars but acknowledged that such refusal caused difficulties to Polish noblemen: "All know, however, if any Polish nobleman, when that takes place which is called in Polish the *pospolite ruszenie* [the general call of the nobility to arms], prefers not to proceed to war, he submits to penalties of such a character, which could easily be the cause that he himself would perish with his family, not only with respect to what pertains to this life and its comforts but even to what pertains to the future life, because in the measure he is reduced to extreme poverty he can most easily be driven to many shameful deeds, first he himself, then his wife, then their sons, then his daughters. Besides it is certain that it touches upon turmoil, which is even linked with future scandal, that such a man is commonly held to be a deserter and traitor to his fatherland, all of which things are most diligently to be avoided, so long as no one commits anything against the precepts of Christ."

54. Cited in English in Kot, *Socinianism in Poland*, 21.

55. *Acta Synodalia Ecclesiarum Poloniae Reformatarum, 1560–1570*, 2: 175.

56. Cited in Jarosław Bodniak, "Sprawa wygnania arjan w r. 1566," *Reformacja w Polsce* 5, no. 19 (1928): 58.

57. Kazimierz Kłoda, "Sprawa ariańska w czasie bezkrólewia 1648 roku," *Odrodzenie i Reformacja w Polsce* 22 (1977): 185. For the text of this clause see *Volumina Legum*, 3: 345–6.

58. *Acta Synodalia Ecclesiarum Poloniae Reformatarum, 1560–1570*, 2: 175.

59. Maria Sipayłło, ed., *Acta Synodalia Ecclesiarum Poloniae Reformatarum, 1571–1632*, vol. 3, *Akta synodów różnowierczych w Polsce* (Warsaw: Wydawnictwa Uniwersytetu Warszawskiego, 1983), 11.

60. Tazbir, *A State without Stakes*, 173–4. Kłoda, "Sprawa ariańska w czasie bezkrólewia 1648 roku," 185. *Volumina Legum*, 3: 345–6.

61. *Volumina Legum*, 4: 94.

62. See Maria Sipayłło, ed., *Acta Synodalia Ecclesiarum Poloniae Reformatarum, 1550–1559*, vol. 1, *Akta synodów różnowierczych w Polsce* (Warsaw: Wydawnictwa Uniwersytetu Warszawskiego, 1966); *Acta Synodalia Ecclesiarum Poloniae Reformatarum, 1560–1570; Acta Synodalia Ecclesiarum Poloniae Reformatarum, 1571–1632*.

63. *Acta Synodalia Ecclesiarum Poloniae Reformatarum, 1550–1559*, 1: 36.

64. *Acta Synodalia Ecclesiarum Poloniae Reformatarum, 1550–1559*, 1: 36.

65. For the text of the 1576 synod, see *Acta Synodalia Ecclesiarum Poloniae Reformatarum, 1571–1632*, 3: 15. See also the case of Stanisław Steffanowicz, who converted to Catholicism after being persuaded by Jesuits; he then became a member of a municipal council in Cracow and eventually committed suicide because "his conscience bothered him"; in Węgierski, *Kronika zboru ewangelickiego krakowskiego*, 70–1.

66. *Acta Synodalia Ecclesiarum Poloniae Reformatarum, 1571–1632*, 3: 380.

67. Some anti-Trinitarians remained faithful to this idea and still in the seventeenth century demanded that priests engage in manual labor. See the satirical poem by Wacław Potocki, "Dziesięcina," in Dürr-Durski, ed., *Arianie polscy*, 108–09.

68. *Acta Synodalia Ecclesiarum Poloniae Reformatarum, 1560–1570*, 2: 59.

69. *Acta Synodalia Ecclesiarum Poloniae Reformatarum, 1560–1570*, 2: 71.

70. *Acta Synodalia Ecclesiarum Poloniae Reformatarum, 1560–1570*, 2: 206.

71. *Acta Synodalia Ecclesiarum Poloniae Reformatarum, 1571–1632*, 3: 37. For money needed for schools, see also *Acta Synodalia Ecclesiarum Poloniae Reformatarum, 1560–1570*, 2: 71, as well as *Acta Synodalia Ecclesiarum Poloniae Reformatarum, 1571–1632*, 3: 104.

72. *Acta Synodalia Ecclesiarum Poloniae Reformatarum, 1560–1570*, 2: 53.

73. *Acta Synodalia Ecclesiarum Poloniae Reformatarum, 1571–1632*, 3: 183.

74. *Acta Synodalia Ecclesiarum Poloniae Reformatarum, 1550–1559*, 1: 84.

75. *Acta Synodalia Ecclesiarum Poloniae Reformatarum, 1550–1559*, 1: 85.

76. *Acta Synodalia Ecclesiarum Poloniae Reformatarum, 1550–1559*, 1: 111.

77. *Acta Synodalia Ecclesiarum Poloniae Reformatarum, 1560–1570*, 2: 110.

78. *Acta Synodalia Ecclesiarum Poloniae Reformatarum, 1571–1632*, 3: 7.

79. *Acta Synodalia Ecclesiarum Poloniae Reformatarum, 1571–1632*, 3: 221.

80. *Acta Synodalia Ecclesiarum Poloniae Reformatarum, 1550–1559*, 1: 99.

81. *Acta Synodalia Ecclesiarum Poloniae Reformatarum, 1550–1559*, 1: 100–01. See also the 1558 Synod in Włodzisław, in *Acta Synodalia Ecclesiarum Poloniae Reformatarum, 1550–1559*, 1: 277.

82. *Acta Synodalia Ecclesiarum Poloniae Reformatarum, 1571–1632*, 3: 105.

83. Marriage was not a sacrament according to Protestant teachings. Moreover, Protestants allowed divorce. In this context exempla such as the one evoked by Paweł Misiakiewicz, in which he pointed out that Joseph from Genesis was married by the Pharaoh and was soon bored with his wife, casting her off with a letter of divorce, was of a polemical nature. Paweł Misiakiewicz, "Korona Braterska nowo na świat rodzącą się Przenajświętszą P. Maryą koronuiącą iey koronacyą w przecudownym Sokalskim obrazie sprowadzona," in *Słuszna sprawa koron Jezusa y Maryi za dekretem O. S. papieża Innocentego XIII przez cała okrawę truymfalnego aktu koronacyi cudownego sokalskiego obrazu Nayświętszey Maryi Panny obwołana* (Lwów, 1727), 118–22. See also a diatribe against Protestant marriages and divorce in Jakób Wujek, *Postilla katholicka mneysza, to iest krótkie kazania abo wykłady świętych ewangeliey, na każdą niedzielę y na każde święto, przez cały rok według nauki prawdziwej kościoła chrześcijanskiego powszechnego* (Cracow: 1870–1 <1617>), 156–8. For the Sejm's decisions, see *Akt osobny pierwszey zawieraiący w sobie wolno ści y prerogàtywy Greków orientalnych, nieunitów, dyssydentów* (Warsaw, n.d.), 49, paragraph X. For a discussion of the Church reactions, see chapter 3.
84. *Acta Synodalia Ecclesiarum Poloniae Reformatarum, 1560–1570*, 2: 13.
85. On the Jesuit education system in Poland, see for example Bronisław Batoński, "Szkolnictwo jezuickie w dobie kontrreformacji," in *Z dziejów szkolnictwa jezuickiego w Polsce*, ed. Jerzy Paszenda (Cracow: WAM-Księża Jezuici, 1994).
86. Dürr-Durski, ed., *Arianie polscy*, 17.
87. Laws of the school in Raków published in English in Williams, *The Polish Brethren*, 1: 78.
88. *Acta Synodalia Ecclesiarum Poloniae Reformatarum, 1571–1632*, 3: 104.
89. For evidence of such debates, see Wiszowaty in Williams, *The Polish Brethren*, 1: 28.
90. *Acta Synodalia Ecclesiarum Poloniae Reformatarum, 1571–1632*, 3: 113.
91. *Acta Synodalia Ecclesiarum Poloniae Reformatarum, 1571–1632*, 3: 350.
92. *Acta Synodalia Ecclesiarum Poloniae Reformatarum, 1571–1632*, 3: 350.
93. *Acta Synodalia Ecclesiarum Poloniae Reformatarum, 1571–1632*, 3: 386.
94. *Acta Synodalia Ecclesiarum Poloniae Reformatarum, 1571–1632*, 3: 476.
95. "Dyskursik o sinodzie," in *Dwa nieznane rękopisy z dziejów polskiej Reformacji*, ed. Aleksander Woyde (Warsaw: Universitas Liberae Poloniae, Wolna Wszechnica Polska, 1922), 9.
96. *Acta Synodalia Ecclesiarum Poloniae Reformatarum, 1571–1632*, 3: 63.
97. *Acta Synodalia Ecclesiarum Poloniae Reformatarum, 1571–1632*, 3: 67.
98. *Acta Synodalia Ecclesiarum Poloniae Reformatarum, 1571–1632*, 3: 82–3.
99. "Dyskursik o Sinodzie," 9.
100. Cited in English in Kot, *Socinianism in Poland*, 112.
101. See for example Miller, "The Origins of Polish Arianism," 245–9. Wacław Potocki mocked these values and the importance of wealth; see his satirical poems "Zbytki polskie" and "Za pieniądze wszystko złe" in Dürr-Durski, ed., *Arianie polscy*, 112–14.
102. *Acta Synodalia Ecclesiarum Poloniae Reformatarum, 1571–1632*, 3: 331.
103. *Acta Synodalia Ecclesiarum Poloniae Reformatarum, 1560–1570*, 2: 288.
104. For an overview of this process, see Norman Davies' chapter "Antemurale: Bulwark of Christendom," in his *God's Playground: A History of Poland*, vol. 1, *The Origins to 1795* (New York: Columbia University Press, 1982). See also, Janusz Tazbir, "Sarmatyzacja katolicyzmu w XVII wieku," in *Wiek XVII–kontrreformacja–barok: prace*

z historii kultury, ed. Janusz Pelc (Wrocław: Zakład Narodowy im. Ossolińskich, 1970), 13–14.

105. There is a large body of literature on this subject; the most recent studies include Edward Fram, "Creating a Tale of Martyrdom in Tulczyn, 1648," in *Jewish History and Jewish Memory: Essays in Honor of Yosef Hayim Yerushalmi*, ed. Elisheva Carlebach, John M. Efron, and David N. Myers (Hanover, NH: University Press of New England, 1998); Edward Fram, "Bein 1096 ve 1648–49 – 'iyun me hadash," *Zion* 61, no. 2 (1996); Edward Fram, "Ve-'adayin en bein 1096 le-1648–49," *Zion* 62, no. 1 (1997); Hayyim Jonah Gurland, *Le-korot ha-gezerot al yisrael* (Przemyśl: 1887); Nathan Nata Hannover, *Abyss of Despair (Yeven Metzulah)*, trans. Abraham J. Mesch, Judaica Series (New Brunswick, NJ: Transaction, 1983); Nathan Nata Hannover, *Sefer yeven mezulah: gezerot tah-tat* (Kibbuz Ha-Meuhad: Ha-Histadrut ha-kalkalit shel 'ovadim ha-'ivriim be-erez Israel, 1945); Joel Raba, *Bein zikaron le-hakhhashah: gezerot 408 ve–409 be-reshimot bene ha-zeman uve-ro'i ha-khetivah ha-historit*, vol. 98 (Tel-Aviv: Makhon le-heker ha-tefuzot, 1994); Joel Raba, *Between Remembrance and Denial: The Fate of the Jews in the Wars of the Polish Commonwealth During the Mid-Seventeenth Century as Shown in Contemporary Writings and Historical Research*, (Boulder: East European Monographs, 1995); Bernard D. Weinryb, *The Jews of Poland: A Social and Economic History of the Jewish Community in Poland from 1100 to 1800* (Philadelphia: Jewish Publication Society of America, 1973), 181–205; Howard Aster, Peter J. Potichnyj, and Canadian Institute of Ukrainian Studies, *Ukrainian-Jewish Relations in Historical Perspective*, 2nd ed. (Edmonton: Canadian Institute of Ukrainian Studies, University of Alberta, 1990); Frank Sysyn, "A Contemporary's Account of the Causes of the Khmel'nytskyi Uprising," *Harvard Ukrainian Studies* 1, no. 2 (1981); Frank Sysyn, "The Jewish Factor in the Khmiel'nytskyi Uprising," in *Ukrainian-Jewish Relations in Historical Perspective*, ed. Howard Aster and Peter Potichnyi (Edmonton: Canadian Institute of Ukrainian Studies, University of Alberta, 1990). *Jewish History* 17 (2) is devoted entirely to the Chmielnicki uprising.

106. Jerzy Lukowski, *Liberty's Folly: The Polish-Lithuanian Commonwealth in the Eighteenth Century, 1697–1795* (New York: Routledge, 1991), 7–8.

107. To see this, one need only compare sizes of the towns in the sixteenth and early seventeenth centuries and in the late seventeenth and eighteenth centuries. Maria Bogucka, "Polish Towns between the Sixteenth and Eighteenth Centuries," in *A Republic of Nobles: Studies in Polish History to 1864*, ed. J. K. Fedorowicz (New York: Cambridge University Press, 1982), 138–41; Lukowski, *Liberty's Folly*, 62–3.

108. MS. 590 "Księga synodów generalnych z lat 1633–1678" in Biblioteka Uniwersytetu Warszawskiego, fol. 248.

109. MS. 590 "Księga synodów generalnych z lat 1633–1678" in Biblioteka Uniwersytetu Warszawskiego, for example fols. 121–122, 245–248.

110. *Volumina Legum*, 4: 238. For an English translation see Williams, *The Polish Brethren*, 1: 39–40.

111. *Volumina Legum*, 4: 238.

112. See for example Lubieniecki, *History of the Polish Reformation: And Nine Related Documents*, and Williams, *The Polish Brethren*, 1: 44–49. For an account of the impact of the exile decree on the most committed anti-Trinitarians, see Jonas Sztychling's letter to a pastor in Holland published in Williams, *The Polish Brethren*, 2: 639–56.

113. Jesuit sources, such as Litterae Annuae from the second half of the seventeenth century, suggest such conversions. See for example MS. Pol. 53 "Historia 1648–1670" in

ARSI (Archivium Romanum Societatis Iesu) in Rome, Annuae Proviniciae Poloniae for Lublin (1665, 1666), Cracow (1666), Krosno (Crosno, 1678), Jarosław (1662, 1667, 1670).

114. Aside from the explicitly religious charges, the right of Potocki's wife to own property was questioned because of her Arianism. See Stanislaw Grzeszczuk, "Wacław Potocki," in *Polski słownik biograficzny*, ed. Stefan Kieniewicz et al. (Wrocław: Zakład Narodowy im. Ossolińskich, 1985), vol. 28/2: 221–2.

115. Williams, *The Polish Brethren*, 2: 663–4.

116. Henryk Wisner, "Dysydenci litewscy wobec wybuchu wojny polsko-szwedzkiej (1655–1660)," *Odrodzenie i Reformacja w Polsce* 15 (1970). Dürr-Durski, ed., *Arianie polscy*, 299. See also Wiszowaty in Williams, *The Polish Brethren*, 1: 36, 61 n. 123.

117. Williams, *The Polish Brethren*, 2: 576.

118. Samuel Twardowski, *Woyna domowa z Kozaki i Tatary, Moskwą, potym Szwedami i z Węgry przez lat dvvanascie [sic] za panowania nayjaśnieyszego Iana Kazimierza króla polskiego tocząca się* (Kalisz: Typis Societatis Jesu, 1681), "Woyny domowey czwartey, punkt wtory," 138–9.

119. *Volumina Legum*, 4: 272.

120. Marek Wajsblum, *Ex Regestro Arianismi: szkice z dziejów upadku protestantyzmu w Małopolsce* (Cracow: Towarzystwo Badań Dziejów Reformacji w Polsce, 1937), 45.

121. Williams, *The Polish Brethren*, 2: 646–7.

122. Davies, *God's Playground: A History of Poland*, 1: 454, 466.

123. *Volumina Legum*, 4: 323.

124. Williams, *The Polish Brethren*, 2: 647.

125. *Volumina Legum*, 4: 389. The anti-Trinitarians themselves saw wars that started in 1648 as punishment for sins of the Polish-Lithuanian Commonwealth. But the sins were not theirs. An anonymous writer left a counter-Gospel modeled on Matthew 18:23ff, in which he enumerated all the sins of the Commonwealth, beginning with idolatry, all the way through the whole Decalogue. Dürr-Durski, ed., *Arianie polscy*, 199–205, especially, 199–202.

126. *Volumina Legum*, 4: 389.

127. Dürr-Durski, ed., *Arianie polscy*, 208 (the whole poem: 207–10).

128. Dürr-Durski, ed., *Arianie polscy*, 208. Potocki's adamant reaction to the law against husbands protecting their wives is partly linked to his deep love for his wife, beautifully expressed in his poem written after her death in 1686. Dürr-Durski, ed., *Arianie polscy*, 151–6. On the consequences of the anti-Arian laws, see also Potocki's poem "Summum Ius Summa Iniuria," Dürr-Durski, ed., *Arianie polscy*, 217.

129. The Uniates were a denomination resulting from the 1596 Union of Brest Litovsk according to which a faction of Eastern Orthodox Christians accepted the authority of the Pope, but was allowed to retain their own religious rites.

130. *Volumina Legum*, 4: 484.

131. Wajsblum, *Ex Regestro Arianismi*, 65 ff.

132. *Volumina Legum*, 5: 355.

133. *Volumina Legum*, 6: 220.

134. See Wajsblum, *Ex Regestro Arianismi*, 67.

135. *Volumina Legum*, 4: 286.

136. *Volumina Legum*, 4: 286.

137. *Volumina Legum*, 4: 11.

138. *Volumina Legum*, 4: 133.
139. See the discussion below of a Jewish convert to Catholicism during the Northern War with Sweden.
140. Davies, *God's Playground: A History of Poland*, 1: 404–5. Józef Andrzej Gierowski, *Historia Polski, 1505–1864* (Warsaw: Państwowy Instytut Wydawniczy, 1978), 1: 383–4.
141. *Akt osobny pierwszy zawieraiący w sobie wolności y prerogatywy Greków orientalnych, nieunitów dyssydentów, obywatelów y mieszkańców w państwach nayiaśnieyszey Rzeczpospolitey Polskiey w przyłączonych do niey prowincyach*, published in volume VII of *Prawa, konstytucye i przywileie Królestwa Polskiego y Wielkiego Xięstwa Litewskiego y wszystkich prowincyi należących: na walnych seymiech koronnych od Seymu wiślickiego roku pańskiego 1347 aż do ostatniego Seymu uchwalone* (Warsaw, n.d.)
142. See for example the following MSS in Biblioteka Uniwersytetu Warszawskiego: 590 "Księga synodów generalnych z lat 1633–1678"; 594 "Acta y conclusie albo canony synodów zboru districtu lubelskiego 1636–1708"; 596 "Akta synodow prowincjonalnych małopolskich 1719–1766." In the 1690s, the authors of the "Discourse on the synod" stated that neither could they burden one person with the costs and responsibilities of a printing house, nor could they do without these. "Dyskursik o sinodzie," 7. See also Wojciech Kriegseisen, *Ewangelicy polscy i litewscy w epoce saskiej* (Warsaw: Semper, 1996).
143. *Akty izdavaemye vilenskoiu kommisieiu dla razbora drevnikj aktov*, vol. V (Vilna: 1871), 173.

CHAPTER 4: "BAD AND CRUEL CATHOLICS": CHRISTIAN SINS AND SOCIAL
INTIMACIES BETWEEN JEWS AND CHRISTIANS

1. MS. 263 "Kazania: 55 kazań na różne okoliczności" in Archiwum O. O. Franciszkanów Reformatów in Cracow, Sermon 33, no pagination. In a late eighteenth-century sermon, Franciscan preacher Józef Męciński continued to use the metaphor of Jews murdering Jesus in underlining Christian sins, MS. 274 in Archiwum O. O. Franciszkanów Reformatów in Cracow, fols. 19v, 20v–21 r.
2. On the Counter-Reformation and social discipline and on the level of education of the laity, see for instance R. Po-chia Hsia, *Social Discipline in the Reformation: Central Europe, 1550–1750*, Christianity and Society in the Modern World (New York: Routledge, 1989), especially 129–35, 152, 183; and R. Po-chia Hsia, *The World of Catholic Renewal* (New York: Cambridge University Press, 1998), 115–17.
3. On this issue in the West, see Jean Delumeau, *Catholicism between Luther and Voltaire: A New View of the Counter-Reformation* (Philadelphia: Westminster Press, 1977), 159–202. See also Louis Châtellier, *The Religion of the Poor: Rural Missions in Europe and the Formation of Modern Catholicism, C. 1500-C. 1800* (New York: Cambridge University Press, 1997). On the Jesuit missions and education, see John W. O'Malley, *The First Jesuits* (Cambridge, MA: Harvard University Press, 1993), 70, 117–20, 126–7, 272. See also, Hsia, *The World of Catholic Renewal*, 116–17, 198.
4. Jakub Radliński, *Prawda chrześcianska od nieprzyiaciela swego zeznana* (Lublin: W Drukarni Coll: Soc: Jesu, 1733), 427–32. See also for example Krzysztof Jan Szembek, *Krótkie zebranie nauki chrześcianskiey* (Cracow: Drukarnia Franciszka Cezarego, 1719), 93, 131.

5. Preaching was, as Patrick Ferry stated, "a way of connecting the theological teachings and pastoral concerns of the clergy with the religious ideas and spiritual practices of the people." Patrick Ferry, "Confessionalization and Popular Preaching: Sermons against Synergism in Reformation Saxony," *Sixteenth Century Journal* 28, no. 4 (1997): 1143. The emphasis on preaching was also reflected in the ecclesiastical architecture. New churches were more intimate and their shape and acoustics allowed for preaching. Older, gothic churches, not suitable for preaching, were increasingly furnished with new preaching stands usually placed on the side of the main nave.

6. R. Po-chia Hsia, *The World of Catholic Renewal,* 198–9. See also Châtellier, *The Religion of the Poor,* 15–19, 23–4, 32–6.

7. Jacob Marchand, *Katechizm abo nauka chrześcijanska* (Cracow: 1682 <1648>), 50–2. To ensure privacy, confessionals were introduced too. Merry E. Wiesner, *Women and Gender in Early Modern Europe,* New Approaches to European History (New York: Cambridge University Press, 1993), 201.

8. Jan Krosnowski, SJ, *Pochodnia słowa bożego w kazaniach niedzielnych całego roku na oświecenie i zapalenie rozumów i afektów chrześciańskich przez Iana Krosnowskiego Societatis Iesu wystawiona roku Boga w ciele ludzkim oświecaiącego 1689 w Lublinie w Drukarni Koleium [sic] Societatis IESU* (Lublin: Typis Societatis Jesu, 1689), 185.

9. Krosnowski, *Pochodnia Słowa Bożego,* 185.

10. This phrase has been borrowed from W. David Myers, *"Poor, Sinning Folk": Confession and Conscience in Counter-Reformation Germany* (Ithaca, NY: Cornell University Press, 1996).

11. MS. 280 "Zebranie obiaśniaiących w głębokich niewiadomości cieniach pogrążonych serc ludzi prostych kondycyi nauk podczas missyi w kazaniach materyi według potrzeby wyrażonych roku pańskiego 1756 w Krakowie na Stradomiu" in Archiwum OO. Reformatów in Cracow, "Conciones de Sanctificatione Festorum," folios 219 ff.

12. Julius Ruff noted that "weekend" violence was a serious issue in early modern Europe. Julius R. Ruff, *Violence in Early Modern Europe, 1500–1800,* New Approaches to European History 22 (New York: Cambridge University Press, 2001), 128–9.

13. It is the preachers' job to point to the sins of the society and to attempt to correct them. As such, though problematic as a source of information about the audiences, sermons serve as a source in gauging the clergy's ideals and concerns. Indeed, as Ferry pointed out, "sermon material tells us much more about the preachers than about the auditors." Ferry, "Confessionalization and Popular Preaching," 1146.

14. Gershon David Hundert, *The Jews in a Polish Private Town: The Case of Opatów in the Eighteenth Century,* Johns Hopkins Jewish Studies (Baltimore: Johns Hopkins University Press, 1992), 64–8. See also Jacob Goldberg, "Poles and Jews in the Seventeenth and Eighteenth Centuries: Rejection and Acceptance," *Jahrbücher für Geschichte Osteuropas* 22 (1974): 260–1. On halakhic problems related to this activity see Jacob Katz, *Goi Shel Shabat* (Jerusalem: Merkaz Zalman Shazar, 1983), and Jacob Katz, *The "Shabbes Goy": A Study in Halakhic Flexibility* (Philadelphia: Jewish Publication Society, 1989), 96–8. In prewar Poland, the Jews, who continued to run taverns, became symbols of the social ills of Polish Catholic society, stemming from the lack of temperance. They were blamed for Poles' inebriety.

15. Jan Alexander Lipski, *Epistola Pastoralis ad Clerum et Populum Dioecesis Cracoviensis. Ex Mandato Eminentissimi et Reverendissimi Domini Ioanni Alexandri Divina Miseratione S. R. E. Presbyterii Cardinalis Lipski Episcopi Cracoviensis, Ducis Severiae* (1737).

16. *Constitutiones et Decreta Synodi Dioecesana Plocensi sub Illustrissimo Excellentissimo Reverendissimo Domino D. Andrea Stanislao Kostka in Zaluskie Zaluski Dei et Apostolicae Sedis Gratia Episcopo Plocensi Pultoviae Anno Domini M.D. CC.XXXIII Die 4 Augusti Celebratae* (Warsaw: Typis Societatis Jesu, 1735), 12. Elisheva Carlebach is currently working on the Jewish calendars, and *sifre 'evronot*, which indicate that Jews were acutely aware of the Christian calendar, and noted Christian holidays in their calendars, sometimes with a polemical twist.

17. Andrzej Stanislaw Kostka Zaluski, "Edictum contra Judaeos" in MS. "Edicta et Mandata Diocesis Cracoviensis 1737–1772" in AKM in Cracow.

18. For more on this, see for example Gershon David Hundert, *The Jews in a Polish Private Town*, 64–8; Murray Jay Rosman, *The Lords' Jews: Magnate-Jewish Relations in the Polish-Lithuanian Commonwealth During the Eighteenth Century* (Cambridge, MA: Harvard University Press, 1990), 113–20.

19. See also chapter five.

20. Franciszek Antoni Kobielski, *List pasterski: Wszem i wobec i każdemu z osobna a osobliwie niewiernym rabinom kahalnym* (Łuck: 1741); Lipski, *Epistola Pastoralis*; Józef Eustachy Szembek, *List pasterski wyraźne w sobie naywyższey stolicy apostolskiey uwagi y napomnienia dostateczne zawieraiący, dla zabieżenia y z gruntu wyniszczenia niegodziwych występkow, przez niewierne żydowstwo z oczywistym uszczerbkiem wiary świętey y prawa duchownego y oyczystego, zagęszczonych w dyecezyi chełmskiey w roku 1752 ogłoszony* (Zamość: Drukarnia B. Jana Kantego, 1752); Załuski, "Edictum contra Judaeos." The problem of servile labor on Sundays and holidays had already been legislated against in the Carolingian Empire. One of the rulings attributed to Charlemagne was that the Jews could own Christian slaves, provided they did not make them work on Sundays. See Walter Pakter, *Medieval Canon Law and the Jews* (Ebelsbach: R. Gremer, 1988), 96; Grayzel and Stow, *The Church and the Jews in the XIIIth Century*, 161, n. 6; see also 157–62 for an example of a papal letter dealing with this issue – a bull by Honorius IV of November 30, 1286.

21. Lipski, *Epistola Pastoralis*. I2 verso.

22. For examples of the parish priests' responsibility to prevent and report on the violations of decrees regarding conduct of Jews and Christians, see *Synodus Dioecesana ab Illustrissimo et Reverendissimo D. Casimiro a Łubna Łubienski Dei et Apostolica Sedis Gratia Episcopo Cracoviensis Duce Severiae Celebrata Cracoviae in Ecclesia Archipresbyteriali A.D. 1711* (Cracow: Franciszek Cezary, 1711), 47; *Constitutiones et Decreta Synodi Plocensis (1733)*, "De Judaeis," 8–15; *Decreta, Sanctiones et Universa Acta Synodi Dioecesanae ab Illustrissimo, Excellentissimo ac Reverendissimo Domino D. Constantino Casimiro Brzostowski* (Wilno: Typis Societatis Jesu, 1717), 76–7. For an example of priests' responsibility to monitor Christian conduct more broadly, see for instance a decree of the synod of Płock in 1733, which ordered priests to investigate and report on those "infected with heresy." *Constitutiones et Decreta Synodi Plocensis (1733)*, "De Hereticis," 4–8.

23. AIVAK, vol. XXVIII: "Akty o evreiakh," 224–5.

24. AIVAK, 28: 270. The case continues on 251–2, 269–72.

25. AIVAK, 28: 272. Another case from 1646 shows Jewish leaseholders forcing Christian peasants to work on Christian holidays, 284–6.

26. AIVAK, vol. V, 182–3, doc. 495. In 1652, a complaint was sent to Prince Albrecht Stanisław Radziwiłł by Mikołaj Baranowicz of Motole (a small town) concerning a brawl that

happened after Baranowicz scolded Jews and their helpers for working on Sundays. See AIVAK, 28: 345–6, doc. 283.

27. For this line of argument see Yehudit Kalik, "Ha-knesiyah ha-katolit ve-ha-yehudim be-mamlekhet Polin-Lita ba-meot ha-17–18." (Ph.D. dissertation, Hebrew University, 1998), 81.

28. See also chapters two and six.

29. For a discussion of the tensions between the halakhic ideals and the reality, see Edward Fram, *Ideals Face Reality: Jewish Law and Life in Poland, 1550–1655* (Cincinnati: Hebrew Union College Press, 1997).

30. See for instance *Shulḥan 'Aruk*, Yoreh De'ah 113, especially Isserles on 113.4. For a detailed halakhic study of the question of non-Jewish servants see Katz, *Goi Shel Shabat*, and *The "Shabbes Goy."* For instance rabbis prohibited Jewish women to nurse non-Jewish children and to help non-Jewish women in labor, the latter on the grounds that they would be helping them to bring "idolaters" into this world. Mishnah AZ 2:1. See also Maimonides' explanation in *Mishnah 'im perush rabenu Mosheh ben Maimon* (Jerusalem, 1964/5), 2:228. *Shulḥan 'Aruk*, Yoreh De'ah, 154.1–2. Judith Kalik argues that Church laws influenced also decisions made by Jewish communal leaders. She gives an example of a 1595 takkanah from Cracow prohibiting Jews from keeping Christian servants overnight. See Kalik, "Ha-knesiyah ha-katolit ve-ha-yehudim be-mamlekhet Polin-Lita ba-meot ha-17–18," 85–6.

31. For examples of Church law, see Grayzel, *The Church and the Jews in the XIIIth Century*, "Etsi Judaeos": 114–17; III Lateran Council 1179: 296–7.

32. The laws of *niddah* and *yiḥud* created difficulties for Jewish men to interact with Jewish female servants; Edward Fram, "A Lamb among the Lions," paper delivered at the conference "Jews and Burgers in the Nobles' Republic," Warsaw, September 29–October 2, 2002. For a discussion of Jewish female servants, see Hundert, *The Jews in a Polish Private Town*, 71–5.

33. Merry Wiesner argues that "domestic service was probably the largest employer of women in most cities," citing Cissie Fairchild's and Judith Brown's research showing that in France and Florence two-thirds of domestic servants were female. Wiesner, *Women and Gender in Early Modern Europe*, 92. Sometimes women were hired as domestic servants as part of the welfare system in early modern cities, whereby they would receive support in exchange for work, albeit with a lower payment. On early modern welfare, see Abel Athouguia Alves, "The Christian Social Organism and Social Welfare: The Case of Vives, Calvin and Loyola," *Sixteenth Century Journal* 20, no. 1 (1989); Marco H. D. van Leeuwen, "Logic of Charity: Poor Relief in Preindustrial Europe," *Journal of Interdisciplinary History* 24, no. 4 (1994); Nicholas Terpstra, "Apprenticeship in Social Welfare: From Confraternal Charity to Municipal Poor Relief in Early Modern Italy," *Sixteenth Century Journal* 25, no. 1 (1994); Nicholas Terpstra, "Confraternal Prison Charity and Political Consolidation in Sixteenth-Century Bologna," *Journal of Modern History* 66, no. 2 (1994). See also Bronisław Geremek, *Poverty: A History* (Oxford: Blackwell, 1997), especially 142–77.

34. See for instance Moses Isserles' gloss on *Shulḥan 'Aruk*, Yoreh De'ah 81.7

35. Wiesner, *Women and Gender in Early Modern Europe*, 93. Pope Benedict XIV, *Epistola Encyclica ad Primatem, Archiepiscopos et Episcopos Regni Poloniae. De His Quae Vetita Sunt Hebraeis Habitantibus in Iisdem Civitatibus et Locis in Quibus Habitant Christiani* (Rome: 1751); Pope Benedict XIV, *List pasterski wyraźne w sobie naywyższey*

stolicy apostolskiey uwagi y napomnienia dostateczne zawieraiący, dla zabieżenia y z gruntu wyniszczenia niegodziwych występkow, przez niewierne żydowstwo z oczywistym uszczerbkiem wiary świętey y prawa duchownego y oczywistego, zagęszczonych w dyecezyi chełmskiey w roku 1752 ogłoszony (Zamość: Jan Kanty, 1752). Poor Jewish women were sometimes employed as servants in exchange for financial support from the community. On this see Hayyim Hillel Ben-Sasson, *Hagut ve-hanhagah: Hashkafotehem ha-ḥevratiyot shel yehudei Polin be-shilhe yeme ha-beynayim* (Jerusalem: Mosad Bialik, 1959), 156–7.

36. *Shulḥan ʾAruk*, Yoreh Deʿah, 154.1, based on Mishnah, AZ 2.1. See Yehudit Kalik, "Christian Servants Employed by Jews in the Polish-Lithuanian Commonwealth in the Seventeenth and Eighteenth Centuries," *Polin* 14 (2001): 266–7.

37. Renaissance Italians had similar concerns, as Rudolph Bell has shown; Rudolph M. Bell, *How to Do It: Guides to Good Living for Renaissance Italians* (Chicago: University of Chicago Press, 1999), 126–37. On secret baptism, see for instance Pope Benedict XIV's ruling that secret baptism by wet nurses was valid. Pope Benedict XIV, *De baptismo Judaeorum*. See also the tale of a Jewish child who was stolen by a Christian servant and became a pope, popularized in an early seventeenth-century Yiddish collection of tales, *Mayse Bukh*. For the English translation, see Moses Gaster, *Maʾaseh Book: Book of Jewish Tales and Legends* (Philadelphia: Jewish publication Society of America, 1981), 410–18.

38. *Acta, Constitutiones & Decreta Synodi Diaecesis Vilnensis, Praesidente Illustrissimo ac Reverendissimo Domino Domino Alexandro Michaele Kotowicz* (Wilno: Typis Academicis Societatis Jesu, 1685), 34. Further in the paragraph it is stated that Christian women were talked into selling their children to Jews for their abuses.

39. Already in the Middle Ages, the Church was concerned with the religious corruption of Christian women serving in Jewish homes as midwives and wet nurses. Pope Alexander III in his bull *Licet universis* admonished that Christian women should not accept such jobs for fear of corruption. Pakter, *Medieval Canon Law and the Jews*, 132, n. 69. This letter was initially addressed to the bishops in England.

40. *Synodus Diaecesana Chelmensis ab Illustrissimo et Reverendissimo Domino D. Christophoro Ioanne in Slupow Szembek, Dei et S. Sedis Apostolicae Gratia Episcopo Chelmensi, Nominato Premislensi etc, Crasnostaviae in Ecclesia Cathedrali Praesente Universo Dioecesis Clero Celebrata Die Decima Mensis Julii et Aliis Duobus Sequentibus Diebus, Anno Domini M.D.CC.XVII* (Zamość: 1717), R2.

41. *Constitutiones Synodi Dioecesana Vilnensis ab Illustrissimo, Excellentissimo ac Reverendissimo Domino D. Michaele Joanne Zienkowicz Dei et Apostolicae Sedis Gratia Episcopo Vilnensi* (Wilno: Typis Societatis Jesu, 1744), 4.

42. On this letter as an attempt to assert ecclesiastical authority on non-Catholics, see Magdalena Teter, "Jewish Conversions to Catholicism in the Polish-Lithuanian Commonwealth of the Seventeenth and Eighteenth Centuries," *Jewish History* 17, no. 3 (2003): 265–6.

43. Kobielski, *List pasterski* (1741): "Pod zakładem tysiąca grzywien, niemacie sobie prywatnych wystawiać szkoł, y niektórzy przez powagę nienależytą po domach swoich wystawiać szkółki albo buznice [sic], którym nabożeństwem waszym prywatnym nie których Chrześcijan zarażacie, tak że zostające u was na służbie Chrześcijanki pacierz z waszemi dziećmi po żydowsku mówic potrafią."

44. See numerous cases of "apostasy" noted in the Jesuit reports to Rome and found in the Archivum Romanum Societatis Jesu (ARSI). See for instance Polonia 67; Polonia 84; see also Jesuit *fructus spiritualis* published in *Istoriko-iuridicheskie materialy izvlechennye iz*

aktov knig gubernii vitebskoi i mogilevskoi khraniashchikhsia v tsentralnom arkhive v Vitebske i izdannye pod redaktseiu arkhivariusa sego arkhiva M. Verevkina, ed. M. Verevkin, 32 vols. (Vitebsk: 1890), 20: 267–315 [henceforth *Istoriko-iuridicheskie materialy*]; *Istoriko-iuridicheskie materialy*, 19: 337–410. Prohibitions concerning Catholic servants also were aimed at Armenians, Eastern Orthodox Christians ("Schismatics"), and Turks. See for instance the 1644 synod of Chełm, chapter XXIII, paragraph 14; also *Constitutiones Synodorum Matropolitanae Ecclesiae Gnesnensis Provincialium* (Cracow: 1761 <1636>), 270.

45. *Arkhiv iugo-zapadnoi Rossii*, ed. Komissiia dlia razbora drevnikh aktov (Kiev: 1859–), (Kiev, 1869), vol. 1/5: 267–70.
46. *Arkhiv iugo-zapadnoi Rossii*, vol. 1/5: 270.
47. *Arkhiv iugo-zapadnoi Rossii*, vol. 1/5: 270.
48. *Arkhiv iugo-zapadnoi Rossii*, vol. 1/5: 267–70.
49. *Arkhiv iugo-zapadnoi Rossii*, vol. 1/5: 268.
50. *Arkhiv iugo-zapadnoi Rossii*, vol. 1/5: 268.
51. Both women fell under two sets of secular law. According to the Magdeburg Laws, apostasy from Catholicism was punishable by death; see Bartlomiej Groicki, *Porządek sądów i spraw miejskich prawa majdeburskiego w Koronie Polskiej* (Warszawa: Wydawnictwa Prawnicze, 1953), 199. According to the 1658 Sejm law against anti-Trinitiarians that was later on expanded to include any actions threatening to Catholicism, apostasy was punishable by death. And in 1685, an amendment included judaizing as one of the transgressions punishable by this law. *Volumina Legum: Przedruk zbioru praw staraniem xx. pijarów w Warszawie od roku 1732 do roku 1782 wydanego*, 2nd ed., 10 vols. (Petersburg: Jozafat Ohryzka, 1859; reprint, 1980), 5: 355, 729. As late as 1768, when the Polish parliament was considering legal reforms, apostasy from Catholicism was considered a criminal act; the punishment, however, was no longer death but expulsion from Poland. See *Akt osobny pierwszy zawieraiący w sobie wolności y prerogatywy Greków orientalnych, nieunitów, dyssydentów, obywatelów y mieszkańców w państwach nayiaśnieyszey Rzeczpospolitey Polskiey w przyłączonych do niey prowincyach*, 38, paragraph III, art. I, published in volume VII of *Prawa konstytucye y przywileie Królestwa Polskiego y Wielkiego Xięstwa Litewskiego y wszystkich prowincyi należących: na walnych weymiech koronnych od seymu wiślickiego roku pańskiego 1347 aż do ostatniego seymu uchwalone* (Warsaw: n.d.): "Considering Catholic Religion rules in Poland *inter iura cardinalia*, we declare leaving the Roman Church for any other Religion in the Polish Crown, the Great Duchy of Lithuanian and *in annexis provinciis* a criminal act; therefore anyone who would dare it, should be exiled from the territories of the Republic."
52. Groicki, *Porządek sądów*, 62. The idea of linking Jewish-Christian marriage to adultery is not an invention of the Magdeburg law and can be traced to Theodosian Code, CTh 3.7.2 and 9.7.5: "Let no Jew receive a Christian woman in mariage nor any Chrisitian choose marriage with a Jewess. For if he should commit anything like this, his crime will stand as if he had committed adultery." As cited and translated in Pakter, *Medieval Canon Law and the Jews*, 266, also 271 and 289–91. Jewish law also discouraged proselytism and had a very complicated attitude to converts to Judaism. See Jacob Katz, *Exclusiveness and Tolerance: Studies in Jewish-Gentile Relations in Medieval and Modern Times* (New York: Schocken Books, 1973), especially chapters "Apostates and Proselytes" and "The Attitude of Estrangement."

53. *Istoriko-iuridicheskie materialy*, 15: 229–38. See infra for more examples.
54. *Istoriko-iuridicheskie materialy*, 15: 229.
55. *Istoriko-iuridicheskie materialy*, 15: 231.
56. Bartłomiej Groicki, *Artykuły prawa majdeburskiego. Postępek sądów koło karania na gardle. Ustawa płacej u sądów* (Warsaw: Wydawnictwa Prawnicze, 1954), 62, 199; Groicki, *Porządek sądów*, 112, 53–4, 57, 59.
57. *Istoriko-iuridicheskie materialy*, 15: 232.
58. *Istoriko-iuridicheskie materialy*, 15: 232.
59. For a discussion of laws concerning sexual relations between Jews and Christians in Polish towns see Groicki, *Porządek sądów*.
60. MS. AEp 78, in AKM in Cracow, folios 331 verso-334.
61. Grayzel, *The Church and the Jews in the XIIIth Century*, "Etsi Judaeos": 114–17: III Lateran Council 1179: 296–7; Council of Paris 1213: 306–7.
62. Grayzel, *The Church and the Jews in the XIIIth Century*, 308–9. See also 106–7, Pope Innocent III's to the King of France: "Moreover although it was enacted in the [III] Lateran Council that the Jews are not permitted to have Christian servants in their homes, either under pretext of rearing their children, nor for domestic service, nor for any other reason whatever . . . they do not hesitate to have Christian servants and nurses, with whom, at times they work such abominations as are more fitting that you should punish, than proper that we should specify." And 198–9, a 1233 letter by Pope Gregory IX: "They have, moreover, Christian nurses and maid-servants in their homes, and they commit among these servants enormities that are an abomination and a horror to hear." Even earlier at the Council of Nicea, the Christian authorities were concerned with the possibility of corruption of Christian women by non-Christian, that is, Jewish and pagan, men. Pakter, *Medieval Canon Law and the Jews*, 264.
63. David Nirenberg, *Communities of Violence: Persecution of Minorities in the Middle Ages* (Princeton, NJ: Princeton University Press, 1996), especially chapter five "Sex and Violence between Majority and Minority"; David Nirenberg, "Conversion, Sex and Segregation: Jews and Christians in Medieval Spain," *American Historical Review* 107, no. 4 (2002). See also Kenneth R. Stow, *Catholic Thought and Papal Jewry Policy, 1555–1593* (New York: Jewish Theological Seminary of America, 1977), 105–7. Pakter, *Medieval Canon Law and the Jews*, 289–91. On the sexual relation between Jewish men and Christian women as a violation against the "holy Church of God," see also Pakter, *Medieval Canon Law and the Jews*, 289–90.
64. *S. Congregationis Relationes Statu ad Limina*, 667 Dioecesis Premisliensis in Archivio Segreto Vaticano, fol.26: "Christianam enim familiam utriusque sexus, pro annuo servito conductam et conventam fovent, ab iis frequenter diversa scandala, crimina, adulteria, fornicationes cum Christianis sibi famulantibus committuntur." Jacek Krochmal discussed the legislation concerning Jews of the Przemyśl diocese in his "Ha-yahasim bein ha-ʿironim ve-ha-knesiyah be-Przemyśl le-vein ha-yehudim bashanim 1559–1772" *Gal-Ed* 15–16 (1997): 15–33, especially 25 ff.
65. *S. Congregationis Relationes Statu ad Limina*, 217 Chełmensis in Archivio Segreto Vaticano, fol.105: "Familiam Christianam utriusque sexus quilibet Judaeus in domo sua ad continua servitia de anno in annum frequenter cum gravi offensa Dei et scandalo ut nuper sub tempus eiusdem visitationis per inquisitiones Juratorias de multiplicatis cum mulieribus Christianis enormibus adulteriis et fornicationibus, judicialiter mihi constitit tenet."

66. *Edicta et Mandata Dioecesis Cracoviensis 1737–1772*, in AKM in Cracow, document no. 26 *Edictum contra Judaeos* 1751. Some Jewish sources confirm that there was sexual attention given to Christian female servants employed in Jewish homes. For example, Solomon Maimon, an eighteenth century Polish Jew, in his memoir described how the girl who served in their home aroused him as a boy. Solomon Maimon, *An Autobiography* (New York: Schocken, 1947), 20. On the question of Christian servants in Jewish homes see also Kalik, "Christian Servants Employed by Jews in the Polish-Lithuanian Commonwealth in the Seventeenth and Eighteenth Centuries," *Polin* 14 (2001): 259–70. Adam Kaźmierczyk, "The Problem of Christian Servants as Reflected in the Legal Codes of the Polish-Lithuanian Commonwealth During the Second Half of the Seventeenth Century and in the Saxon Period," *Gal-Ed* 15–16 (1997): 23–40.

67. MS. "Edicta et Mandata Dioecesis Cracoviensis 1737–1772" in Archiwum Archidiecezji Metropolitalnej w Krakowie, document no. 26: "Edictum contra Judaeos" (1751).

68. Stefan Żuchowski, *Process kryminalny of niewinne dziecię Jerzego Krasnowskiego* (Sandomierz: n.p., after 1718), 80–1.

69. Żuchowski, *Process kryminalny*, 81.

70. *Constitutiones Synodorum Matropolitanae Ecclesiae Gnesnensis Provincialium*. Stanislaw Kutrzeba, *Historja źródeł dawnego prawa polskiego*, 2 vols. (Lwów: Wydawnictwo Zakładu Narodowego im. Ossolińskich, 1925), 2: 118.

71. Karol Estreicher, *Bibliografia polska*, 14: 381; 30: 131 ff. and 32: 404.

72. This was, in fact, a very common punishment for adultery, even between two Christians. Women were usually flogged and expelled.

73. Worth noting is the fact that if a noble woman married a commoner she lost her noble status, while if a noble man married a commoner, his wife gained the noble status. Henryk Wisner, *Najjaśniejsza Rzeczpospolita: szkice z dziejów Polski szlacheckiej XVI–XVII wieku* (Warsaw: Państwowy Instytut Wydawniczy, 1978), 141; Andrzej Wyczański, *Polska Rzeczą Pospolitą szlachecką* (Warsaw: PWN, 1991), 375. See Nirenberg, *Communities of Violence*, especially chapter five "Sex and Violence between Majority and Minority."

74. For a discussion of a similar dynamic of relations between European settlers and native Americans, see Saliha Belmessous, "Assimilation and Racialism in Seventeenth and Eighteenth Century French Colonial Policy," *American Historical Review* 110 no. 2 (2005): 322–49.

75. A year later, the council of Vienne also included such a clause prohibiting sexual relations between Jewish men and Christian women, except that the punishment for a Jew included incarceration. For the texts of rulings regarding the Jews at the Wrocław and Vienne Councils, see Grayzel and Stow, *The Church and the Jews*, 244–9. See also Pakter, *Medieval Canon Law and the Jews*, 289–90, 299.

76. On the importance of this codification of Church law in Poland see Kutrzeba, *Historja źródeł prawa polskiego*, 2:117–18.

77. The Magdeburg law in use in most cities in Poland-Lithuania had specific prohibitions and more severe penalties concerning sexual relations between Jews and Christians. They were to be treated as adultery and thereby punished by death. See the discussion above and the case of Abram Michelevich, a Jew from Mohilev, and his Christian partner, Paraska Daniłowna, tried in Mohilev in 1748. *Istoriko-iuridicheskie materialy*, 15: 229–38.

78. Lay and episcopal court records provide concrete examples of these sexual relations between Jews and Christian women and of other "sins" that ensued because of Christians' employment in Jewish homes. There are also early modern Polish rabbinic sources

that indicate the existence of sexual relations between Jews and Christians. See also Magdalena Teter, "Kilka uwag na temat podziałów społecznych i religijnych pomiędzy Żydami i chrześcijanami we wschodnich miastach dawnej Rzeczpospolitej [Some Remarks on Social and Religious Divisions between Jews and Christians in Eastern Cities of Old Poland]," *Kwartalnik Historii Żydów (Jewish History Quarterly*, Poland*)* 207, no. 3 (2003).

79. Filip Sulimierski and Bronislaw Chlebowski, *Słownik geograficzny Królestwa Polskiego i innych krajów słowianskich,* 15 vols. (Warsaw: Wiek, 1880), 4: 205–7. Henceforth *Słownik geograficzny Królestwa Polskiego.*

80. AIVAK, vol. VI, 527–8.

81. *Słownik geograficzny Królestwa Polskiego,* 2: 599–600.

82. AIVAK, vol. VI, 528.

83. Ruff, *Violence in Early Modern Europe, 1500–1800,* 150.

84. Bishop Załuski in his "Edictum contra Judaeos" of 1751 states that Jews harm Christians not only healthwise but they also harm Christian souls by making them drink, steal, lie, and swear falsely. See MS. "Edicta et Mandata Dioecesis Cracoviensis 1737–1772" in Archiwum Archidiecezji Metropolitalnej in Cracow, document no. 26.

85. Załuski, "Edictum contra Judaeos."

86. "Białogłowom chrześciańskim [nie godzi się] ... dzieci żydowskich, *chybaby od głodu umierać miały* za mamki karmić ..." A different kind of concession was made in Isserles' glosses to the *Shulḥan 'Aruk.* To the prohibition against Jewish women serving as wet nurses to Christian children, he added "unless she has [too much] milk and suffers from it." It emphasized the well-being of the Jewish woman. *Shulḥan 'Aruk,* Yoreh De'ah 154.2.

87. See for instance rulings of the Council of Paris 1213 in Grayzel, *The Church and the Jews,* 306–7. There is a parallel prohibition in Jewish law concerning assistance during childbirth and nursing children. See the Mishnah, 'Avodah Zarah 2:1: "An Israelite girl should not serve as a midwife to a gentile woman because she serves to bring forth a child for the service of idolatry, but a gentile woman may serve as a midwife to an Israelite girl; An Israelite girl should not give suck to the child of a gentile woman, but a gentile woman may give suck to the child of an Israelite girl, when it is by permission," cited in English after *The Mishnah,* trans. J. Neusner (New Haven: Yale University Press, 1988), 662. See also *Shulḥan 'Aruk,* Yoreh De'ah, 154.2: "A Jewish woman is not allowed to nurse a child of a gentile, even for payment [Isserles: Unless she has milk and suffers from it, then she is allowed] and should not help a gentile woman in childbirth unless she is known to the woman who is giving birth then it is permitted for payment [Isserles: it is prohibited to teach gentiles craft]." It is clear that the rabbis tried to prevent friendships. See also BT 'Avodah Zarah 26a.

88. For instance, a Polish nobleman, Marcin Matuszewicz, mentioned in his memoirs an incident from the end of the seventeenth century. He mentioned a noblewoman who, having studied the Bible, began practicing Judaism and eventually left Poland for Amsterdam with her Jewish estate administrator, where she converted to Judaism. Her husband eventually followed and also converted. But the stress is placed on the study and reading of the Bible and not the sexual relations between her and the Jew. Marcin Matuszewicz, *Diariusz życia mego* (Warsaw: PIW, 1986), 385–6. Daniel Stone discussed this case in Daniel Stone, "Knowledge of Foreign Languages among Eighteenth Century Polish Jews," *Polin* 10 (1997): 215–16. See also this story retold in a polemical work of an eighteenth-century Jesuit, Jan Poszakowski, *Antidotum contra "Antidotum abo*

zbawienna przestroga," ze lekarstwo duszne przeciwko apostazyi Woyciecha Węgierskiego
niegdy superintendenta zborów ewangelickich sporządzone y wygotowane teraz świeżo w
Królewcu roku pańskiego 1750 drukiem opublikowane y ogłoszone (Wilno: Typis Societatis
Jesu, 1754), 4.

89. For example, noblemen's memoirs from the period show little evidence of their socializing with Jews. See Matuszewicz, *Diariusz życia mego.*

90. See the section below.

91. Jewish law also restricted socializing; special regulations concerning food and wine
were to prevent such contacts. However, as Edward Fram has shown, despite rabbinic
prohibitions such contacts occurred and Jews ate in non-Jewish homes as well. Fram,
Ideals Face Reality, 29–32.

92. Załuski, "Edictum contra Judaeos." Passover was commonly referred to in these documents as Easter [*Wielkanoc*]. On non-Jewish doctors and barbers used by Jews, see
Shulḥan ʾAruk, Yoreh Deʾah 155 and 156, and discussion below.

93. *Constitutiones Synodorum Matropolitanae Ecclesiae Gnesnensis Provincialium*, 266; *Synodus Diaecesana Chelmensis (1717)*, Chapter XXI, page preceding R2. See also *Constitutiones Synodales Luceoriensis et Brestensis ab Ill. Excellent. et Reverendiss. D.D.
Stephano Boguslao a Rupniew in Januszowice Rupniewski* (Warsaw: Typis Scholarum
Piarum, 1726); Josaphat Michał Karp, *Epistola Pastoralis ad Clerum Diocesis Samogitiensis ex Mandato Illustrissimi Excellentissimi Domini D. Josaphati Michaelis Karp
Espiscopi Samogitiensis Edita et Impressa* (Wilno: Typis Societatis Jesu, 1737).

94. *Constitutiones Synodi Dioecesana Vilnensis ab Illustrissimo, Excellentissimo ac Reverendissimo Domino D. Michaele Joanne Zienkowicz Dei et Apostolicae Sedis Gratia
Episcopo Vilnensi, Synodus Diaecesana Chelmensis (1717).* For examples of socializing and even dancing together of Jews and Christians, see Edward Fram, "Two
Cases of Adultery and the Halakhic Decision-Making Process," *AJS Review* 26, no. 2
(2002).

95. Jan Wężyk, *Constitutiones Synodorum Metropolitae Ecclesiae Gnesnensis Provincialium
Authoritate Synodi Provincialis Gembicianae* (Cracow: 1630; reprint, 1761).

96. MS. 3698 I: "Kazania misyjne" in Biblioteka X. Czartoryskich in Cracow, fol. 227.

97. Krzysztof Kraiński, *Postylla kościoła powszechnego apostolskiego słowem bożym ugruntowana na Jezusie Chrystusie. Spisana ku chwale Bogu w Tróycy S. iedynemu przez księdza
Krzysztofa Kraińskiego* (n.p.: n.p., after 1611), 440–1. The epistles of Ignatius of Antioch
(b. ca. 50 C.E.) are not extant and are only known to us through references to them in
the writings of Eusebius and Jerome. John B. O'Connor, "Ignatius of Antioch," in *The
Catholic Encyclopedia* (New York: The Encyclopedia Press, 1913), 7:644–7.

98. Szembek, *List Pasterski*, D.

99. See Grayzel and Stow, *The Church and the Jews*, 246–8. Indeed the prohibition of feasting
with Jews was a remarkably old one, which goes back as far as the Council of Vannes
in Breton. See Grayzel and Stow, *The Church and the Jews*, 161–2, n.8. Moreover, the
prohibition regarding eating matzoth can also be found in Canon law. See Grayzel and
Stow, *The Church and the Jews*, 69, n.2. Also Pakter, *Medieval Canon Law and the Jews*,
122, n. 131.

100. Edward Fram discusses briefly the ambiguity of Jewish attitudes toward Poles in his
Ideals Face Reality, 22–3.

101. See also BT, especially the tractate ʾAvodah Zarah but not restricted to that tractate, and
infra discussion of the *Shulḥan ʾAruk*, which follows the Tur.

102. On parallel language of discourse about the Other within Christianity and Judaism, see for example Israel Yuval, "Jews and Christians in the Middle Ages: Shared Myths, Common Language," in *Demonizing the Other*, ed. Robert Wistrich (Amsterdam: Harwood Academic Publishers, 1999); Israel Jacob Yuval, *Shene goyim be-vitnekh: Yehudim ve-nozrim dimuyim h-adadiyim* (Tel-Aviv: 'Alma 'Am 'Oved, 2000).

103. For instance in the *Shulḥan 'Aruk*, Yoreh De'ah 148.9, it is stated that a Jew is not allowed to enter the house of a gentile on non-Jewish holidays and give him greetings. A Jew, however, is allowed to greet a non-Jew outside but should speak with the non-Jew unenthusiastically and with seriousness [*aval i'amar lo be safa rafa u-bi-khvod rosh*]. See also a discussion in BT 'Avodah Zarah 35b-36b.

104. *Shulḥan 'Aruk*, Yoreh De'ah 148, "Dinei ḥagei ha-elilim." On the *Shulḥan 'Aruk* see for example Joseph Davis, "The Reception of the Shulḥan 'Arukh and the Formation of Ashkenazic Jewish Identity," *AJS Review* 26, no. 2 (2002); Menachem Elon, *Jewish Law: History, Sources, Principles*, trans. Bernard Auerbach and Melvin Syks (Philadelphia: Jewish Publication Society of America, 1994), 3: 1320ff; Stephen M. Passamaneck, "Toward the Sunrise in the East, 1300–1565," in *An Introduction to the History and Sources of Jewish Law*, ed. Bernard Jackson et al. (Oxford: Oxford University Press, 1996); Isadore Twersky, "The Shulḥan 'Aruk: Enduring Code of Jewish Law," in *The Jewish Expression*, ed. Judah Goldin (New Haven: Yale University Press, 1970).

105. Much of Isserles' views is based on Tosafot, 'Avodah Zarah 2a. I thank Edward Fram of Ben Gurion University for pointing this out to me.

106. *Shulḥan 'Aruk*, Yoreh De'ah 152. In the Talmud, see BT 'Avodah Zarah 8a.

107. On the intermarriage see BT 'Avodah Zarah 35b. See also BT 'Avodah Zarah 36b and Rashi's commentary there that wine would lead the man to lewdness, and consequently to idolatry.

108. Meir ben Gedaliah (Maharam) of Lublin, *Shu"T* (Venice, 1618) no. 15. Later editions replaced the acronym *'akum* (gentiles, idol worshippers that in early modern Poland meant Christians) used in the original 1618 edition with *ishmaelim* (Muslims). See for instance Meir ben Gedaliah of Lublin, *Shu"T* (Metz, 1769 and Warsaw, 1881). See also Hundert, *The Jews in a Polish Private Town*, 171, n. 72.

109. See Ben-Zion Katz, *Le-korot ha-yehudim be-Rusyia, Polin ve-Lita* (1899), 13.

110. Wężyk, *Constitutiones Synodorum Metropolitae Ecclesiae Gnesnensis*, 268. *Synodus Diaecesana Chelmensis (1717)*, Chapter XXII "De Judeis," unnumbered page preceding R2. See also Franciszek Antoni Kobielski, *List pasterski wszystkiemu duchowieństwu, świeckim i zakonnym, tudzież i wszystkim swoiemi honorami, godnościami prerogatywami ozdobnym y dystyngowanym panom, dziedzicom y possesorom, także uczciwym y pracowitym oboyga płci* (1752).

111. Moses Isserles, *Darkei Moshe* on Tur, Yoreh De'ah 153.3.

112. Mishnah 'Avodah Zarah 2.1; BT 'Avodah Zarah 22a-b.

113. Israel Halpern and Israel Bartal, eds., *Pinkas va'ad arb'a arazot* (Jerusalem: 1989 <1945>), 17, takkanah 50. Also cited and discussed in Edward Fram, "Hagvalat motarot ba-kehilah ha-yehudit be-Krakov be-shilhe ha-meah ha-16 u-ve-reshit ha-meah ha-17 [Sumptuary Laws in the Jewish Community of Krakow at the End of the Sixteenth and the Beginning of the Seventeenth Centuries]," *Gal-Ed* 18 (2002): 14 (Hebrew).

114. In a 1613 law, Polish nobles prohibited non-nobles from wearing expensive clothes. Though this was a sumptuary law, it also externally defined who belonged to this group. See Fram, "Hagvalat Motarot," 15 (Hebrew).

115. See *Siftei Cohen* there. David ben Shmuel ha-Levi, the author of another commentary on the Shulḥan 'Aruk, *Turei Zahav*, accepted the prohibition but seems to have been concerned with the possibility of homosexual relations. He is reluctant to allow nudity even among Jews themselves. *Turei Zahav* on Isserles' commentary on Shulḥan 'Aruk, Yoreh De'ah 153.

116. See above on Jews and Christian women in this chapter.

117. See also Isserles, *Darkei Moshe* on Tur, Yoreh De'ah 154.

118. Mishnah, 'Avodah Zarah 2.1. See also *Mishnah 'im perush rabenu Mosheh Ben Maimon* (Jerusalem: Mossad Ha-Rav Kook, 1964 or 1965), the same section in 'Avodah Zarah, p. 228.

119. *Turei Zahav* on Shulḥan 'Aruk, Yoreh De'ah, 154.2. See also Tur, Yoreh De'ah 154, and commentaries, *Beit Yosef* and *Beit ḥadash*.

120. See BT 'Avodah Zarah 26a; Tur and Shulḥan 'Aruk, Yoreh De'ah, 154.2.

121. Tur, Yoreh De'ah 154.1. BT 'Avodah Zarah 26b.

122. Isserles' gloss on Shulḥan 'Aruk, Yoreh De'ah, 81.7. See also *Beit Yosef* on Tur, Yoreh De'ah 154.1.

123. Żuchowski, *Process kryminalny*, 126–7.

124. Żuchowski, *Process kryminalny*, 126–7.

125. Lyndal Roper, "Witchcraft and Fantasy in Early Modern Germany," in *Witchcraft in Early Modern Europe: Studies in Culture and Belief*, ed. Gareth Roberts (New York: Cambridge University Press, 1996), 207–36. Barbara Ehrenreich and Deirdre English, *Witches, Midwives, and Nurses: A History of Women Healers* (New York: The Feminist Press at City University of New York, 1973).

126. For example, *Synodus Diaecesana Chelmensis (1717)*, Chapter XXI, "De Judeis," unnumbered page preceding R2. For the text of Pope Paul IV's bull *Cum Nimis Absurdum*, see Stow, *Catholic Thought and Papal Jewry Policy, 1555–1593*, 291–8, par. 10; on physicians, ibid. 293, 296.

127. See also Mishnah 'Avodah Zarah 2.2, BT 'Avodah Zarah 27a.

128. See also Isserles, *Darkei Moshe* on Tur, Yoreh De'ah 155.1 (4). In both the Shulḥan 'Aruk and *Darkei Moshe* Isserles refers to *Sefer Mordekhai* by Mordekhai ben Hillel ha-Kohen (d. 1298).

129. "Franciscan Friars Minor Reformed Conventuals," in Polish "Franciszkanie Reformaci," in Italian "frati riformati de' Minori Conventuali."

130. Archiwum OO. Franciszkanów Reformatów in Cracow, MS. 258 "Kazania w Krakowie, 1733", fol. 30.

131. Yuval, "Jews and Christians."

132. Fram, "Two Cases of Adultery."

133. Benjamin Aaron ben Abraham Slonik, *Mas'at Binyamin: Ve-hem she'elot u-teshuvot* (Cracow: M. N. Meisels, 1632), no. 86. This responsum was excised from later editions. See also Fram, *Ideals Face Reality*, 28, 30–1.

134. Teter, "Kilka Uwag," 331.

135. MS. 534 "Exempla" in Archiwum O.O. Dominikanów in Cracow, Exemplum 9. See also Magdalena Teter, "Jewish Conversions to Catholicism in the Polish-Lithuanian Commonwealth of the Seventeenth and Eighteenth Centuries," *Jewish History* 17, no. 3 (2003): 268–9, and chapter below, "Warding Off Heretical Depravity."

136. The number of days is perhaps not coincidental. Jesus is believed to have been on earth forty days after his resurrection, before ascending to heaven.

137. Church legislation concerning Christian servants in Poland is discussed in Kalik, "Christian Servants"; Kalik, "Ha-knesiyyah ha-katolit ve-ha-yehudim be-mamlekhet Polin-Lita ba-me'ot ha-17–18"; Kaźmierczyk, "The Problem of Christian Servants"; Magdalena Teter, "Jews in the Legislation and Teachings of the Catholic Church in Poland 1648–1772" (Ph.D. dissertation, Columbia University, 2000).
138. This word is generally used to refer to Jewish synagogues; it is therefore possible that the "pagans" here might be Jews.
139. Jan Krosnowski, *Pochodnia słowa Bożego*, 185.
140. MS. Jan Choynacki, "Kazania na piątki postne o dziesięciu przykazaniach," in Archiwum i Biblioteka OO. Bernardynow in Cracow, 32. See also a sermon in MS. 280, "Zebranie obiaśniaiących w głębokich niewiadomości cieniach pogrążonych serc ludzi prostych kondycyi" in Archiwum OO. Franciszkanów-Reformatów, 223–4. The preacher complained that Catholics engage in business affairs and go to fairs on Sundays and contrasts this with Lutheran cities that have legislation against such activities and with Jews whose Sabbath observance is laudable. The synod of Łuck and Brest in 1726 also emphasized the Christian sins of violating holidays by drinking, fighting, working, and attending fairs, and contrasted this behavior with heretics and Jews, who "piously celebrate their holidays." *Constitutiones Synodales Luceoriensis et Brestensis ab Ill. Excellent. et Reverendiss. D. D. Stephano Boguslao a Rupniew in Januszowice Rupniewski*, 12–13.
141. MS. 3011 I "Zbiór kazań" in Biblioteka X. Czartoryskich in Cracow, 194–5.
142. Fortunat Łosiewski, *Powtórna męka Chrystusa Jezusa w nayświętszym sakramencie* (Warsaw, 1729), 60–1.
143. MS. 274 "Józef Męciński" in Archiwum OO. Franciszkanów Reformatów, fols. 20v–21r.
144. MS. 281 Roch Trucki "Messis de Semine Verbi Dei in Agro Eccclesiae in Amnipulos Collecta, seu Conciones in Dominica et Festa Conscripta" in Archiwum OO. Franciszkanów-Reformatów, 163.
145. MS. 3698 I "Kazania misyjne" in Biblioteka X. Czartoryskich in Cracow, 263. See also Jakob Wujek, *Postilla katholicka mneysza, to iest krótkie kazania abo wykłady świętych ewangeliey, na każda niedziele y na każde święto, przez cały rok według nauki prawdziwej kościoła chrześcijanskiego powszechnego* (Cracow: 1870–1 <1617>), 220.
146. MS. 61 A. Zapartowicz, "Nauki o grzechach krótko dla pamięci zebrane" in Archiwum OO. Franciszkanów-Reformatów, fol. 138.
147. See chapter three above for a Protestant preacher claiming the same.
148. This is a corrupted version of Matthew 5:7 "Beati misericordes quia ipsi misericordiam consequentur [Blessed are the merciful for they will receive mercy]." "Misericordiam volo [I desire mercy]," Matthew 9:13.
149. Jakub Filipowicz, *Kazania na niedziele całego roku* (Lwów, 1725), 28. Judith Kalik discussed a similar example in which a Catholic preacher contrasted alleged Jewish communal cohesiveness and solidarity with Christian impiety and disregard for fellow Christians. Kalik, "Polish Attitudes to Jewish Spirituality," 79.
150. MS. 255 "Kazania głoszone w 1731 r." in Archiwum OO. Franciszkanów-Reformatów, Cracow, folio 133 verso.
151. See for instance an anonymous preacher who in his sermon delivered in 1731 stated: "and with your repeated sins you crucify Him more cruelly than the Jews!" MS. 255 "Kazania głoszone w 1731" in Archiwum OO. Franciszkanów-Reformatów, folio 61 V. See also Adrian Seriewicz, *Dyalog albo komedya męki Jezusowej w siedmiu scenach lub*

kazaniach reprezentowane y zgromadzonemu słuchaczowi na passyach wtorkowych w Lublinie ogłoszone (Lwów, 1738), N4 verso.

CHAPTER 5: "A SHAMEFUL OFFENCE": THE NOBLES AND THEIR JEWS

1. MS. 58 "Kazania w. XVII" in Archiwum OO. Franciszkanów Reformatów, fol. 314.
2. Jakub Radliński, *Prawda chrześciańska od nieprzyiaciela swego zeznana* (Lublin: Typis Societatis Jesu, 1733), 527–8.
3. Radliński, *Prawda chrześciańska*, 527–8.
4. Judith Kalik has studied economic and political relations between Jews and the Church in seventeenth and eighteenth-century Poland-Lithuania. See Yehudit Kalik, "Ha-knesiyah ha-katolit ve-ha-yehudim be-Krakow ve-be-Kazimierz ʾad halukoth Polin," in *Kroke-Kazimierz-Krakow*, ed. Elchanan Reiner (Tel Aviv: The Diaspora Research Institute / Center for the History of Polish Jewry, 2001); Yehudit Kalik, "Ha-knesiyah ha-katolit ve-ha-yehudim be-mamlekhet Polin-Lita ba-meot ha-17-18." (Ph.D. dissertation, Hebrew University, 1998); Yehudit Kalik, "Patterns of Contact between the Catholic Church and the Jews in the Polish-Lithuanian Commonwealth: Jewish Debts," in *Studies in the History of the Jews in Old Poland in Honor of Jacob Goldberg*, ed. Adam Teller (Jerusalem: Magnes Press, 1998).
5. Kalik, "Ha-knesiyah ha-katolit ve-ha-yehudim be-mamlekhet Polin-Lita" especially 211–46.
6. Kalik, "Ha-knesiyah ha-katolit ve-ha-yehudim be-mamlekhet Polin-Lita," 136–7, 180. See also MSS. in AKM in Cracow, AEp 11, fol. 288–288v; AEp12, fol. 21v–22, 41, 42–42v, 79–80, 83v–84, 89–89v, 94, 94v, 95; AEp 18, fol. 55v–56.
7. Kasper Balsam, *Kazania na święta całego roku* (Poznań: Typis Societatis Jesu, 1762), 265–6.
8. Balsam, *Kazania na święta całego roku*, 265–6.
9. For example, Judith Kalik has shown the magnates intervention on behalf of Jews in cases of conflict between Jews and local priests. Kalik, "Ha-knesiyah ha-katolit ve-ha-yehudim be-mamlekhet Polin-Lita," 164–8, 176–7.
10. Jan Skarbek, "Edictum Contra Judaeos," in *Edicta et Mandata Dioecesis Cracoviensis (1737–1772)*, AKM (Cracow: 1717), no. 29.
11. This is a reference to Lamentations 1:5: "Her foes have become the masters and her enemies prosper."
12. Skarbek, "Edictum contra Judaeos."
13. Skarbek, "Edictum contra Judaeos."
14. MS. "S. Concilii Relationes Statu ad Limina: 667 Premisliensis" in Archivio Segreto Vaticano, *relatio* from 1666.
15. MS. "S. Concilii Relationes Statu ad Limina: 667 Premisliensis" in Archivio Segreto Vaticano, *relatio* from 1743, fol. 26.
16. MSS. in Archivio Segreto Vaticano: "S. Concilii Relationes Statu ad Limina: 272 Cracoviensis," *relatio* from 1751; "217 Chelmensis," *relatio* from 1743, 1749; "445 Leopoliensis," *relatio* from 1731; "651 Plocensis," *relatio* from 1665.
17. See infra. Pope Benedict XIV, *Benedicti Divina Providentia Papae XIV Epistola Encyclica ad Primatem, Archiepiscopos et Episcopos Regni Poloniae. De His Quae Vetita Sunt Hebraeis Habitantibus in Iisdem Civitatibus et Locis in Quibus Habitant Christiani* (Rome: 1751).

18. Pope Benedict XIV, *Epistola Encyclica ad Primatem, Archiepiscopos et Episcopos Regni Poloniae.*

19. It did not control the most land, but was perhaps the largest single land owner, along with the Crown. It controlled 10–15 percent of land, the Crown 15 percent, but the latter's land was often in the hands of the nobles under life-long leases. Jerzy Lukowski, *Liberty's Folly: The Polish-Lithuanian Commonwealth in the Eighteenth Century, 1697–1795* (New York: Routledge, 1991), 11–12; Daniel Stone, *The Polish-Lithuanian State, 1386–1795*. Vol. 4, *History of East Central Europe* (Seattle: University of Washington Press, 2001), 42.

20. On the questions of permits to establish cemeteries and to build and restore synagogues, see Kalik, "Ha-knesiyah ha-katolit ve-ha-yehudim be-mamlekhet Polin-Lita," 144–8. Protestants often challenged this claim of authority in other courts; see Wojciech Kriegseisen, *Ewangelicy polscy i litewscy w epoce saskiej* (Warsaw: Semper, 1996), 40–1.

21. Radliński, *Prawda chrześciańska*, 557–60. One has to remember, however, the size of most towns in early modern Poland. The furthest street from the main square was often within one or two short blocks. And so for instance, Zamość – founded in the sixteenth century as a prominent Renaissance town in Małopolska – in 1860 had a square market place and only twelve streets. That meant two streets starting from each corner of the market square (totaling eight) and one street paralleling each side of the square. Filip Sulimierski, Bronisław Chlebowski, and Władysław Walewski, *Słownik geograficzny Królestwa Polskiego i innych krajów słowiańskich* (Warszawa: Wydawnictwa Artsytyczne i Filmowe, 1975 <1880>), vol. 15. Moshe Rosman noted that in the towns owned by the Czartoryski-Sieniawski family, Jews tended to live in central locations (the marketplace) and in the more expensive (stone) homes; Rosman, *The Lords' Jews*, 48–9.

22. See for instance *Arkhiv iugo-zapadnoi Rossii*, ed. Komissiia dlia razbora drevnikh aktov, vol. 1/5 (Kiev: 1869), 371.

23. MS. "S. Concilii Relationes Statu ad Limina: 272 Cracoviensis" in Archivio Segreto Vaticano, *relatio* from 1751.

24. Jan Alexander Lipski, *Epistola Pastoralis ad Clerum et Populum Dioecesis Cracoviensis. Ex Mandatio Eminentissimi et Reverendissimi Domini Ioanni Alexandri Divina Miseratione S. R. E. Presbyterii Cardinalis Lipski Episcopi Cracoviensis, Ducis Severiae* (1737).

25. According to canon 67 of the IV Lateran Council, Jews were to be compelled "to make satisfaction for the tithes and offerings due to the churches, which the Christians were accustomed to supply from their houses and other possessions before these properties, under whatever title fell into the hands of the Jews and thus the churches may be safeguarded against loss." Henry Joseph Schroeder, *Disciplinary Decrees of the General Councils, Text, Translation, and Commentary* (St. Louis: B. Herder Book Co., 1937), 290. For the Latin text see Schroeder, *Disciplinary Decrees*, 583.

26. Concerning fees paid by Jews, see Kalik, "Ha-knesiyah ha-katolit ve-ha-yehudim be-mamlekhet Polin-Lita," 150–1, and 249–99 on business relations with Jews.

27. Henryk Samsonowicz, "The Agreement between the Bishop of Płock and the Jews of Ostrów Mazowiecka in 1721," in *Studies in the History of the Jews in Old Poland in Honor of Jacob Goldberg*, ed. Adam Teller (Jerusalem: Magnes Press, 1998).

28. Kriegseisen, *Ewangelicy polscy*, 33.

29. Kriegseisen, *Ewangelicy polscy*, 130.

30. The fight over tithing and fees can be seen as a part of the Church's larger struggle for influence and control, for the demand and collection of tithes, or fees in their stead,

was also an assertion of authority, as was the ability to issue sanctions. For examples
of the conflict over tithes in the east, see a complaint by "Poles, Ruthenians and Jews"
of Luboml against a Catholic priest forcing them to pay tithes to the church, AIVAK,
vol. XXIII, 158–9. See also a royal decree forcing all inhabitants of Chełm, "both of
Roman and Ruthenian faith," to pay tithes to the local Roman Catholic church, AIVAK,
vol. XXIII, doc. 222. One has to remember also that not paying the tithes was considered
a sin serious enough to merit excommunication. See for instance *Acta Synodi Diaecesis
Vilnensis. Praesidente Illustrissimo ac Reverendissimo Domino D. Alexandro in Maciejow
Sapieha Dei et Apostolica Sedis Gratia Episcopo Vilnensi* (Wilno: Typis Societatis Jesu,
1669), unnumbered pages. Section "Polonico idiomate redditum in Casibus Nostras
Regiones concernentibus."

31. Sometimes these cases involved conflicts between different churchmen, but often it was
    the nobles who took the opportunity to seize tithes from the Church. Both AEp in
    the AKM in Cracow and Acta Actorum Capitulorum in the AKW provide numerous
    examples, too numerous to cite here, of the conflicts over tithes. See for instance MSS.
    in AKM, AEp 15, fols. 31, 36, and AEp 18, fols. 226, 333v.

32. Kalik, "Ha-knesiyah ha-katolit ve-ha-yehudim be-mamlekhet Polin-Lita," 192–3. For
    the document see AIVAK, vol. XXIX, 143–4.

33. Benedict XIV, *Epistola Encyclica ad Primatem, Archiepiscopos et Episcopos Regni Poloniae.*

34. *Acta Synodi Diaecesis Vilnensis* (1669), Canon "Bona Ecclesiastica Iudaeis Non
    Arendentur."

35. *Synodus Dioecesana ab Illustrissimo et Reverendissimo D. Casimiro a' Lubna Lubienski
    Dei et Apostolica Sedis Gratia Episcopo Cracoviensi Duce Severiae Celebrata Cracoviae
    in Ecclesia Archipresbyteriali ad 1711* (Cracow: Franciszek Cezary, 1711), chapter XXXIX
    "De Iudaeis."

36. *Synodus Luceoriensis et Brestensis per Illustrissimum ac Reverendissimum Dominum
    Dominum Stanislaum in Magna Witwica Witwicki* (Warsaw: Carolus Schreiber, 1684),
    14–15. See also Zenon Chodyński and Edward Likowski, eds., *Decretales Summorum
    Pontificum pro Regno Poloniae et Constitutiones Synodorum Provincialium et Dioece-
    sanarum Regni Eiusdem ad Summam Collectae cum Annotationibus, Declarationibus,
    Admonitionibus et Additionibus ex Historia, Jure Ecclesiastico Universali et Jure Civili
    Regni Curantibus Plerisque Sacerdotibus Posnanensibus Editae*, 3 vols. (Poznań: Typis
    Augustini Schmaedicke, 1869), 2:91.

37. "Taceo quod sicubi desunt, peius Judaizare dolemus Christianos, si tamen Christianos,
    et non magis baptizatos Judaeos convenit appellari." Bernard of Clairvaux, *Epistolae*,
    ed. J. P. Migne, Patrologiae Cursus Completus: Series Latina, 182, pt.1 (Paris: Garnieri
    Fratres et al., 1879), letter 363, col. 567, par. 7. For the English translation see Bernard of
    Clairvaux, *The Letters of St Bernard of Clairvaux*, trans. Bruno Scott James (Kalamazoo,
    MI: Cistercian Publications, 1998), 463, letter 391. On Bernard of Clairvaux and the Jews
    see David Berger, "The Attitude of St. Bernard of Clairvaux toward Jews," *Proceedings
    of the American Academy of Jewish Research* 40 (1972). See also Léon Poliakov, *Jewish
    Bankers and the Holy See: From the Thirteenth to the Seventeenth Century* (London:
    Routledge and Kegan Paul, 1977), 14.

38. MS. Jan Alexander Lipski, "Letter to the Cathedral Chapter," Libri Archivi vol. 29 in
    AKW, doc. 114.

39. The word used in this document is *wyrugować* and it may mean expel, remove, eliminate,
    etc. It is not clear whether the bishop meant eliminate from the positions of leaseholders

or whether he meant an expulsion of Jews from the ecclesiastical domains. The context of leaseholding would indicate that it meant ending the economic ties and applying the directives issued by the bishop.

40. Lipski, "Letter to the Cathedral Chapter," Libri Archivi vol. 29 in AKW, doc. 115.

41. MS. AEp 78 in AKM in Cracow, document of October 22, 1721, folio 333.

42. MS. AEp 90, document "Conservationis Judaeorum in Bonis Spiritualis contra Parochem Gołaszowiensis et Mielczensis" in AKM in Cracow, folios 271–271 v.

43. This may have required cooperation with secular authorities.

44. MS. AEp 90, document "Submission Infidelis Abram Józefowicz Neocorcinensis super Non Arendandis Spiritualis Bonis," November 19, 1750, folio 275.

45. Benedict XIV, *Epistola Encyclica ad Primatem, Archiepiscopos et Episcopos Regni Poloniae.*

46. For a study of some of these ties see Kalik, "Ha-knesiyah ha-katolit ve-ha-yehudim be-mamlekhet Polin-Lita."

47. AIVAK, vol. V, 252–4. The specific mention of the Church *jurydyka* is on 253.

48. Ber of Bolechow, *The Memoirs of Ber of Bolechow (1723–1805)*, trans. Mark Wischnitzer (London: Oxford University Press, 1922), 119.

49. The question of Jewish involvement in the wine trade and the sale of wine to priests, potentially for ritual use, was also a serious matter for both the Church officials, who would have found it insulting to use Jewish-made wine, and Jewish authorities, who would object to benefiting from wine to be used in idolatrous practices. See for example a letter from Pope Innocent III to the Count of Nevers from 1208, in Solomon Grayzel, *The Church and the Jews in the XIIIth Century* (Philadelphia: The Dropsie College, 1933), 127–9.

50. Bolechow, *The Memoirs of Ber of Bolechow*, 174.

51. See for example Israel Halpern and Israel Bartal, eds., *Pinkas va'ad arb'a arazot* (Jerusalem: 1989 <1945 >), takanah 639 of 1739. See also Moshe Rosman, "The Indebtedness of the Lublin Kahal in the Eighteenth Century," in *Studies in the History of the Jews in Old Poland*, ed. Adam Teller (Jerusalem: Magnes Press, 1998); Kalik, "Ha-knesiyah ha-katolit ve-ha-yehudim be-mamlekhet Polin-Lita," especially 247–98; Kalik, "Patterns of Contact"; and Benedict XIV, *Epistola Encyclica ad Primatem, Archiepiscopos et Episcopos Regni Poloniae.*

52. MS. "S. Concilii Relationes Statu ad Limina: 272 Cracoviensis," in Archivio Segreto Vaticano, *relatio* from 1751: "Verum infidelium Judaeorum propago adeo in hoc Regno et Mea D. multiplicatur ut numero suo videtur jam Christianitatem exaequare." And in fol. 120v–121 there is a summary of the whole document in Italian: "Si duole nel fine della Relazione Monsg. che nella sua Diocesi, ed in tutto il Regno di Polonia siano talmente moltiplicarti i Giudei, che non solo nel numero uggualiano gli Cattolici, ma che occupando ancora tutti gli negozii, e per sino l'ammministrazione de' Beni ecclesiastici gli reducono in tale angustia, che costretti sono a vendere a medesimi Giudei le proprie case, e ritirarsi ad abitare ne sobborghi."

53. MS. Libri Archivi, Epistolae Variarum Personarum, vol. 27 in AKW, doc. 68: Stanisław Potocki, "Letter to the Cathedral Chapter, 1658." Similar traces of this conflict emerge also in polemical and homiletic works from that time.

54. See for instance *Acta Synodi Diaecesis Vilnensis (1669).*

55. MS. 3698 I, "Kazania misyjne" in Biblioteka X. Czartoryskich in Cracow, fol. 87.

56. *Synodus Dioecesana Chelmensis per Illustrissimum et Reverendissimum Dominum Stanislaum Hyacynthum Świecicki Episcopum Chelmensem Abbatem Lublinensem*

Crasnostaviae Celebrata Anno Domini 1694 Die 15 Septembris (Warsaw: Collegium Scholarum Piarum, 1696), unnumbered page that precedes E.

57. Paulina Buchwald-Pelcowa, *Cenzura w dawnej Polsce: Między prasą drukarską a stosem* (Warsaw: Wydawnictwo Stowarzyszenia Bibliotekarzy Polskich, 1997). Zdzisław Kaczmarczyk and Bogusław Leśniodorski, *Historia państwa i prawa Polski*, ed. Juliusz Bardach, 3rd ed., 2 vols. (Warsaw: PWN, 1968), 2:68.

58. Josaphat Michał Karp, *Epistola Pastoralis ad Clerum Diocesis Samogitiensis ex Mandato Illustrissimi Excellentissimi Domini D. Josaphati Michaelis Karp Espiscopi Samogitiensis Edita et Impressa* (Wilno: Typis Societatis Jesu, 1737), 4: "filios liberae filiis Agar ancillae eiiciendis subijcere non verentur."

59. Augustine, *City of God*, Book XV, chapter 2, "On the children of the flesh and the children of the promise:" "As for the statement 'The elder will be servant to the younger,' hardly anyone of our people has taken it as meaning anything else but that the older people of the Jews was destined to serve the younger, the Christians." This interpretation finally was applied to the Roman law and the later canon law concerning Jews holding public office. In Roman law this ban was applied to offices that might cause harm to Christians. See Amnon Linder, *The Jews in Roman Imperial Legislation* (Detroit: Wayne State University Press, 1987), 75–7. In his *Collectarium canonum* or *Decretum*, Burchard of Worms prohibited the appointment of Jews as administrators of villages or Christian households: "Ne Judaeis administratorio usu sub ordine villicorum atque actorum Christianam familiam regere audeant, nec eis hoc a quoquam fieri praecipiatur. Si quis vero contra haec agere praesumpserit, si episcopus, presbyter, aut diaconus fuerit, proprio summoveatur gradu si vero monachus fuerit, communione privertur. Similiter et laicus. Et si perseveraverint inobedientes, anathematizentur." Cited in Walter Pakter, *Medieval Canon Law and the Jews*, Abhandlungen Zur Rechtswissenschaftlichen Grundlagenforschung 68 (Ebelsbach: R. Gremer, 1988), 229, n. 33. The twelfth-century decretists also agreed that unconverted Jews should not hold public office. In the thirteenth century the canon *Cum sit nimis absurdum* at the IV Lateran Council prohibited Jews from holding public offices; see Grayzel, *The Church and the Jews*, 310–11. See also Innocent III's *Etsi Iudaeos* and Innocent IV's May 9, 1244, letter to the king of France, both in Grayzel, *The Church and the Jews*, 114–15 and 250–1, respectively. This canon prohibits Jews from holding public office because it "offers them a pretext to vent their wrath." The 1267 Council of Wrocław also included this prohibition in its mandates. For an extensive discussion of the question of Jews in public office see Pakter, *Medieval Canon Law and the Jews*. For the text of the Council of Wrocław, see Solomon Grayzel and Kenneth R. Stow, *The Church and the Jews in the XIIIth Century*, vol. 2, *1254–1314* (Detroit: Wayne State University Press, 1989), 244–6.

60. Lipski, *Epistola Pastoralis*, I2.

61. MS. "S. Concilii Relationes Statu ad Limina: 667 Premisliensis" in Archivio Segreto Vaticano, *relatio* from 1743, fol. 26.

62. See for instance Pope Innocent III's letters of 1205 to Alphonso, king of Castille, to Cantor of Seguntium of 1207, to Count of Nevers of 1208; all are in Grayzel, *The Church and the Jews*, 112–13, 122–3, 126–7.

63. See for example Karp, *Epistola Pastoralis*, 4. Also Lipski, *Epistola Pastoralis*, I2.

64. Benedict XIV, *Epistola Encyclica ad Primatem, Archiepiscopos et Episcopos Regni Poloniae*; Benedict XIV, *List pasterski wyraźne w sobie naywyższey stolicy apostolskiey uwagi y napomnienia dostateczne zawieraiacy, dla zabieżenia y z gruntu wyniszczenia niegodziwych*

występków, przez niewierne żydowstwo z oczywistym uszczerbkiem wiary świętey y prawa duchownego y oczywistego, zagęszczonych w dyecezyi chełmskiey w roku 1752 ogłoszony (Zamość: Jan Kanty, 1752). The encyclical has been discussed by Gershon Hundert in Gershon David Hundert, *Jews in Poland-Lithuania in the Eighteenth Century: A Genealogy of Modernity* (Berkeley: University of California Press, 2004), 59–64.

65. My emphasis in the translation. The Latin text reads "Quo sit, ut illi infelices ab auctoritate hominis Judaeis, *tamquam* subditi de nutu et potestate domini dependant." See Benedict XIV, *Epistola Encyclica ad Primatem, Archiepiscopos et Episcopos Regni Poloniae.*

66. "Y stąd pochodzi, że owi nieszczęśliwi ludzie Chrześcijanie rozumieią bydź Panem y dziedzicem swoim Żyda, od którego skinienia, woli, y rozkazu, owi Poddani mienią się bydź dependuiacem." See Benedict XIV, *List Pasterski,* B.

67. Benedict XIV, *List Pasterski,* B.

68. See Benedict XIV, *Epistola Encyclica ad Primatem, Archiepiscopos et Episcopos Regni Poloniae.*

69. Benedict XIV, *Epistola Encyclica ad Primatem, Archiepiscopos et Episcopos Regni Poloniae.*

70. Pakter, *Medieval Canon Law and the Jews,* 85–142. See also III Lateran Council of 1179, paragraph 68; Council of Paris of 1213 and Innocent III's *Etsi Judaeos* in Grayzel, *The Church and the Jews,* 114–17, 306–7.

71. *Synodus Diaecesana Chelmensis ab Illustrissimo et Reverendissimo Domino D. Christophoro Ioanne in Slupow Szembek, Dei et S. Sedis Apostolicae Graita Episcopo Chelmensi, Nominato Premislensi Etc, Crasnostaviae in Ecclesia Cathedrali Praesente Universo Dioecesis Clero Celebrata Die Decima Mensis Julii et Aliis Duobus Sequentibus Diebus, Anno Domini M.D.CC.XVII* (Zamość: 1717), unnumbered page that precedes R2. Franciszek Antoni Kobielski, *Literae Pastorales ad Universum Clerum, et Populum Utriusque Diaecesis Illustrissimi & Reverendissimi Domini Francisci Antonii in Dmenin Kobielski Episcopi Luceoriensis et Brestensis, Serenissimae Reginalis Maiestatis Cantellarii cum Annexis de Verbo ad Verbum in Testimonium Legis Suae Sanctissimi Domoni Nostri Benedicti Papae XIV Constitutionibus et Litteris in Anno 1740 Et 1741 Ac Praesenti 1742* (no place: 1742), D3.

72. MS. "Edicta et Mandata Diocesis Cracoviensis 1737–1772" in AKM in Cracow, doc. 26; Andrzej Stanisław Kostka Załuski, "Edictum contra Judaeos."

73. Franciszek Antoni Kobielski, *List pasterski wszystkiemu duchowieństwu, świeckim i zakonnym, tudzież i wszystkim swoiemi honorami, godnościami prerogatywami ozdobonym y dystyngowanym panom, dziedzicom y possesorom, także uczciwym y pracowitym oboyga płci* (1752), 2. In 1670 King Michał Korybut Wiśniowiecki issued a universal decree concerning Christian servants in Jewish homes. The document did not prohibit daily service but rather yearly contracts. AIVAK, vol. V, 195–6.

74. Karp, *Epistola Pastoralis,* 4.

75. Józef Eustachy Szembek, *List pasterski wyraźne w sobie naywyższey stolicy apostolskiey uwagi y napomnienia dostateczne zawieraiący, dla zabieżenia y z gruntu wyniszczenia niegodziwych występków, przez niewierne żydowstwo z oczywistym uszczerbkiem wiary świętey y prawa duchownego y oyczystego, zagęszczonych w dyecezyi chełmskiey w roku 1752 ogłoszony. Y do należytego zachowania pzrez [sic] podane niżey wszelkim stanom sposoby, dla uśmierzenia do tąd szerzacey sią w wyuzdanym żydowstwie zuchwałości, przełożony* (Zamość: Drukarnia B. Jana Kantego, 1752), C2v-D.

76. Załuski, "Edictum contra Judaeos."

77. AEp 67 in AKM w Krakowie, folios 27–28, AEp 78, folios 16–18.

194   NOTES TO PAGES 90–93

78. Szembek, *List pasterski*, D. Kobielski, *List pasterski* (1752), 2. Lipski, *Epistola Pastoralis*, I3. See also *Constitutiones Synodales Luceoriensis et Brestensis ab Ill. Excellent. et Reverendiss. D. D. Stephano Bogulsao a Rupniew in Januszowice Rupniewski* (Warsaw: Typis Scholarum Piarum, 1726), D2v.
79. Kobielski, *List pasterski* (1752), 2.
80. On Jews and non-Jews during Purim, see Elliot Horowitz, "'Ve-nahafokh hu': yehudim mul soneihem be-ḥagigot ha-Purim ["And It Was Reversed": Jews and Their Enemies in the Festivities of Purim]," *Zion* 59 (1994). Codex Theodosianus, 16:8:18 prohibited Jews from celebrating Purim as a mockery of Christianity. See Linder, *The Jews in Roman Imperial Legislation*, 237–8.
81. Szymon Hubicki, *Żydowskie okrucieństwa* (Cracow: 1602), 25.
82. This presumably referred to Jewish inns and the profit they made renting rooms to travelers.
83. Stefan Żuchowski, *Process kryminalny o niewinne dziecię Jerzego Krasnowskiego* (Sandomierz: n.p., after 1718), 119–20. Also Przecław Mojecki, *Żydowskie okrucieństwa, mordy i zabobony* (Cracow: 1589), 21v. Cited also in Kazimierz Bartoszewski, *Antysemityzm w literaturze polskiej* (Warsaw: Geberthner & Wolff, 1914), 47. Pope Innocent III used this phrase as well, and Pope Benedict XIV reminded the bishops about it in his encyclical *A Quo Primum*. Benedict XIV, *Epistola Encyclica ad Primatem, Archiepiscopos et Episcopos Regni Poloniae*.
84. Żuchowski, *Process kryminalny*, 119–20.
85. Żuchowski, *Process kryminalny*, 73–4. This text is influenced by works by Sebastyan Śleszkowski, to whom Żuchowski referred on p. 72. In fact, Śleszkowski uses the term "Jewish Christians [żydochrześcianie]" in his Sebastyan Śleszkowski, *Dostateczna genealogia żydowska* (Brunsberg: n.p., 1622).
86. Żuchowski, *Process kryminalny*, 73–4.
87. See above chapters two and three, and also Joannicyusz Galatowski *Messyasz prawdziwy Iezus Chrystus syn boży od poczatku świata przez wszystkie wieki ludziom od Boga obrócony y od ludziey oczekiwany y w ostatnie czasy dla zbawienia ludzkiego na świat posłany* (Czernihow, 1672), 293–293v.
88. Żuchowski, *Process kryminalny*, 69–75. See also Mojecki, *Żydowskie okrucieństwa*, chapter XVIII, 26v–27v.
89. Żuchowski, *Process kryminalny*, 71–3, especially 71.
90. For sources and scholarship on the uprising see Edward Fram, "Bein 1096 ve 1648–49 – 'iyun me-ḥadash," *Zion* 61, no. 2 (1996); Edward Fram, "Ve-'adayin en bein 1096 le-1648–49," *Zion* 62, no. 1 (1997); Hayyim Jonah Gurland, *Le-korot ha-gezerot al israel* (Przemyśl: 1887); Joel Raba, *Between Remembrance and Denial* (Boulder: East European Monographs, 1995). See also articles in *Jewish History* 17/2 (2003) devoted to this 1648 uprising. Nathan Nata Hannover, *Abyss of Despair (Yeven Metzulah)*, trans. Abraham J. Mesch, Judaica Series (New Brunswick, NJ; Transaction, 1983); Nathan Nata Hannover and Meir Shabbetai ben, *Yeven meẓulah* (Toronto: Ozarenu, 1990).
91. Neither Hanna Węgrzynek nor Zenon Guldon and Jacek Wijaczka mention these cases. Zenon Guldon and Jacek Wijaczka, *Procesy o mordy rytualne w Polsce w XVI–XVIII wieku* (Kielce: DCF, 1995), 96–101; Hanna Węgrzynek, *"Czarna legenda" Żydów: Procesy o rzekome mordy rytualne w dawnej Polsce* (Warsaw: Wydawnictwo "Bellona" Fundacja Historia pro Futuro, 1995), 182–94.
92. Żuchowski, *Process kryminalny*, 73–4.

93. Indeed, he cited the famous Franciscan preacher, Węgrzynowicz, when referring to punishments against protectors of both Jews and heretics. Żuchowski, *Process kryminalny*, 71. On the historiographical perception of the Chmielnicki uprising see Joel Raba, *Ben zikkaron le-hakhhashah: Gezerot 408 ve-409 be-reshimot bene ha-zeman uve-ro'i ha-khetivah ha-historit*, vol. 98 (Tel-Aviv: Makhon le-heker ha-tefuẓot, 1994). In English, see Raba, *Between Remembrance and Denial*.

94. Adam Teller has studied the situation of Jews on the Radziwiłł estates in the eighteenth century. Adam Teller, "Tafkidam ha-kalkali u-me'amadam ha-ḥevrati shel yehudim be-aḥuzot bet Radziwil be-Lita ba-meah 18" (Ph.D., Hebrew University, 1997).

95. Żuchowski, *Process kryminalny*, 69.

96. S. G. F. Brandon, "History or Theology? The Basic Problems of the Evidence of the Trial of Jesus," in *Essential Papers on Judaism and Christianity in Conflict: From Late Antiquity to the Reformation*, ed. Jeremy Cohen (New York: New York University Press, 1991 <1968>), 118.

97. Józef Potocki (1673–1751).

98. Radliński, *Prawda chrześciańska*, 557–60.

99. For instance, in his *Collectarium canonum* or *Decretum*, Burchard of Worms prohibited the appointment of Jews as administrators of villages or Christian households: "Ne Judaeis administratorio usu sub ordine villicorum atque actorum Christianam familiam regere audeant, nec eis hoc a quoquam fieri praecipiatur. Si quis vero contra haec agere praesumpserit, si episcopus, presbyter, aut diaconus fuerit, proprio summoveatur gradu si vero monachus fuerit, communione privertur. Similiter et laicus. Et si perseveraverint inobedientes, anathematizentur." (Cited after Pakter, *Medieval Canon Law and the Jews*, 229, n. 33.)

100. Szembek, *List Pasterski*, C2.

101. Skarbek, "Edictum Contra Judaeos." *Constitutiones Synodales Editae et Promulgatae ab Illustrissimo etc. Andrea Stanislao Kostka Zaluski Episcopo Culmensi et Pomesaniensi, Abbate Commendatario Czervinensi et Paradisiensi, Supremo Regni Cancellario in Dioecesana Synodo Celebrata in Ecclesia Archipresbyteriali Lubaviensi Diebus XVI, XVII Et XVIII Mensis Septembris Anno Domini MDCCXLV* (Brunsberg [Braniewo]: Typis Societatis Jesu, 1746). Załuski, "Edictum contra Judaeos." Lipski, *Epistola Pastoralis*, I2 and the preceding unnumbered page. Karp, *Epistola Pastoralis*, 4.

102. Skarbek, "Edictum contra Judaeos."

103. Fortunat Łosiewski, *Powtórna męka Chrystusa Jezusa w nayświętszym sakramencie we czwartki postu wielkiego kazaniami prezentowana* (Warsaw: 1729), 13–16.

104. Radliński, *Prawda chrześciańska*, 557–60.

105. See a similar tale, which ends with a miracle, in Joan Young Gregg, *Devils, Women, and Jews: Reflections of the Other in Medieval Sermon Stories* (Albany: State University of New York Press, 1997), 212–13.

106. Mikołaj Popławski, *Stół duchowny rozliczeń nauk zbawiennych historyi y przykładów przy reflexyach na całego roku tygodnie, niedziele y święta* (Warsaw, 1704), 2157.

107. The issue of Jewish and Christian real estate ownership evoked concern also among Jewish leaders, but from a different perspective. In Poland, Joel Sirkes wrote a responsum concerning the purchase of a property from Christians in a predominantly Jewish district. The situation described in the responsum indicated that some Jewish leaders preferred it when Christians lived among Jews because they believed that it would be less likely that Christians would set fire in Jewish quarters if they lived there. *Shu"T Ba"*

Ḥ *(yashanot)*, no. 4. What is still interesting about this responsum and other Jewish and Christian sources is that both Jewish and Christian leadership perceived the Other as harmful and dangerous.

108. In the nineteenth century, this idea of Poland as the Christ of nations will be found in works by Adam Mickiewicz.

109. Alfonso de Espina, *Fortalitium Fidei, in Universos Christiane Religionis Hostes Judeorum [et] Saracenorum No[n] Invalido Brevis Nec Minus Lucidi Compendii Vallo Rabiem Cohibens Fortitudinis Turris No[n] abs Re Appellatum Quinq[Ue] Turriu[M] Inexpugnabilium Munimine Radians: Succincte Admodum [et] Adamussim Quinq[Ue] Partium Librorum Farragine Absolutum* (Lyon: 1525), Liber Tertius, unnumbered pages. Kenneth R. Stow, *Catholic Thought and Papal Jewry Policy, 1555–1593* (New York: Jewish Theological Seminary of America, 1977), 145–8.

110. Scholars of Jewish converts to Christianity have shown that converts often attacked their former society rather than the new one. See, for instance, the cases of Pablo Christiani in the Middle Ages or Johanness Pfefferkorn in early modern German lands. For further discussion of this issue, see Elisheva Carlebach, *Divided Souls: Converts from Judaism in Early Modern German Lands, 1500–1750* (New Haven: Yale University Press, 2001). Bogdan Rok seems to believe that Jan Lewek was indeed a Jewish convert; Bogdan Rok, "Z literatury antyżydowskiej w Polsce XVIII Wieku," in *Z historii ludności żydowskiej w Polsce i na Śląsku*, ed. Krystyn Matwijowski (Wrocław: Wydawnictwo Uniwersystetu Wrocławskiego, 1994), 214. For a detailed analysis of this text, see also Magdalena Teter, "Jewish Conversions to Catholicism in the Polish-Lithuanian Commonwealth of the Seventeenth and Eighteenth Centuries," *Jewish History* 17, no. 3 (2003): 269–72.

111. Jan Lewek, *List pewnego statysty, zawierajacy w sobie niektóre przyczyny, dla których z teraźniejszych żydów ledwie który do wiary świętey katolickiey nawracan bywa* (1728), Av.

112. Lewek, *List pewnego statysty*, A3 [unnumbered]. Jakub Radliński in his *Prawda chrześciańska*, 26, while discussing Jewish exile, wrote: "Here in Poland, Jews are allowed everything; they receive far more respect and rights to administer estates from some lords than Christians themselves."

113. See also Teter, "Jewish Conversions to Catholicism," 269–72, and Magdalena Teter, "Jews in the Legislation and Teachings of the Catholic Church in Poland 1648–1772" (Ph.D. dissertation, Columbia University, 2000), 158–62.

114. Kenneth Stow has discussed this motif in Counter-Reformation Church Jewry policy in his work; see, for instance, Stow, *Catholic Thought and Papal Jewry*.

115. *Parch*, scab or a skin ailment, a pejorative term for Jews. MS 303/R "Kazania świątecze (1706–1730)" in Archiwum i Biblioteka O. O. Bernardynów in Cracow, folio 200 R-200V. In Hebrew, *perekh* means tyranny/oppression.

116. This was a clear exaggeration, for only Catholic noblemen could seat in the senate. Eugeni od Sw. Mateusza, *Protekcya od tronu łaski Anny S. dysgracyom nieba na ziemi awizowana, na placu zguby płaczu znaleziona* (Cracow: 1736), E. Similar claims concerning the alleged Jewish control of political leaders would later be developed more sophisticatedly in modern anti-Semitism.

117. "Hiberna": between 1649 and 1775, a tax from royal and Church domains to support the army.

118. *Machlarstwo/machlojstwo* closely resembles the Hebrew *mahloket/mahloykes*, contention, discord, and sometimes "shady business."

119. *Bachor* is a pejorative term denoting a child; it closely resembles, and probably stems from, the Hebrew *bahur/boher*, a young man.
120. Żuchowski, *Process kryminalny*, 74.
121. Jan Stanisław Bystroń, *Dzieje obyczajów w dawnej Polsce, wiek XVI–XVIII* (Warsaw: PIW, 1994), 1:71. See also Gershon D. Hundert, "Poland: Paradisus Judaeorum," *Journal of Jewish Studies [Great Britain]* 48, no. 2 (1997).
122. Biblioteka X. Czartoryskich in Cracow, MS. 3011 I "Zbiór kazań," 94.
123. Guido Ruggiero, *Binding Passions: Tales of Magic, Marriage and Power at the End of the Renaissance* (New York: Oxford University Press, 1993), 9, 17–8, 99, 136.
124. It is interesting to note that in a Polish film from the 1930s, *Szczęśliwa trzynastka*, this folk belief was central to the plot. The protagonist and his friend went out of their ways to see as many bearded Jews as possible for "good luck." The opposite, the belief in priests bringing bad luck, was reported by a nineteenth-century traveler to Russia, John Foster Fraser. Fraser wrote, "so much indeed is the priestly class held in abhorrence that men spit on the ground as they walk by and a Russian merchant when leaving his house on important business in the morning will turn back if he sees a priest, rather than court ill-luck for the rest of the day by passing him." His remark is based on his observations of the southern parts of the Russian empire, and admittedly refer to Eastern Orthodox priests. See John Foster Fraser, *Round the World on a Wheel* (London, 1899), 31–2. I thank Shawn Hill for bringing this text to my attention.

CHAPTER 6: "COUNTLESS BOOKS AGAINST COMMON FAITH": CATHOLIC
INSULARITY AND ANTI-JEWISH POLEMIC

1. See for instance the classic study by Joshua Trachtenberg in which he distinguished between the two kinds of accusations; Joshua Trachtenberg, *The Devil and the Jews: The Medieval Conception of the Jew and Its Relation to Modern Antisemitism* (Philadelphia: Jewish Publication Society of America, 1983), 124–55.
2. One Catholic catechism addressed the question of Jesus' presence in each wafer, emphasizing that he is present in whole even when a wafer is torn into smaller pieces. *Katechizm prostych albo krótkie zebranie potrzebnieyszych wiary naszey artykułów. Dla prostych ludzi y dzieci na pytania y odpowiedzi krótkie rozłożony* (n.p.: 1600?), 6–7.
3. For a more recent study of tales of host desecration, see Miri Rubin, *Gentile Tales: The Narrative Assault on Late Medieval Jews* (New Haven, CT: Yale University Press, 1999).
4. Gavin I. Langmuir, *Toward a Definition of Antisemitism* (Berkeley: University of California Press, 1990), chapter "Ritual Cannibalism," 263–81.
5. R. Po-chia Hsia, *The Myth of Ritual Murder: Jews and Magic in Reformation Germany* (New Haven: Yale University Press, 1988). See also Kenneth Stow's forthcoming book on Jewish dogs.
6. For examples of these beliefs explicated in a Polish Protestant catechism see questions 78 and 80: *Katechizm albo krótkie w iedno mieysce zebranie wiary y powinności krześcijanskiey z pasterstwem zborowym y domowym, z modlitwami, psalmami y piosnkami na cześć a chwałę Panu Bogu a zborowi iego ku zbudowaniu teraz znowu za pilnym przeyrzeniem y poprawieniem wydany* (Wilno: n.p., 1600?), 96, 98. For an example of the same issue in a Catholic catechism see *Katechizm prostych albo krótkie zebranie potrzebnieyszych wiary naszey artykułów. Dla prostych ludzi y dzieci na pytania y odpowiedzi krótkie rozłożony* (1600), 6–7. The book itself has the 1600 date (MDC) but

both the catalogue of the Jagiellonian Library in Cracow and Karol Estreicher claim it comes from mid-eighteenth century. See also sermons by Krzysztof Kraiński. Krzysztof Kraiński, *Postylla kościoła powszechnego apostolskiego słowem bożym ugruntowana na Jezusie Chrystusie. Spisana ku chwale Bogu w Tróycy S. iedynemu przez księdza Krzysztofa Kraińskiego* (n.p.: n.p., after 1611), 214.

7. *Fortalitium Fidei* saw several editions: Strasbourg, 1471; Basle, 1475; Lyon (Lugundi), 1487, 1511, and 1525; Nuremberg, 1485, 1494; *Historia maior:* London 1570, 1571, 1640, 1644, 1684, 1686; Paris 1644 (based on the 1571 London edition); Zurich (Tiguri), 1586.

8. See also Bernard D. Weinryb, *The Jews of Poland: A Social and Economic History of the Jewish Community in Poland from 1100 to 1800* (Philadelphia: Jewish Publication Society of America, 1973), 130–1.

9. Gelasius I became a saint and his feast is held on November 21. John F. Murphy, "Gelasius I," in *The Catholic Encyclopedia,* ed. Charles Herbermann et al. (New York: The Encyclopedia Press, 1913), 6:406.

10. Julian Bukowski, *Dzieje Reformacyi w Polsce: Od jej wejścia do Polski aż do jej upadku* (Cracow: Nakładem Autora, 1883), 167. According to the archivists in the archive of the Archdiocese of Cracow (AKM w Krakowie), the volume of trial records, AEp 2, which Bukowski used for his study, was lost during the Second World War, although one scholarly work published in 1972 refers to it. See Kazimierz Gabryel, "Działalność Kościelna Biskupa Tomickiego 1464–1535," in *Studia historii kościoła w Polsce* (Warsaw: Akademia Teologii Katolickiej, 1972). It is unclear whether Gabryel saw the volume or copied references to it from some prewar publication. Excerpts can be found also in the notes by the nineteenth-century Catholic author and historian Żegota Pauli, now in the manuscript collection of the Library of the Jagiellonian University in Cracow. This case is noted in MS. 5357 in Biblioteka Uniwersytetu Jagiellońskiego, vol. 9, fol. 70v. According to Pauli's notes, this case was in AEp 2 in AKM in Cracow, fol. 69.

11. Stanisław Hoszowski, *Ceny we Lwowie w XVII i XVII wieku* (Lwów: Kasa im. J. Mianowskiego, 1928), 214.

12. See references to the now lost sources in Bukowski, *Dzieje Reformacyi w Polsce,* 168.

13. AKW, Acta Actorum 3, fol. 156.

14. Paulina Buchwald-Pelcowa, *Cenzura w dawnej Polsce,* 25–7.

15. Buchwald-Pelcowa, *Cenzura w dawnej Polsce,* 28. See also *Constitutiones Synodorum Metropolitanae Ecclesiae Gnesnensis, Provincialium, Tam Vetustorum Quam Recentiorum, Usquae ad Annum Domini MD L XX VIII* (Cracow: Andreas Petricovius [Andrzej Piotrowczyk], 1578), 126–7.

16. Bolesław Ulanowski, *Materiały do historii ustawodawstwa synodalnego w Polsce w w. XVII,* Collectanea ex Archivio Collegii Iuridici (Cracow, 1895), 1: 388–90.

17. Ulanowski, *Materiały do historii ustawodawstwa synodalnego,* 390–1.

18. Ulanowski, *Materiały do historii ustawodawstwa synodalnego,* 453.

19. The text can be found in Wiesław Müller, ed., *Relacje o stanie diecezji krakowskiej, 1615– 1765* (Lublin: Katolicki Universytet Lubelski, 1978), 44–5.

20. Benedict Herbest, *Nauka prawego chrześcijanina* (Cracow, 1566), unnumbered page before Aiij. Herbest outlined a chain of transmission of knowledge: the priest should instruct the male head of the household [*gospodarz*], who then should instruct his daughters, sons, journeymen, and neighbors. The head of the household is not to teach anything new about religion and only transmit what the preacher taught him. Herbest, *Nauka prawego chrześcijanina,* Aiiij [penciled 45].

21. Dariusz Kuźmina sees Herbest's work as the first Polish Catholic catechism, but I would argue that the 1568 *Katechizm rzymski* is the first formal Polish Catholic catechism. Dariusz Kuźmina, *Katechizmy w Rzeczypospolitej XVI i początku XVII wieku,* ed. Marcin Drzewiecki, Nauka-Dydaktyka-Praktyka (Warsaw: Stowarzyszenie Bibliotekarzy Polskich, 2002), 27–33.

22. *Katechizm albo nauka wiary y pobożnosci krześcijanskiey według uchwały s. Tridentskiego Concilium przez uczone a bogoboyne ludzie zebrana y spisana. Przodkiem plebanom y przełożonym kościelnym, potym inszym wsystkim pobożnym krześcianom barzo pożyteczna y potrzebna. Przez księdza Walentego Kuchorskiego archidiakona pomorskiego etc. z łacinskiego na polskie wyłożony,* trans. Walenty Kuchorski (Cracow: Mikołaj Schaffenberg, 1568), "Przedmowa do czytelnika," page unnumbered.

23. See for instance the long discussion of baptism, *Katechizm albo nauka wiary,* 120–47.

24. See for example *Katechizm rzymski to iest, nauka chrześcianska powaga Concilium Tridentskiego y Papieża Piusa V wydane po łacinie; a teraz nowo na polskie pytania y odpowiedzi przełożona; za rozkazaniem jego mości X. Stanisława Karnkowskiego arcybiskupa gnieźnienskiego etc. y iego nakładem wydrukowana* (Kalisz: Drukarnia Jana Wolraba, 1603); *Katechizm rzymski to iest nauka chrześcianska powaga Concilium Tridentskiego y Piusa V Papieża po łacinie wydana; potym za rozkazaniem s. pamięci X. Stanisława Karnkowskiego arcybiskupa gnieźnienskiego, primasa koronnego na polskie pytania y odpowiedzi przełożona; teraz znowy dla ubogich plebanów y gospodarzów katholickich przedrukowana* (Cracow: Drukarnia Franciszka Cezarego, 1643); *Katechizm rzymski z dekretu S. Koncilium Trydentskiego za rozkazem S. Piusa V Papieża po łacinie wydany, na polski ięzyk powagą niegdyś wydany J. O. Xcia Jmci Xiędza Stanisława Karnkowskiego arcybiskupa gnieźnienskiego, prymasa Kor. Po. Y W. X. L. przez pytania y odpowiedzi przetłumaczony y wydrukowany w Kaliszu w R. P. 1603 teraz zaś z niezliczonych omyłek y słów staropolskich dziś nierozumiałych oczyszczony y z oryginałem łacińkim skonfrontowany, a jako dzieło arcybiskupa y prymasa utriusque gentis jaśnie oświeconemu nayprzewielebnieyszemu w Bogu xiążęciu jmci xiędzu Władysławowi Łubienskiemu arcybiskupowi gnieźnienskiemu prymasowi y xiążęciu pierwszemu Kor. Pol. Y W. X. L. sedis apostolicae legato etc. . . . dedykowany* (Wilno: Typis Scholarum Piarum, 1762).

25. *Katechizm prostych.*

26. *Katechizm rzymski* (1603), Przedmowa, page unnumbered.

27. *Katechizm rzymski* (1643). *Katechizm rzymski* (1762). The provincial and diocesan synods in Poland ordered the use of catechisms in regular instruction of the people. See relevant decrees from the synod of Łuck in 1607, Chełm in 1624, Cracow in 1711, Wilno in 1717, and Płock in 1733. Zenon Chodyński and Edward Likowski, eds., *Decretales Summorum Pontificum pro Regno Poloniae et Constitutiones Synodorum Provincialium et Dioecesanarum Regni Eiusdem ad Summam Collectae cum Annotationibus, Declarationibus, Admonitionibus et Additionibus ex Historia, Jure Ecclesiastico Universali et Jure Civili Regni Curantibus Plerisque Sacerdotibus Posnanensibus Editae,* 3 vols. (Poznań: Typis Augustini Schmaedicke, 1869), 1:22–3.

28. *Katechizm rzymski* (1603), Przedmowa, page unnumbered, quire iiii v.

29. *Katechizm rzymski* (1603), 3. *Katechizm rzymski* (1643), 2–3.

30. Jan Poszakowski, *Antidotum contra 'Antidotum abo zbawienna przestroga,' że lekarstwo duszne przeciwko apostazyi Woyciecha Węgierskiego niegdy superintendenta zborów ewangelickich sporządzone y wygotowane teraz świeżo w Królewcu roku pańskiego 1750 drukiem opublikowane y ogłoszone* (Wilno: Typis Societatis Jesu, 1754), 100.

31. The text of this pamphlet was printed in Aleksander Woyde, *Dwa nieznane rękopisy z dziejów polskiej Reformacji: Deux manucrits inconnus concernant la Reformation en Pologne*, vol. 7, *Bibliotheca Universitatis Liberae Polonae* (Warsaw: Wolna Wszechnica Polska, 1922), 7.

32. See for example Maria Sipayłło, ed., *Acta Synodalia Ecclesiarum Poloniae Reformatarum, 1550–1559*, vol. 1, *Akta synodów różnowierczych w Polsce* (Warsaw: Wydawnictwa Uniwersytetu Warszawskiego, 1966), 179, 264, 308–9; Maria Sipayłło, ed., *Acta Synodalia Ecclesiarum Poloniae Reformatarum, 1571–1632*, vol. 3, *Akta synodow różnowierczych w Polsce* (Warsaw: Wydawnictwa Uniwersytetu Warszawskiego, 1983), 82, 439, 495–6; Maria Sipayłło, ed., *Acta Synodalia Ecclesiarum Poloniae Reformatarum, 1560–1570*, vol. 2, *Akta synodów różnowierczych w Polsce* (Warsaw: Wydawnictwa Uniwersytetu Warszawskiego, 1972), 61.

33. "Dyskursik o Sinodzie," in *Dwa nieznane rękopisy z dziejów polskiej Reformacji*, ed. Aleksander Woyde (Warsaw: Universitas Liberae Poloniae, Wolna Wszechnica Polska 1922), 11.

34. *Katechizm albo nauka wiary* (1568), "Przedmowa do czytelnika"; *Katechizm rzymski* (1643), 3.

35. *Katechizm albo nauka wiary* (1568), "Przedmowa do czytelnika."

36. *Katechizm rzymski* (1643), 3.

37. See the author's introduction to the second edition of this catechism. Krzysztof Jan Szembek, *Krótkie zebranie nauki chrześcianskiey zlecenia nayprzelewiebneyszego w Chrystusie Panu jaśnie wielmożnego I. MC. Krzysztofa Jana Szembeka, Biskupa przemyskiego, proboszcza y generała miechowskego etc. dziatkom chrześciańskim przez pytanie y odpowiedź według porządku y podzielenia catech: S. Concil: Trinden.* (Cracow: Drukarnia Franciszka Cezarego, 1719), pages unnumbered.

38. Chodyński and Likowski, eds., *Decretales Summorum Pontificum pro Regno Poloniae*, 1:25.

39. *Katechizm rzymski* (1762), "Do czytelnika," page unnumbered.

40. Ulanowski, *Materiały do historii ustawodawstwa synodalnego*, 436–7.

41. Ulanowski, *Materiały do historii ustawodawstwa synodalnego*, 444–5.

42. The text of the report is published in Müller, ed., *Relacje o stanie diecezji*, 44–5.

43. See also other synods before mid-eighteenth century – for example, the provincial synod of Piotrków of 1577, the diocesan synods of Wilno in 1669, 1685, and 1717, and the 1690 synod of Samogitia. In 1737, Bishop Jan Alexander Lipski also addressed some of these issues in his *Epistola pastoralis*. Synod of Chełm in 1694 included sending sons to "heretical schools" among sins that could not be absolved by a regular priest. See also rulings by the synod of Brest and Łuck dioceses in 1726 and the 1744 synod of Wilno.

44. Bronisław Batoński, "Szkolnictwo jezuickie w dobie kontrreformacji," in *Z Dziejów szkolnictwa jezuickiego w Polsce*, ed. Jerzy Paszenda (Cracow: WAM-Księża Jezuici, 1994), 46–54; Stanisław Obirek, *Jezuici w Rzeczpospolitej Obojga Narodów 1564–1668* (Cracow: Wydział Filozoficzny Towarzystwa Jezusowego, 1996), 77.

45. Wojciech Kriegseisen, *Ewangelicy polscy i litewscy w epoce saskiej* (Warsaw: Semper, 1996), 122–49.

46. Poszakowski, *Antidotum contra 'Antidotum'*.

47. Poszakowski, *Antidotum contra 'Antidotum'*, 83.

48. They were taught briefly and with a lot of suspicion. Henryk Barycz, *Historia Uniwersytetu Jagiellońskiego w epoce humanizmu* (Cracow: Uniwersytet Jagielloński, 1935),

NOTE TO PAGE 105

79, 87. In contrast, in the West, Hebrew was taught by Elijah Levita in Padua; Matteus Adrianus, a Spanish Jew, at the Collegium Trilingue in Louvain; Jacon Jonah in Tübingen; Anthonius Margharita in Vienna; Werner Einhorn (referred to as Wernerus Einhorn de Bacharach hebreus baptizatus) in Erfurt; Johannes Böschlingen de Esslingen in Wittenberg and then in Heidelberg; Johannes Cellarius in Leipzig and in Frankfurt on Oder; Johannes Reuchlin in Ingolstadt and Tübingen.

49. Barycz, *Historia Uniwersytetu*: on the Greek see 67–84; on the Hebrew see 84–95. Władysław Smereka, "Biblistyka polska (wiek XVI–XVIII)," in *Dzieje teologii katolickiej w Polsce*, ed. Marian Rechowicz (Lublin, 1975), vol. 2/1, 221–66. For examples of books on Hebrew grammar published in Poland see Joannes Campensis and Elias Levita, *Ex Variis Libellis Eliae Grammaticorum Omnium Doctissimi, Huc Fere Congestum Est Opera Ioannis Campensis, Quicquid ad Absolutam Grammaticen Hebraicam Est Necessarium* (Cracow: Ex Officina Ungleriana, 1534). Also the now lost Franciszek Stankar, *Gramatica Institutio Linguae Hebreae* (Cracow: Johannes Helicz, 1548). This is the Polish edition of *Francisci Stancari Mantuani, Suae Ebreae Grammaticae Compendium* (Basilea, 1547). On teaching Hebrew and Greek in Braunsberg, see "Motiva pro erigenda studio generali sue universitate in Collegio Brunsbergensis SJ in Prussia in diaecesi Varmensi" in ARSI, MS. Pol. 78 "Epistolae (1670–1700)," fols. 174–5.

50. See the note above.

51. Such works were to be found on the peripheries of the Polish-Lithuanian Commonwealth, in places with larger numbers of Protestants. For example, in 1740, a book on the history of printing in Poland was published in Gdańsk [Danzig]. The author of the book, Johannes Daniel Hoffman, used the book by Johannes Christian Wolf on Hebrew books to provide information about Hebrew printing in the Commonwealth. Johannes Daniel Hoffman, *De Typographiis Earumque Initiis et Incrementis in Regno Poloniae et Magno Ducatu Lithuaniae cum Variis Observationibus Rem et Literariam et Typographicam Utriusque Gentis Aliqua ex Parte Illustrantibus* (Gdańsk [Dantisci]: Apud Georgium Marcum Knochium, 1740 [1983?]), 10, 13–14. The book by Wolf was Johannes Christian Wolf, *Bibliotecae Hebreae* (Hamburg: 1715–1721). On Christian Hebraism in the West, see Stephen G. Burnett, "Distorted Mirrors: Antonius Margaritha, Johann Buxtorff and Christian Enthographies of the Jews," *Sixteenth Century Journal* 25 (1994); Stephen G. Burnett, *From Christian Hebraism to Jewish Studies: Johannes Buxtorf (1564–1629) and Hebrew Learning in the Seventeenth Century* (Leiden: Brill, 1996); Elisheva Carlebach, *Divided Souls: Converts from Judaism in Early Modern German Lands, 1500–1750* (New Haven, CT: Yale University Press, 2001); R. Po-chia Hsia, "Christian Ethnographies of the Jews in Early Modern Germany," in *The Expulsion of the Jews: 1492 and After*, ed. Raymond B. Waddington and Arthur Williamson (New York: Garland Press, 1994); Aaron L. Katchen, *Christian Hebraists and Dutch Rabbis: Seventeenth Century Apologetics and the Study of Maimonides' Mishneh Torah*, Harvard Judaic Texts and Studies (Cambridge, MA: Harvard University Press, 1984); Frank Rosenthal, "The Study of the Hebrew Bible in Sixteenth Century Italy," *Studies in the Renaissance* 1 (1954). Some Christian Hebraists even defended Jews and Jewish writings against attacks; see Johannes Reuchlin, *Recommendation Whether to Confiscate, Destroy and Burn All Jewish Books: A Classic Treatise against Anti-Semitism* (New York: Paulist Press, 2000).

52. Few Polish clergymen appreciated the value of Hebrew, and even fewer knew it. One of the few exceptions might be Marek Korona (1590–1651), a Franciscan polemicist, who encouraged the study of Hebrew, which he called *lingua sacra et casta*, to fully

understand the meaning of the Scriptures, and even "Christ himself." We, however, have little information about his knowledge of Hebrew. See more on Korona in chapter seven, "Warding Off Heretical Depravity." See also works by Jan Poszakowski (d. 1755). For examples of library catalogues, see MS. 2626 in Biblioteka Uniwersytetu Jagiellońskiego in Cracow, and MS. AKK 50 in Biblioteka i Archiwum OO. Kapucynów in Cracow. Waldemar Kowalski has shown that in 1610 a parish in Jędrzejów in Little Poland (Małopolska) had only "the Bible, Gratian's *Decrees*, and three volumes of sermons." Waldemar Kowalski, "Change in Continuity: Post-Tridentine Rural and Township Parish Life in the Cracow Diocese," *Sixteenth Century Journal* 35, no. 3 (2004): 704.

53. Burnett, *From Christian Hebraism to Jewish Studies*, 240.

54. Ms. 238 Tomasz Nargielewicz, "Kazania, Prov. S. Hyacinthi in Russia, OP, Leopoli in Conventu SS. Corporis Christi, A.D. 1689, Maj 31," in Archiwum Prowincji Polskiej OO. Dominikanów in Cracow, 9r.

55. Jan Poszakowski, *Antidotum contra 'Antidotum'*, 2–4. See also Marcin Matuszewicz, *Diariusz życia mego*, 2 vols. (Warsaw: Państwowy Instytut Wydawniczy, 1986), 1: 385–6. See also Daniel Stone, "Knowledge of Foreign Languages among Eighteenth-Century Polish Jews," *Polin* 10 (1997): 215–16.

56. Still in 1717, for instance, the diocesan synod of Chełm prohibited Catholics from reading the Bible in the vernacular. MS. "Archivio della Nunziatura di Varsovia" in Archivio Segreto Vaticano, vol. 171, folio 13. See also Janusz Tazbir, *A State without Stakes: Polish Religious Toleration in the Sixteenth and Seventeenth Centuries* (Warsaw: Państwowy Instytut Wydawniczy, 1973), 143. On the medieval misgivings about the vernacular Bibles, see for example Leonard Boyle, "Innocent III and Vernacular Versions of Scripture," in *The Bible in the Medieval World: Essays in Honor of Beryl Smalley*, ed. Katherine Walsh and Diana Wood (New York: Blackwell, 1985).

57. Elisheva Carlebach pointed out that some Protestant Hebraists were surprised how little knowledge of Jewish customs Catholics had and used it in anti-Catholic polemic. Elisheva Carlebach, *The Death of Simon Abeles: Jewish-Christian Tension in Seventeenth Century Prague*, Third Annual Herbert Berman Memorial Lecture (New York: Center for Jewish Studies, Queens College, City University of New York, 2001), 33–4.

58. Eliyahu ben Shemuel of Lublin, *Shu"T: Yad Eliyahu* (Amsterdam, 1712), no. 48. BT Sanhedrin 59a says that a non-Jew studying the Torah deserves death because the Torah was permitted "to us" and not "to them." BT Hagigah 13a, to which R. Eliyahu refers right at the beginning of his lengthy answer, uses the term *masar*, "to inform against/betray"; in the context of teaching the Torah to non-Jews, it can also mean transmit. Commentary on this section by the Polish rabbi Joel Sirkes reinforces the idea that it is prohibited to teach a non-Jew the Torah, except for the seven Noahide commandments. In contrast, BT 'Avodah Zarah 3a states that "even a heathen/idolator who studies the Torah is equal to High Priest." BT Sanhedrin 59a also mentions this opinion but limits it to the seven Noahide commandments. Tosafot on BT 'Avodah Zarah 3a also reiterated that the statement "a heathen/idolator who studies the Torah is equal to High Priest" applies only to the Noahide commandments and not the rest of the Torah, for which he deserves death as mentioned in BT Sanhedrin 59a.

59. On the Noahide commandments, see BT 'Avodah Zarah 2b and BT Sanhedrin 56a–6. See also BT Sanhedrin 59a, Tosafot and Rashi's commentary to this passage. See Eliyahu ben Shmuel of Lublin's responsum (note 58) and the responsum of Elia Menachem Halfan on teaching Hebrew to non-Jews. Halfan permits teaching Hebrew

but prohibits teaching oral traditions. The responsum was published by David Kaufman in David Kaufman, "Elia Menachem Chalfan on Jews Teaching Hebrew to Non-Jews," *Jewish Quarterly Review* 9 (1897). For this reference I am indebted to Daniel Kokin's talk "Jewish Messianism and Christian Hebraism: A Quiet Partnership?" at the 34th AJS Annual Conference, Los Angeles, December 17, 2003.

60. He refers to Cardinal Egidio.

61. Elias Levita, *Massoreth ha-Massoreth of Elias Levita Being an Exposition of the Massoretic Notes on the Hebrew Bible or the Ancient Critical Apparatus of the Old Testament, in Hebrew with an English Translation and Critical and Explanatory Notes*, ed. Norman Henry Snaith, trans. Christian D. Ginsburg (New York: Ktav, 1968), 95–6. I have modified the English translation slightly.

62. Kaufman, "Elia Menachem Chalfan on Jews Teaching Hebrew to Non-Jews," 500.

63. On the sense of permanency of the ghetto setting see Kenneth R. Stow, "The Consciousness of Closure: Roman Jewry and Its *Ghet*," in *Essential Papers on Jewish Culture in Renaissance and Baroque Italy*, ed. David Ruderman (New York: New York University Press, 1992). For instances of this kind of interaction, see Mark R. Cohen, "Leone Da Modena's *Riti*: A Seventeenth-Century Plea for Social Toleration of Jews," in *Essential Papers on Jewish Culture in Renaissance and Baroque Italy*, ed. David Ruderman (New York: New York University Press, 1992). Leone Modena and Mark R. Cohen, *The Autobiography of a Seventeenth-Century Venetian Rabbi: Leon Modena's Life of Judah* (Princeton, NJ: Princeton University Press, 1988). For examples of ambivalence see a responsum by Elijah Menahem Halfan of 1544 published by David Kaufman in *Jewish Quarterly Review* 9 (1897): 503–8. See also the introduction to Elias Levita's *Masoreth ha-Masoret* (1538), in which he is apologetic about the instruction of non-Jews in rabbinic sources.

64. Sebastian Miczyński, *Zwierciadło Korony Polskiey: Urázy ciężkie y utrapienia wielkie, które ponosi od Żydów wyrażaiące synom koronnym ná seym walny w roku pańskim 1618* (Cracow: Máciej Jędrzeiowczyk, 1618); Sebastyan Śleszkowski, *Dostateczna genealogia żydowska* (Brunsberg: n.p., 1622); Sebastyan Śleszkowski, *Jasne dowody o doktorach żydowskich, ze nie tylko duszę ale y ciało swoie w niebespieczenstwo zginienia wiecznego wdaią, którzy Żydów, Tatarów y innych niewiernych, przeciwko zakazaniu kościoła świętego powszechnego za lekarzów używaia* (n.p.: n.p., 1623). Subsequent editions 1649, 1758.

65. See chapter four above and chapter seven below.

66. David d'Avray called preaching "distillation of some aspects of society, especially if one pictures society as saturated with thoughts and values." He also emphasized the long term impact of preaching on the social values: "The long term impact on the mind of at least a significant portion of listeners was probably much greater than that of the revivalist sermon. It might be described as drip-drip method of inculcating beliefs. The same or similar topoi would be greatly repeated year in, year out and eventually they would become assumptions. Moreover, since preachers all over Europe would be borrowing material from the same internationally available model sermon collections, almost the same ideas and formulae would reach people in many different countries and – since the model of collections often had a long life – over an extended period." David d'Avray, "Method of the Study of Medieval Sermons," in *Modern Questions About Medieval Sermons: Essays on Marriage, Death, History and Sanctity*, ed. Nicole Beriou and David d'Avray (Spoleto: Centro italiano di studi sull'alto medioevo, 1994), 7, 9. Still, it is worthwhile to remember that within the whole body of works published by the Polish

Catholic clergy Jews were not a central element. In a somewhat problematic estimate, Daniel Tollet assessed that anti-Jewish literature accounted for only 0.4 percent of overall literary output in Poland between 1588–1668. He took into account only explicit anti-Jewish books, and did not consider a wider range of homiletic and polemical works. Daniel Tollet, "La littérature antisémite polonaise, de 1588 à 1668," *Revue francaise d'histoire du livre* 14 (1977): 73–105.

67. John Y. B. Hood, *Aquinas and the Jews*, Middle Ages Series (Philadelphia: University of Pennsylvania Press, 1995), ix.

68. See for example Maimonides, *Iggeret teman le-rabenu Mosheh ben Maimon*, ed. Abraham Halkin (New York: 1952), Hebrew on 12–13, English on iii. See also *Sefer Toledot Yeshu sive Liber de Ortu Origine Jesu ex Editione Wagenseiliana Transcriptus et Explicatus*, ed. L. Edman (Upsala, 1857), Hebrew on 20 and 22, Latin on 21 and 23. For the English translation of *Toledot Yeshu* see *The Jewish Life of Christ being the Sepher Toldoth Jeshu or Book of the Generation of Jesus*, trans.G. W. Foote and J. M. Wheeler (London, 1885). For a less explicit acceptance of this accusation, see David Berger, *The Jewish-Christian Debate in the High Middle Ages: A Critical Edition of the Nizzahon Vetus*, Judaica, Texts and Translations 4 (Philadelphia, 1979), Hebrew section on 24–5 and 81; English on 64–5 and 136.

69. See for example Antoni Siarkiewicz, *Miecz sprawiedliwości bożey* (Lwów: Typis Societatis Jesu, 1718). Anonymous, *Kazania w Jarosławiu i Lublinie* (n.p.: n.p., 1740?), 298–310.

70. See for instance the catechisms *Katechizm prostych*, 4; *Katechizm rzymski (1643)*, 29–30.

71. Woyciech Tylkowski, *Problemata święte abo pytania około wyrozumienia świętey Ewangeliey od kościoła powszechnego tak na niedziele iako i na święta rozłożony* (Poznań, 1688), Oo4v. See also Paweł Kaczyński, *Kazania na niedziele całego roku* (Kalisz, 1675), 76; Marceli Dziewulski, *Prezerwatywa powietrza mororwego reskrypcji kaznodziejskiej* (Cracow, 1720), B1v; Paweł Kaczyński, *Kazania na niedziele całego roku* (Kalisz, 1675), 76; Mikołaj Popławski *Stół duchowny rozliczeń nauk zbawiennych historyi y przykładów przy reflexyach na całego roku tygodnie, niedziele y święta, nie tylko dla nabożnych dusz, ale y kaznodziejów, spowiedników, potrawkami zastawiony* (Warsaw, 1704), 587; Jan Poszakowski *Głos pasterza Jezusa Chrystusa wzywającego oświecenie do owczarni swoiey abo nauka katholicka* (Vilno, 1737), 49; MS. 62 "Manuale seu Sacri Oratoris Notata seu Conciones in Ecclessiis Leopoliensis Auditae Harum Nonnullarum Brevis Annotatio Prioprioque Labore Collecta ex Anno Quo de Exedra Crucis Spinis Coronatus Orator Verbum Incarnatum Peroravit Orbi 1738–1744" in Archiwum Prowincji Polskiej O O. Dominikanów in Cracow, 475–6. Gospels of Mathew 27:11–31; Mark 15:1–15; Luke 23:1–25; John 18:28–19:16. In Matthew 27:11ff and Mark 15 Jews are not actively present; in Luke 23 and John 18:12–40, Jews are present and Pilate can find "no guilt" in Jesus.

72. Popławski, *Stół duchowny*, 193–4.

73. Popławski, *Stół duchowny*, 538. Popławski referred to Paul's Epistle to Galatians 4:22–7: "For it is written that Abraham had two sons, one by a slave woman and the other by a free woman. One, the child of the slave, was born according to the flesh; the other, the child of the free woman, was born through the promise. Now this is an allegory: these women are two covenents. One woman in fact is Hagar, from Mount Sinai, bearing children for slavery. Now Hagar is Mount Sinai in Arabia and corresponds to the present Jerusalem, for she is in slavery with her children. But the other woman corresponds to the Jerusalem above, she is free and she is our mother."

74. Henry Phillips, "Sacred Text and Sacred Image: France in the Seventeenth Century," *Bulletin of the John Rylands University Library of Manchester* 81, no. 3 (1999).
75. Mieczysław Brzozowski, "Teoria kaznodziejska (wiek XVI–XVIII)," in *Dzieje teologii katolickiej w Polsce*, ed. Marian Rechowicz (Lublin: Towarzystwo Naukowe Katolickiego Uniwersytetu Lubelskiego, 1975), vol. 2/1, 410. See also Janusz Tazbir, "Sarmatyzacja katolicyzmu w XVII wieku," in *Wiek XVII – kontrreformacja – barok: prace z historii kultury*, ed. Janusz Pelc (Wrocław: Zakład Narodowy im. Ossolinskich, 1970). For an example from the period, see Tomasz Młodzianowski, *Kazania i homilyie na święta uroczystsze także pogrzeby dla większey chwały Boga, króla królów: nayiaśnieyszey na zawsze królowy polskiy Bogarodzicy Panny, czci* (Poznań: Collegium Societatis Iesu, 1681), title, 296–7.
76. Młodzianowski, *Kazania i homilye*, 296.
77. Młodzianowski, *Kazania i homilye*, 297.
78. MS. 279 "O. Bernard, Reformata, Kazania misjonarskie, 1758" in Archiwum O O. Franciszkanów-Reformatów w Krakowie, folio 17: "Pro Dominica infra Octavam Epiphaniae."
79. Luke 2:41–7: "Now every year his parents went to Jerusalem for the festival of the Passover. And when he was twelve years old, they went up as usual for the festival. When the festival was ended and they started to return, the boy Jesus stayed behind in Jerusalem, but his parents did not know it. Assuming that he was in the group of travelers, they went a day's journey. Then they started to look for him among their relatives and friends. When they did not find him, they returned to Jerusalem to search for him. After three days they found him in the temple, sitting among the teachers, listening to them and asking them questions. And all who heard him were amazed at his understanding and his answers." In Luke 2:48, Mary does express her anxiety "Child, why have you treated us like this? Look, your father and I have been searching for you in great anxiety."
80. See for example "Akty o evreiakh," AIVAK, vol. XXVIII, 392–5. Zenon Guldon and Jacek Wijaczka, *Procesy o mordy rytualne w Polsce w XVI–XVIII wieku* (Kielce: DCF, 1995); Hanna Węgrzynek, *"Czarna legenda" Żydów: procesy o rzekome mordy rytualne w dawnej Polsce* (Warsaw: Bellona, 1995). Even though each separate case raises questions about the extent to which this myth was accepted and believed in Poland, many used this myth to attack Jews.
81. On this, see for example Israel Yuval, "Ha-nakam ve-ha-klalah, ha-dam ve ha-'alilah: Me-'alilot kedushim le-'alitot dam," *Zion* 48, no. 1 (1993); Yuval, "Jews and Christians in the Middle Ages: Shared Myths, Common Language," in *Demonizing the Other*, ed. Robert Wistrich (Amsterdam: Harwood Academic Publishers, 1999); Yuval, "'They Tell Lies; You Are the Man': Jewish Reactions to Ritual Murder Accusations," in *Religious Violence between Christians and Jews*, ed. Anna Sapir Abulafia (Hampshire: Palgrave, 2002).
82. Piotr Hyacynt Pruszcz, *Forteca duchowna Królestwa Polskiego z żywotów świętych, tak iuż kanonizowanych y beatyfikowanych, iako też świątobliwie żyiących patronów polskich, także z obrazów Chrystusa Pana y Matki iego przenayświętszey w oyczyźnie naszey cudami wielkimi błyszących* (Cracow: Drukarnia Stanislawa Lenczewskiego, 1662), 182–5.
83. AIVAK, vol. V, 230–1. In the Middle Ages, the popes also opposed such accusations. Pope Innocent IV in several letters condemned Christian accusations that Jews murder Christian children. See for instance his letter of May 28, 1247 to the archbishop of Vienne,

his letter of June 5, 1247 to the archbishops and bishops of Germany, and his constitution *Sicut Judaeis* to "all faithful Christians" of July 9, 1247, reissued by Pope Gregory X in 1272. Gregory also issued a bull *Lachrymabilem Judaeorum* on July 7, 1274 in which he again condemned such accusations against Jews. Sometimes local Church officials did not accept these documents as defense. Stefan Żuchowski, the instigator of blood libels in Sandomierz in Poland, claimed that they were forgeries because the popes knew and believed that Jews killed Christian children, which is clear from the beatification or canonization of victims. He rejected that the popes would issue such bulls of protection because they could know that according to "canon law, those defending Jews are to be anathemized." Stefan Żuchowski, *Process kryminalny*, 190–3.

84. Popławski, *Stół duchowny*, 394.

85. *Kazania w Jarosławiu i Lublinie*, 144. Its only known copy can be found at the Jagiellonian Library in Cracow, but it lacks the frontispiece; Biblioteka Uniwersytetu Jagiellońskiego, call number: 58822 II. Karol Estreicher estimated that they were published before 1714. Karol Estreicher, *Bibliografia polska* (Cracow, 1903), 19:199.

86. *Kazania w Jarosławiu i Lublinie*, 144.

87. *Kazania w Jarosławiu i Lublinie*, 144.

88. On exempla in Poland, see Teresa Szostek, *Exemplum w polskim średniowieczu* (Warsaw: Instytut Badań Literackich, 1997).

89. Augustyn Adam Wessel, *Morze miłosierdzia y dobroci Bożey pokazane grzesznikowiy grzesznicy w uwagach y reflexiach na całą mękę Jezusa* (Lwów, 1735), 23, 36, 76, 87, 242–3, 255, 854–5. See also Antoni Szermierski, SJ, *Strzał Jonaty (kazania niedzielne)* (Wilno, 1728), 225, 240; MS. 228/R "Kazania wielkopostne (2 poł. XVII wieku)" in Biblioteka Prowincji OO. Bernardynów in Cracow, 50 v.

90. MS. 443 Łac-Pol. (1708) "Kazania pasyjne autorstwa kapłana zakonu kaznodziejskiego," parts "Wiązanie Jezusa" in Archiwum OO. Dominikanów in Cracow, "Prowadzenie na trybunał Jezusa" (folios unnumbered).

91. Joan Young Gregg, *Devils, Women, and Jews: Reflections of the Other in Medieval Sermon Stories* (Albany: State University of New York Press, 1997). Another typology fairly common in homiletic works was that of the Antichrist as a Jew. See for example Poszakowski, *Antidotum contra 'Antidotum,'* 42, 46. Antoni Węgrzynowicz (d. 1721), a famous Franciscan preacher, presented Jews as "sons of the Devil," thereby disassociating them from Christians, since Jesus was after all the son of God. MS. 58 "Antoni Węgrzynowicz: Kazania w. XVII" [noted on the manuscript: "1690s and early eighteenth century, sermons delivered in Pińczów and Lwów"] in Archiwum OO. Franciszkanów-Reformatów in Cracow, 312. Karol Estreicher does not note these sermons in his *Bibliografia polska*, vol. 33, under Antoni Węgrzynowicz. On medieval use of this stereotype, see Jeremy Cohen, *The Friars and the Jews: A Study in the Development of Medieval Anti-Judaism* (Ithaca: Cornell University Press, 1982), 146–7, 179–80, 231–2. Kenneth R. Stow, *Alienated Minority: the Jews of Medieval Latin Europe* (Cambridge, MA: Harvard University Press, 1992), 234. Also the Gospels, especially the Gospel of John, provided a typology for this association, whereas the Revelation introduced the concept of the Synagogue of Satan: John 8:39–59, especially 44; Revelation 2:9–13, 3:9. In fact, an early eighteenth-century Jesuit preacher, Mikołaj Kieremowicz (1672–1739), directly cited John 8:44 in his sermon, emphasizing the fury of Jews against Jesus. See MS. 535 Pol. (1711–1725), Mikołaj Kieremowicz, SJ, "Kazania na niedziele całego roku" in Archiwum OO. Dominikanów in Cracow, 352.

92. MS. 295 Pol. 1756 "Kazania na święta roczne niedziele adventowe y pasyonalne zebrane z róznych poważnych autorów przez księdza Woyciecha Józefa Barańskiego na ten czas komendarza kościoła farnego Rybitwickiego, kazane y spisane anno dni 1756" in Archiwum OO. Dominikanów in Cracow, 202. This exemplum has its roots in Pope Gregory the Great's *Dialogues*; for another medieval retelling of this exemplum, see Gregg, *Devils, Women, and Jews*, 205–11.

93. MS. 295 Pol. (1756) "Kazania" in Archiwum O O. Dominikanów in Cracow, 202.

94. Kraiński, *Postylla kościoła powszechnego*, 527.

95. Kasper Balsam *Kazania na święta całego roku* (Poznań, 1762), 265–6.

96. Jan Poszakowski, *Antidotum contra 'Antidotum,'* 42.

97. See for instance the works of the sixteenth-century Protestant polemicist and former Catholic priest, Marcin Krowicki. Two of his brochures were republished in 1969. Marcin Krowicki, *Chrzescijańskie a żałobliwe napominanie*, ed. Zbigniew Ogonowski, Lech Szczucki, and Janusz Tazbir, Biblioteka Pisarzy Reformacyjnych 7 (Warsaw: Polska Akademia Nauk, 1969); Marcin Krowicki, *Obraz a kontrefet własny Antykrystów z Pisma Świętego dostatecznie wymalowany y wystrychniony przez sługę słowa Pana Krystusowego, Marcina Krowickiego, dla przestrogi ludziom krześcianskim*, ed. Zbigniew Ogonowski, Lech Szczucki, and Janusz Tazbir, Biblioteka Pisarzy Reformacyjnych 7 (Warsaw: Polska Akademia Nauk, 1969).

98. Poszakowski, *Antidotum contra 'Antidotum,'* 46–7. For an example of linking the pope with the Antichrist see Kraiński, *Postylla kościoła powszechnego*, 508v-16.

99. *Katechizm rzymski (1643)*, 65.

100. Popławski, *Stół duchowny*, 2157.

101. See chapter seven below, "Warding Off Heretical Depravity." Protestants were also often demonized and associated with the devil. See for example Jan Krosnowski, SJ, *Pochodnia słowa Bożego w kazaniach niedzielnych całego roku na oświecenie i zapalenie rozumów i afektów chrześcianskich przez Iana Krosnowskiego Societatis Jesu wystawiona* (Lublin, 1689), 83. See also MS. 3699 I in Biblioteka X. Czartoryskich in Cracow, 311 –19: "Sermo pro Dominica prima quadrogesimae: Gdy pościł czterdzieści dni," 313; MS 534 in Archiwum Prowincji Polskiej OO. Dominikanów in Cracow, fol. 686 "exemplum 6"; MS. 60 "Kazania niedzielne i swiąteczne, w. XVII." in Archiwum OO. Franciszkanów-Reformatów in Cracow, 52v: "In resurrectione Christi concio pomeridiana."

102. *Katechizm albo krótkie w iedno mieysce zebranie wiary y powinności krześcijańskiey*, part II: 8.

103. *Katechizm albo krótkie w iedno mieysce zebranie wiary y powinności krześcijańskiey*, part II: 115.

104. Kraiński, *Postylla kościoła powszechnego*, 466.

105. Kraiński, *Postylla kościoła powszechnego*, 522v-23.

106. Whereas this myth of ritual murder in its most gruesome form emerged in the West in the Middle Ages, by the end of the sixteenth century the trials of Jews for these "crimes" virtually ceased there. In Poland, by contrast, the trials began in the sixteenth century and persisted through the eighteenth century. See R. Po-chia Hsia, *The Myth of Ritual Murder: Jews and Magic in Reformation Germany* (New Haven, CT: Yale University Press, 1988); Guldon and Wijaczka, *Procesy o mordy rytualne w Polsce*; and Węgrzynek, *"Czarna legenda" żydów*.

107. The reasons for this disappearance in Poland were not the same as in Protestant countries, where they were related to rejection of the Catholic doctrine of transubstantiation.

208   NOTES TO PAGES 113–115

108. A prime example of that is Pruszcz, *Forteca duchowna Królestwa Polskiego.*
109. See for instance the discussion of the Eucharist and transubstantiation by the Jesuit polemicist Jan Poszakowski (1684–1757) in his work against Lutherans. Jan Poszakowski, *Nauka katholicka o przenayświetszey Eucharystiey: Z nauka Protestantów konfessyey auzburskiey w xięgach ich symbolicznych zawarta* (Wilno, 1737), vol. 2.
110. On the use of the term "arrendator [*arendarz*]" to denote Jews, see Rosman, *The Lords' Jews,* 110.
111. A village in southern Poland or in the eastern territories of the Polish-Lithuanian Commonwealth. Filip Sulimierski and Bronisław Chlebowski, *Słownik geograficzny królestwa polskiego i innych krajów słowianskich* (Warsaw, 1880), 10: 562–3.
112. Stefan Żuchowski, *Process kryminalny,* 51–3.
113. *Istoriko-iuridicheskie materialy,* ed. Sozonov, 32 vols. (Vitebsk, 1871–), 15: 326–33.
114. For instance a case of Jewish church robbers in Komaje in 1700. AIVAK, vol. XXIX, 241–53. "Komaje" Sulimierski and Chlebowski, *Słownik geograficzny Królestwa Polskiego,* 4: 297. For examples of Christians accused of Church robbery see *Istoriko-iuridicheskie materialy,* 8: 264–70. See also a 1719 case against two Jews of Brest who broke into the tomb of the wife of the Royal Treasurer of Lithuania, Mrs. Pociej, which was in the vaults of the Bernardine Church in Brest. AIVAK, vol. XX: 409–11.
115. MS. "Acta Maleficiorum," vol. 198 (microfilm 110213) in Wojewódzkie Archiwum Państwowe w Lublinie, folio 206.
116. In 1255, the Jews of Lincoln were accused of ritual murder. On the case of Hugh of Lincoln, see Trachtenberg, *The Devil and the Jews,* 131. See also Cecil Roth, *A History of the Jews in England* (Oxford: Clarendon Press, 1964), 57; and Joseph Jacobs, "Little St. Hugh of Lincoln: Researches in History, Archeology and Legend," in *The Blood Libel Legend,* ed. Alan Dundes (Madison: University of Wisconsin Press, 1991 <1896>).
117. Matthew's text is cited in Jacobs, "Little St. Hugh of Lincoln: Researches in History, Archeology and Legend," 44.
118. Radliński, *Prawda chrześciańska,* 531.
119. Żuchowski, *Process kryminalny,* 87–8. Alfonso de Espina, *Fortalitium Fidei* (Lugduni [Lyon]: Gulielmus Balsarin, 1487), "Liber Tertius," 121–121 v. See also Alfonso de Espina, *Fortalitium Fidei, in Universos Christiane Religionis Hostes Judeorum [et] Saracenorum No[n] Invalido Brevis Nec Minus Lucidi Compendii Vallo Rabiem Cohibens Fortitudinis Turris No[n] abs Re Appellatum Quinq[ue] Turriu[m] Inexpugnabilium Munimine Radians: Succincte Admodum [et] Adamussim Quinq[ue] Partium Librorum Farragine Absolutum* (Lugduni [Lyon]: Stephano Gueynard, 1525), 188bv-189av. This story by Espina is cited also in Ben Zion Netanyahu, *The Origins of the Inquisition in Fifteenth Century Spain* (New York: Random House, 1995), 826–7. I would like to thank Elisheva Carlebach of Queens College (CUNY) for pointing me to this source. The referred food is *haroset,* consumed during Passover Seder. For *haroset* as a symbol and resemblance of blood within Jewish tradition (Talmud Yerushalmi, Pesahim 10:3; *Minhagei Maharil*), see Yuval, "Jews and Christians," 102.
120. See for example *Liber Cronicarum* (Nuremberg: Anton Korberger, 1493), folio CCLIIII verso. See also R. Po-Chia Hsia, *Trent 1475: Stories of a Ritual Murder Trial* (New Haven: Yale University Press, 1992), 57ff.
121. Żuchowski, *Process kryminalny,* 99.
122. MS. 295 Pol. "Kazania na święta roczne niedziele adwentowe y pasyonalne zebrane z różnych poważnych autorów przez księdza Woyciecha Józefa Barańskiego na ten czas

komendarza kościoła farnego rybitwickiego y promotora szkaplerza świętego kazane i spisane anno dni 1756" in Archiwum OO. Dominikanów in Cracow, 328.

123. See Grayzel, *The Church and the Jews in the XIIIth Century*, 126–7. On practices and conflicts in Umbria, see Ariel Toaff, *Love, Work, and Death: Jewish Life in Medieval Umbria* (London: Littman Library of Jewish Civilization, 1996), 61–74.

124. See especially the end of *Or Zaru'a*, "Hilkot basae," no. 478, (Żytomir, 1882), 1:139. The English summary can be found in Irving A. Agus, *Urban Civilization in Pre-Crusade Europe: A Study of Organized Town-Life in Northwestern Europe During the Tenth and Eleventh Centuries Based on the Responsa Literature* (New York: Yeshiva University Press, 1965), 2:750. See also Rashi, *Shu"T*, end of no. 60, paraphrased in English in Agus, *Urban Civilization*, 2:759–60.

125. The text was reprinted in Adam Kaźmierczyk, ed., *Żydzi polscy 1648–1772: Źródła*, Studia Judaica Cracoviensia 6 (Cracow: Uniwersytet Jagielloński Katedra Judaistyki, 2001), 36–8.

126. See for instance Augustine, *City of God*, Book XVI, chapter 32: "Moreover, after the father [Abraham] had been prevented from striking his son, since it was not right that Isaac should be slain, who was the ram whose immolation completed the sacrifice by blood of symbolic significance? Bear in mind that when Abraham saw the ram it was caught by the horns in a thicket. Who then was symbolized by the ram but Jesus, crowned with Jewish thorns before he was offered in sacrifice?" See also the introduction *Katechizm rzymski (1762)*.

127. Żuchowski, *Process kryminalny*, 108.

128. Stefan Żuchowski, *Odgłos processów criminalnych* (n. p.: n. p., 1700), page unnumbered at the end of the rhymed description of the trial:

> Przewiodłem process, prawdę opisałem,
> dla którey niewiem czyć się spodobałem,
> w czym mi niewierzysz y sam nie masz wiary,
> bo przez żydowskie czytasz okulary.

129. Trachtenberg, *The Devil and the Jews*, 142, 147–51.

130. Żuchowski, *Process kryminalny*, 117.

131. Żuchowski, *Process kryminalny*, 117–18.

132. For the menstrual bleeding, see Żuchowski, *Process kryminalny*, 116. For the use of Christian blood in circumcision and postpartum, see 119.

133. Żuchowski, *Process kryminalny*, 112. According to laws of kashrut, eggs with a blood spot are not considered kosher.

134. Żuchowski, *Process kryminalny*, 113.

135. Żuchowski, *Process kryminalny*, 120; for the whole section see 112–34. See also Mojecki, *Żydowskie okrucieństwa*, 21–3. See also a copy of an alleged testimony of Jan Serafinowicz incriminating Jews for using Christian blood, Biblioteka Universitety Jagiellońskiego in Cracow, MS. 949 vol. 101 "Copia Recognitionis per Rabinum ad Fidem Orthodoxam Romanam Mirabiliter Vocatum, contra Judaeos Facta," (1713), folio 175.

136. Mojecki, *Żydowskie okrucieństwa*. Szymon Hubicki, *Żydowskie okrucieństwa*.

137. That is in fact how Żuchowski refers to Jews. See for instance his description of Jewish women, Żuchowski, *Process kryminalny*, 126–7, and infra, chapter seven.

138. For a discussion of an exceptional work from this period, see Judith Kalik, "Polish Attitudes Towards Jewish Spirituality in the Eighteenth Century," *Polin* 15 (2003): 80–1.

139. Radliński, *Prawda chrześcijańska*, 490. See for instance Espina, *Fortalitium Fidei*. Also Trachtenberg, *The Devil and the Jews*, 42.

140. These claims were not entirely unsubstantiated. Jewish prayers did indeed contain some anti-Christian statements. See infra for more detail.

141. Jan Poszakowski *Zohar co znaczy splendor* (Warsaw, 1749), 190–1. Also Przecław Mojecki mentions that Jews curse Christians in a prayer *velam schumadim*. Mojecki, *Żydowskie okrucieństwa*, 13.

142. On these prayers, see Carlebach, *Divided Souls*, 26–8. I would like to thank Edward Fram from Ben-Gurion University, Israel, and David Wachtel of the Jewish Theological Seminary for referring me to *Avinu Malkenu*, and an anonymous reader from Cambridge University Press for noting that the words *ve-la-meshumadim* are related to the daily 'Amidah prayer, where instead of *meshumadim* there is *malshinim*.

143. Hubicki, *Żydowskie okrucieństwa*, chapter 4, "Czemu Żydowie pastwią się nad Sakramentem?"

144. On the medieval period, see for example Yuval, "Ha-nakam ve-ha-klalah."

145. *Selihot*, (Cracow: Helicz, late 1530s). For example *selihot* nos.: 8, 11, 17, 25, 81, 114, 140. On this book, see Edward Fram and Magdalena Teter, "Matai hithil ha-defus ha-'ivri be-Polin? [When Did Hebrew Printing Begin in Poland?]," *Gal-Ed* 20 (2005).

146. The title page bears the date 1713 but the final page contains material from 1718.

147. Żuchowski, *Process kryminalny*, 199.

148. Pruszcz, *Forteca duchowna Królestwa Polskiego*, 182–5, chapter titled "O okrutnym dziateczek niewinnych od jaszczurowego Narodu na różnych mieyscach żydowskiego morderstwie."

149. Cecil Roth, "The Feast of Purim and the Origins of the Blood Accusation," in *The Blood Libel Legend*, ed. Alan Dundes (Madison: University of Wisconsin Press, 1991 <1933>), 269.

150. See Alan Dundes, "The Ritual Murder or Blood Libel Legend: A Study of Anti-Semitic Victimization through Projective Inversion," in *The Blood Libel Legend*, ed. Alan Dundes (Madison: University of Wisconsin Press, 1991 <1989>), 354.

151. Dundes, "The Ritual Murder or Blood Libel Legend," 336. See also Langmuir, *Toward a Definition of Antisemitism*, 269–71.

152. This may be a reference to BT 'Avodah Zarah 2b.

153. Alexander Dowgiało, *Kaidan żelazny doczesney niewoli przerobiony od Boga na łańcuch złoty wieczney wolności ofiarowany. Przy pogrzebowym akcie w Bogu zeszłego J. M. Pana Stephana Moroza sekretarza aktualnego J. K. M. woyta wileńskiego* (Wilno: Typis Franciscanis, n.d. 1706?), D3-E1 v.

154. Dowgiało, *Kaidan żelazny*, D3-E1 v. Since the Middle Ages, there was a debate among Jewish rabbis concerning the status of Christianity as idolatry. There were serious practical repercussions should Christianity continue to be classified as such. Maimonides, who lived in Muslim lands, could afford to classify it in such a way. European rabbis' opinions were not unanimous. Some reclassified Christianity and removed from it the stigma of idolatry; some continued to regard it as idolatry. This discussion continued also in early modern Poland; see for example the glosses of Moses Isserles on the *Shulhan 'Aruk*, especially Yoreh De'ah, Hilkot 'Avodat Kokhavim, or Benjamin Slonik, *Shu"T: Mas'at Binyamin* (Cracow, 1632), no. 86. See also Edward Fram, *Ideals Face Reality*, 28.

155. This rule is based on Mishnah Berakhot 4.5. I would like to thank Edward Fram for this reference. See also BT Berakhot 28b. Rashi in his gloss on this passage specified that one should turn one's face toward Jerusalem. Rashi on BT Berakhot 28b.

156. Bernard of Clairvaux, *The Letters of St. Bernard of Clairvaux*, trans. Bruno Scott James (Kalamazoo: Cistercian Publications, 1998 <1953>), letters 391 and 393. On Bernard of Clairvaux and Jews, see David Berger, "The Attitude of St. Bernard of Clairvaux toward Jews," *Proceedings of the American Academy of Jewish Research* 40 (1972); Robert Chazan, "Twelfth-Century Perceptions of the Jews: A Case Study of Bernard of Clairvaux and Peter the Venerable," in *From Witness to Witchcraft: Jews and Judaism in Medieval Christian Thought*, ed. Jeremy Cohen (Wiesbaden: Harrassowitz Verlag, 1996).

157. MS. 3698 I "Kazania misyjne" in Biblioteka X. Czartoryskich in Cracow, 276.

158. MS. 153 "Kazania na różne okoliczności (XVIII wiek)" in Archiwum OO. Dominikanów in Cracow, 271.

159. MS. 534 Pol. "Materiały kaznodziejskie" in Archiwum OO. Dominikanów in Cracow, 286.

160. MS. 3006 I "Nauka Religii w pytaniach i odpowiedziach" in Biblioteka X. Czartoryskich, 60–1. Elisheva Carlebach pointed out to me that a similar question concerning converts that aimed at preventing them from relapsing to Judaism was also popular in Lutheran sources in German lands.

161. Shlomo Simonsohn, *Apostolic See and the Jews* (Toronto, ON: Pontifical Institute of Mediaeval Studies, 1988), document no. 5.

162. In his 1146 letter to the archbishop of Mainz, St. Bernard of Clairvaux reiterated the point of value of Jewish converts. Protesting violence against Jews, he stated: "Is it not a far better triumph for the Church to convince and convert Jews than to put them all to sword?" See Robert Chazan, *Church, State, and Jew in the Middle Ages*, Library of Jewish Studies (New York: Behrman House, 1980), 105. *The Letters of St. Bernard of Clairvaux*, 466, letter 393. Pope Benedict XIV, *Epistola Encyclica ad Primatem, Archiepiscopos et Episcopos Regni Poloniae* (Rome: 1751).

163. See, for example, MS. 534 "Exempla" in Archiwum Prowincji Polskiej OO. Dominikanów in Cracow, especially the exempla of "The Fallen Agnieszka" and "Rachel the Jewish Girl Who Became a Nun." I have discussed some of these exempla in Magdalena Teter, "Jewish Conversions to Catholicism in the Polish-Lithuanian Commonwealth of the Seventeenth and Eighteenth Centuries," *Jewish History* 17, no. 3 (2003).

164. Teter, "Jewish Conversions to Catholicism."

CHAPTER 7: "WARDING OFF HERETICAL DEPRAVITY": "WHOM DOES THE CATHOLIC CHURCH REJECT, CONDEMN, AND CURSE?"

1. See, among many examples, Marceli Dziewulski, *Dobry znak w który słońce sprawiedliwości przy wcieleniu swoim na pociechę całemu światu weszło nayświętsza Marya Panna* (Cracow: Franciszek Cezary, 1721); Paweł Kaczyński, *Kazanie na niedziele całego roku* (Kalisz: Typis Societatis Jesu, 1675); Jan Morawski, *Duchowna theologia abo kościół ducha świętego* (Lwów: n.p., 1695); Jakub Radliński, *Oktawa Bożego Ciała na cały rok rozporzadzona albo sposób nawiedzania nayświętszego sakramentu, tak przez oktawę Bożego Ciała, iako i cały rok* (Lublin: Typis Societatis Jesu, 1731); Stanisław Szembek, *Zebranie kazań na Wielką Noc, Boże Narodzenie, uroczystości Nayświętszey Marii Panny y niektórych świętych* (Brunsbergae [Braniewo]: Typis Societatis Jesu, 1726); Andrzej Chryzostom Załuski, *Kazania które się na prędce zebrać mogły* (Warsaw: Typis Scholarum Piarum, 1996).

2. Wojciech Węgierski, *Antidotum abo lekarstwo duszne przeciwko apostasiey, y odstąpieniu od prawdy, na iedynym fundamencie Ss. proroków y apostołów ugruntowaney* (Baranów: Gerzy [sic] Twardomeski, 1646), 68.

3. Lidia Kwiatkowska-Frejlich, *Sztuka w służbie kontrreformacji* (Lublin: Wydawnictwo Uniwersytetu Marii Curie-Skłodowskiej, 1998).

4. Kwiatkowska-Frejlich, *Sztuka w służbie kontrreformacji*, 43; for the discussion of art in this church see 44–128.

5. Frederick Holweck, "Immaculate Conception," in *The Catholic Encyclopedia*, ed. Charles Herbermann et al. (New York: The Encyclopedia Press, 1910), 7:674–81.

6. See for instance Benedykt Herbest, *Chrzesciańska porządna odpowiedź na tę Confessią która pod tytułem braciey zakonu christusowego niedawno iest wydana, przydana też iest historya kacerstwa Hussowego, zbiiaią się pzy tym osszczepieństwa dzisieyszych inych nowowiernikó* (Cracow: Mattheusz Siebeneycher, 1567), pages unnumbered. Tomasz Młodzianowski, *Kazania i homilyce na święta uroczystsze także pogrzeby dla większey chwały Boga, króla królów: nayiaśnieyszey na zawsze królowy Polskiy Bogarodzicy Panny, czci* (Poznań: Collegium Societatis Iesu, 1681), 292–339.

7. See Catholic sermons for various festivals. Even in the eighteenth century, Catholic sermons paralleled the structure followed by Kraiński. See for example MS. 279 "O. Bernard, Reformata, Kazania misjonarskie, 1758" in Archiwum OO. Franciszkanów-Reformatów in Cracow.

8. Krzysztof Kraiński, *Postylla kościoła powszechnego* (n.p.: n.p., after 1611), 551 v-6. The controversy around the immaculate conception erupted in the twelfth century. One major medieval figure who disagreed with the concept of "immaculate conception" was Thomas Aquinas. Holweck, "Immaculate Conception."

9. Kraiński, *Postylla kościoła powszechnego*, 696v-7.

10. Kraiński, *Postylla kościoła powszechnego*, 687v.

11. Kraiński, *Postylla kościoła powszechnego*, 604, also 697–97v. This passage may have come from Hieronim Moszkowski: "they ascribe[d] to Mary the Virgin what one can only ascribe to God." Hieronim Moskorzowski, *Zawstydzenie księdza Skargi* (Raków: 1606), 42. Cited in Kwiatkowska-Frejlich, *Sztuka w służbie kontrreformacji*, 52. On the Assumption of Mary see also Kraiński, *Postylla kościoła powszechnego*, 686–91 v.

12. Kwiatkowska-Frejlich, *Sztuka w służbie kontrreformacji*, 85–102.

13. The famous late seventeenth-century preacher, Tomasz Młodzianowski, devoted a large section of his sermons on various Catholic holidays to these themes; see Młodzianowski, *Kazania i homilyie*, 292–339.

14. Alexander Dowgiało, *Purpura zbawienna to jest męka jezusowa na dni dziesięć rozdzielona* (Wilno: Drukarnia Akademicka, SJ, 1747 <1707>), 66–70.

15. Dowgiało, *Purpura zbawienna*, 162–3. Protestants criticized it. See for example Krzysztof Kraiński's critique of the Catholic teaching that "It is not enough that Christ suffered for you, you also have to suffer if you want to be saved" by the famous sixteenth-century Catholic preacher Jakub Wujek. Kraiński, *Postylla kościoła powszechnego*, 210v.

16. Kraiński, *Postylla kościoła powszechnego*, 603v-4. See also Kraiński, *Postylla kościoła powszechnego*, 614.

17. Krzysztof Kraiński, *Forma odprawowania nabożenstwa czyli mała agendka*, 2nd ed. (Łaszczów: n.p., 1602); Krzysztof Kraiński, *Porządek nabożeństwa kościoła powszechnego apostolskiego* (Toruń: n.p., 1599); Krzysztof Kraiński, *Porządek nabożeństwa kościoła powszechnego apostolskiego* (n.p.: n.p., 1614).

18. Kraiński, *Porządek nabożenstwa* (1599), "Przedmowa," page unnumbered, par. V.
19. Wieslaw Müller, ed., *Relacje o stanie diecezji krakowskiej, 1615–1765* (Lublin: Katolicki Uniwersytet Lubelski, 1978), 101.
20. For the synodal decree see *Synodus Dioecesana ab Illustrissimo et Reverendissimo D. Casimiro á Łubna Łubienski* (Cracow: Franciszek Cezary, 1711), 46. For the text of Łubieński's report, see Müller, ed., *Relacjie o stanie diecezji*, 111.
21. Konstantyn Felicjan Szaniawski, *Edictum contra Dissidentes* (Kielce: n.p., 1725).
22. See also *Agenda albo forma porządku usługi świętey w zborach ewangelickich koronnych y Wielkiego Xięstwa Litewskiego* (Gdańsk: Andrzey Hüncfeldt, 1637), 19–40. It is highly derivative of Kraiński, *Porządek nabożenstwa*.
23. See for instance Kraiński, *Postylla kościoła powszechnego*, 439, also 126v, 516, 523, 551–51 v.
24. Węgierski, *Antidotum abo lekarstwo duszne*, 53.
25. As Elukin pointed out in his article on Jacques Basnage, Protestants also drew parallels between Jews and Catholics. Basnage highlighted parallels between canon law and halakhah, and between both Catholic and Jewish reliance on tradition rather than directly on biblical texts. Jonathan Elukin, "Jacques Basnage and the History of the Jews: Anti-Catholic Polemic and Historical Allegory in the Republic of Letters," *Journal of the History of Ideas* 53, no. 4 (1992): 606, 619, 621–3. See also Kraiński's sporadic use of Jews in his attacks on Catholicism in Kraiński, *Postylla kościoła powszechnego*.
26. See for example Jakub Radliński, *Prawda chrześcijańska od nieprzyjaciela swego zeznana* (Lublin: Typis Societatis Jesu, 1733); Marek Korona, *Rozmowa theologa katolickiego z rabinem żydowskim przy arianinie nieprawym chrześcijaninie* (Lwów: Typis Societatis Jesu, 1645); Jan Poszakowski, *Kalendarz jezuicki większy na rok przestępny MDCXL* (Wilno: Typis Societatis Jesu, 1740). See also a manuscript by Antoni Węgrzynowicz, "Tractatus Compendiarius Constrovertisticus in Quo Praecipua Fundamenta Articulorum Verae Fidei Proponuntur et Satisfit Obiectionibus Sectariorum," in Archiwum OO. Franciszkanów-Reformatow in Cracow (1698). See also MS. 215 in Archiwum OO. Franciszkanów-Reformatów, 87v-98 on proofs concerning the Messiahship of Jesus. Contrast this with the thirteenth-century anti-Jewish polemic that used post-biblical Jewish literature and the above-discussed Protestant anti-Jewish polemic in the early modern period. Sometimes the use of rabbinic literature served as a polemic against "judaizers" to discredit contemporary Judaism and thereby discourage judaizing. Elukin, "Jacques Basnage and the History of the Jews," 620. Perhaps the most prolific anti-Protestant polemicist was the Jesuit, Jan Poszakowski. See Jan Poszakowski, *Antidotum contra "Antidotum abo zbawienna przestroga"* (Wilno: Typis Societatis Jesu, 1754); Jan Poszakowski, *Firmament prawdy trzema gwiazdami rozumy dyssydentów oświecaiący to iest nauka katolicka o wzywaniu świętych, o modlitwie za umarłych y o czyścu* (Wilno: Typis Societatis Jesu, 1737); Jan Poszakowski, *Historya luterska: O początkach y rozkrzewieniu się tey sekty, oraz niektóre rewolucye w sobie zawieraiąca* (Wilno: Typis Societatis Jesu, 1745); Jan Poszakowski, *Historyi kalwińskiey część trzecia w którey opisuie okazya y sposób rozmnożenia tey herezyi w Belgium albo w Niderlandach*, 3 vols., vol. 3 (Warsaw: Typis Societatis Jesu, 1749); Jan Poszakowski, *Konfessya albo wyznanie wiary jednostaynym konsensem y zgodą wszystkich zborów kalwińskich ogłoszone* (Warsaw: Typis Societatis Jesu, 1742); Jan Poszakowski, *Lilia między cierniami prawda między błędami to iest nauka katholicka o usprawiedliwieniu z nauka Protestantów konfessyey auzgburskiey w xięgach ich symbolicznych zawarty* (Wilno: Typis Societatis Jesu, 1738); Jan Poszakowski, *Nauka katholicka o przenayświętszey Eucharystiey z nauka Protestantów*

konfessyey auzburskiey w xięgach ich symbolicznych zawarta (Wilno: Typis Societatis Jesu, 1737); Jan Poszakowski, *Rozdział światła y ciemności to iest nauka katholicka o przenayświetszey Eucharystyey z nauka Protestantów konfessyey auzgburskiey zawarty* (Wilno: 1737).

27. On the use of Jews and works ostensibly concerning only Jews in anti-Catholic polemics see Elukin, "Jacques Basnage and the History of the Jews," 603–30.

28. See chapter 6 above, "'Countless Books against Common Faith': Catholic Insularity and Anti-Jewish Polemic." For examples of such literature see Piotr Hyacynt Pruszcz, *Forteca duchowna Królestwa Polskiego z żywotów świętych, tak iuż kanonizowanych y beatyfikowanych, iako też świątobliwie żyiących patronów polskich, także z obrazów Chrystusa Pana y Matki iego przenayświętszey w oyczyźnie naszey cudami wielkimi słyszących* (Cracow: Drukarnia Stanisława Lenczewskiego, 1662); Przecław Mojecki, *żydowskie okrucieństwa, mordy i zabobony* (Cracow: 1589); Stefan Żuchowski, *Process kryminalny o niewinne dziecię Jerzego Krasnowskiego* (Sandomierz: n.p., after 1718).

29. On medieval anti-Jewish polemics and changes that took place in the thirteenth century, see for instance Robert Chazan, *Barcelona and Beyond: The Disputation of 1263 and Its Aftermath* (Berkeley: University of California Press, 1992); Robert Chazan, *Daggers of Faith: Thirteenth-Century Christian Missionizing and Jewish Response* (Berkeley: University of California Press, 1989); Jeremy Cohen, *The Friars and the Jews: A Study in the Development of Medieval Anti-Judaism* (Ithaca: Cornell University Press, 1982); Gilbert Dahan, *The Christian Polemic against the Jews in the Middle Ages* (Notre Dame: University of Notre Dame Press, 1998).

30. MSS. S. Concilii Relationes Statu ad Limina: 217 Chelmensis, *relatio* from 1717 and 1740; 464 Luceoriensis *relatio* from 1749; and 667 Premisliensis *relatio* from 1666 in Archivio Segreto Vaticano.

31. See for instance the laws of 1658, 1662, 1668, 1685, 1699, 1726 and 1733. *Volumina Legum*, 4: 515, 829; 5: 264; 6: 581. On the subject of anti-Socinian laws, see Marek Wajsblum, *Ex Regestro Arianismi: szkice z dziejów upadku protestantyzmu w Małopolsce* (Cracow: Towarzystwo Badań Dziejów Reformacji w Polsce, 1937).

32. Załuski, *Kazania które się na prędce zebrać mogły*, O03 verso.

33. See Qur'an, Sura 5:15: "Oh, People of the Book, now there has come to you Our Messenger, making clear to you many things you have been concealing of the Book and effacing many things"; or 5:45: "The Jews who listen to falsehood, listen to other folk who have not come to thee, perverting words from their meaning," as translated by A. J. Arberry. Ahmed Ali's translation (Princeton, 1988) is much more explicit about this: "Jews . . . who distort the words of the Torah." The notion of Jews as witnesses follows. See also Sura 3:78. See also Camilla Adang, *Muslim Writers on Judaism and the Hebrew Bible: From Ibn Rabban to Ibn Hazm*, Islamic Philosophy, Theology, and Science 22 (New York: E. J. Brill, 1996).

34. On the distortion of the Bible by Jews within Christian anti-Jewish polemic, see for instance Cohen, *The Friars and the Jews*, especially 124, 148, 159. On the change of attitudes see also the collection of essays edited by Jeremy Cohen, *From Witness to Witchcraft: Jews and Judaism in Medieval Christian Thought* (Wiesbaden: Harrassowitz, 1996).

35. Cohen, *The Friars and the Jews*, 145–52.

36. For a medieval example see David Berger, *The Jewish-Christian Debate in the High Middle Ages: A Critical Edition of the Nizzahon Vetus* (Philadelphia: Jewish Publication

Society of America, 1979), for example chapter 145, Hebrew 94–5, English 150–1. For a sixteenth-century version of the same argument, see for example Solomon Ibn Verga, *Sefer Shevet Yehuda*, ed. Azriel Shohet and Yitzhak Baer (Jerusalem: Mosad Bialik, 1946), 87–8.

37. Cohen, *The Friars and the Jews*, 175.

38. On Christian Hebraism see Stephen G. Burnett, "Calvin's Jewish Interlocutor: Christian Hebraism and Anti-Jewish Polemics During the Reformation," *Bibliotheque d'humanisme et renaissance* 55 (1993); Stephen G. Burnett, "Distorted Mirrors: Antonius Margaritha, Johann Buxtorff and Christian Enthographies of the Jews," *Sixteenth Century Journal* 25 (1994); Stephen G. Burnett, *From Christian Hebraism to Jewish Studies: Johannes Buxtorf (1564–1629) and Hebrew Learning in the Seventeenth Century* (Leiden: Brill, 1996); Stephen G. Burnett, "Hebrew Censorship in Hanau: A Mirror of Jewish-Christian Coexistence in Seventeenth-Century Germany," in *The Expulsion of the Jews: 1492 and After*, ed. Raymond B. Waddington and Arthur Williamson (New York: Garland Press, 1994); Elisheva Carlebach, *Divided Souls: Converts from Judaism in Early Modern German Lands, 1500–1750* (New Haven, CT: Yale University Press, 2001); Aaron L. Katchen, *Christian Hebraists and Dutch Rabbis: Seventeenth Century Apologetics and the Study of Maimonides' Mishneh Torah*, Harvard Judaic Texts and Studies (Cambridge, MA: Harvard University Press, 1984); Frank Rosenthal, "The Study of the Hebrew Bible in Sixteenth Century Italy," *Studies in the Renaissance* 1 (1954).

39. English translation from *The Canons and Decrees of the Sacred and Oecumenical Council of Trent*, ed. and trans. J. Waterworth (London: Dolman, 1848), 19. For a discussion of the debate over the biblical canon during the Council of Trent, see Hubert Jedin, *A History of the Council of Trent*, 2 vols. (London, New York: T. Nelson, 1961), 2:52–98.

40. Zenon Chodyński and Edward Likowski, eds., *Decretales Summorum Pontificum pro Regno Poloniae et Constitutiones Synodorum Provincialium et Dioecesanarum Regni Eiusdem*, 3 vols. (Poznań: Typis Augustini Schmaedicke, 1869), 1:13.

41. Kraiński, *Postylla kościoła powszechnego*, 350v. This was somewhat disingenuous because even Martin Luther did not approve of individual reading of the Bible without the guidance of the clergy. And individual Bible reading only became popular in the eighteenth century. Richard Gawthrop and Gerald Strauss, "Protestantism and Literacy in Early Modern Germany," *Past and Present* 104 (1984).

42. Woyciech Tylkowski, *Problemata święte abo pytania około wyrozumienia świętey ewangeliey od kościoła powszechnego tak na niedziele iako y na święta rozłożoney* (Poznań: Typis Societatis Jesu, 1688), G3 verso.

43. For Korona's works see Karol Estreicher and Stanislaw Estreicher, *Bibliografia polska. stólecie XV-XVIII*, 34 vols. (Kraków: Uniwersytet Jagielloński, 1878–1951), pt. 1, vol. 9: 93–5.

44. Korona, *Rozmowa theologa katholickiego z rabinem żydowskim*, 3–4.

45. Korona, *Rozmowa theologa katholickiego z rabinem żydowskim*, 3.

46. Korona, *Rozmowa theologa katholickiego z rabinem żydowskim*, B3. It is unclear if he knew Hebrew himself. Some Polish writers used Latin texts that explained the Hebrew meaning of the text. See for instance sermons by Tomasz Młodzianowski. He sometimes discussed the Hebrew words or translations, but gave Latin meanings. It is very difficult to identify works that these writers may have used; they often do not cite their sources, and when they do they give very fragmentary references. For example, Młodzianowski provided a marginal reference to "Lectio Hebr." or "Interpretatio Hebraica." This could

possibly be *Hebraicorum Chaldaeorum Graecorum Nominum Interpretatio* (Lyon: Apud Sebastianum Honoratum, 1562) now in the collection of the Jagiellonian University. See for example Młodzianowski, *Kazania i Homilyie*, 203, 205, 293, 315, 329.

47. Alodia Kawecka-Gryczowa, ed., *Bogowie fałszywi: nieznany pamflet antykatolicki z XVI wieku* (Warsaw: Biblioteka Narodowa, 1983), 57.

48. A reference to currency.

49. Kawecka-Gryczowa, ed., *Bogowie fałszywi*, 59.

50. In the Gospel of John 1:3–4 the verse is "omnia per ipsum facta sunt et sine ipso factum est nihil quod factum est (4) in ipso vita erat et vita erat lux hominum." (RSV: all things were made through him, and without him was not anything made that was made. In him was life, and the life was the light of men.)

51. Korona, *Rozmowa theologa katholickiego z rabinem żydowskim*, 27.

52. Korona, *Rozmowa theologa katholickiego z rabinem żydowskim*, 27.

53. Korona, *Rozmowa theologa katholickiego z rabinem żydowskim*, 27.

54. Berger, *Nizzaḥon Vetus*, English 41, Hebrew 3. See also 233, note on verses 10–11.

55. Korona, *Rozmowa theologa katholickiego z rabinem żydowskim*, 40, 46, 49ff. "Ironically" because the Bible was not widely known to Catholics because the Council of Trent did not allow individual Bible study unmitigated by a Catholic priest.

56. Korona, *Rozmowa theologa katholickiego z rabinem żydowskim*, 52.

57. Korona, *Rozmowa theologa katholickiego z rabinem żydowskim*, 148.

58. See for instance Jakob Wujek, *Postilla katholicka mneysza, to iest krótkie kazania abo wykłady świętych ewangeliey, na każdą niedzielę y na każde święto, przez cały rok według nauki prawdziwej kościoła chrześcijańskiego powszechnego* (Cracow: 1870–1 <1617>).

59. MS. 281, Roch Trucki "Messis de Semine Verbi Dei in Agro Ecclesiae in Amnipulos Collecta, seu Conciones in Dominicae et Festa Conscripta 1741" in Archiwum OO. Franciszkanów-Reformatów in Cracow, 430.

60. MS. 534 "Exempla" in Archiwum OO. Dominikanów in Cracow, Exemplum 9. See also Magdalena Teter, "Jewish Conversions to Catholicism in the Polish-Lithuanian Commonwealth of the Seventeenth and Eighteenth Centuries," *Jewish History* 17, no. 3 (2003): 268–9.

61. MS. 534 "Exempla" in Archiwum OO. Dominikanów in Cracow, Exemplum 10.

62. Stanisław Bielicki, SJ, *Święta kaznodziejskie to iest kazania doroczne na uroczystości świętych bożych* (Kalisz: Typis Societatis Jesu, 1717), 164. See also Teter, "Jewish Conversions to Catholicism in the Polish-Lithuanian Commonwealth," 268.

63. Kazimierz Lubieński and Theodor Potocki.

64. See for instance Wujek, *Postylla katholicka mnieysza*, 199: "At the end of this century, in the new world, in America, Peru, Mexico, Japan and Brazil, the Catholics converted numerous pagan people and they convert more every day, including many Jews and Turks. Where did the Lutherans convert anyone? Even though they compare themselves to Apostles and Evangelists they have many Jews and Turks as neighbors in Germany and Poland." For instances of Mary's role in converting Jews, see an exemplum of the fallen Agnieszka below and an exemplum of a Jewish girl, Rachel, who, "inspired by Mary," converted to Catholicism. MS. 534 in Archiwum OO. Dominikanów in Cracow, exemplum 10.

65. Kraiński, *Porządek nabożeństwa*, 107.

66. Poland was not unique in that some French anti-Protestant pamphlets used this analogy as well. In France it was purely rhetorical, for there were officially no Jews there since the last expulsion in 1397. See for instance a reference to a 1586 pamphlet by Louis Dorleans,

NOTE TO PAGE 131

Advertissement des catholiques anglois aux francois catholiques, in Arthur Tilley, "Some Pamphlets of the French Wars of Religion," *The English Historical Review* 14, no. 55 (1899): 459.

67. Woyciech Ochabowicz, *Tarcza wiary świętey rzymskiey katolickiey przeciwko różnych ich nieprzyjaciół impetom wystawiona albo theologia polska kontrowersye y konkluzye katolickie dla prawowiernych katolików, polskim stylem y alphabetycznym porządkiem w sobie zamykaiąca* (Lublin: Typis Societatis Jesu, 1736), 309. See also Wujek, *Postylla katholicka mnieysza*, 195.

68. Providing a list of Catholic saints, Dziewulski wrote: "In 1475, the Jews crucified the little Simon, a little boy who was only twenty nine months old, in Trent." Marceli Dziewulski, *Prezerwatywa powietrza morowego reskrypcyi kaznodzieyskiey* (Cracow: Jakob Matuszkiewicz, 1720), A1v.

69. Dziewulski, *Prezerwatywa powietrza morowego*, B1v.

70. See for instance the exemplum discussed in chapter 3 above and used by Mikołaj Popławski to discourage the sale of houses to Jews. Mikołaj Popławski, *Stół duchowny* (Warsaw, 1704), 2157.

71. An eighteenth-century manuscript, MS. 263 "Kazania: 55 Kazań na różne okoliczności" in Archiwum OO. Franciszkanów-Reformatów in Cracow, "Kazanie 33 na Wielki Czwartek." For an example of an iconoclastic poem see Wacław Potocki, "Do Zelanta sine Scientia," in Jan Dürr-Durski, ed., *Arianie polscy w świetle własnej poezji: zarys ideologii i wybór wierszy* (Warsaw: Państwowe Zakłady Wydawnictw Szkolnych, 1948), 76.

72. For the use of the term "Christian" in reference to Catholicism see for instance numerous synodal decrees; see also Tomasz Młodzianowski, *Kazania i homilie na święta uroczyste także pogrzeby* (Poznań: Typis Societatis Jesu, 1681), 398; Woyciech Wiiuk Kojałowicz, *O rzeczach do wiary należących rozmowy theologa z różnemi wiary prawdziwej przeci-wnikami* (Cracow: Drukarnia Stanisława Piotrowczyka, 1671), for example, his discus-sion about Calvin, 66. Woyciech Ochabowicz also appears to use the term "Christian" in reference to Catholics; however, he does acknowledge that even heretics believe that the promised Messiah was Jesus Christ. Woyciech Ochabowicz, *Tarcza wiary świętey rzymskiey katolickiey przeciwko różnych iey nieprzyiaciół impetom wystawiona* (Lublin: Collegium Societatis Jesu, 1736), 124. Preacher Adam Abramowicz asked a rhetorical question whether or not "these Christian religions, for instance Luther's, Calvin's, Arian or Catholic are all one faith." To which he responds that the Catholic Church rejects the non-Catholic religions and condemns them for fallacy. Adam Abramowicz, *Kazania niedzielne* (Wilno: Typis Societatis Jesu, 1753), 475. Jan Felix Szaniawski, bishop of Chełm, in his votive sermon before the election of the new king in Poland in 1733 used the term *dualitas* to indicate the reasons for the country's ruin. In this term he casts Catholics on one side and "dissidents, Schismatics and others" on the other side, perhaps intending to classify them with non-Christians, Jews and Muslims, and perhaps anti-Trinitarians.

73. In the thirteenth century, after the bull by Pope Urban IV of 1269, which instituted the festival *Corpus Christi*, Dominicans were behind founding the first confraternities devoted to the worship of the Eucharist. A similar process took place in the sixteenth century with the rise of similar confraternities that were aimed at strengthening the cult of the "Holy Sacrament." Louis Châtellier, "Rinnovamento della pastorale e società dopo il concilio Di Trento," in *Il concilio di Trento e il moderno*, ed. Paolo Prodi and Wolfgang Reinhard (Bologna: Il Mulino, 1996), 142.

74. See, for instance, Hanna Węgrzynek, *"Czarna legenda" Żydów: procesy o rzekome mordy rytualne w dawnej Polsce* (Warszawa: "Bellona" Wydawnictwo Fundacji Historia pro Futuro, 1995). See also Janusz Tazbir, *A State without Stakes: Polish Religious Toleration in the Sixteenth and Seventeenth Centuries*, trans. A. T. Jordan (Warsaw: Państwowy Instytut Wydawniczy, 1973), 75–6. For an example on the use of the host desecration stories in the context of Protestantism, see Benedict Herbest, *Nauka prawego chrześcijanina* (Cracow: Mateusz Siebeneycher, 1566), paragraph 253. See also Wujek, *Postylla katholicka mnieysza*, 545. For a lengthy exposition of Catholic teachings on the Eucharist in a polemic against Protestant beliefs see Wujek, *Postylla katholicka mnieysza*, 287, 292–306. For the earlier tales of desecration of the host, see Miri Rubin, *Gentile Tales: The Narrative Assault on Late Medieval Jews* (New Haven, CT: Yale University Press, 1999).

75. Kawecka-Gryczowa, ed., *Bogowie fałszywi*, 52. For other examples, see Węgierski, *Antidotum abo lekarstwo duszne*, 98–9.

76. Kawecka-Gryczowa, ed., *Bogowie fałszywi*, 51.

77. Herbest, *Nauka Prawego chrześcijanina*, paragraphs 253–4.

78. Stefan Żuchowski in his *Process kryminalny* claimed that a blind Jewish woman was healed after she had used the blood from the profaned host. Żuchowski, *Process kryminalny*, 47.

79. Popławski, *Stół duchowny*, 394, 538, 587, 677, 1114–15, 1289. See also chapter 2 supra.

80. Popławski, *Stół duchowny*, 1736. Interestingly, the Protestants claimed that it was the Catholics who were idolaters for worshiping the Eucharist as Christ himself. See for example Węgierski, *Antidotum abo lekarstwo duszne*, 91–3.

81. In his homilies, Wujek urged the following of Church teachings on that, juxtaposing them to Protestant attitudes. Wujek, *Postylla katholicka mnieysza*, 287. Fortunat Łosiewski shuddered that the Eucharist was sold to Jews, heretics, and witches. Fortunat Łosiewski, *Powtórna męka Chrystusa Jezusa w nayświętszym Sakramencie* (Warsaw: Drukarnia J. K. M. OO. Scholarum Piarum, 1729), 13–16.

82. MS. 303/R "Kazania świąteczne (1706–1730)" in Archiwum i Biblioteka OO. Bernardynów in Cracow, 4.

83. MS. 534 in Archiwum OO. Dominikanów in Cracow, folio 686, exemplum 6.

84. On viewing a church as *Domus Dei*, see Elżbieta Gieysztor-Miłobędzka, "Church Interior in Later Counter-Reformation Period: Presuppositions and Practice," in *Late Baroque Art in the Eighteenth Century in Poland, Bohemia, Slovakia and Hungary*, ed. Lech Kalinowski (Cracow: MN, 1990), 14–16.

85. See for example a statement made in a sermon by an early eighteenth-century preacher that "Jewish malice is worse than that of the devil" in MS. 443 Łac-Pol. (1708) "Kazania pasyjne autorstwa kapłana zakonu kaznodziejskiego" in Archiwum OO. Dominikanów in Cracow, sermon VII "Złość żydowska gorsza aniżeli dyabelska." See also Joan Young Gregg, *Devils, Women, and Jews*.

86. MS. 3699 I in Biblioteka X. Czartoryskich in Cracow, "Sermo pro Dominica Prima Quadrogesimae: Gdy pościł czterdzieści dni," 313. For the passage in Krosnowski, see Jan Krosnowski, *Pochodnia słowa bożego w kazaniach niedzielnych całego roku na oświecenie i zapalenie rozumow i afektów chrześcijańskich* (Lublin: Typis Societatis Jesu, 1689), 83: "Any fast, [Luther] says, is so ugly and detestable in the eyes of God that guzzling [*obżarstwo*], drunkenness, gluttony [*żarłoctwo*] are more pleasing to God than observing fasts. This is the reasoning concerning prescribed Fasts of this heresiarch who used to gorge worse than a beast every day: I believe that the Devil himself would be ashamed to

say what the blasphemer said with his ignominious tongue and wrote with his ignominious pen. Another blasphemer similar to Luther, no less objecting to fasting is
Calvin."

87. Matthew 4:1 –11; Mark 1 :12–13; Luke 4:1 –13. Also Benedict Herbest bluntly stated that
all heretics [*kacerze*] give themselves to Satan. Herbest, *Nauka prawego chrześcijanina*,
Aiiijv and M-Mv. See also the reference to the "devil's teachings" in Wujek,
Postylla katholicka mnieysza, 65, 100. See also Jacob Marchand, *Katechizm abo nauka
chrześcijańska. Nie tylko świeckim, ale i pannom zakonnym, także i plebanom wielce
użyteczny* (Cracow: Łukasz Kupisz <1682, SJ>, 1648), 123.

88. Kraiński, *Postylla kościoła powszechnego*, 110.

89. Kraiński, *Postylla kościoła powszechnego*, 110.

90. Kraiński, *Postylla kościoła powszechnego*, 110v.

91. Maria Sipayłło, ed., *Acta Synodalia Ecclesiarum Poloniae Reformatarum, 1571–1632*,
vol. 3, *Akta synodów różnowierczych w Polsce* (Warsaw: Wydawnictwa Uniwersytetu
Warszawskiego, 1983), 367.

92. Sipayłło, ed., *Acta Synodalia Ecclesiarum Poloniae Reformatarum, 1571–1632*, 3:367.

93. "Dyskursik o Sinodzie," in *Dwa nieznane rękopisy z dziejów polskiej Reformacji*, ed.
Aleksander Woyde (Warsaw: Universitas Liberae Poloniae, Wolna Wszechnica Polska,
1922), 19, n. 1.

94. See for instance Daniel Boyarin, *Carnal Israel: Reading Sex in Talmudic Culture*
(Berkeley: University of California Press, 1993). In the introduction Boyarin deals with
the early Christian representations of Jews as carnal. Jews also perceived non-Jews as
carnal. The representation of non-Jews as oversexualized is common in rabbinic literature. The laws in the Mishnah already signal this image; see for example Mishnah,
'Avodah Zarah. On parallels of imagery of gentiles in Jewish thought see also a brief discussion in Joseph M. Davis, *Yom-Tov Lipmann Heller: Portrait of a Seventeenth-Century
Rabbi* (Portland: Littman Library of Jewish Civilization, 2004), 92–5.

95. See the juxtaposition of physical versus spiritual circumcision in Paul's Epistle to
Romans 2:28–9 (RSV): "For he is not a real Jew who is one outwardly, nor is true
circumcision something external and physical. He is a Jew who is one inwardly, and
real circumcision is a matter of the heart, spiritual and not literal. His praise is not from
men but from God." See also Ephesians 2:11 and II Corinthians 3, 5. On the impossibility
of salvation through the flesh, see I Corinthians 15:50. An eighteenth-century preacher,
Abramowicz, also included Muslims in the category of lewd carnality. Muslims, like
Jews, practice circumcision. Abramowicz, *Kazania niedzielne* (Wilno, 1753), 463–5.

96. Indeed, the seven deadly sins have a mirroring seven heavenly virtues. The virtue
corresponding to gluttony is temperance, and the virtue corresponding to lust, another
deadly carnal sin, is self-control. The other deadly sins and their corresponding virtues
are pride/humility, avarice or greed/generosity, envy/love, anger/kindness, sloth/zeal.

97. Kraiński, *Postylla kościoła powszechnego*, 126v.

98. See for instance Alexander Lorencowicz, *Kazania na niedziele całego roku. Część pierwsza*
(Kalisz: Kolegium Soc. Jesu, 1671), 111. On the opposite side, the Protestant Jacques
Basnage, for instance, drew on the observance of fasts by Jews and used it in his anti-
Catholic polemic. See Elukin, "Jacques Basnage and the History of the Jews," 626.

99. See supra, chapter four.

100. In France, where there were technically no Jews since the last expulsion in 1394, Jews
were not central in Catholic polemic against Protestants. The image of the Protestants,

however, resembles that presented by Polish clergy but emphasizes sexuality, violence, and general carnality even more. See G. Wylie Sypher, "'Faisant Ce Qu'il a Plaisir': The Image of Protestantism in French Catholic Polemic on the Eve of the Religious Wars," *Sixteenth Century Journal* 11, no. 2 (1980): especially 59–60, 69–72.

101. Lorencowicz, *Kazania na niedziele całego roku*, 111. For an excellent study of religious issues related to fasting, albeit in the Middle Ages, see Caroline Bynum, *Holy Fast and Holy Feast* (Berkeley: University of California Press, 1987). See also Wujek, *Postylla katholicka mnieysza*, 65.

102. *Kazania w Jarosławiu* (Lublin, 1740), 196–8.

103. Jacob Marchand, *Katechizm abo nauka chrześcijanska* (Cracow: 1682 <1648>), 10–11: "Question: What are the sources of heresy? Answer: Haughtiness and carnality in particular."

104. Samuel Bogumił Linde, *Słownik języka polskiego*, 3rd ed., 6 vols. (Warszawa: Państwowy Instytut Wydawniczy, 1951), 1:296.

105. MS. 3699 I in Biblioteka X. Czartoryskich in Cracow, "Sermo pro dominica prima quadrogesimae: Gdy pościł czterdzieści dni," 313. See also Krosnowski, *Pochodnia słowa bożego*, 83.

106. Krosnowski, *Pochodnia słowa bożego*, 181–90.

107. MS. 291 "Kazania calego roku (1742–1747)" in Archiwum OO. Dominikanów in Cracow, 98.

108. Wujek, *Postylla katholicka mnieysza*, 168. Krzysztof Kraiński, a contemporary Protestant preacher familiar with Wujek's *Postylla*, compared the Roman Catholic Church to a body infected with leprosy, drawing on the parallels from the Scripture and the significance of leprosy there. Kraiński, *Postylla kościoła powszechnego*, 418v ff.

109. Marchand, *Katechizm abo nauka chrześcijanska*, 10–11. The idea of heretics as an infectious disease is found also in MS. 298/R "Kazania misjonarskie o rzeczach ostatecznych y o grzechach" in Biblioteka i Archiwum OO. Bernardynów in Cracow, 293–4. These sermons were delivered by Bernardine preachers in the town of Zasław in the first half of the eighteenth century.

110. *Constitutiones Synodales Editae et Promulgatae ab Illustrissimo Etc. Andrea Stanislao Kostka Zaluski Episcopo Culmensi et Pomesaniensi* (Brunsberg [Braniewo]: Typis Societatis Jesu, 1746), 30.

111. *Constitutiones Synodi Dioecesana Vilnensis ab Illustrissimo, Excellentissimo ac Reverendissimo Domino D. Michaele Joanne Zienkowicz Dei et Apostolicae Sedis Gratia Episcopo Vilnensi* (Wilno: Typis Societatis Jesu, 1744).

112. MS. 404 "Kazania świąteczne" in Archiwum OO. Dominikanów in Cracow, 564, "a sermon delivered in 1718 in *conventu P. Fransicanorum Cracoviae.*" On the next page the preacher refers to "our Carmelite Order."

113. MS. 404 "Kazania świąteczne" in Archiwum OO. Dominikanów in Cracow, 564.

114. Jan Lewek, *List pewnego statysty, zawierający w sobie niektóre przyczyny, dla których z teraźniejszych Żydow ledwie który do wiary świętey katolickiey nawracan bywa* (n.p.: n.p., 1728), A3 (unnumbered). Jakub Radliński in his *Prawda chrześciańska*, 26, while discussing Jewish exile, wrote: "Here in Poland, Jews are allowed everything; they receive far more respect and rights to administer estates from some lords than Christians themselves." See also Żuchowski, *Process kryminalny*, 119–20; and Przecław Mojecki *Żydowskie okrucieństwa, mordy i zabobony* (Cracow, 1589), 21v. Cited also in Kazimierz Bartoszewski, *Antysemityzm w literaturze polskiej XV-XVII w.* (Warsaw: Geberthner &

Wolff, 1914), 47. Eugeni od Św. Mateusza, *Protekcya od tronu łaski Anny S. dysgracyom nieba na ziemi awizowana* (Cracow: Drukarnia Kollegium Większego, 1736), E.

115. Lorencowicz, *Kazania na niedziele całego roku*, 1:5.

116. For a version of this ideal see Dowgiało, *Purpura zbawienna*, 45.

117. Krzysztof Jan Szembek, *Krótkie zebranie nauki chrześciańskiey* (Cracow: Drukarnia Franciszka Cezarego, 1719), 54.

118. This doctrine was affirmed in Pope Boniface VIII's bull *Unam Sanctam* of 1302. Ernst Hartwig Kantorowicz, *The King's Two Bodies: A Study in Mediaeval Political Theology* (Princeton, NJ: Princeton University Press, 1957; reprint, 1981), 194.

119. Julian Bukowski, *Dzieje Reformacyi w Polsce: od jej wejścia do Polski aż do jej upadku* (Cracow: Nakładem Autora, 1883), 1:165. We know of these cases only from the late nineteenth-century history of the Reformation in Poland by a Polish Catholic priest, Julian Bukowski, who had access to Church archives and the trial records at the Episcopal court, including the now apparently lost volume II of Acta Episcopalia.

120. Bukowski, *Dzieje Reformacyi w Polsce*, 166. See also MS. 5358, vol. II, Biblioteka Uniwersytetu Jagiellońskiego in Cracow, folio 14, for a case of Salomon Imbris "suspected of Lutheran heresy."

121. These and other cases are mentioned in the excerpts from the now-lost volume II of Acta Episcopalia taken by Żegota Pauli. MS. 5357 vol. 9, fol. 70 in Biblioteka Uniwersytetu Jagiellońskiego in Cracow.

122. Bolesław Ulanowski, *Materyały do historii ustawodawstwa synodalnego w Polsce w wieku XVI*, Archiwum Komisyi Prawniczey (Collectanea Ex Archivo Collegii Iuridici) 1 (Cracow: Akademia Umiejętności, 1895), 378, par. 1.

123. *Katechizm rzymski to iest nauka chrześciańska* (Cracow: Drukarnia Franciszka Cezarego, 1643), 58.

124. Szaniawski, *Edictum contra Dissidentes*.

125. For sources see Müller, ed., *Relacje o stanie diecezji*, 101, 111; *Synodus Dioecesana ab Illustrissimo et reverendissimo D. Casimiro á Lubna Łubienski 1711*, 46. Szaniawski, *Edictum contra Dissidentes*. Wojciech Kreisgseisen briefly discussed this in Wojciech Kriegseisen, *Ewangelicy polscy i litewscy w epoce saskiej* (Warsaw: Semper, 1996), 40–1.

126. A good example of the Church's awareness of the ineffectiveness of its policies is a 1742 complaint by a nuncio that Jews, despite prohibitions against settling in Livonia, nonetheless open schools and run businesses. MS. 393 "Archivio Nunziatura di Polonia" in *Archivio Segreto Vaticano*, 447–447v, no. 6. Wojciech Kriegseisen noted that on occasion Protestants turned to the Catholic Church to validate their marriages. Kriegseisen, *Ewangelicy polscy*, 40.

127. *Wszem wobec y każdemu z osobna, osobliwie niewiernym rabinom kahalnym, y całemu pospólstwu żydowstwa w diecezyi naszey łuckiey y brzeskiey zostaiącym* (Łuck, 1741). Also published in *Literae Pastorales ad Universum Clerum, et Populum Utriusque* (n. p.: n. p., 1742), E3-Fv. More recently in Goldberg, *Ha-mumarim be-mamlekhet Polin-Lita*, 76–81; and Adam Kaźmierczyk, *Żydzi polscy 1648–1772*, 53–7.

128. The ruling by Theodosius II in 438 limiting the number of synagogues to one synagogue per town can be found in Codex Theodosianus 16.8.25. By the thirteenth century it found its way into canon law. In 1221, Pope Honorius III recommended that newly built synagogues be destroyed. Similar opinion was voiced in Paul IV's *Cum Nimis Absurdum* in 1555 (paragraph 2). See also Solomon Grayzel, *The Church and the Jews in the XIIIth Century* (Philadelphia: The Dropsie College, 1933), 106–7. For the text of

Cum Nimis Absurdum see Kenneth R. Stow, *Catholic Thought and Papal Jewry Policy,*
1555–1593 (New York: Jewish Theological Seminary of America, 1977), 291–8. See also
Walter Pakter, *Medieval Canon Law and the Jews* (Ebelsbach: Verlag Rolf Gremer, 1988),
41 n. 8.

129. *Constitutiones Synodi Archidioecesis Gnesnensis sub D. Stanislao in Słupow Szembek*
(Warsaw: Typis Scholarum Piarum, 1720), chapter titled "De Haeresi."

130. Jan Alexander Lipski, *Epistola Pastoralis ad Clerum et Populum Dioecesis Cracoviensis*
(1737), I2. *Constitutiones et Decreta in Dioecesana Synodo Plocensi* (Płock: 1643); *Consti-*
tutiones Synodales Luceoriensis et Brestensis (Warsaw: Typis Scholarum Piarum, 1726);
Constitutiones Synodi Archidioecesis Gnesnensis sub D. Stanislao in Slupow Szembek, Syn-
odus Diaecesana Chelmensis ab Illustrissimo et Reverendissimo Domino D. Christophoro
Ioanne in Slupow Szembek (Zamość: 1717).

131. Judith Kalik illustrated the mechanisms at work in granting permits to Jews for
their cemeteries and synagogues in Kalik, "Ha-knesiyyah ha-katolit ve-ha-yehudim
be-mamlekhet Polin-Lita ba-meot ha-17–18," (Ph.D. dissertation, Hebrew University,
1998), 144–7. For a discussion of the Church's efforts to eradicate Protestant worship
and churches, see Kriegseisen, *Ewangelicy polscy,* 194–8.

132. George Huntston Williams, *The Polish Brethren: Documentation of the History and*
Thought of Unitarianism in the Polish-Lithuanian Commonwealth and in the Diaspora,
1601–1685 (Missoula, MT: Scholars Press for Harvard Theological Review, 1980), 2:367,
373, and images A on 368 and E on 370.

133. Wacław Hieronim Sierakowski (1700–80) became the archbishop of Lwów in 1759. See
Polski słownik biograficzny (Warsaw: Polska Akademia Nauk, 1996), vol. 37/2: 306–13.

134. Ber of Bolechow, *The Memoirs of Ber of Bolechow (1723–1805)*, trans. Mark Wischnitzer
(London: Oxford University Press, 1922), 113.

135. *Constitutiones et Decreta Synodi Dioecesana Plocensi sub Illustrissimo Excellentissimo*
Reverendissimo Domino D. Anrea Stanislao Kostka in Zaluskie Zaluski (Warsaw: Typis
Societatis Jesu, 1735), 6. For examples of laws concerning Jews, see Jan Skarbek,
"Edictum contra Judaeos" (1717) in "Edicta et mandata Dioecesis Cracoviensis 1737–
1772" in AKM in Cracow; Józef Eustachy Szembek, *List pasterski* (Zamość: Drukarnia
B. Jana Kantego, 1752). For an example concerning Jews from polemical literature and
sermons see infra on Łosiewski, *Powtórna męka Chrystusa Jezusa,* 13–16.

136. Skarbek, "Edictum contra Judaeos." Szembek, *List pasterski,* C2v. *Constitutiones et*
Decreta Synodi Plocensis (1733), 10. *Constitutiones Synodales Editae et Promulgatae ab*
Illustrissimo Etc. Andrea Stanislao Kostka Zaluski Episcopo Culmensi et Pomesaniensi
(1746), 56. Andrzej Stanisław Kostka Załuski, "Edictum contra Judaeos" (1751) in *Edicta*
et Mandata Diocesis Cracoviensis 1737–1772 in AKM in Cracow, doc. 26.

137. *Decreta, Sanctiones et Universa Acta Synodi Dioecesanae ab Illustrissimo, Excellentis-*
simo ac Reverendissimo Domino D. Constantino Casimiro Brzostowski, (Wilno: Typis
Academiciis Societatis Jesu, 1717), 77.

138. Kraiński, *Porządek nabożeństwa,* 130. The minutes of the 1582 Protestant synod in Tur-
obin report funerary rituals in which the Protestant community "led the body of our
late brother appropriately singing Christian songs." This funeral, though, was also
attended by Catholic priests, some of whom "in tears praised the deceased." Sipayłło,
ed., *Acta Synodalia Ecclesiarum Poloniae Reformatarum, 1571–1632,* 3:72.

139. *Constitutiones Synodales Luceoriensis et Brestensis ab Stephano Boguslao a Rupniew*
in Januszowice Rupniewski; Lipski, *Epistola Pastoralis* (1737); *Synodus Dioecesana ab*
Illustrissimo et Reverendissimo D. Casimiro á Łubna Łubienski (1711).

140. *Constitutiones Synodales Luceoriensis et Brestensis*; *Constitutiones Synodi Dioecesana Vilnensis* (Warsaw: Typis S. R. M in Collegio Scholarum Piarum, 1696). For a summary of many of those laws see *Constitutiones Synodorum Matropolitanae Ecclesiae Gnesnensis Provincialium* (Cracow: 1761 <1636>).

141. MS. 3006 I in Biblioteka X. Czartoryskich in Cracow, 10–11.

142. According to canon law, marriage between Jews and Christians was forbidden and if contracted considered null. In contrast, marriage between a heretic and a Catholic – though still prohibited – if contracted was considered valid. See Pakter, *Medieval Canon Law and the Jews*, 271–2.

143. Müller, *Relacje o stanie diecezji krakowskiej*, 74.

144. MS. 57 "Kazania niedzielne i świąteczne 1681" in Archiwum OO. Kapucynów in Cracow, 41.

145. *Synodus Dioecesana ab Illustrissimo et Reverendissimo D. Casimiro á Łubna Łubienski* (1711), 46. *Constitutiones Synodales Luceoriensis et Brestensis*. Lipski, *Epistola pastoralis*, "De haereticis." Josaphat Michal Karp, *Epistola Pastoralis ad Clerum Diocesis Samogitiensis* (Wilno: Typis Acedemicis Societatis Jesu, 1737), chapter II.

146. Szaniawski, *Edictum contra Dissidentes*.

147. Wujek, *Postylla katholicka mnieysza*, 158.

148. Szembek, *Krótkie zebranie nauki chrześciańskiey*, 131.

149. Szaniawski, *Edictum contra Dissidentes*. See also Kriegseisen, *Ewangelicy polscy*, 40–1.

150. MS. 3006 I in Biblioteka X. Czartoryskich in Cracow, 11.

151. *Constitutiones Synodi Dioecesana Vilnensis ab Illustrissimo, Excellentissimo ac Reverendissimo Domino D. Michaele Joanne Zienkowicz Dei et Apostolicae Sedis Gratia Episcopo Vilnensi*, 3. See also a report from 1746 in MS. "S. Congregatione Concilii Relationes Statu ad Limina," Archivio Segreto Vaticano, 366A Gnesnensis.

152. The Protestant clergy also guarded these boundaries, perhaps even more. The case of baptism is a good example. In Catholicism, in cases of danger anyone can baptize an infant, not only a priest, but also any lay person, man or woman, and even a Jew, if the intention is correct. In Protestant churches, this was not so. Despite the claims that the clergy was like anyone else in the congregation, an assertion that was to counter the special quality of Catholic clergy, the Protestant clergy still claimed exclusive right, or "power" as one Polish manual said, to baptize infants. "It is a dangerous and impious thing for a woman to baptize [an infant]. Indeed it is against the Law of God. If a woman were allowed to baptize, Christ would have been baptized by his mother and not by John. And indeed, we do not permit any lay person to baptize [infants], nor do we give power to do so to any clerics, such as lectors, cantors . . . or other servants. Only the Bishops and the presbyters in service to deacons [have such power]." *Agenda albo forma porządku*, 42–3.

153. *Synodus Dioecesana* (1711), 46–7.

154. *Synodus Dioecesana* (1711), 46–7.

155. *Constitutiones et Decreta Synodi Plocensis* (1733), 6. *Constitutiones Synodorum Matropolitanae Ecclesiae Gnesnensis Provincialium*, 271.

156. See, for example, Müller, *Relacje o stanie diecezji krakowskiej 1615–1765*, 74, 110.

157. See, for example, Jerzy Kłoczowski, *History of Polish Christianity*, trans. Małgorzata Sady (Cambridge: Cambridge University Press, 2000), 108–16: "Victory of Catholicism." Janusz Tazbir, *Historia kościoła katolickiego w Polsce (1460–1795)* (Warsaw: Wiedza Powszechna, 1966), 139 ff; Janusz Tazbir, *Reformacja, kontrreformacja, tolerancja: A to Polska właśnie* (Wrocław: Wydawnictwo Dolnośląskie, 1996), chapter 5 "Triumf

kontrreformacji," 127–81; Kalik, "Ha-knesiyyah ha-katolit ve-ha-yehudim be-mamlekhet Polin-Lita ba-meot ha-17–18," 165; Gershon Hundert, *Jews in Poland-Lithuania in the Eighteenth Century: A Genealogy of Modernity* (Berkeley: University of California Press, 2004), chapter 3.

158. See also Teter, "Jewish Conversions to Catholicism."

CONCLUSION: DID THE COUNTER-REFORMATION TRIUMPH IN POLAND?

1. See, for example, Wacław Sobieski, *Nienawiść wyznaniowa tłumów za rzadów Zygmunta III–go* (Warsaw: Nakładem S. Dembego, 1902); Jerema Maciszewski, "Mechanizmy kształtowania sie opinii publicznej w Polsce doby kontrreformacji," in *Wiek XVIII–kontrreformacja-barok: Prace z historii kultury*, ed. Janusz Tazbir (Wrocław: Zakład Narodowy im. Ossolińskich, 1970), 68. Janusz Tazbir, *Szlachta i teologowie: studia z dziejów polskiej kontrreformacji* (Warsaw: Wiedza Powszechna, 1987), especially chapter 13. Gershon David Hundert, *Jews in Poland-Lithuania in the Eighteenth Century: A Genealogy of Modernity* (Berkeley: University of California Press, 2004), chapter 3.

2. There were fifty-nine non-Catholic senators in 1572, forty-one in 1586, and six in 1632. Tazbir, *Szlachta i teologowie*, 273.

3. Norman Davies, *God's Playground: A History of Poland* (New York: Columbia University Press, 1982), 1: 197.

4. Richard J. Plantinga, ed., *Christianity and Plurality: Classic and Contemporary Readings* (Oxford: Blackwell, 1999), 124–5.

5. Sara Lipton has shown in her work on medieval iconography that Jews were often used to symbolize other challengers to the Church authority; see Sara Lipton, *Images of Intolerance: The Representation of Jews and Judaism in the Bible Moralisée* (Berkeley: University of California Press, 1999), especially chapters 4 and 5.

Selected Bibliography

ARCHIVAL SOURCES

Archivio Segreto Vaticano (ASV, Rome):
  "S. Congregationis Relationes Statu ad Limina": 217 Chełmensis; 272 Cracoviensis; 366A Gnesnensis; 464 Luceoriensis; 651 Plocensis; 667 Dioecesis Premisliensis.
  "Archivio della Nunziatura di Varsovia": vol. 171.
Archivium Romanum Societatis Iesu (ARSI, Rome):
  Pol. 53 "Historia 1648–1670."
  Pol. 78 "Epistolae 1670–1700."
Archiwum Kapituły na Wawelu (AKW, Cracow):
  Acta Actorum Rmi Capituli Cathedr. Ecclesiae Cracoviensis Liber III (a. d. 3 Februarii 1524-ad d. 16 Julii 1543).
  Libri Archivi, vol. 27"Epistolae Variarum Personarum"; vol. 29.
  Libri Privilegiorum 7/2.
Archiwum Kurii Metropolitalnej w Krakowie (AKM, Cracow):
  Acta Episcopalia (AEp) 12; AEp 13; AEp 15; AEp 16; AEp 18; AEp 67; AEp 78; AEp 90.
  Edicta et Mandata Dioecesis Cracoviensis 1737–72.
Archiwum Państwowe w Poznaniu
  D 580 "Rescriptum SS. Augusti III Varsaviae 16 Mensis Octobris 1756 Ratione Transmurationis Judaeorum Posnaniae."
Biblioteka Prowincji OO. Bernardynów w Krakowie (Regional Archive of the Bernardine Friars, Cracow):
  228/R "Kazania wielkopostne (2 poł. XVII wieku)."
  298/R "Kazania misjonarskie o rzeczach ostatecznych y o grzechach."
  303/R "Kazania światecze (1706–1730)."
Archiwum Prowincji Polskiej OO. Dominikanów w Krakowie or Archiwum OO.
  Dominikanów (Archive of the Dominican Friars in the Province of Poland, Cracow):
  62 "Manuale seu Sacri Oratoris Notata seu Conciones in Ecclessiis Leopoliensis Auditae Harum Nonnullarum Brevis Annotatio Prioprioque Labore Collecta ex Anno Quo de Exedra Crucis Spinis Coronatus Orator Verbum Incarnatum Peroravit Orbi 1738–1744."
  153 "Kazania na różne okoliczności (XVIII wiek)."
  238 Tomasz Nargielewicz, "Kazania, Prov. S. Hyacinthi in Russia, OP, Leopoli in Conventu SS. Corporis Christi, A.D. 1689, Maj 31."
  291 "Kazania całego roku (1742–1747)."
  295 Pol. 1756 "Kazania na święta roczne niedziele adventowe y pasyonalne zebrane z różnych poważnych autorów przez księdza Woyciecha Józefa Barańskiego anno dni 1756."
  404 "Kazania świąteczne."

443 Łac-Pol. (1708) "Kazania pasyjne autorstwa kapłana zakonu kaznodziejskiego."
534 "Exempla."
534 Pol. "Materiały kaznodziejskie."
535 Pol. 1711–1725 Mikołaj Kieremowicz, SJ, "Kazania na niedziele całego roku."
Archiwum OO. Franciszkanów-Reformatów w Krakowie (Archive of Franciscan Friars Minor Reformed Conventuals, Reformed Franciscans):
58 Antoni Węgrzynowicz, "Tractatus Compendiarius Controvertisticus in Quo Praecipua Fundamenta Articulorum Verae Fidei Proponuntur et Satisfit Obiectionibus Sectariorum." Cracow, 1698, and "Kazania w. XVII."
60 "Kazania niedzielne i świąteczne, w. XVII."
61 Antoni Zapartowicz, "Nauki o grzechach krótko dla pamięci zebrane"; 255 "Kazania głoszone w 1731 r."
258 "Kazania w Krakowie, 1733."
263 "Kazania: 55 kazań na różne okoliczności."
274 "Józef Męciński: Kazania."
279 "O. Bernard, Reformata, Kazania misjonarskie, 1758."
280 "Conciones de Sanctificatione Festorum."
281 Roch Trucki "Messis de Semine Verbi Dei in Agro Eccclesiae in Amnipulos Collecta, seu Conciones in Dominica et Festa Conscripta."
Biblioteka i Archiwum OO. Kapucynów (The Archive and Library of the Capuchin Friars, Cracow):
50 "Katalog."
57 "Kazania niedzielne i świąteczne 1681."
Biblioteka Uniwersystetu Jagiellońskiego (Jagiellonian University Library, Cracow):
2626; 5357, vol. 9; 5358 II: "Notaty z kalendarzy dawnych krakowskich XVI, XVII, XVII w."
Biblioteka Uniwersytetu Warszawskiego (Warsaw University Library, Warsaw):
590 "Księga synodów generalnych z lat 1633–1678."
594 "Acta y conclusie albo canony synodów zboru districtu lubelskiego 1636–1708."
596 "Akta synodów prowincjonalnych małopolskich 1719–1766."
Biblioteka X. Czartoryskich (The Czartoryski Library, Cracow):
3011 I "Zbiór kazań."
3006 I "Nauka religii w pytaniach i odpowiedziach."
3698 I "Kazania misyjne."
3699 *I Wojewódzkie Archiwum Państwowe w Lublinie: Acta Maleficiorum*, vol. 198 (microfilm 110213).

PUBLISHED PRIMARY SOURCES

Abramowicz, Adam. *Kazania niedzielne jaśniewielmożnemu Bogu nayprzewielebnieyszemu jego mości X. hrabi na Zasławiu, Bychowie, Dąbrowie etc. Józefowi Sapieże.* Wilno [Vilnius]: Typis Societatis Jesu, 1753.
Acta, Constitutiones & Decreta Synodi Diaecesis Vilnensis, Praesidente Illustrissimo ac Reverendissimo Domino Domino Alexandro Michaele Kotowicz. Wilno [Vilnius]: Typis Academicis Societatis Jesu, 1685.
Acta Synodi Diaecesis Vilnensis. Praesidente Illustrissimo ac Reverendissimo Domino D. Alexandro in Maciejow Sapieha Dei et Apostolica Sedis Gratia Episcopo Vilnensi. Wilno [Vilnius]: Typis Academicis, 1669.

Agenda albo forma porządku usługi świętey w zborach ewangelickich koronnych y Wielkiego Xięstwa Litewskiego na wieczną cześć y chwale Oycu, Synowi y Duchu S. Bogu w Tróycy jedynemu, za zgodna zborów wszystkich uchwałą, teraz nowo przeyzrzana y wydana. Gdańsk: Andrzey Hüncfeldt, 1637.

Akty izdavaemye vilenskoiu arkheograficheskoiu kommiseiu. Vol. 23 Vilna [Vilnius], 1896.

Akty izdavaemye vilenskoiu kommisieiu dla razbora drevnikh aktov. Vol. 29 Vilna [Vilnius], 1902.

Akty izdavaemye vilenskoiu kommisieiu dla razbora drevnikh aktov. Vol. 5 Vilna [Vilnius], 1871.

Akty izdavaemye vilenskoiu kommisieiu dla razbora drevnikh aktov. Vol. 17 Vilna [Vilnius]: Tipografia A. G. Syrkina, 1890.

Akty o evreiakh. Vol. 28, *Akty izdavaemye vilenskoiu kommisieiu dla razbora drevnikh Aktov.* Vilna [Vilnius], 1901.

Anonymous. *Kazania w Jarosławiu i Lublinie.* N.p.: n.p., 1740?

Arba'ah turim shalem. Jerusalem: Hoẓaot Mosdot Shirat Devorah, Mekhon Yerushalayim, 1989.

Arkhiv iugo-zapadnoi Rossii, edited by Komissiia dlia razbora drevnikh aktov. Vol. 1/5. Kiev, 1869.

Augustine. *The City of God.* Translated by Henry Bettenson. New York: Penguin Books, 1984.

Balsam, Kasper. *Kazania na święta całego roku.* Poznań: Typis Societatis Jesu, 1762.

Balsam, Kasper. *Kazanie pobudzaiące do modlitwy, na uproszenie szczęśliwego powodzenia seymowi walnemu w roku 1754.* Cracow, 1754.

Baranowski, Bohdan, ed. *Instrukcje gospodarcze dla dóbr magnackich i szlacheckich z XVII– XIX wieku, źródła do historii kultury materialnej.* Wrocław: Zakład Narodowy im. Ossolińskich and PAN, 1958.

Benedict XIV, Pope. *Benedicti Divina Providentia Papae XIV Epistola Encyclica ad Primatem, Archiepiscopos et Episcopos Regni Poloniae. De His Quae Vetita Sunt Hebraeis Habitantibus in Iisdem Civitatibus et Locis in Quibus Habitant Christiani.* Rome, 1751.

Benedict XIV, Pope. *List pasterski wyraźne w sobie naywyższey stolicy apostolskiey uwagi y napomnienia dostateczne zawieraiący, dla zabieżenia y z gruntu wyniszczenia niegodziwych występkow, przez niewierne żydowstwo z oczywistym uszczerbkiem wiary świętey y prawa duchownego y oczywistego, zagęszczonych w dyecezyi chełmskiey w roku 1752 ogłoszony.* Zamość: Jan Kanty, 1752.

Bershadskii, Sergei Aleksandrovich, ed. *Dokumenty i regesty k istorii litovskikh evreev.* 3 vols. St. Petersburg: A. E. Landau, 1882.

Bersohn, Mathias. *Dyplomataryusz dotyczący Żydów w dawnej Polsce, na źródłach archiwalnych osnuty (1388–1782).* Warsaw: Druk E. Nicz i s-ka, 1910.

Bielicki, Stanisław, SJ. *Święta kaznodziejskie to iest kazania doroczne na uroczystości świętych bożych.* Kalisz: Typis Societatis Jesu, 1717.

Bielski, Marcin. *Kronika.* Sanok: Karol Pollak, 1856 <Cracow: Siebeniecher, 1597>.

Bolechow, Ber of. *The Memoirs of Ber of Bolechow (1723–1805).* Translated by Mark Wischnitzer. London: Oxford University Press, 1922.

Campensis, Joannes, and Elias Levita. *Ex Variis Libellis Eliae Grammaticorum Omnium Doctissimi, Huc Fere Congestum Est Opera Ioannis Campensis, Quicquid ad Absolutam Grammaticen Hebraicam Est Necessarium. Quod Ultima Pagella Magis Indicabit. Adiecta Est Ipsius Elie Tabula, ut Vocant, Coniugandi Omnis Generic Verba, Que Priori Editioni, Propter Inopiam Characterum Hebraicorum Addi Non Poterat.* Cracow: Ex Officina Ungleriana, 1534.

Chazan, Robert. *Church, State, and Jew in the Middle Ages.* New York: Behrman House, 1980.

Chodyński, Zenon, and Edward Likowski, eds. *Decretales Summorum Pontificum pro Regno Poloniae et Constitutiones Synodorum Provincialium et Dioecesanarum Regni Eiusdem ad Summam Collectae cum Annotationibus, Declarationibus, Admonitionibus et Additionibus ex Historia, Jure Ecclesiastico Universali et Jure Civili Regni Curantibus Plerisque Sacerdotibus Posnanensibus Editae.* 3 vols. Poznań: Augustyn Schmaedicke, 1869.

Chrysostom, John, and Mervyn Maxwell. "Chrysostom's Homilies against the Jews: An English Translation." Ph.D. diss., University of Chicago, 1966.

Clairvaux, Bernard of. *Epistolae.* Edited by J. P. Migne. Patrologiae Cursus Completus: Series Latina, 182, pt. 1. Paris: Garnieri Fratres et al., 1879.

Clairvaux, Bernard of. *The Letters of St. Bernard of Clairvaux.* Translated by Bruno Scott James. Kalamazoo, MI: Cistercian Publications, 1998 <1953>.

Constitutiones et Decreta in Dioecesana Synodo Plocensi. Płock, 1643.

Constitutiones et Decreta Synodi Dioecesana Plocensi sub Illustrissimo Excellentissimo Reverendissimo Domino D. Andrea Stanislao Kostka in Zaluskie Zaluski Dei et Apostolicae Sedis Gratia Episcopo Plocensi Pultoviae Anno Domini M.D. CC.XXXIII Die 4 Augusti Celebratae. Warsaw: Typis Societatis Jesu, 1735.

Constitutiones Synodales Editae et Promulgatae ab Illustrissimo Etc. Andrea Stanislao Kostka Zaluski Episcopo Culmensi et Pomesaniensi, Abbate Commendatario Czervinensi et Paradisiensi, Supremo Regni Cancellario in Dioecesana Synodo Celebrata in Ecclesia Archipresbyteriali Lubaviensi Diebus XVI, XVII et XVIII Mensis Septembris Anno Domini Mdccxlv. Brunsberg [Braniewo]: Typis Societatis Jesu, 1746.

Constitutiones Synodales Luceoriensis et Brestensis ab Ill. Excellent. et Reverendiss. D.D. Stephano Bogulsao a Rupniew in Januszowice Rupniewski. Warsaw: Typis Scholarum Piarum, 1726.

Constitutiones Synodi Archidioecesis Gnesnensis sub D. Stanislao in Słupów Szembek. Warsaw: Typis Scholarum Piarum, 1720.

Constitutiones Synodi Dioecesana Vilnensis ab Illustrissimo, Excellentissimo ac Reverendissimo Domino D. Michaele Joanne Zienkowicz Dei et Apostolicae Sedis Gratia Episcopo Vilnensi. Wilno [Vilnius]: Typis Societatis Jesu, 1744.

Constitutiones Synodorum Metropolitanae Ecclesiae Gnesnensis Provincialium. Cracow, 1761 <1636>.

Constitutiones Synodorum Metropolitanae Ecclesiae Gnesnensis, Provincialium, Tam Vetustorum Quam Recentiorum, Usquae ad Annum Domini M.D. L XX VIII. Cracow: Andreas Petricovius [Andrzej Piotrowczyk], 1579.

de Espina, Alfonso. *Fortalitium Fidei, in Universos Christiane Religionis Hostes Judeorum [et] Saracenorum No[n] Invalido Brevis Nec Minus Lucidi Compendii Vallo Rabiem Cohibens Fortitudinis Turris No[n] abs Re Appellatum Quinq[ue] Turriu[m] Inexpugnabilium Munimine Radians: Succincte Admodum [et] Adamussim Quinq[ue] Partium Librorum Farragine Absolutum.* Lugundi[Lyon], 1525.

Decreta, Sanctiones et Universa Acta Synodi Dioecesanae ab Illustrissimo, Excellentissimo ac Reverendissimo Domino D. Constantino Casimiro Brzostowski. Wilno [Vilnius]: Typis Societatis Jesu, 1717.

Deresiewicz, Janusz. *Transakcje chłopami w rzeczypospolitej szlacheckiej w w. XVI–XVIII.* Warsaw: Książka i Wiedza, 1959.

Dowgiało, Alexander. *Purpura zbawienna to jest męka Jezusowa na dni dziesięć rozdzielona, y od rospamietywania, a duchowney w utrapieniach pociechy, pobożnemu czytelnikowi roku 1707 od W.J.M.X. Alexandra Dowgiały, S. Th. L. kaznodziei ordynaryinego wileńskiego S. Ducha Z. K. ofiarowana; znowu na usilne zadanie dusz w rozmyślaniach teyże męki kochaiących się staraniem X. Józefa Grzegorza Szymaka S. Theol. actualnego bakałarza tegoż Zak. Kazn.* Wilno: J. K. M. Akademicka, SJ, 1747 <1707>.

Dürr-Durski, Jan, ed. *Arianie polscy w świetle własnej poezji: zarys ideologii i wybór wierszy.* Warsaw: Państwowe Zakłady Wydawnictw Szkolnych, 1948.

"Dyskursik o sinodzie." In *Dwa nieznane rękopisy z dziejów polskiej Reformacji,* edited by Aleksander Woyde. Warsaw: Universitas Liberae Poloniae, Wolna Wszechnica Polska, 1922.

Dziewulski, Marceli. *Dobry znak w który słońce sprawiedliwości przy wcieleniu swoim na pocieche całemu światu weszło nayświętsza Marya Panna.* Cracow: Franciszek Cezary, 1721.

Dziewulski, Marceli. *Prezerwatywa powietrza morowego reskrypcyi kaznodzieyskiey.* Cracow: Jakob Matuszkiewicz, 1720.

Eliyahu ben Shemuel of Lublin. *Shu"T: Yad Eliyahu.* Amsterdam, 1712.

Eugeni od Św. Mateusza. *Protekcya od tronu łaski Anny S. dysgracyom nieba na ziemi awizowana.* Cracow: Drukarnia Kollegium Większego, 1736.

Gaster, Moses, ed. *Ma'aseh Book: Book of Jewish Tales and Legends.* Philadelphia: Jewish Publication Society of America, 1981.

Grayzel, Solomon. *The Church and the Jews in the XIIIth Century: A Study of Their Relations During the Years 1198–1254.* Philadelphia: The Dropsie College, 1933.

Grayzel, Solomon, and Kenneth R. Stow. *The Church and the Jews in the XIIIth Century.* Vol. 2, *1254–1314.* New York: Jewish Theological Seminary of America, 1989.

Groicki, Bartłomiej. *Artykuły prawa majdeburskiego. Postępek sądów około karania na gardle. Ustawa płacej u sądów.* Warsaw: Wydawnictwa Prawnicze, 1954.

Groicki, Bartłomiej. *Porządek sądów i spraw miejskich prawa majdeburskiego w Koronie Polskiej.* Warsaw: Wydawnictwa Prawnicze, 1953 <1616>.

Gurland, Hayyim Jonah. *Le-korot ha-gezerot al israel.* Przemyśl, 1887.

Halpern, Israel, ed. *Bet israel be-Polin.* Tel-Aviv: Youth Department of the Zionist Organization, 1953.

Halpern, Israel, ed. *Pinkas va'ad arb'a arazot.* Jerusalem: Mosad Bialik, 1945.

Halpern, Israel, and Israel Bartal, eds. *Pinkas va'ad arb'a arazot.* Jerusalem, 1989.

Hannover, Nathan Nata. *Abyss of Despair (Yeven Metzulah): The Famous 17th Century Chronicle Depicting Jewish Life in Russia and Poland During the Chmielnicki Massacres of 1648–1649.* Translated by Abraham J. Mesch. Judaica Series. New Brunswick, NJ: Transaction, 1983.

Hannover, Nathan Nata. *Sefer yeven mezulah: Gezerot Taḥ-Tat.* Kibbuẓ ha-meuḥad: Hahistadrut ha-kalkalit shel ovadim ha-'ivriim be-ereẓ Israel, 1945.

Herbest, Benedykt. *Chrześciańska porządna odpowiedź na tę confessią która pod tytułem braciey zakonu christusowego niedawno iest wydana, przydana też iest historya kacerstwa Hussowego, zbiiaią się przy tym osszczepieństwa dzisieyszych inych nowowierników.* Cracow: Mattheusz Siebeneycher, 1567.

Herbest, Benedykt. *Nauka prawego chrześcijanina.* Cracow: Mateusz Siebeneycher, 1566.

Hoffman, Johannes Daniel. *De Typographiis Earumque Initiis et Incrementis in Regno Poloniae et Magno Ducatu Lithuaniae cum Variis Observationibus Rem et Literariam et Typographicam Utriusque Gentis Aliqua ex Parte Illustrantibus.* Dantisci [Gdańsk]: Georgius Marcus Knochius [Gregory Mark Knoch], 1740 [1983?].

Hubicki, Szymon. *Żydowskie okrucieństwa.* Cracow, 1602.

Ibn Verga, Solomon. *Sefer shevet Yehuda.* Edited by Azriel Shohet and Yiẓhak Baer. Jerusalem: Mosad Bialik, 1946.

Istoriko-iuridicheskie materialy izvlechennye iz aktov knig gubernii vitebskoi i mogilevskoi khraniashchikhsia v tsentralnom arkhive v Vitebske i izdannye pod redaktseiu arkhivariusa sego arkhiva M. Verevkina, ed. M. Verevkin. 32 vols. Vitebsk: 1890.

The Jewish Life of Christ being the Sepher Toldoth Jeshu or Book of the Generation of Jesus. Translated by G. W. Foote and J. M. Wheeler. London, 1885.

Kaczyński, Paweł. *Kazanie na niedziele całego roku.* Kalisz: Typis Societatis Jesu, 1675.

Karp, Josaphat Michał. *Epistola Pastoralis ad Clerum Diocesis Samogitiensis ex Mandato Illustrissimi Excellentissimi Domini D. Josaphati Michaelis Karp Espiscopi Samogitiensis Edita et Impressa.* Wilno: Typis Societatis Jesu, 1737.

Katechizm albo krótkie w iedno mieysce zebranie wiary y powinności krześcijańskiey z pasterstwem zborowym y domowym, z modlitwami, psalmami y piosnkami na cześć a chwałę Panu Bogu a zborowi iego ku zbudowaniu teraz znowu za pilnym przeyrzeniem y poprawieniem wydany. Wilno, 1600 [?].

Katechizm albo nauka wiary y pobożnosci krześcijanskiey według uchwały S. tridentskiego concilium przez uczone a bogoboyne ludzie zebrana y spisana. Przodkiem plebanom y przełożonym kościelnym, potym inszym wszystkim pobożnym krześcianom barzo pożyteczna y potrzebna. Przez księdza Walentego Kuchorskiego archidiakona pomorskiego etc. z łacinskiego na polskie wyłożony. Translated by Walenty Kuchorski. Cracow: Mikolaj Schaffenberg, 1568.

Katechizm prostych albo krótkie zebranie potrzebnieyszych wiary naszey artykułów. Dla prostych ludzi y dzieci na pytania y odpowiedzi krótkie rozłożony. N.p., 1600 [?].

Katechizm rzymski to iest, nauka chrześciańska powaga Concilium Tridentskiego y papieża Piusa V wydane po łacinie. A teraz nowo na polskie pytania y odpowiedzi przełożona. Za rozkazaniem jego mości X. Stanisława Karnkowskiego arcybiskupa gnieźnieńskiego etc. y iego nakładem wydrukowana. Kalisz: Drukarnia Jana Wolraba, 1603.

Katechizm rzymski to iest, nauka chrześciańska powaga Concilium Tridentskiego y Piusa V papieża po łacinie wydana. Potym za rozkazaniem s. pamięci X. Stanisława Karnkowskiego arcybiskupa gniezneńskiego, primasa koronnego na polskie pytania y odpowiedzi przełożona. Teraz znowu dla ubogich plebanów y gospodarzów katholickich przedrukowana. Cracow: Drukarnia Franciszka Cezarego, 1643.

Katechizm rzymski z dekretu S. Koncilium Trydentskiego za rozkazem S. Piusa V papieża po łacinie wydany, na polski ięzyk powagą niegdyś wydany J. O. Xcia Jmci Xiędza Stanisława Karnkowskiego arcybiskupa gnieźnieńskiego, prymasa Kor. Po. Y W. X. L. przez pytania y odpowiedzi przetłumaczony y wydrukowany w Kaliszu w r.p. 1603 teraz zaś z niezliczonych omyłek y słów staropolskich dziś nierozumiałych oczyszczony y z oryginałem łacińskim skonfrontowany, a jako dzieło arcybiskupa y prymasa utriusque gentis jaśnie oświeconemu nayprzewielebnieyszemu w Bogu xiążęciu jmci xiędzu Władysławowi Lubieńskiemu arcybiskupowi gnieznienskiemu prymasowi y xiążęciu pierwszemu Kor. Pol. Y W. X. L. Sedis Apostolicae Legato etc. oraz j. oo. j. ww. nayprzewielebnieyszym w Bogu imc xięży arcybiskupom, biskupom, senatorom Kor. Pol. Y W. X. L. y całemu nayprzewielebnieyszemu duchowieństwu pasterska około dusz funkcya bawią cemu się … dedykowany. Wilno [Vilnius]: Typis Scholarum Piarum, 1762.

Kawecka-Gryczowa, Alodia, ed. *Bogowie fałszywi: nieznany pamflet antykatolicki z XVI wieku.* Warsaw: Biblioteka Narodowa, 1983.

Kaźmierczyk, Adam, ed. *Żydzi polscy 1648–1772: Źródła.* Studia Judaica Cracoviensia 6. Cracow: Uniwersytet Jagielloński Katedra Judaistyki, 2001.

Kobielski, Franciszek Antoni. *List pasterski wszystkiemu duchowieństwu, świeckim i zakonnym, tudzież i wszystkim swoiemi honorami, godnościami prerogatywami ozdobionym y dystyngowanym panom, dziedzicom y possesorom, także uczciwym y pracowitym oboyga płci,* 1752.

Kobielski, Franciszek Antoni. *List pasterski: wszem i wobec i każdemu z osobna a osobliwie niewiernym rabinom kahalnym.* Łuck [Luck]: 1741.

Kobielski, Franciszek Antoni. *Literae Pastorales ad Universum Clerum, et Populum Utriusque Diaecesis Illustrissimi & Reverendissimi Domini Francisci Antonii in Dmenin Kobielski Episcopi Luceoriensis et Brestensis, Serenissimae Reginalis Maiestatis Cantellarii cum Annexis de Verbo ad Verbum in Testimonium Legis Suae Sanctissimi Domini Nostri Benedicti Papae XIV Constitutionibus et Litteris in Anno 1740 et 1741 ac Praesenti 1742.* n.p., 1742.

Kojałowicz, Woyciech Wiiuk. *O rzeczach do wiary należących rozmowy theologa z różnemi wiary prawdziwej przeciwnikami.* Cracow: Drukarnia Stanisława Piotrowczyka, 1671.

Korona, Marek. *Rozmowa theologa katholickiego z rabinem żydowskim przy arianinie nieprawym chrześcijaninie.* Lwów: Typis Societatis Jesu, 1645.

Kraiński, Krzysztof. *Forma odprawowania nabożeństwa czyli mała agendka.* 2nd ed. Laszczów: n.p., 1602.

Kraiński, Krzysztof. *Porządek nabożeństwa kościoła powszechnego apostolskiego, słowem bożym ugruntowanego y zbudowanego, na Iezusie Krystusie spisany, ku chwale Bogu w Troycy iedynemu roku 1602 przez starsze kościołów reformowanych w Małey Polszcze, za rada y dozwoleniem synodu provincialnego ożarowskiego, włodzisławskiego y łańcutskiego powtóre drukowano roku 1614.* N.p.: n.p., 1614.

Kraiński, Krzysztof. *Porządek nabożeństwa kościoła powszechnego apostolskiego, słowem bożym zbudowanego, na Iezusie Krystusie, który iest Bogiem izraelskim, synem bożym przedwiecznym, spolistnym z oycem, zbawicielem, kapłanem, przyczyńca, iedynym namiestnika nie maiacym, y dosyć czynieniem za grzechy ludzkie. Spisany, ku chwale Bogu w Troycy iedynemu roku 1598 przez xiędza Krzysztofa Kraińskiego superintendenta kościołów reformowanych w Małey Polszcze, za rada y dozwoleniem braciey destriktu lubelskiego.* Toruń: n.p., 1599.

Kraiński, Krzysztof. *Postylla kościoła powszechnego apostolskiego słowem bożym ugruntowana na Jezusie Chrystusie. Spisana ku chwale Bogy w Troycy S. iedynemu przez księdza Krzysztofa Kraińskiego.* N.p.: n.p., after 1611.

"Kronika od r. 1507 do 1541 spisana (z rękopismu 1549)." In *Biblioteka Starożytna Pisarzy Polskich,* 1–38. Warsaw: n.p., 1854.

Krosnowski, Jan. *Pochodnia słowa bożego w kazaniach niedzielnych całego roku na oświecenie i zapalenie rozumów i afektów chrześcijanskich.* Lublin: Typis Societatis Jesu, 1689.

Krowicki, Marcin. *Chrześcijańskie a żałobliwe napominanie.* Edited by Zbigniew Ogonowski, Lech Szczucki, and Janusz Tazbir. Biblioteka Pisarzy Reformacyjnych 7. Warsaw: Polska Akademia Nauk, 1969.

Krowicki, Marcin. *Obraz a kontrefet własny Antykrystów z Pisma Świętego dostatecznie wymalowany y wystrychniony przez sługe słowa pana Krystusowego, Marcina*

Krowickiego, dla przestrogi ludziom krześciańskim. Edited by Zbigniew Ogonowski, Lech Szczucki, and Janusz Tazbir. Biblioteka Pisarzy Reformacyjnych 7. Warsaw: Polska Akademia Nauk, 1969.

Leskiewiczowa, Janina, and Jerzy Michalski, eds. *Supliki chłopskie XVIII wieku. Z archiwum prymasa Michała Poniatowskiego: Materiały do dziejów wsi polskiej.* Warsaw: Książka i Wiedza, 1954.

Levita, Elias. *Massoreth ha-Massoreth of Elias Levita Being an Exposition of the Massoretic Notes on the Hebrew Bible or the Ancient Critical Apparatus of the Old Testament, in Hebrew with an English Translation and Critical and Explanatory Notes.* Translated by Christian D. Ginsburg. Edited by Norman Henry Snaith. New York: Ktav, 1968.

Lewek, Jan. *List pewnego statysty, zawierający w sobie niektóre przyczyny, dla których z teraźniejszych Żydow ledwie który do wiary świętey katolickiey nawracan bywa.* N.p.: n.p., 1728.

Liber Cronicarum. Nuremberg: Anton Korberger, 1493.

Linder, Amnon. *The Jews in Roman Imperial Legislation.* Detroit: Wayne State University Press, 1987.

Lipski, Jan Alexander. *Epistola Pastoralis ad Clerum et Populum Dioecesis Cracoviensis. Ex Mandatio Eminentissimi et Reverendissimi Domini Ioanni Alexandri Divina Miseratione S. R. E. Presbyterii Cardinalis Lipski Episcopi Cracoviensis, Ducis Severiae,* 1737.

Lorencowicz, Alexander. *Kazania na niedziele całego roku. Część pierwsza.* Kalisz: Kollegium Societatis Jesu, 1671.

Łosiewski, Fortunat. *Powtórna męka Chrystusa Jezusa w nayświetszym sakramencie; na sześciu dyscyplinach archi konfraterni tegoż nayświetszego sakramentu w kościele S. Jana Chrzciciela przesławney kollegiaty warszawskiey we czwartki postu wielkiego, kazaniami reprezentowana.* Warsaw, 1729.

Lubieniecki, Stanislaw. *History of the Polish Reformation: And Nine Related Documents.* Translated by George Huntston Williams. Minneapolis: Fortress Press, 1995.

Lublin, Meir ben Gedaliah *She'elot u-teshuvot.* Venice: Pietro e Lorenzo Bragadin, 1618 <Metz, 1769; Warsaw; 1881 >

Maimon, Salomon. *An Autobiography.* New York: Schocken Books, 1947.

Maimonides. *Iggeret Teman le-rabenu Mosheh ben Maimon.* Edited by Abraham Halkin. New York, 1952.

Małecki, Jan, ed. *Jewish Trade in Cracow at the End of the Sixteenth Century and in the Eighteenth Century: Selected Records from Cracow Customs Registers, 1593–1683.* Cracow: Polska Akademia Umiejętności, 1995.

Marchand, Jacob. *Katechizm abo nauka chrześcijańska. Nie tylko świeckim, ale i pannom zakonnym, także i plebanom wielce użyteczny.* Cracow: Łukasz Kupisz <1682, SJ>, 1648.

Marcus, Jacob Rader, and Marc Saperstein. *The Jew in the Medieval World: A Source Book, 315–1791.* Rev. ed. Cincinnati: Hebrew Union College Press, 1999.

Martyr, Justin the. *Justin Martyr, the Dialogue with Trypho.* Translated by A. Lukyn Williams, *Translations of Christian Literature;.* London S.P.C.K.: New York, 1930.

Martyr, Justin the. *Justin Martyr's Dialogue with Trypho the Jew.* Translated by Henry Brown. London: Macmillan Barclay and Macmillan, 1846.

Mateusza, Eugeni od Sw. *Protekcya od tronu łaski Anny S. dysgracyom nieba na ziemi awizowana; na placu zguby płaczu znaleziona.* Cracow, 1736.

Matuszewicz, Marcin. *Diariusz życia mego.* 2 vols. Warsaw: Państwowy Instytut Wydawniczy, 1986.

Miczyński, Sebastian. *Zwierciadło Korony Polskiey: urazy ciężkie y utrapienia wielkie, które ponosi od Żydow wyrażaiące synom koronnym na seym walny w roku pańskim 1618.* Cracow: Máciej Jedrzeiowczyk, 1618.

Misiakiewicz, Paweł. *Korona braterska księgę rodzaiu nowo na świat rodząca się przenayśw. P. Maryę koronuiącą na tryumfalną iey koronacyą w Sokalskim obrazie sprwadzona.* N.p.: n.p., 1724.

Młodzianowski, Tomasz. *Kazania i homilye na święta uroczystsze także pogrzeby dla większey chwały Boga, króla królów: nayiaśnieyszey na zawsze królowy polskiy bogarodzicy panny, czci.* Poznań: Collegium Societatis Jesu, 1681.

Modena, Leone, and Mark R. Cohen. *The Autobiography of a Seventeenth-Century Venetian Rabbi: Leon Modena's Life of Judah.* Princeton, NJ: Princeton University Press, 1988.

Mojecki, Przecław. *Żydowskie okrucieństwa, mordy i zabobony.* Cracow, 1589.

Morawski, Jan. *Duchowna theologia abo kościół Ducha Świętego.* Lwów [Lviv]: n.p., 1695.

Moskorzowski, Hieronim. *Zawstydzenie księdza Skargi.* Raków, 1606.

Müller, Wiesław. *Relacje o stanie diecezji krakowskiej 1615–1765.* Lublin: KUL, 1978.

Ochabowicz, Woyciech. *Tarcza wiary świętey rzymskiey katolickiey przeciwko różnych ich nieprzyjaciół impetom wystawiona albo theologia polska kontrowersye y konkluzye katolickie dla prawowiernych katolików, polskim stylem y alphabetycznym porządkiem w sobie zamykaiąca.* Lublin: Typis Societatis Jesu, 1736.

Or Zaru'a. Żytomir, 1882.

Pollak, Roman, Stanisław Drewniak, and Marian Kaczmarek, eds. *Antologia pamiętników polskich XVI wieku.* Wrocław: Zakład Narodowy im. Ossolińskich, 1966.

Popławski, Mikołaj. *Stół duchowny rozliczeń nauk zbawiennych historyi y przykładów przy reflexyach na całego roku tygodnie, niedziele y święta, nie tylko dla nabożnych dusz, ale y kaznodziejów, spowiedników, potrawkami zastawiony.* Warsaw, 1704.

Poszakowski, Jan. *Antidotum contra "Antidotum abo zbawienna przestroga," że lekarstwo duszne przeciwko apostazyi Woyciecha Węgierskiego niegdy superintendenta zborów ewangelickich sporządzone y wygotowane teraz świeżo w Królewcu roku pańskiego 1750 drukiem opublikowane y ogłoszone.* Wilno [Vilnius]: Typis Societatis Jesu, 1754.

Poszakowski, Jan. *Firmament prawdy trzema gwiazdami rozumy dyssydentów oświecaiący to iest nauka katholicka o wzywaniu świętych, o modlitwie za umarłych y o czyścu.* Wilno [Vilnius]: Typis Societatis Jesu, 1737.

Poszakowski, Jan. *Historya luterska: O początkach y rozkrzewieniu się tey sekty, oraz niektóre rewolucye w sobie zawieraiąca.* Wilno [Vilnius]: Typis Societatis Jesu, 1745.

Poszakowski, Jan. *Historyi kalwinskiey część trzecia w którey opisuie okazya y sposób rozmnożenia tey herezyi w Belgium albo w Niderlandach.* 3 vols. Warsaw: Typis Societatis Jesu, 1749.

Poszakowski, Jan. *Kalendarz jezuicki większy na rok przestępny MDCXL.* Wilno [Vilnius]: Typis Societatis Jesu, 1740.

Poszakowski, Jan. *Konfessya albo wyznanie wiary jednostaynym konsensem y zgodą wszystkich zborów kalwińskich ogłoszone.* Warsaw: Typis Societatis Jesu, 1742.

Poszakowski, Jan. *Lilia między cierniami prawda między błędami to iest nauka katholicka o usprawiedliwieniu z nauka protestantów konfessyey auzgburskiey w xięgach ich symbolicznych zawarty.* Wilno [Vilnius]: Typis Societatis Jesu, 1738.

Poszakowski, Jan. *Nauka katholicka o przenayświętszey Eucharystiey z nauka protestantów konfessyey auzburskiey w xięgach symbolicznych zawarta.* Wilno [Vilnius]: Typis Societatis Jesu, 1737.

Poszakowski, Jan. *Rozdział światła y ciemności to iest nauka katholicka o przenayświetszey eucharystyey z nauka Protestantów konfessyey auzgburskiey zawarty*. Wilno [Vilnius], 1737.

Pruszcz, Piotr Hyacynt. *Forteca duchowna Królestwa Polskiego z żywotów świętych, tak iuż kanonizowanych y beatyfikowanych, iako też świątobliwie żyiących patronów polskich, także z obrazów Chrystusa pana y matki iego przenayświętszey w oyczyźnie naszey cudami wielkimi słyszących*. Cracow: Drukarnia Stanisława Lenczewskiego, 1662 (1737).

Radliński, Jakub. *Oktawa bożego ciała na cały rok rozporządzona albo sposób nawiedzania nayświetszego sakramentu, tak przez oktawę bożego ciała, iako i cały rok*. Lublin: Typis Societatis Jesu, 1731.

Radliński, Jakub. *Prawda chrześciańska od nieprzyiaciela swego zeznana: to iest traktat rabina Samuela, pokazuiący błędy żydowskie około zachowania prawa mojżeszowego, y przyścia messyaszowego, którego Żydzi czekaią*. Lublin: Typis Societatis Jesu, 1733.

Reuchlin, Johannes. *Recommendation Whether to Confiscate, Destroy and Burn All Jewish Books: A Classic Treatise against Anti-Semitism, Studies in Judaism and Christianity*. New York: Paulist Press, 2000.

Sawicki, Jakub, ed. *Wybór tekstów źródłowych z historii państwa i prawa polskiego*. Warsaw, PWN, 1952.

Schroeder, Henry Joseph. *Disciplinary Decrees of the General Councils, Text, Translation, and Commentary*. St. Louis: B. Herder Book Co., 1937.

Sefer Toledot Yeshu sive Liber de Ortu Origine Jesu ex Editione Wagenseiliana Transcriptus et Explicatus. Edited by L. Edman. Upsala, 1857.

Seliḥot. Cracow: Helicz, late 1530s.

Siarkiewicz, Antoni. *Miecz sprawiedliwości bożey*. Lwów [Lviv]: Typis Societatis Jesu, 1718.

Simonsohn, Shlomo, ed. *The Apostolic See and the Jews*. 8 vols. Toronto, ON: Pontifical Institute of Mediaeval Studies, 1988.

Shulḥan 'Aruk.

Sipayłło, Maria, ed. *Acta Synodalia Ecclesiarum Poloniae Reformatarum, 1550–1559*. 4 vols. Vol. 1, *Akta synodów różnowierczych w Polsce*. Warsaw: Wydawnictwa Uniwersytetu Warszawskiego, 1966.

Sipayłło, Maria, ed. *Acta Synodalia Ecclesiarum Poloniae Reformatarum, 1560–1570*. 4 vols. Vol. 2, *Akta synodów różnowierczych w Polsce*. Warsaw: Wydawnictwa Uniwersytetu Warszawskiego, 1972.

Sipayłło, Maria, ed. *Acta Synodalia Ecclesiarum Poloniae Reformatarum, 1571–1632*. 4 vols. Vol. 3, *Akta synodów różnowierczych w Polsce*. Warsaw: Wydawnictwa Uniwersytetu Warszawskiego, 1983.

Skarbek, Jan. "Edictum Contra Judaeos." In *Edicta et Mandata Dioecesis Cracoviensis (1737– 1772)*, *Archiwum Kurii Metropolitalnej w Krakowie*, No. 29. Cracow, 1717.

Śleszkowski, Sebastyan. *Dostateczna genealogia żydowska. A zatym y przednieysze ustawy Talmudu żydowskiego, którymi iako własna nauka ichże samych rabinów starszych, iaśnie dowodzimy, że to wszystko cokolwiek o niewypowiedzianych złościach y niezaliczonych zbrodniach żydowskich zdawna piszą, prawda iest nieomylna; wszystkie się bowiem te nic-noty żydowskie w ich ustawiach obficie nayduią. Tak samym Żydom, iako y wszystkim niewiernikom, pomocnikom żydowskim, y Żydo-Chrześcianom, na poznanie z nich zat-wardzenia, y ślepoty swey serdeczney bardzo potrzebne y pożyteczne. Z sześciset y trzynaści ustaw Talmudu żydowskiego (tylo ich bowiem w nim maiaą), krótko zebrane, a teraz nowo z obiaśnieniem ich sensu dostatecznym a prawdziwym wydane*. Brunsberg [Braniewo], 1622.

Śleszkowski, Sebastyan. *Jasne dowody o doktorach żydowskich, że nie tylko dusze ale y ciało swoie w niebespieczeństwo zginienia wiecznego wdaią, którzy Żydów, Tatarów y innych niewiernych, przeciwko zakazaniu kościoła świętego powszechnego za lekarzów używaia.* N.p.: n.p., 1623 <1649, 1758>.

Slonik, Benjamin Aaron ben Abraham. *Mas'at Binyamin: Ve-hem she'elot u-teshuvot.* Cracow: M. N. Meisels, 1632.

Słuszna sprawa koron Jezusa y Maryi za dekretem O. S. papieża Innocentego XIII przez cała okrawę truymfalnego aktu koronacyi cudownego sokalskiego obrazu Nayświętszey Maryi Panny obwołana. Lwów[Lviv]: n.p., 1727.

Stankar, Franciszek. *Gramatica Institutio Linguae Hebreae.* Cracow: Johannes Helicz, 1548.

Statut Velikago Kniazhestva Litovskago: s podvedeniem v nadlezhashchikh mestakh ssylki na konstitutsii, prilichnyia soderzhaniiu pnago: perevod s polskago. Sankt Petersburg: Pravitel-stvuiushchii Senat, 1811.

Synodus Diaecesana Chelmensis ab Illustrissimo et Reverendissimo Domino D. Christophoro Ioanne in Slupów Szembek, Dei et S. Sedis Apostolicae Gratia Episcopo Chelmensi, Nominato Premislensi etc, Crasnostaviae in Ecclesia Cathedrali Praesente Universo Dioecesis Clero Celebrata Die Decima Mensis Julii et Aliis Duobus Sequentibus Diebus, Anno Domini M.D.CC.XVII. Zamość, 1717.

Synodus Dioecesana ab Illustrissimo et Reverendissimo D. Casimiro a Łubna Łubienski Dei et Apostolica Sedis Gratia Episcopo Cracoviensi Duce Severiae Celebrata Cracoviae in Ecclesia Archipresbyteriali ad 1711. Cracow: Franciszek Cezary, 1711.

Synodus Dioecesana Chelmensis per Illustrissimum et Reverendissimum Dominum Stanislaum Hyacynthum Święcicki Episcopum Chelmensem Abbatem Lublinensem Crasnostaviae Celebrata Anno Domini 1694 Die 15 Septembris. Warsaw: Typis S.R.M in Collegio Scholarum Piarum, 1696.

Synodus Luceoriensis et Brestensis per Illustrissimum ac Reverendissimum Dominum Dominum Stanislaum in Magna Witwica Witwicki. Warsaw: Carolus Schreiber, 1684.

Szaniawski, Jan Felix. *Kazanie na solenney wotywie o Duchu Świętym przy zaczynaiącey się elekcyi roku 1733 dnia 25 augusta w kollegiacie warszawskiey świętego Jana miane.* Warsaw, 1733.

Szaniawski, Konstantyn Felicjan. *Edictum contra Dissidentes.* Kielce: n.p., 1725.

Szembek, Józef Eustachy. *List pasterski wyraźne w sobie naywyższey stolicy apostolskiey uwagi y napomnienia dostateczne zawieraiący, dla zabieżenia y z gruntu wyniszczenia niegodziwych wystepków, przez niewierne Żydowstwo z oczywistym uszczerbkiem wiary świętey y prawa duchownego y oyczystego, zagęszczonych w dyecezyi chełmskiey w roku 1752 ogłoszony. Y do należytego zachowania pzrez [sic] podane niżey wszelkim stanom sposoby, dla uśmierzenia do tąd szerzącey się w wyuzdanym Żydowstwie zuchwałości, przełożony.* Zamość: Drukarnia B. Jana Kantego, 1752.

Szembek, Krzysztof Jan. *Krótkie zebranie nauki chrześcianskiey zlecenia nayprzelewiebneyszego w Chrystusie Panu jaśnie wielmożnego i. mc Krzysztofa Jana Szembeka, biskupa przemyskiego, proboszcza y generała miechowskiego etc. dziatkom chrześcianskim przez pytanie y odpowiedź według porządku y podzielenia catech: S. Concil: Trinden:.* Cracow: Drukarnia Franciszka Cezarego, 1714.

Szembek, Stanisław. *Zebranie kazań na Wielką Noc, Boże Narodzenie, uroczystości naysswietszey Marii Panny y niektórych świętych.* Brunsbergae [Braniewo]: Typis Societatis Jesu, 1726.

Szermierski, Antoni, SJ. *Strzał Jonaty (kazania niedzielne).* Wilno [Vilnius]: n.p., 1728.

Talmud Bavli (The Babylonian Talmud).

Tanner, Norman P. *Decrees of the Ecumenical Councils.* Washington, DC: Georgetown University Press, 1990.

Tertullian, and Immacolata Aulisa. *Polemica con i giudei.* Collana di testi patristici 140. Rome: Città nuova, 1998.

Twardowski, Samuel. *Woyna domowa z Kozaki i Tatary, Moskwa, potym Szwedami i z Węgry przez lat dvvanascie [sic] za panowania nayjasnieyszego Iana Kazimierza króla polskiego toczaca się.* Kalisz: Typis Societatis Jesu, 1681.

Tylkowski, Woyciech. *Problemata święte abo pytania około wyrozumienia świętey ewangeliey od kościoła powszechnego tak na niedziele iako y na święta rozłożoney.* Poznań: Typis Societatis Jesu, 1688.

Ulanowski, Boleslaw. *Materyały do historii ustawodawstwa synodalnego w Polsce w wieku XVI.* Archiwum Komisyi Prawniczey (Collectanea Ex Archivo Collegii Iuridici) 1. Cracow: Akademia Umiejętności, 1895.

Ulanowski, Boleslaw, Jan Fijałek, and Adam Vetulani, eds. *Statuty synodalne wielunsko-kaliskie Mikołaja Trąby z R. 1420.* Studia i Materiały do Historii Ustawodawstwa Synodalnego w Polsce 4. Cracow: Polska Akademia Umiejętności, 1915–51.

Volumina Legum: Przedruk zbioru praw staraniem xx. pijarów w Warszawie od roku 1732 do roku 1782 wydanego. 2nd ed. 10 vols. St. Petersburg: Jozafat Ohryzka, 1859. Reprint, 1980.

Węgierski, Wojciech. *Antidotum abo lekarstwo duszne przeciwko apostasiey, y odstąpieniu od prawdy, na iedynym fundamencie ss. proroków y apostołów ugruntowaney.* Baranów: Gerzy [sic] Twardomeski, 1646.

Węgierski, Wojciech. *Kronika zboru ewangelickiego krakowskiego.* Cracow: n.p., 1817 <1651>.

Wessel, Augustyn Adam. *Morze miłosierdzia y dobroci Bożey pokazane grzesznikowi y grzesznicy w uwagach y reflexiach na całą mękę Jezusa.* Lwów [Lviv]: n.p., 1735.

Wielowieyski, Stefan. *Nabożeństwo dla ludzi zabawnych, którzy czasy nie maią, dla tych, którzy nie mogą, dla niedbałych, którym się nie chce modlić.* Poznań: n.p., 1693.

Williams, George Huntston. *The Polish Brethren: Documentation of the History and Thought of Unitarianism in the Polish-Lithuanian Commonwealth and in the Diaspora, 1601–1685.* Harvard Theological Studies 30. Missoula, MT: Scholars Press for Harvard Theological Review, 1980.

Wolf, Johannes Christian. *Bibliotecae Hebreae.* Hamburg, 1715–21.

Woyde, Aleksander. *Dwa nieznane rękopisy z dziejów polskiej Reformacji: Deux manucrits inconnus concernant la Reformation en Pologne.* Bibliotheca Universitatis Liberae Polonae 7. Warsaw: Wolna Wszechnica Polska, 1922.

Wujek, Jakob. *Postilla katholicka mneysza, to iest krótkie kazania abo wykłady świętych ewangeliey, na każdą niedzielę y na każde święto, przez cały rok według nauki prawdziwej kościoła chrześcijanskiego powszechnego.* Cracow, 1870–1 <1617>.

Wyrozumska, Bożena, ed. *The Jews in Mediaeval Cracow: Selected Records from Cracow Municipal Books.* Cracow: Polska Akademia Umiejętności, 1995.

Załuski, Andrzej Chryzostom. *Kazania które się na prędce zebrać mogły.* Warsaw: Typis Scholarum Piarum, 1696.

Załuski, Andrzej Stanisław Kostka. "Edictum contra Judaeos." In Archiwum Kurii Metropolitalnej w Krakowie: "Edicta et Mandata Diocesis Cracoviensis 1737–1772." Cracow, 1751.

Załuski, Józef Andrzej. *Dwa miecze katolickiej w królestwie ortodoksyjnym odsieczy przeciwko natarczywym pp. dysydentów polskich zamachom.* Warsaw: n.p., 1731.

Żuchowski, Stefan. *Odgłos processów criminalnych na Żydach o różne excessy, także morderstwo dzieci, osobliwie w Sandomierzu roku 1698 przeświadczone. W prześwietnym Trybunale Koronnym przewiedzionych dla dobra pospolitego wydany od X. Stephana Żuchowskiego oboyga prawa doktora.* N.p.: n.p., 1700.

Żuchowski, Stefan. *Process kryminalny o niewinne dziecię Jerzego Krasnowskiego iuż to trzecie, roku 1710 dnia 18 sierpnia w Sendomirzu okrutnie od Żydów zamordowane. Dla odkrycia iawnych kryminalów żydowskich, dla przykładu sprawiedliwości potomnym wiekom.* Sandomierz: n.p., after 1718.

SECONDARY SOURCES

Adang, Camilla. *Muslim Writers on Judaism and the Hebrew Bible: From Ibn Rabban to Ibn Hazm.* Islamic Philosophy, Theology, and Science 22. New York: E. J. Brill, 1996.

Ådna, Jostein, and Hans Kvalbein. *The Mission of the Early Church to Jews and Gentiles.* Wissenschaftliche Untersuchungen zum neuen Testament 127. Tübingen: Mohr Siebeck, 2000.

Agus, Irving A. *Urban Civilization in Pre-Crusade Europe: A Study of Organized Town-Life in Northwestern Europe during the Tenth and Eleventh Centuries Based on the Responsa Literature.* New York: Yeshiva University Press, 1965.

Alves, Abel Athouguia. "The Christian Social Organism and Social Welfare: The Case of Vives, Calvin and Loyola." *Sixteenth Century Journal* 20, no. 1 (1989): 3–22.

Asch, Ronald G. *The Thirty Years War: The Holy Roman Empire and Europe, 1618–1648.* European History in Perspective. New York: St. Martin's Press, 1997.

Aster, Howard, and Peter J. Potichnyj, eds. *Ukrainian-Jewish Relations in Historical Perspective.* 2nd ed. Edmonton, ON: Canadian Institute of Ukrainian Studies, University of Alberta, 1990.

Audisio, Gabriel. *The Waldensian Dissent: Persecution and Survival, C. 1170–C. 1570.* Cambridge Medieval Textbooks. New York: Cambridge University Press, 1999.

Bałaban, Majer. *Historja i literatura żydowska, ze szczególnem uwzględnieniem historji Żydów w Polsce, dla klas wyższych szkół średnich.* 3 vols. Lwów [Lviv]: Zakład Narodowy imienia Ossolińskich, 1924.

Bałaban, Majer. *Historja Żydów w Krakowie i na Kazimierzu: 1304–1868.* 2 vols. Cracow: Krajowa Agencja Wydawnicza, 1991.

Barber, Malcolm. *The Cathars, the Medieval World.* Harlow, UK: Longman, 2000.

Barclay, John M. G., Morna Dorothy Hooker, and J. P. M. Sweet. *Early Christian Thought in Its Jewish Context.* Cambridge: Cambridge University Press, 1996.

Barkat, Amiram. "Shnei ha-rabanim ha-roshiim nifgashu le-rishona 'im apifior be-vatikan," *Ha'aretz,* January 18, 2004, 4A.

Baron, Salo Wittmayer. "'Plenitude of Apostolic Powers' and Medieval 'Jewish Serfdom'." In *Ancient and Medieval Jewish History,* edited by David M. Feldman. New Brunswick, NJ: Rutgers University Press, 1972.

Baron, Salo Wittmayer. *Poland-Lithuania 1500–1650.* Vol. 16, *A Social and Religious History of the Jews.* New York: Columbia University Press and Jewish Publication Society of America, 1976.

Bartoszewski, Kazimierz. *Antysemityzm w literaturze polskiej XV–XVII w.* Warsaw: Geberthner & Wolff, 1914.

Barycz, Henryk. *Historia Uniwersytetu Jagiellońskiego w epoce humanizmu.* Cracow: Uniwersytet Jagielloński, 1935.

Batoński, Bronisław. "Szkolnictwo jezuickie w dobie kontrreformacji." In *Z dziejów szkolnictwa jezuickiego w Polsce,* edited by Jerzy Paszenda, 29–57. Cracow: WAM-Księża Jezuici, 1994.

Belmessous, Saliha. "Assimilation and Racialism in Seventeenth and Eighteenth Century French Colonial Policy." *American Historical Review* 110 no. 2 (2005): 322–49.

Ben-Sasson, Hayyim Hillel. *Hagut ve-hanhagah: Hashkafotehem ha-ḥevratiyot shel yehudei Polin be-shilhe yeme ha-beynayim.* Jerusalem: Mosad Bialik, 1959.

Berger, David. "The Attitude of St. Bernard of Clairvaux toward Jews." *Proceedings of the American Academy of Jewish Research* 40 (1972): 89–108.

Berger, David. *The Jewish-Christian Debate in the High Middle Ages: A Critical Edition of the Nizzahon Vetus.* Judaica, Texts and Translations 4. Philadelphia: Jewish Publication Society of America, 1979.

Bershadskii, Sergei A. *Avram Ezofovich Rebichkovich, podskarbii zemskii, chlen rady Velikago Kniazhestva Litovskago: Otryvok iz istorii vnutrennikh otnoshenii Litvy v nachalie XVI veka.* Kiev: Tip. G. T. Korchak-Novitskago, 1888.

Bireley, Robert. *The Refashioning of Catholicism, 1450–1700: A Reassessment of the Counter Reformation.* Washington, DC: Catholic University of America Press, 1999.

Bodniak, Jarosław. "Sprawa wygnania arjan w r. 1566." *Reformacja w Polsce* 5, no. 19 (1928): 52–9.

Bogucka, Maria. "Polish Towns between the Sixteenth and Eighteenth Centuries." In *A Republic of Nobles: Studies in Polish History to 1864,* edited by J. K. Fedorowicz, 135–52. New York: Cambridge University Press, 1982.

Bowersock, G. W. *Martyrdom and Rome, The Wiles Lectures Given at the Queen's University of Belfast.* New York: Cambridge University Press, 1995.

Boyarin, Daniel. *Carnal Israel: Reading Sex in Talmudic Culture.* Berkeley: University of California Press, 1993.

Boyle, Leonard. "Innocent III and Vernacular Versions of Scripture." In *The Bible in the Medieval World: Essays in Honor of Beryl Smalley,* edited by Katherine Walsh and Diana Wood, 97–107. New York: Blackwell, 1985.

Brandon, S. G. F. "History or Theology? The Basic Problems of the Evidence of the Trial of Jesus." In *Essential Papers on Judaism and Christianity in Conflict: From Late Antiquity to the Reformation,* edited by Jeremy Cohen, xiv, 578. New York: New York University Press, 1991 <1968>.

Brzozowski, Mieczysław. "Teoria kaznodziejska (wiek XVI–XVIII)." In *Dzieje teologii katolickiej w Polsce,* edited by Marian Rechowicz. Lublin: Towarzystwo Naukowe Katolickiego Uniwersytetu Lubelskiego, 1974–5.

Buchwald-Pelcowa, Paulina. *Cenzura w dawnej Polsce: między prasą drukarską a stosem.* Warsaw: Wydawnictwo Stowarzyszenia Bibliotekarzy Polskich, 1997.

Bukowski, Julian. *Dzieje Reformacyi w Polsce: od jej wejścia do Polski aż do jej upadku.* Cracow: Nakładem Autora, 1883.

Buliński, Melchior. *Monografija miasta Sandomierza.* Sandomierz: Wydawnictwo Diecezjalne, 1999 <1879>.

Burnett, Stephen G. "Calvin's Jewish Interlocutor: Christian Hebraism and Anti-Jewish Polemics During the Reformation." *Bibliotheque d'humanisme et renaissance* 55 (1993).

Burnett, Stephen G. "Distorted Mirrors: Antonius Margaritha, Johann Buxtorff and Christian Enthographies of the Jews." *Sixteenth Century Journal* 25 (1994).

Burnett, Stephen G. *From Christian Hebraism to Jewish Studies: Johannes Buxtorf (1564–1629) and Hebrew Learning in the Seventeenth Century.* Studies in the History of Christian Thought. Leiden: Brill, 1996.

Burnett, Stephen G. "Hebrew Censorship in Hanau: A Mirror of Jewish-Christian Coexistence in Seventeenth-Century Germany." In *The Expulsion of the Jews: 1492 and After,* edited by Raymond B. Waddington and Arthur Williamson. New York: Garland Press, 1994.

Bynum, Caroline. *Holy Fast and Holy Feast.* Berkeley: University of California Press, 1987.

Bystroń, Jan Stanisław. *Dzieje obyczajów w dawnej Polsce, wiek XVI–XVIII.* Warsaw: Państwowy Instytut Wydawniczy, 1994.

Cantor, Norman F. *Medieval History: The Life and Death of a Civilization.* New York: Macmillan, 1969.

Carlebach, Elisheva. *The Death of Simon Abeles: Jewish-Christian Tension in Seventeenth Century Prague.* Third Annual Herbert Berman Memorial Lecture. New York: Center for Jewish Studies, Queens College, City Universtiy of New York, 2001.

Carlebach, Elisheva. *Divided Souls: Converts from Judaism in Early Modern German Lands, 1500–1750.* New Haven, CT: Yale University Press, 2001.

Châtellier, Louis. *The Religion of the Poor: Rural Missions in Europe and the Formation of Modern Catholicism, C.1500–C.1800.* New York: Cambridge University Press, 1997.

Châtellier, Louis. "Rinnovamento della pastorale e società dopo il concilio di Trento." In *Il concilio di Trento e il moderno,* edited by Paolo Prodi and Wolfgang Reinhard. Bologna: Il Mulino, 1996.

Chazan, Robert. *Barcelona and Beyond: The Disputation of 1263 and Its Aftermath.* Berkeley: University of California Press, 1992.

Chazan, Robert. *Church, State, and Jew in the Middle Ages.* Library of Jewish Studies. New York: Behrman House, 1980.

Chazan, Robert. *Daggers of Faith: Thirteenth-Century Christian Missionizing and Jewish Response.* Berkeley: University of California Press, 1989.

Chazan, Robert. "Twelfth-Century Perceptions of the Jews: A Case Study of Bernard of Clairvaux and Peter the Venerable." In *From Witness to Witchcraft: Jews and Judaism in Medieval Christian Thought,* edited by Jeremy Cohen. Wiesbaden: Harrassowitz Verlag, 1996.

Cohen, Jeremy. *The Friars and the Jews: A Study in the Development of Medieval Anti-Judaism.* Ithaca: Cornell University Press, 1982.

Cohen, Jeremy, ed. *From Witness to Witchcraft: Jews and Judaism in Medieval Christian Thought.* Wolfenbütteler Mittelalter-Studien 11. Wiesbaden: Harrassowitz, 1996.

Cohen, Mark R. "Leone Da Modena's *Riti*: A Seventeenth-Century Plea for Social Toleration of Jews." In *Essential Papers on Jewish Culture in Renaissance and Baroque Italy,* edited by David Ruderman. New York: New York University Press, 1992.

Cohen, Shaye J. D. *From the Maccabees to the Mishnah.* Library of Early Christianity 7. Philadelphia: Westminster Press, 1987.

Courtenay, William J. "Between Pope and King: The Parisian Letters of Adhesion of 1303." *Speculum* 71, no. 3 (1996): 577–605.

Czapliński, Władysław. "Myśl polityczna w Polsce w dobie kontrreformacji (1573–1655)." In *Wiek XVII–kontrreformacja–barok: prace z historii kultury,* edited by Janusz Pelc. Wrocław: Zakład Narodowy im. Ossolińskich, 1970.

Dahan, Gilbert. *The Christian Polemic against the Jews in the Middle Ages.* Notre Dame: University of Notre Dame Press, 1998.

Davies, Norman. *God's Playground: A History of Poland*. Vol. 1, *The Origins to 1795*. Reprinted edition (with corrections). Oxford: Clarendon Press and in the U.S. by Columbia University Press, 1982.

Davis, Joseph. "The Reception of the Shulhan 'Arukh and the Formation of Ashkenazic Jewish Identity." *AJS Review* 26, no. 2 (2002): 251–76.

Davis, Joseph. *Yom-Tov Lipmann Heller: Portrait of a Seventeenth-Century Rabbi*. Portland: Littman Library of Jewish Civilization, 2004.

d'Avray, David. "Method of the Study of Medieval Sermons." In *Modern Questions About Medieval Sermons: Essays on Marriage, Death, History and Sanctity*, edited by Nicole Beriou and David d'Avray. Spoleto: Centro italiano di studi sull'alto medioevo, 1994.

Delumeau, Jean. *Catholicism between Luther and Voltaire: A New View of the Counter-Reformation*. Philadelphia: Westminster Press, 1977.

Dubnow, Simon. *History of the Jews in Russia and Poland*. Translated by I. Friedlander. Bergenfield, NJ: Avotaynu, 2000.

Dundes, Alan. *The Blood Libel Legend: A Casebook in Anti-Semitic Folklore*. Madison: University of Wisconsin Press, 1991.

Dzięgielewski, Jan. "Biskupi rzymskokatoliccy końca XVI-pierwszej połowy XVII wieku i ich udział w kształtowaniu stosunków wyznaniowych w Rzeczypospolitej." In *Między monarchią a demokracją: Studia z dziejów Polski XV–XVIII wieku*, edited by Anna Sucheni-Grabowska and Małgorzata Zaryń, 191–210. Warsaw: Wydawnictwa Sejmowe, 1994.

Edwards, M. J., Martin Goodman, S. R. F. Price, and Christopher Rowland. *Apologetics in the Roman Empire: Pagans, Jews, and Christians*. Oxford: Oxford University Press, 1999.

Ehrenreich, Barbara, and Deirdre English. *Witches, Midwives, and Nurses: A History of Women Healers*. New York: The Feminist Press at City University of New York, 1973.

Elon, Menachem. *Jewish Law: History, Sources, Principles*. Translated by Bernard Auerbach and Melvin Syks. Philadelphia: Jewish Publication Society of America, 1994.

Elukin, Jonathan. "Jacques Basnage and the History of the Jews: Anti-Catholic Polemic and Historical Allegory in the Republic of Letters." *Journal of the History of Ideas* 53, no. 4 (1992): 603–30.

Estreicher, Karol, and Stanisław Estreicher. *Bibliografia polska. Stólecie XV–XVIII*. 34 vols. Cracow: Uniwersytet Jagielloński, 1878–1955.

Ettinger, Shmuel. "The Council of Four Lands." In *The Jews in Old Poland, 1000–1795*, edited by Antony Polonsky, Jakub Basista, and Andrzej Link-Lenczowski, 93–109. New York: I. B. Tauris / Institute for Polish-Jewish Studies, 1993.

Ettinger, Shmuel. "Ma'amadam ha-mishpati ve-ha-ḥevrati shel yehudei Ukraina ba-meot ha-15–17." *Zion* 20 (1955): 128–52.

Evans, Robert John Weston. *The Making of the Habsburg Monarchy, 1550–1700*. Oxford: Clarendon Press, 1979.

Ferry, Patrick. "Confessionalization and Popular Preaching: Sermons against Synergism in Reformation Saxony." *Sixteenth Century Journal* 28, no. 4 (1997): 1143–66.

Fram, Edward. "Bein 1096 ve 1648–49 – 'iyun me ḥadash." *Zion* 61, no. 2 (1996): 159–82.

Fram, Edward. "Creating a Tale of Martyrdom in Tulczyn, 1648." In *Jewish History and Jewish Memory: Essays in Honor of Yosef Hayim Yerushalmi*, edited by Elisheva Carlebach, John M. Efron, and David N. Myers, xv, 462. Hanover, NH: University Press of New England, 1998.

Fram, Edward. "Hagvalat motarot ba-kehilah ha-yehudit be-Krakov be-shilhe ha-meah ha-16 u-ve-reshit ha-meah ha-17 [Sumptuary Laws in the Jewish Community of Krakow at

SELECTED BIBLIOGRAPHY   241

the End of the Sixteenth and the Beginning of the Seventeenth Centuries." *Gal-Ed* 18 (2002): Hebrew section on 11–23.

Fram, Edward. *Ideals Face Reality: Jewish Law and Life in Poland, 1550–1655*. Monographs of the Hebrew Union College 21. Cincinnati: Hebrew Union College Press, 1997.

Fram, Edward. "Ve-'adayin en bein 1096 le-1648–49." *Zion* 62, no. 1 (1997): 31–46.

Fram, Edward, and Magdalena Teter. "Matai hithil ha-defus ha-'ivri be-Krakov [When Did the Hebrew Printing Start in Cracow]." *Gal-Ed* 20 (2005).

Fredriksen, Paula. "Divine Justice and Human Freedom: Augustine on Jews and Judaism, 392–398." In *From Witness to Witchcraft: Jews and Judaism in Medieval Christian Thought*, edited by Jeremy Cohen. Wiesbaden: Harrassowitz Verlag, 1996.

Frend, W. H. C. *Martyrdom and Persecution in the Early Church: A Study of a Conflict from the Maccabees to Donatus*. New York: New York University Press, 1967.

Gabryel, Kazimierz. "Działalność kościelna biskupa Tomickiego 1464–1535." In *Studia kistorii kościoła w Polsce*. Warsaw: ATK, 1972.

Gawthrop, Richard, and Gerald Strauss. "Protestantism and Literacy in Early Modern Germany." *Past and Present* 104 (1984): 31–55.

Geremek, Bronisław. *Poverty: A History*. Oxford: Blackwell, 1997.

Gierowski, Józef Andrzej. *Historia Polski, 1505–1864*. 2 vols. Vol. 1. Warsaw: Państwowy Instytut Wydawniczy, 1978.

Gierowski, Józef Andrzej. *The Polish-Lithuanian Commonwealth in the Eighteenth Century: From Anarchy to Well-Organised State*. Translated by Henry Leeming. Rozprawy Wydziału Historyczno-Filozowicznego 82. Cracow: Polska Akademia Umiejętności, 1996.

Gieysztor, Aleksander, ed. *History of Poland*. 2d ed. Warszawa: Państwowe Wydawnictwo Naukowe, 1979.

Gieysztor-Miłobędzka, Elżbieta. "Church Interior in Later Counter-Reformation Period: Presuppositions and Practice." In *Late Baroque Art in the Eighteenth Century in Poland, Bohemia, Slovakia and Hungary*, edited by Lech Kalinowski. Cracow: MN, 1990.

Given, James. "The Inquisitors of Languedoc and the Medieval Technology of Power." *American Historical Review* 94, no. 2 (1989): 336–59.

Goldberg, Jacob. *Jewish Privileges in the Polish Commonwealth: Charters of Rights Granted to Jewish Communities in Poland-Lithuania in the Sixteenth to Eighteenth Centuries*. Jerusalem: The Israel Academy of Sciences and Humanities, 1985.

Goldberg, Jacob. "Poles and Jews in the Seventeenth and Eighteenth Centuries: Rejection and Acceptance." *Jahrbücher für Geschichte Osteuropas* 22 (1974): 248–82.

Goldberg, Jacob. "Władza dominalna żydów-arendarzy dóbr ziemskich nad chłopami w XVII–XVIII w." *Przegląd Historyczny* 81 (1990).

Grayzel, Solomon. *The Church and the Jews in the XIIIth Century: A Study of Their Relations During the Years 1198–1254*. Philadelphia: The Dropsie College, 1933.

Grayzel, Solomon. "The Papal Bull *Sicut Judaeis*." In *Essential Papers on Jewish Culture in Renaissance and Baroque Italy*, edited by David Ruderman, 386–400. New York: New York University Press, 1992 <1962>.

Grayzel, Solomon, and Kenneth R. Stow. *The Church and the Jews in the XIIIth Century*. Vol. 2, *1254–1314*. Detroit: Wayne State University Press, 1989.

Gregg, Joan Young. *Devils, Women, and Jews: Reflections of the Other in Medieval Sermon Stories*. SUNY Series in Medieval Studies. Albany: State University of New York Press, 1997.

242 SELECTED BIBLIOGRAPHY

Grzeszczuk, Stanislaw. "Wacław Potocki." In *Polski słownik biograficzny*, edited by Stefan Kieniewicz et al., 28: 220–24. Wrocław: Zakład Narodowy im. Ossolińskich, 1985.

Guldon, Zenon, and Jacek Wijaczka. "The Accusation of Ritual Murder in Poland, 1500–1800." *Polin* 10 (1997).

Guldon, Zenon, and Jacek Wijaczka *Procesy o mordy rytualne w Polsce w XVI–XVIII wieku*. Kielce: DCF, 1995.

Guterman, Simeon L. *Religious Toleration and Persecution in Ancient Rome*. Westport, CT: Greenwood Press, 1971 <1951>.

Halpern, Israel, ed. *Bet israel be-Polin*. Tel-Aviv: Youth Department of the Zionist Organization, 1953.

Hamilton, Bernard. "The Albigesian Crusade and Heresy." In *The New Cambridge Medieval History. Volume V: C.1198–C.1300*, edited by David Abulafia. Cambridge: Cambridge University Press, 1999.

Hare, Douglas R. *The Theme of Jewish Persecution of Christians in the Gospel According to St. Matthew*. Society for New Testament Studies Monograph Series 6. Cambridge: Cambridge University Press, 1967.

Harrington, Joel, and Helmut Walser Smith. "Confessionalization, Community, and State Building in Germany, 1555–1870." *Journal of Modern History* 69, no. 1 (1997): 77–101.

Holweck, Frederick. "Immaculate Conception." In *The Catholic Encyclopedia*, edited by Charles Herbermann et al., 674–81. New York: The Encyclopedia Press, 1910.

Hood, John Y. B. *Aquinas and the Jews*. Middle Ages Series. Philadelphia: University of Pennsylvania Press, 1995.

Hood, John Y. B. *Aquinas and the Jews, Middle Ages Series*. Philadelphia: University of Pennsylvania Press, 1995.

Horowitz, Elliot. " 'Ve-nahafokh hu': yehudim mul soneihem be-hagigot ha-Purim ['And It Was Reversed': Jews and Their Enemies in the Festivities of Purim]." *Zion* 59 (1994).

Hoszowski, Stanisław. *Ceny we Lwowie w XVI i XVII wieku*. Lwów [Lviv]: Kasa im. J. Mianowskiego, 1928.

Howe, John. "The Nobility's Reform of the Medieval Chuch." *American Historical Review* 93, no. 2 (1988): 317–39.

Hsia, R. Po-chia. "Christian Ethnographies of the Jews in Early Modern Germany." In *Expulsion of the Jews: 1492 and After*, edited by Raymond B. Waddington and Arthur Williamson. New York: Garland Press, 1994.

Hsia, R. Po-chia. *The Myth of Ritual Murder: Jews and Magic in Reformation Germany*. New Haven, CT: Yale University Press, 1988.

Hsia, R. Po-chia. *Social Discipline in the Reformation: Central Europe, 1550–1750*. Christianity and Society in the Modern World. New York: Routledge, 1989.

Hsia, R. Po-chia. *Trent 1475: Stories of a Ritual Murder Trial*. New Haven, CT: Yale University Press, published in cooperation with Yeshiva University Library, 1992.

Hsia, R. Po-chia. *The World of Catholic Renewal, 1540–1770*. New Approaches to European History 12. New York: Cambridge University Press, 1998.

Hundert, Gershon David. *Jews in Poland-Lithuania in the Eighteenth Century: A Genealogy of Modernity*. Berkeley: University of California Press, 2004.

Hundert, Gershon David. *The Jews in a Polish Private Town: The Case of Opatów in the Eighteenth Century*. Johns Hopkins Jewish Studies. Baltimore: Johns Hopkins University Press, 1992.

Hundert, Gershon David. "Jews, Money and Society in Seventeenth-Century Polish Commonwealth: The Case of Cracow." *Jewish Social Studies* 43, no. 3–4 (1981): 261–74.

Hundert, Gershon David. "The *Kehilla* and the Municipality in Private Towns at the End of the Early Modern Period." In *The Jews in Old Poland, 1000–1795*, edited by Antony Polonsky, Jakub Basista, and Andrzej Link-Lenczowski, 172–85. New York: I. B. Tauris/ Institute for Polish-Jewish Studies, 1993.

Hundert, Gershon David. "Poland: Paradissus Judaeorum." *Journal of Jewish Studies [Great Britain]* 48, no. 2 (1997): 335–48.

Innes, Matthew. "Charlemagne's Will: Piety, Politics and the Imperial Succession." *The English Historical Review* 112, no. 448 (1997): 833–55.

Jarocki, Robert "Biskup pada. . . ." *Rzeczpospolita* 258, November 4, 2000.

Jedin, Hubert. *A History of the Council of Trent.* 2 vols. New York: T. Nelson, 1961.

Jeske-Choiński, Teodor. *Neofici polscy: Materyały historyczne.* Warsaw: Druk P. Laskauera, 1904.

Jordan, William Chester. "The Capetians from the Death of Phillip II to Phillip IV." In *The New Cambridge Medieval History. Volume V: C. 1198–C. 1300*, edited by David Abulafia. Cambridge: Cambridge University Press, 1999.

Kaczmarczyk, Zdzisław, and Bogusław Leśnodorski. *Historia państwa i prawa Polski*, edited by Juliusz Bardach. 3rd ed. 2 vols. Warsaw: Państwowe Wydawnictwo Naukowe, 1968.

Kalik, Yehudit. "Christian Servants Employed by Jews in the Polish-Lithuanian Commonwealth in the Seventeenth and Eighteenth Centuries." *Polin* 14 (2001): 259–70.

Kalik, Yehudit. "Ha-knesiya ha-katolit ve-ha-yehudim be-Krakov ve-be-Kazimierz 'ad halukoth Polin." In *Kroke-Kazimierz-Krakow*, edited by Elchanan Reiner, 69–88. Tel Aviv: The Diaspora Research Institute / Center for the History of Polish Jewry, 2001.

Kalik, Yehudit. "Ha-knesiyah ha-katolit ve-ha-yehudim be-mamlekhet Polin-Lita ba-meot ha-17–18." Ph.D. dissertation, Hebrew University, 1998.

Kalik, Yehudit. "Patterns of Contact between the Catholic Church and the Jews in the Polish-Lithuanian Commonwealth: Jewish Debts." In *Studies in the History of the Jews in Old Poland in Honor of Jacob Goldberg*, edited by Adam Teller, 102–22. Jerusalem: Magnes Press / Hebrew University, 1998.

Kalik, Yehudit. "Polish Attitudes Towards Jewish Spirituality in the Eighteenth Century." *Polin* 15 (2003): 77–85.

Kamiński, Andrzej Sulima. *Republic vs. Autocracy: Poland-Lithuania and Russia 1686–1697.* Harvard Series in Ukrainian Studies, ed. George Grabowicz. Cambridge, MA: Harvard Ukrainian Research Institute, 1993.

Kantorowicz, Ernst Hartwig. *The King's Two Bodies: A Study in Mediaeval Political Theology.* Princeton, NJ: Princeton University Press, 1957. Reprint, 1981.

Katchen, Aaron L. *Christian Hebraists and Dutch Rabbis: Seventeenth Century Apologetics and the Study of Maimonides' Mishneh Torah.* Harvard Judaic Texts and Studies. Cambridge, MA: Harvard University Press, 1984.

Katz, Jacob. *Exclusiveness and Tolerance: Studies in Jewish-Gentile Relations in Medieval and Modern Time.* Oxford: Oxford University Press, 1961.

Katz, Jacob. *Goi Shel Shabat.* Jerusalem: Merkaz Zalman Shazar, 1983.

Katz, Jacob. *The "Shabbes Goy": A Study in Halakhic Flexibility.* Philadelphia: Jewish Publication Society of America, 1989.

Kaufman, David. "Elia Menachem Chalfan on Jews Teaching Hebrew to Non-Jews." *Jewish Quarterly Review* 9 (1897): 500–8.

Kaźmierczyk, Adam. "The Problem of Christian Servants as Reflected in the Legal Codes of the Polish-Lithuanian Commonwealth During the Second Half of the Seventeenth Century and in the Saxon Period." *Gal-Ed* 15–16 (1997): 23–40.

Kłoczowski, Jerzy. *History of Polish Christianity.* Translated by Małgorzata Sady et al. Cambridge: Cambridge University Press, 2000.

Kłoda, Kazimierz. "Sprawa ariańska w czasie bezkrólewia 1648 roku." *Odrodzenie i Reformacja w Polsce* 22 (1977).

Kot, Stanisław. *Socinianism in Poland.* Boston: Starr King Press, 1957.

Kowalski, Waldemar. "Change in Continuity: Post-Tridentine Rural and Township Parish Life in the Cracow Diocese." *Sixteenth Century Journal* 35, no. 3 (2004): 689–715.

Kowalski, Waldemar. "'W obronie wiary': Ks. Stefan Żuchowski – między wzniosłością a okrucieństwem." In *Żydzi wśród chrześcijan w dobie szlacheckiej rzeczypospolitej*, 221–33. Kielce: KTN, 1996.

Krasiński, Valerian. *Historical Sketch of the Rise, Progress and Decline of the Reformation in Poland.* London: Murray, 1838–40.

Kriegseisen, Wojciech. *Ewangelicy polscy i litewscy w epoce saskiej.* Warsaw: Semper, 1996.

Krochmal, Jacek. "Ha-yaḥasim ben ha-'ironim ve-ha-knesiyah be-Przemyśl le-vein ha-yehudim bashanim 1559–1772." *Gal-Ed* 15–16 (1997): 15–33.

Kutrzeba, Stanisław. *Historja źródeł dawnego prawa polskiego.* Lwów: Wydawnictwo Zakładu Narodowego im. Ossolińskich, 1925.

Kuźmina, Dariusz. *Katechizmy w Rzeczypospolitej XVI i początku XVII wieku.* Nauka-Dydaktyka-Praktyka, ed. Marcin Drzewiecki. Warsaw: Stowarzyszenie Bibliotekarzy Polskich, 2002.

Kwiatkowska-Frejlich, Lidia. *Sztuka w służbie kontrreformacji.* Lublin: Wydawnictwo Uniwersytetu Marii Curie-Skłodowskiej, 1998.

Lambert, Malcolm. *Medieval Heresy: Popular Movements from the Gregorian Reform to the Reformation.* 2nd ed. Oxford: Blackwell, 1992.

Langmuir, Gavin I. *Toward a Definition of Antisemitism.* Berkeley: University of California Press, 1990.

Leeuwen, Marco H. D. van. "Logic of Charity: Poor Relief in Preindustrial Europe." *Journal of Interdisciplinary History* 24, no. 4 (1994): 589–613.

Leff, Gordon. "Heresy and the Decline of the Medieval Church." *Past and Present* 20 (1961): 36–51.

Linde, Samuel Bogumił. *Słownik języka polskiego.* 3rd ed. 6 vols. Warszawa: Państwowy Instytut Wydawniczy, 1951.

Lipton, Sara. *Images of Intolerance: The Representation of Jews and Judaism in the Bible Moralisée.* Berkeley: University of California Press, 1999.

Łozinski, Jerzy, and Barbara Wolff, eds. *Wojewodztwo kieleckie: Powiat sandomierski.* Katalog Zabytków Sztuki w Polsce 3/11, ed. Jerzy Łozinski. Warsaw: Instytut Sztuki PAN, 1962.

Lukowski, Jerzy. *Liberty's Folly: The Polish-Lithuanian Commonwealth in the Eighteenth Century, 1697–1795.* New York: Routledge, 1991.

Maciszewski, Jerema. "Mechanizmy kształtowania się opinii publicznej w Polsce doby kontrreformacji." In *Wiek XVIII-kontrreformacja-barok: prace z historii kultury,* edited by Janusz Tazbir. Warsaw: Zakład Narodowy im. Ossolińskich, 1970.

Maciszewski, Jerema. *Szlachta i jej państwo.* Warsaw: Państwowe Wydawnictwo Naukowe, 1984.

MacLennan, Robert S. *Early Christian Texts on Jews and Judaism.* Brown Judaic Studies 194. Atlanta: Scholars Press, 1990.

Mączak, Antoni. "The Structure of Power in the Commonwealth of the Sixteenth and Seventeenth Centuries." In *A Republic of Nobles: Studies in Polish History to 1864*, edited by J. K. Fedorowicz, 91–108. New York: Cambridge University Press, 1982.

Małecki, Jan, ed. *Jewish Trade in Cracow at the End of the Sixteenth Century and in the Eighteenth Century: Selected Records from Cracow Customs Registers, 1593–1683.* Cracow: Polska Akademia Umiejętności, 1995.

Markus, R. A. "Introduction: The West." In *The Cambridge History of Medieval Political Thought C. 350–C. 1450*, edited by J. H. Burns. New York: Cambridge University Press, 1988.

Markus, R. A. "The Latin Fathers." In *The Cambridge History of Medieval Political Thought C. 350–C. 1450*, edited by J. H. Burns. New York: Cambridge University Press, 1988.

Maxwell, C. Mervyn. "Chrysostom's Homilies against the Jews: An English Translation." Ph.D. dissertation, University of Chicago, 1966.

McCready, D. William. "Papal Plenitudo Potestatis and the Source of Temporal Authority in Late Medieval Papal Hierocratic Theory." *Speculum* 48, no. 4 (1973): 654–74.

McKitterick, Rosamond, ed. *The New Cambridge Medieval History. Volume II, C. 700–C. 900.* New York: Cambridge University Press, 1995.

Miller, James. "The Origins of Polish Arianism." *Sixteenth Century Journal* 16, no. 2 (1985): 229–56.

Moll, Herman. *The World Described, or, A New and Correct Sett of maps: Shewing the Several Empires, Kingdoms, Republics... in All the Known Parts of the Earth.* London: J. Bowles, 1709–20.

Müller, Wieslaw. *Relacje o stanie diecezji krakowskiej 1615–1765.* Lublin: KUL, 1978.

Murphy, John F. "Gelasius I." In *The Catholic Encyclopedia*, edited by Charles Herbermann et al., 406. New York: The Encyclopedia Press, 1913.

Musurillo, Herbert comp. *The Acts of the Christian Martyrs.* Oxford Early Christian Texts. Oxford: Clarendon Press, 1972.

Myers, W. David. *"Poor, Sinning Folk": Confession and Conscience in Counter-Reformation Germany.* Ithaca: Cornell University Press, 1996.

Nadav, Modekhai. "Ma'aseh alimut ha-dadiyyim bin yehudim le-lo-yehudim be-Lita lifney 1648." *Gal-Ed* 7–8 (1985): 41–56.

Netanyahu, Ben Zion. *The Origins of the Inquisition in Fifteenth Century Spain.* New York: Random House, 1995.

Nicol, D. M. "Byzantium." In *The Cambridge History of Medieval Political Thought C. 350–C. 1450*, edited by J. H. Burns. Cambridge: Cambridge University Press, 1988.

Nirenberg, David. *Communities of Violence: Persecution of Minorities in the Middle Ages.* Princeton, NJ: Princeton University Press, 1996.

Nirenberg, David. "Mass Conversion and Genealogical Mentalities: Jews and Christians in Fifteenth-Century Spain." *Past and Present* 174 (2002): 3–41.

Obirek, Stanisław. *Jezuici w Rzeczpospolitej Obojga Narodów 1564–1668.* Cracow: Wydział Filozoficzny Towarzystwa Jezusowego, 1996.

Olszewski, Henryk. "Ustrój polityczny rzeczypospolitej." In *Polska XVII wieku*, edited by Janusz Tazbir, 52–83. Warsaw: Wiedza Powszechna, 1969.

O'Connor, John B. "Ignatius of Antioch." In *The Catholic Encyclopedia*. New York: The Encyclopedia Press, 1913.

O'Malley, John W. *The First Jesuits*. Cambridge, MA: Harvard University Press, 1993.

Ozment, Steven E. *The Age of Reform (1250–1550): An Intellectual and Religious History of Late Medieval and Reformation Europe*. New Haven, CT: Yale University Press, 1980.

Pakter, Walter. *Medieval Canon Law and the Jews*. Abhandlungen zur Rechtswissenschaftlichen Grundlagenforschung 68. Ebelsbach: Verlag Rolf Gremer, 1988.

Passamaneck, Stephen M. "Toward the Sunrise in the East, 1300–1565." In *An Introduction to the History and Sources of Jewish Law*, edited by Bernard Jackson, Stephen M. Passamaneck, et al. Oxford: Oxford University Press, 1996.

Paszenda, Jerzy. *Z dziejów szkolnictwa jezuickiego w Polsce: Wybór artykułów*. Cracow: Wydawnictwo WAM-Księża Jezuici, 1994.

Perkins, Judith. *The Suffering Self: Pain and Narrative Representation in the Early Christian Era*. New York: Routlege, 1995.

Peters, Edward. *Heresy and Authority in Medieval Europe: Documents in Translation*. Philadelphia: University of Pennsylvania Press, 1980.

Phillips, Henry. "Sacred Text and Sacred Image: France in the Seventeenth Century." *Bulletin of the John Rylands University Library of Manchester* 81, no. 3 (1999): 299–319.

Plantinga, Richard J., ed. *Christianity and Plurality: Classic and Contemporary Readings*. Oxford: Blackwell, 1999.

Pociecha, Wladyslaw. "Ezofowicz, Rabinkowicz Michel." In *Polski słownik biograficzny*, edited by Władysław Konopczyński, 6: 331–3. Cracow: Polska Akademia Umiejętności, 1948.

Poliakov, Léon. *Jewish Bankers and the Holy See: From the Thirteenth to the Seventeenth Century*. London: Routledge and Kegan Paul, 1977.

Pollak, Roman, Stanislaw Drewniak, and Marian Kaczmarek, eds. *Antologia pamiętników polskich XVI wieku*. Wrocław: Zakład Narodowy im. Ossolińskich, 1966.

Pritsak, Omelijan. "The Pre-Ashkenazic Jews of Eastern Europe in Relation to the Khazars, the Rus' and the Lithuanians." In *Ukrainian-Jewish Relations in Historical Perspective*, edited by Howard Aster. Edmonton, ON: Canadian Institute of Ukrainian Studies, 1988.

Prodi, Paolo. "Il 'Sovrano Pontifice'." *Storia d'Italia: Annali* 9: La Chiesa e il potere politico dal medioevo all'età contemporanea (1995): 195–216.

Prodi, Paolo. *The Papal Prince: One Body and Two Souls: The Papal Monarchy in Early Modern Europe*. New York: Cambridge University Press, 1987.

Prodi, Paolo, and Carla Penuti, eds. *Disciplina dell'anima, disciplina del corpo e disciplina della società tra medioevo ed età moderna*. Bologna: Società editrice il Mulino, 1994.

Raba, Joel. *Ben zikaron ke-hakhhashah: gezerot 408 ve-409 be-reshimot bene ha-zeman uve-ro'i ha-khetivah ha-historit*. Tel-Aviv: Makhon le-ḥeker ha-tefuẓot, 1994.

Raba, Joel. *Between Remembrance and Denial: The Fate of the Jews in the Wars of the Polish Commonwealth During the Mid-Seventeenth Century as Shown in Contemporary Writings and Historical Research*. East European Monographs 428. Boulder: East European Monographs, 1995.

Ravid, Benjamin. "From Geographical Realia to Historiographical Symbol: The Odyssey of the Word Ghetto." In *Essential Papers on Jewish Culture in Renaissance and Baroque Italy*, edited by David Ruderman. New York: New York University, 1992.

Ravid, Benjamin. "The Venetian Government and the Jews." In *The Jews of Early Modern Venice*, edited by Benjamin Ravid and Robert Davis. Baltimore: Johns Hopkins University Press, 2001.

Rechowicz, Marian. *Dzieje teologii katolickiej w Polsce.* Lublin: Towarzystwo Naukowe Katolickiego Uniwersytetu Lubelskiego, 1974–5.

Ricciotti, Giuseppe. *The Age of Martyrs: Christianity from Diocletian to Constantine.* Milwaukee: Bruce Pub. Co., 1959.

Rok, Bogdan. "Z literatury antyżydowskiej w Polsce XVIII wieku." In *Z historii ludności żydowskiej w Polsce i na Śląsku,* edited by Krystyn Matwijowski. Wrocław: Wydawnictwo Uniwersytetu Wrocławskiego, 1994.

Rokeah, David. *Jews, Pagans, and Christians in Conflict.* Studia Post-Biblica 33. Leiden: Jerusalem Magnes Press, Hebrew University, 1982.

Rokeah, David. *Justin Martyr and the Jews.* Jewish and Christian Perspectives Series 5. Leiden: Boston, 2002.

Rokeah, David. *Yustinus Martir veha-yehudim.* Kuntresim, Mekorot U-Meḥkarim 84. Jerusalem: Merkaz Dinur, 1998.

Roper, Lyndal. "Witchcraft and Fantasy in Early Modern Germany." In *Witchcraft in Early Modern Europe: Studies in Culture and Belief,* edited by Gareth Roberts. New York: Cambridge University Press, 1996.

Rosenthal, Frank. "The Study of the Hebrew Bible in Sixteenth Century Italy." *Studies in the Renaissance* 1 (1954).

Rosman, Moshe. "The Indebtedness of the Lublin Kahal in the Eighteenth Century." In *Studies in the History of the Jews in Old Poland,* edited by Adam Teller, 166–83. Jerusalem: Magnes Press, 1998.

Rosman, Moshe. *The Lords' Jews: Magnate-Jewish Relations in the Polish-Lithuanian Commonwealth During the Eighteenth Century.* Cambridge, MA: Harvard University Press, 1990.

Roth, Cecil. *A History of the Jews in England.* Oxford: Clarendon Press, 1964.

Rubin, Miri. *Gentile Tales: The Narrative Assault on Late Medieval Jews.* New Haven, CT: Yale University Press, 1999.

Ruff, Julius R. *Violence in Early Modern Europe, 1500–1800.* New Approaches to European History 22. New York: Cambridge University Press, 2001.

Ruggiero, Guido. *Binding Passions: Tales of Magic, Marriage and Power at the End of the Renaissance.* New York: Oxford University Press, 1993.

Runciman, Steven. *The Medieval Manichee: A Study of the Christian Dualist Heresy.* New York: Viking Press, 1961.

Samsonowicz, Henryk. "The Agreement between the Bishop of Płock and the Jews of Ostrów Mazowiecki in 1721." In *Studies in the History of the Jews in Old Poland in Honor of Jacob Goldberg,* edited by Adam Teller, 184–8. Jerusalem: Magnes Press, 1998.

Schiffman, Lawrence H. *From Text to Tradition: A History of Second Temple and Rabbinic Judaism.* Hoboken, NJ: Ktav Pub. House, 1991.

Schiffman, Lawrence H. *Reclaiming the Dead Sea Scrolls: The History of Judaism, the Background of Christianity, the Lost Library of Qumran.* 1st ed. Philadelphia: Jewish Publication Society of America, 1994.

Schiffman, Lawrence H. *Understanding Second Temple and Rabbinic Judaism.* Jersey City, NJ: Ktav Pub. House, 2003.

Schroeder, Henry Joseph. *Disciplinary Decrees of the General Councils, Text, Translation, and Commentary.* St. Louis: B. Herder Book Co., 1937.

Siemieński, Józef. "Dysydenci w ustawodawstwie." *Reformacja w Polsce* 20 (1928).

Siker, Jeffrey S. *Disinheriting the Jews: Abraham in Early Christian Controversy.* Louisville, KY: Westminster/John Knox Press, 1991.

Sito, Jakub. "Czy usuwać obrazy z kościołów?" *Gazeta Wyborcza* 206, September 4, 2000.

Šmahel, František. "Literacy and Heresy in Hussite Bohemia." In *Heresy and Literacy, 1000–1530*, edited by Peter Biller and Ann Hudson, 237–54. New York: Cambridge University Press, 1996.

Smereka, Władysław. "Biblistyka polska (wiek XVI–XVIII)." In *Dzieje teologii katolickiej w Polsce*, edited by Marian Rechowicz. Lublin: Towarzystwo Naukowe Katolickiego Uniwersytetu Lubelskiego, 1974–75.

Snyder, H. Gregory. *Teachers and Texts in the Ancient World: Philosophers, Jews, and Christians*. Religion in the First Christian Centuries. New York: Routledge, 2000.

Sobieski, Wacław. "Modlitewnik arjański." *Reformacja w Polsce* 1, no. 1 (1921): 58–63.

Sobieski, Wacław. *Nienawiść wyznaniowa tłumów za rządów Zygmunta III-go*. Warsaw: Nakładem S. Dembego, 1902.

Steinlauf, Michael. *Bondage to the Dead: Poland and the Memory of the Holocaust*. Syracuse: Syracuse University Press, 1997.

Stone, Daniel. "Knowledge of Foreign Languages among Eighteenth Century Polish Jews." *Polin* 10 (1997): 200–19.

Stone, Daniel. *The Polish-Lithuanian State, 1386–1795*. History of East Central Europe 4. Seattle: University of Washington Press, 2001.

Stow, Kenneth R. *The "1007 Anonymous" and Papal Sovereignty: Jewish Perceptions of the Papacy and Papal Policy in the High Middle Ages*. Cincinnati: Hebrew Union College – Jewish Institute of Religion, 1984.

Stow, Kenneth R. "The Burning of the Talmud in 1553 in the Light of Sixteenth Century Catholic Attitudes toward the Talmud." *Bibliotheque d'humanisme et renaissance* 34 (1972): 435–59.

Stow, Kenneth R. *Catholic Thought and Papal Jewry Policy, 1555–1593*. New York: Jewish Theological Seminary of America, 1977.

Stow, Kenneth R. "The Church and the Jews." In *The New Cambridge Medieval History. Volume V, C. 1198–C. 1300*, edited by David Abulafia. Cambridge: Cambridge University Press, 1999.

Stow, Kenneth R. "The Consciousness of Closure: Roman Jewry and Its *Ghet*." In *Essential Papers on Jewish Culture in Renaissance and Baroque Italy*, edited by David Ruderman, 386–400. New York: New York University Press, 1992.

Stow, Kenneth R. "The Papacy and the Jews: Catholic Reformation and Beyond." *Jewish History* 6, no. 1–2 (1992): 257–79.

Sucheni-Grabowska, Anna. *Spory królów ze szlachtą w złotym wieku. Wokół egzekucji praw*. Dzieje Narodu i Państwa Polskiego, eds. Feliks Kiryk, Henryk Szydłowski et al. Cracow: Krajowa Agencja Wydawnicza, 1988.

Sulimierski, Filip, Bronisław Chlebowski, and Władysław Walewski. *Słownik geograficzny Królestwa Polskiego i innych krajów słowianskich*. Warszawa: Wydawnictwa Artystyczne i Filmowe, 1975 <1880>.

Synan, Edward A. *The Popes and the Jews in the Middle Ages*. New York: Macmillan, 1965.

Sypher, G. Wylie. "'Faisant Ce Qu'il a Plaisir': The Image of Protestantism in French Catholic Polemic on the Eve of the Religious Wars." *Sixteenth Century Journal* 11, no. 2 (1980): 59–84.

Syryjczyk, Jerzy Waldemar. *Apostazja od wiary w świetle przepisów kanonicznego prawa karnego: Studium prawno-historyczne*. Warsaw: Akademia Teologii Katolickiej, 1984.

Sysyn, Frank. "A Contemporary's Account of the Causes of the Khmel'nytskyi Uprising." *Harvard Ukrainian Studies* 1, no. 2 (1981).

Sysyn, Frank. "The Jewish Factor in the Khmiel'nytskyi Uprising." In *Ukrainian-Jewish Relations in Historical Perspective*, edited by Howard Aster and Peter Potichnyi. Edmonton, ON: Canadian Institute of Ukrainian Studies, University of Alberta, 1990.

Szostek, Teresa. *Exemplum w polskim średniowieczu*. Warsaw: Instytut Badań Literackich, 1997.

Tanner, Norman P. *Decrees of the Ecumenical Councils*. Washington, DC: Georgetown University Press, 1990.

Ta-Shma, Israel. "On the History of the Jews in Twelfth and Thirteenth-Century Poland." *Polin* 10 (1997): 287–317.

Tazbir, Janusz. *Dzieje polskiej tolerancji*. Warsaw: Interpress, 1973.

Tazbir, Janusz. *Historia kościoła katolickiego w Polsce (1460–1795)*. Warsaw: Wiedza Powszechna, 1966.

Tazbir, Janusz. "Problemy wyznaniowe." In *Polska XVII wieku: Państwo, społeczeństwo, kultura*, edited by Janusz Tazbir, 189–219. Warsaw: Wiedza Powszechna, 1969.

Tazbir, Janusz. *Reformacja w Polsce*. Warsaw: Książka i Wiedza, 1993.

Tazbir, Janusz. *Reformacja, kontrreformacja, tolerancja, a to Polska właśnie*. Wrocław: Wydawnictwo Dolnośląskie, 1996.

Tazbir, Janusz. "Sarmatyzacja katolicyzmu w XVII wieku." In *Wiek XVII–kontrreformacja–barok: prace z historii kultury*, edited by Janusz Pelc. Wrocław: Zakład Narodowy im. Ossolińskich, 1970.

Tazbir, Janusz. "Społeczeństwo wobec Reformacji." In *Polska w epoce odrodzenia: państwo, społeczeństwo, kultura*, edited by Andrzej Wyczański, 331–56. Warsaw: Wiedza Powszechna, 1986.

Tazbir, Janusz. *A State without Stakes: Polish Religious Toleration in the Sixteenth and Seventeenth Centuries*. Translated by A. T. Jordan. Warsaw: Państwowy Instytut Wydawniczy, 1973.

Tazbir, Janusz. *Szlachta i teologowie: studia z dziejów polskiej kontrreformacji*. Warsaw: Wiedza Powszechna, 1987.

Teller, Adam. "The Laicization of Early Modern Jewish Society: The Development of Polish Communal Rabbinate in the Sixteenth Century." In *Schöpferische Momente des europäischen Judentums: In der frühen Neuzeit*, edited by Michael Graetz, 333–49. Heidelberg: Winter, 2000.

Teller, Adam. "The Magnates' Attitude to Jewish Regional Autonomy in the Eighteenth Century." In *Studies in the History of the Jews in Old Poland*, edited by Adam Teller, 246–69. Jerusalem: Magnes Press, 1998.

Teller, Adam. "Tafkidam ha-kalkali u-me'amadam ha-hevrati shel yehudim be-ahuzot bet Radziwil be-Lita ba-meah 18." Ph.D. dissertation, Hebrew University, 1997.

Terpstra, Nicholas. "Apprenticeship in Social Welfare: From Confraternal Charity to Municipal Poor Relief in Early Modern Italy." *Sixteenth Century Journal* 25, no. 1 (1994): 101–20.

Terpstra, Nicholas. "Confraternal Prison Charity and Political Consolidation in Sixteenth-Century Bologna." *Journal of Modern History* 66, no. 2 (1994): 217–48.

Teter, Magdalena. "Jewish Conversions to Catholicism in the Polish-Lithuanian Commonwealth of the Seventeenth and Eighteenth Centuries." *Jewish History* 17, no. 3 (2003): 257–83.

Teter, Magdalena. "Jews in the Legislation and Teachings of the Catholic Church in Poland 1648–1772." Ph.D. dissertation, Columbia University, 2000.

Teter, Magdalena. "Kilka uwag na temat podziałów społecznych i religijnych pomiędzy Żydami i chrześcijanami we wschodnich miastach dawnej rzeczpospolitej [Some

Remarks on Social and Religious Divisions between Jews and Christians in Eastern Cities of Old Poland]." *Kwartalnik Historii Żydow (Jewish History Quarterly)* 207, no. 3 (2003): 327–35.

Tilley, Arthur. "Some Pamphlets of the French Wars of Religion." *The English Historical Review* 14, no. 55 (1899): 451–70.

Toaff, Ariel. *Love, Work, and Death: Jewish Life in Medieval Umbria.* London: Littman Library of Jewish Civilization, 1996.

Tollet, Daniel. "La littérature antisemite polonaise, de 1588 à 1668." *Revue francaise d'histoire du livre* 14 (1977).

Tollet, Daniel. "La Pologne au XVIIe siècle: Une puissance en cours de marginalisation." *Dix-septième siècle [France]* 41, no. 1 (1990): 73–86.

Torańska, Teresa. "Sąd nad obrazem." *Gazeta Wyborcza*, no. 252, October 27, 2000.

Torańska, Teresa. "Sąd nad Sądem." Dodatek do *Gazety Wyborczej* no. 3, January 16, 2003.

Trachtenberg, Joshua. *The Devil and the Jews: The Medieval Conception of the Jew and Its Relation to Modern Antisemitism.* 2nd ed. Philadelphia: Jewish Publication Society of America, 1983.

Twersky, Isadore. "The Shulḥan 'Aruk: Enduring Code of Jewish Law." In *The Jewish Expression,* edited by Judah Goldin. New Haven, CT: Yale University Press, 1970.

Tymieniecki, Kazimierz. *Polska w średniowieczu.* Warsaw: Państwowe Wydawnictwo Naukowe, 1961.

Ulanowski, Bolesław, Jan Fijałek, and Adam Vetulani, eds. *Statuty synodalne wieluńsko-kaliskie Mikołaja Trąby z. r. 1420.* Studia i Materiały do Historii Ustawodawstwa Synodalnego w Polsce 4. Cracow: Nakładem Polskiej Akademia Umiejętności, 1915–51.

Wajsblum, Marek. *Ex Regestro Arianismi: szkice z dziejów upadku protestantyzmu w Małopolsce.* Cracow: Towarzystwo Badań Dziejów Reformacji w Polsce, 1937.

Walters, James C. *Ethnic Issues in Paul's Letter to the Romans: Changing Self-Definitions in Earliest Roman Christianity.* Valley Forge, PA: Trinity Press International, 1993.

Watt, J. A. "The Papacy." In *The New Cambridge Medieval History. Volume V: C. 1198– C. 1300,* edited by David Abulafia. Cambridge: Cambridge University Press, 1999.

Węgrzynek, Hanna. *"Czarna legenda" Żydów: procesy o rzekome mordy rytualne w dawnej Polsce.* Warsaw: Wydawnictwo "Bellona" Fundacja Historia pro Futuro, 1995.

Weinryb, Bernard D. *The Jews of Poland: A Social and Economic History of the Jewish Community in Poland from 1100 to 1800.* Philadelphia: Jewish Publication Society of America, 1973.

Wiesner, Merry E. *Women and Gender in Early Modern Europe.* New Approaches to European History. New York: Cambridge University Press, 1993.

Wilken, Robert Louis. *John Chrysostom and the Jews: Rhetoric and Reality in the Late 4th Century.* Vol. 4, *The Transformation of the Classical Heritage.* Berkeley: University of California Press, 1983.

Williams, George Huntston. *The Polish Brethren: Documentation of the History and Thought of Unitarianism in the Polish-Lithuanian Commonwealth and in the Diaspora, 1601–1685.* Harvard Theological Studies 30. Missoula, MT: Scholars Press for Harvard Theological Review, 1980.

Wisner, Henryk. "Dysydenci litewscy wobec wybuchu wojny polsko-szwedzkiej (1655–1660)." *Odrodzenie i Reformacja w Polsce* 15 (1970): 101–42.

Wisner, Henryk. *Najjaśniejsza Rzeczpospolita: szkice z dziejów Polski szlacheckiej XVI–XVII wieku.* Warsaw: Państwowy Instytut Wydawniczy, 1978.

Workman, Herbert B. *Persecution in the Early Church*. Oxford: Oxford University Press, 1980.

Wyczański, Andrzej. "The Problem of Authority in Sixteenth-Century Poland: An Essay of Reinterpretation." In *A Republic of Nobles: Studies in Polish History to 1864*, edited by J. K. Fedorowicz, 91–108. New York: Cambridge University Press, 1982.

Wyczański, Andrzej. *Polska Rzeczą Pospolitą Szlachecką*. 2nd ed. Warsaw: Państwowe Wydawnictwo Naukowe, 1991.

Wyrozumska, Bożena, ed. *The Jews in Mediaeval Cracow: Selected Records from Cracow Municipal Books*. Cracow: Polska Akademia Umiejętności, 1995.

Wyrozumski, Jerzy. *Historia Polski do Roku 1505*. Warsaw: Państwowe Wydawnictwo Naukowe, 1978.

Wyrozumski, Jerzy. "Jews in Medieval Poland." In *The Jews in Old Poland, 1000–1795*, edited by Antony Polonsky, Jakub Basista, and Andrzej Link-Lenczowski,. New York: I. B. Tauris / Institute for Polish-Jewish Studies, 1993.

Yerushalmi, Yosef Hayim. *The Lisbon Massacre of 1506 and the Royal Image in the Shebet Yehudah*. Hebrew Union College Annual. Supplements; no. 1. Cincinnati: Hebrew Union College – Jewish Institute of Religion, 1976.

Yuval, Israel. "Jews and Christians in the Middle Ages: Shared Myths, Common Language." In *Demonizing the Other*, edited by Robert Wistrich, 88–107. Amsterdam: Harwood Academic Publishers, 1999.

Yuval, Israel. "Ha-nakam Ve-ha-klalah, ha-dam ve-ha-'alilah: me-'alilot kedushim le-'alitot dam." *Zion* 48, no. 1 (1993): 33–90.

Yuval, Israel. *Shene goyim be-vitnekh: Yehudim ve-noẓrim dimuyim ha-dadiyim*. Tel-Aviv: 'Alma 'am 'oved, 2000.

Yuval, Israel. "'They Tell Lies; You Are the Man': Jewish Reactions to Ritual Murder Accusations." In *Religious Violence between Christians and Jews*, edited by Anna Sapir Abulafia, 86–106. Hampshire: Palgrave, 2002.

Zivier, E. "Jüdische Bekehrungsversuche im Jahrhundert." In *Beiträge zur Geschichte der deutschen Juden: Festschrift zum siebzigsten Geburtstage Martin Phillippsons*. Leipzig: Gustav Fock GmbH, 1916.

Index

Mary (the Virgin), 109, 122–123, 130–130,
216
  Polonization of, 109
Masiukiewicz, Pawel, 34
Masoret ha-Masoret, 106
Masovia, Duchy of, 139
mass (Catholic), 60, 122
Matuszewicz, Marcin, 183
matzah (matzoth), 69, 99, 118, 184
meat
  kosher, 115
  sold by Jews, 70, 115
Męciński, Józef, 175
medical emergencies. *See also* midwives;
    physicians
  contacts between Jews and non-Jews, 72, 74
medieval anti-Jewish sentiments, 116. *See also*
    anti-Jewish polemic
medieval iconography, Jews in, 224
medievalism
  of Polish anti-Jewish polemic, 113–117
  of Polish Catholicism, 142
Medigo, Elia del, 107
Mennonites, Dutch, 58
menstrual bleeding, 117
menstruating woman, Jesus born of,
    118
merchants, Jews as, 28
Meshullam, Rabbi, 116
Messiah, Jewish as Antichrist, 112
messiahship of Jesus, 213
messianic movement, 33
Metz, 156
Metzger, Rabbi Yona, 1
Michelevich, Abram, 65, 182
Michelewicz, Itzḥak, 35
Michiel, Jewish arrendator, 68
Mickiewicz, Adam, 196
Miczyński, Sebastian, anti-Jewish work by, 29,
    107, 116
midwives, 68–69, 73–74, 183
  Jewish, 74, 178
  Jewish rulings on, 73
Mieczysław, Brzozowski, 109
Mielec (town), 65
Mikhelevich, Esther, 36
military duty, limitations on for nobles, 23
Minsk (royal town), 31
miracles, 113, 132
Mirandola, Pico della, 107
Miriam [Mary], numerical value of, 129
Mishnah, 71
  on assistance during childbirth, 183
  on Jewish midwives, 178

on nursing children, 183
on teaching gentiles crafts, 73
Misiakiewicz, Pawel, 172
mixing of Christians and Jews, 17. *See also*
    socializing
Młodzianowski, Tomasz, 109, 212, 215
Modena, Leon, 107
Mohilev, 65, 114
Mojecki, Przecław, 91, 116, 117, 118, 210
monarchs. *See also* King (Polish)
  electoral process in Poland, 23
  financial weakness of, 25
  Jewish relationship with, 28
  land, 25
  nobles, 22–25, 31, 46–47
  rules for, 24
monarchy
  Catholic Church ties to, 22, 23
  in Lithuania, 30
  papacy as, 16
Moroz, Stefan, funerary sermon for, 119
Moscovite. *See* Muscovite
Moszko "the Senator," 39
Moszkowski, Hieronim, 212
Motole (town), 177
Moyżeszowicz, Jakub, 34
municipal criminal courts, Jews in, 62
Muraszko, Tymoteusz, 32
Muscovite churches as more pious, 78
Muscovite forces, siege of Vitebsk, 58
Muscovy. *See* Russia
Muslims, *also* Saracens, 17, 58, 67, 219
myths, anti-Jewish, 91–95, 100, 107, 119, 207

Nadav, Modekhai, 163
Narew, 29
neighborly love, 111, 120
Nicea, Council of, 18, 181
Nicene Creed, 18
niddah, law of, 178
Nieciecki, Bartłomiej, 33
Niekurza (village), 86
Nihil novi constitution, 23
Nirenberg, David, 67
Noaḥide commandments, 106, 202
nobility. *See also* magnates, nobles
  equality of, 23
  identification with Catholicism, 3, 36, 54, 57
  membership, 23, 26, 36, 57, 185
  multi-religious and multi-ethnic definition of,
    36
  re-Catholicization of, 53
Reformation, 26–27, 45, 47
rise of, 23

Made in the USA
Lexington, KY
27 January 2014